Casebook for Counseling
Lesbian, Gay, Bisexual, and Transgender Persons and Their Families

edited by
Sari H. Dworkin and Mark Pope

American Counseling Association
5999 Stevenson Avenue
Alexandria, VA 22304
www.counseling.org

Casebook for Counseling

Lesbian, Gay, Bisexual, and Transgender Persons and Their Families

10   9   8   7   6   5   4   3   2

American Counseling Association
5999 Stevenson Avenue
Alexandria, VA 22304

Director of Publications   Carolyn C. Baker

Production Manager   Bonny E. Gaston

Editorial Assistant   Catherine A. Brumley

Copy Editor   Beth Ciha

Cover and text design by Bonny E. Gaston

Library of Congress Cataloging-in-Publication Data

Casebook for counseling lesbian, gay, bisexual, and transgender persons
and their families / edited by Sari H. Dworkin and Mark Pope.
   p.   cm.
  ISBN 978-1-55620-306-0 (alk. paper)
1. Lesbians—Counseling of—Case studies.   2. Gays—Counseling of—Case
studies.   3. Bisexuals—Counseling of—Case studies.   4. Transgender
people—Counseling of—Case studies.   5. Counseling—Methodology.   I.
Dworkin, Sari H.   II. Pope, Mark, 1952–
  HQ76.25.C377 2012
  362.89'6086—dc23   2011036419

# Contents

Contents

Contents

Foreword

I have been incredibly fortunate thus far in both my personal and professional lives to have witnessed and/or experienced the ordinary and sometimes extraordinary triumphs associated with our rich and diverse lesbian, gay, bisexual, transgender, queer, questioning, and intersex (LGBTQQI) communities. I have also been in the trenches personally experiencing the pitfalls and soul-wrenching pain that our community faces on a daily basis. It is through many of these experiences that I have had the great fortune to learn from and serve with Drs. Sari Dworkin and Mark Pope and, in doing so, have seen with my own eyes what inner strength, grace under pressure, and unwavering commitment to changing the world for the greater good really is and what one person, or even a small group of people, can do, one day at a time, one person at a time. I am deeply grateful to both Sari and Mark for the paths they forge, the mantles they wear, and the steadfast leadership they provide. This book is yet one more example of their visionary work and extraordinary contribution.

To say that Sari and Mark have done it again would seem unnecessary or at best an understatement, but I will say it anyway . . . yes, they have done it again! Yet again they have gathered together the A-team, the best of the best, the cream of the crop, and asked them to do what they do best: educate, innovate, and advocate. I challenge you to find another group of people who represent this caliber of educators, practitioners, researchers, and all-around earth-shakers . . . the truth is, you won't, but the good news is that they're all here, in one book, ready and willing to move all of us one step closer to the change we want to be. I am fortunate to call many of them friends and absolutely ecstatic that I can call all of them colleagues and team players in the war against prejudice, bigotry, stereotype, and bias.

I promise you that this book is the one book you will turn to throughout your professional career no matter if you are a seasoned scholar-practitioner or a new graduate—this is the go-to resource, bar none. It is this book you will turn to when you need to understand the myriad experiences of the sexual minority client who sits in front of you; it is this book you will turn to when you need to choose a theory or technique, assess, diagnose, or treat sexual minority clients who stare across from you wounded by the world, drowning in the prejudice; and it is this book you will turn to when you really want to help, intervene, and make a difference in the life of a sexual minority client who has nowhere else to turn and no one else who understands or is willing to listen.

Across four broad sections—Developmental Issues, Relationship Issues, Contextual Issues, and Wellness Issues—you will find the rich, powerful, and complex narratives of real people. You will learn how to carefully choose a theoretical approach and select appropriate techniques so that you empathically effect change. You will learn a range of strategies and interventions, and above all you will learn how to develop and sustain compassionate affirmation for your sexual minority clients and their significant others. And, I guarantee, you will learn a lot about yourself, the biases and prejudice that you yourself carry, and how, if left unchecked, they will negatively impact the therapeutic alliance and relationships with your LGBTQQI clients. Period. I'm certainly not saying it is simple work, nor easy work, but I am saying that the rewards both for you and for the people you serve will far outweigh the challenges of really digging in and learning from this material. You will perhaps for the first time have a comprehensive set of tools and resources to guide and support you in this important work. And, as one more reward, you will have a newfound confidence in yourself and your ability to work effectively with sexual minority clients and their significant others. It just doesn't get better than this.

I don't have to remind anyone that these are extraordinary times, the walls opposing same-sex marriage and unions are crumbling, the military ban is folding, and the assumptive constraints against anything but binary sexuality and gender are loosening; yes, these are extraordinary times, and, as such, they call for extraordinary measures. I know of no better way to achieve success as a truly competent multicultural counselor than to immediately start reading the *Casebook for Counseling Lesbian, Gay, Bisexual, and Transgender Persons and Their Families*.

The time is now. If not now, when? If not us, who?

With pride,

—Colleen R. Logan, PhD, LPC, LMFT, NCC
Program Coordinator
Marriage, Couple and Family Counseling Program
Walden University

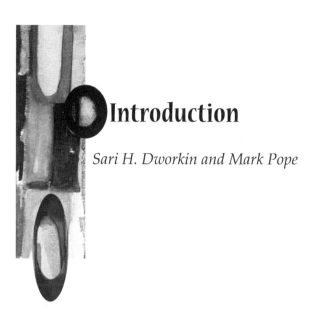

Introduction

Sari H. Dworkin and Mark Pope

Research suggests that most mental health professionals feel their training on lesbian and gay issues has been inadequate at best and nonexistent at worst. Add to this the issues of bisexuality and transgender, not to mention intersex issues, and these feelings of adequacy to deal with the issues of sexual minorities diminish even further.

Ethical codes (American Counseling Association, 2005) and accreditation bodies (Council for Accreditation of Counseling and Related Educational Programs, 2009) now call for training on lesbian, gay, bisexual, and transgender (LGBT) issues. However, even with *bisexuality* or *transgender* in the title of the course, article, book, or workshop, there is often little exploration of the uniqueness of bisexuality and transgender from lesbian and gay issues.

Training on LGBT issues often consists of a section of a course on multicultural counseling, or if a counseling program is truly cutting edge perhaps there will be an entire course on LGBT issues in the curriculum. Supervision during practicum, field experience, and internship tends only to broach LGBT issues if an LGBT client presents for counseling. Even when these issues are discussed, we often hear from students, "What do I do when the client is sitting in front of me? What questions do I ask? What theories and techniques do I use?" Sometimes the supervisor's suggestions get a response similar to "I can say that? I can ask that?" This book was written to answer those questions.

We are fortunate to be living in an era when LGBT-affirmative counseling is the position of all mental health professions and is accepted by most practitioners. A proliferation of scholarly and practical literature has addressed the most pressing concerns of this population. Lesbians and gays avail themselves of therapy in great numbers (Garnets, Hancock, Cochran, Goodchilds, & Peplau, 1991) and for the most part are accepting of and satisfied with the therapy they receive (Page, 2007). This is not the case for bisexuals. Some bisexual clients do not disclose their identity in therapy because they believe that their therapists will not validate their identity and will not have the knowledge or skills needed to treat them adequately (Page, 2007). Because identity is a critical aspect of a person, it is likely that a client who does not disclose a bisexual identity will receive inadequate or even harmful treatment. Transgender clients have the dual problem of believing that they must educate their therapist (confusing the role of therapist and client) and, if they are considering surgery, knowing that their therapist is a gatekeeper who can stop the surgery from happening (Mizock & Fleming, 2011; see the World Professional Association for Transgender Health). Intersex individuals are a newly recognized group of clients with unique issues. They are also likely to feel that they must educate their therapists prior to receiving appropriate care. This book examines actual cases (often composite cases) to help clinicians address appropriate issues within the course of treatment. The identities of clients have been disguised to ensure confidentiality. In all cases the authors have gained permission from their clients to include actual (not composite) cases in this book.

We proposed this book to fill what we considered a gap in the LGBT counseling literature. Students and clinicians desire more information about what to do when faced with particular clients with particular issues. Our invitation to authors outlined the following:

> The chapters in this book should be different from the LGBT counseling books currently in the market. We are *not* looking for a review of the scholarly literature. Authors are being asked to address the following issues, focusing on treatment planning and implementation rather than reviewing the literature about counseling and therapy with this population. The protocol includes the following:
>
> 1. Identifying data (if you are using information on actual clients, please be careful to protect their identities as well as to obtain signed release forms)
> 2. Background information (please provide sufficient information that is especially relevant to your case[s])
> 3. Presenting issues (what specific problems brought the client to you?)
> 4. Diagnoses (as applicable, including a full five-axis diagnosis and rationale)
> 5. Theoretical framework(s) (identify the theory[ies] from which you are working in this case)
> 6. Goals of treatment (initial, negotiated, and final goals, including the process)
> 7. Interventions used (be specific and provide a thorough justification)
> 8. Outcomes (identify all outcomes, both successful and not successful)
> 9. Transference and countertransference issues (as applicable, based on your theoretical framework, identify those that did occur or are potential issues of which the therapist should be mindful)
> 10. Other multicultural and cross-cultural issues (using an inclusive definition of "culture" and including gender issues)
> 11. Crisis issues, if applicable
> 12. Any recommendations for further counseling or training

The chapters of our book follow the Association for Lesbian, Gay, Bisexual and Transgender Issues in Counseling Competencies for Counseling Gay, Lesbian, Bisexual and Transgendered (LGBT) Clients (1997) and Competencies for Counseling With Transgender Clients (2010), both of which have been adopted by the American Counseling Association (see Appendixes A and B, respectively). The chapters are grouped into the following sections: Developmental Issues, Relationship Issues, Contextual Issues, and Wellness Issues. We provide a brief introduction to each section that states the competencies in detail and reviews the pertinent literature (suggested by the authors of the chapters) to provide background. Those who need more background will find that the scholarly literature is easily accessible in books and articles currently in print.

Furthermore, we have assembled many of the best authors and researchers in our field to address these issues. These authors have great insight into their LGBT clients and have produced extremely interesting, readable, and useful narratives of the lives of LGBT persons and their families and how to go about helping them.

We believe that this book is a timely and important resource for professors, students, and practitioners in the counseling profession. It is also a fascinating read. Many issues addressed in coursework on lesbian, gay, bisexual, transgender, queer, questioning, and intersex populations are addressed in these chapters: coming out; family; spouses/significant others; binational couples; religion; addictions; HIV; women's health; conversion therapy; and intersections with race, ethnicity, gender, rural culture, and more. In addition, one chapter specifically deals with intersex individuals, and a number of chapters include issues faced by bisexual and transgender persons.

Most important, we hope that this book helps illuminate the issues that LGBT persons and their families face in their daily lives and better prepares counseling professionals to effectively address them.

References

American Counseling Association. (2005). *ACA code of ethics.* Alexandria, VA: Author.

Association for Lesbian, Gay, Bisexual and Transgender Issues in Counseling. (1997). *Competencies for counseling gay, lesbian, bisexual, and transgendered (LGBT) clients.* Alexandria, VA: Author.

Association for Lesbian, Gay, Bisexual and Transgender Issues in Counseling. (2010). *Competencies for counseling with transgender clients.* Alexandria, VA: Author.

Council for Accreditation of Counseling and Related Educational Programs. (2009). *2009 standards.* Alexandria, VA: Author.

Garnets, L., Hancock, K. A., Cochran, S. E., Goodchilds, J., & Peplau, L. A. (1991). Issues in psychotherapy with lesbians and gay men: A survey of psychologists. *American Psychologist, 46,* 964–972.

Mizock, L., & Fleming, M. Z. (2011). Transgender and gender variant populations with mental illness: Implications for clinical care. *Professional Psychology: Research and Practice, 42,* 208–213.

Page, E. (2007). Bisexual women's and men's experiences of psychotherapy. In B. A. Firestein (Ed.), *Becoming visible: Counseling bisexuals across the lifespan* (pp. 52–71). New York, NY: Columbia University Press.

About the Editors

Sari H. Dworkin, PhD, MFT, is a professor emerita of California State University, Fresno. She taught in the Marriage and Family Therapy master's program for 25 years. Currently she is in a limited private practice, is licensed as a psychologist, and does volunteer counseling and supervision at the Community Counseling Center in San Luis Obispo, California. Her long career has included many publications and presentations on LGBT issues. In addition, she has held positions in both the American Psychological Association (APA) and the American Counseling Association (ACA) advocating for LGBT issues. Some of these positions include president of the Society for the Psychological Study of Lesbian, Gay, Bisexual, and Transgender Issues (APA Division 44), cochair of the Association for Lesbian, Gay, Bisexual and Transgender Issues in Counseling (ACA), and chair of the Committee on Lesbian, Gay, Bisexual, and Transgender Concerns (APA). In 2009 APA's Committee on Lesbian, Gay, Bisexual, and Transgender Concerns presented her with its Outstanding Achievement Award. In 2007 she was elected as an inaugural Legacy Fellow of the Association for Gay, Lesbian, and Bisexual Issues in Counseling.

o o o

Mark Pope, EdD, NCC, MCC, MAC, ACS, is professor and chair of the Division of Counseling and Family Therapy at the University of Missouri–Saint Louis. He is the author of six books, more than 30 book chapters, more than 40 journal articles, and more than 100 professional presentations at the international, national, and state levels. Dr. Pope has written extensively on various aspects of counseling, including counseling with and the career development of ethnic, racial, and sexual minorities; violence in schools; teaching career and multicultural competence in counseling; psychological testing; international issues in counseling, and the history of and public policy issues in career counseling. His work has appeared as books, as conference presentations, and in such journals as the *Journal of Homosexuality, Journal of Lesbian and Gay Social Services, Journal of Counseling & Development, The Career Development Quarterly, The Counseling Psychologist, The Family Journal, Journal of Multicultural Counseling and Development,* and *American Psychologist.* Dr. Pope has served as president of the American Counseling Association; the National Career Development Association; the Association for Lesbian, Gay, Bisexual and Transgender Issues in Counseling; and the Society for the Psychological Study of Lesbian, Gay, Bisexual, and Transgender Issues (APA Division 44). He has been elected a Fellow of the American Counseling Association; American Psychological Association; National Career Development Association; Society of Counseling Psychology; Society for the Psychological Study of Ethnic Minority Issues; and Society for the Psychological Study of Lesbian, Gay, Bisexual, and Transgender Issues. He has also served as the editor of *The Career Development Quarterly,* on the editorial boards of several other professional journals, as well as as the Director of Psychological Services for the American Indian AIDS Institute and the Native American AIDS Project in San Francisco. He has special expertise in Native American, Asian, and sexual minority cultures.

About the Contributors

Theodore R. Burnes, PhD, is an associate professor in the California School of Professional Psychology's Los Angeles campus. He conducts research projects and supervises clinical practice surrounding issues of trauma, gender identity, and mental health and wellness for LGBTQQI people. Dr. Burnes has more than 25 refereed publications and presentations in the area of sexual orientation, social justice, teaching psychology, multicultural counseling, and trauma. He is currently the chair for the section on Supervision and Training for Division 17 of the American Psychological Association.

Connie Callahan, PhD, LMFT, LPCC, has taught more than 50 different courses in psychology, counseling, education, and family studies at three universities, and this has provided her with a solid background in the helping professions. Running Southwestern Counseling Services in Albuquerque, New Mexico, with its complex multicultural mix of denizens, added real-life experience to her work with diverse populations. Dr. Callahan has published on and conducted numerous workshops concerning school safety, diverse populations, advanced counseling skills, dialectical behavior therapy, proper treatment protocols for mental health practitioners, and crisis response to disaster and trauma. She and her partner Nancy, a psychiatric nurse practitioner, have enjoyed 19 committed years together.

Edward P. Cannon, PhD, LPC, LMFT, is an assistant professor at the University of Colorado Denver, where he teaches courses on multicultural counseling as well as gender and sexual orientation. His research agenda is currently focused on the experiences of LGBT clients in counseling. He is a former board member of the Association for Lesbian, Gay, Bisexual and Transgender Issues in Counseling and received its 2009 national service award. Dr. Cannon has produced numerous scholarly publications and national presentations related to LGBT issues.

Laurie A. Carlson, PhD, is an associate professor and program coordinator for the Counseling and Career Development Program at Colorado State University in Fort Collins. She spent 5 years as an English teacher and 4 years as a K–12 school counselor in northern Minnesota prior to obtaining her PhD in counselor education at the University of Arkansas. Shie is a past-cochair of the American Counseling Association Task Force for the National Summit on Sexual Minority Youth in the Schools and currently serves as a trainer for the American Psychological Association's Healthy Lesbian, Gay, and Bisexual Students Project. At the state level, Dr. Carlson is on the regional Parents, Families, and Friends of Lesbians and Gays Committee for Safe Schools and served for 2 years as the Human Rights Chair for the Colorado School Counselors Association.

Armand R. Cerbone, PhD, ABPP, is in independent practice in Chicago, where he has been counseling LGBT individuals and couples since 1978. He is a Fellow of five divisions of the American Psychological Association (APA) and holds an American Board of Professional Psychology diplomate in clinical psychology. He coauthored APA's *Guidelines on Psychotherapy With LGB Clients* and chaired the working group that developed APA's *Resolution on Sexual Orientation and Marriage* and *Resolution on Sexual Orientation, Parents and Children*. Dr. Cerbone is a former member of the APA Board of Directors and past-president of both Division 44 (Society for the Psychological Study of Lesbian, Gay, Bisexual, and Transgender Issues) and the Illinois Psychological Association. He is a former Director of Behavioral Health at the Howard Brown Memorial Health Center, the Midwest's largest LGBT health center. In 2001 he cochaired the first international conference on lesbian, gay, and bisexual psychology. He has received many awards for his contributions to psychology, including the Stanley Sue Award for Distinguished Contributions to Diversity in Clinical Psychology. He is also a member of the City of Chicago Gay and Lesbian Hall of Fame.

Stuart F. Chen-Hayes, PhD, NCC, is a program coordinator and associate professor of counselor education/school counseling in the Counseling, Leadership, Literacy, and Special Education Department at Lehman College of the City University of New York. He was Visiting Professor of Counseling at National Changhua University of Education in Changhua, Taiwan, and with his family regularly lectures in Taiwan and the United States on LGBTQQI and antioppression issues. He cofounded Counselors for Social Justice and is a past-president of this organization and the North Atlantic Region Association for Counselor Education and Supervision. He has authored more than 40 refereed counseling publications and presented more than 200 professional counseling and social justice education workshops. He cofounded the first international LGBTQQI school counselor and educator conference in 2010. He is a member of the editorial boards of the *Journal of LBGT Issues in Counseling, Journal of International Counselor Education,* and *Journal of Counselor Preparation and Supervision.*

Kirstyn Yuk Sim Chun, PsyD, received her doctorate in clinical psychology from Indiana University of Pennsylvania in 2003. She is an associate professor and licensed clinical psychologist at Counseling and Psychological Services at California State University, Long Beach, where she supervises in the American Psychological Association (APA)–accredited predoctoral internship training program. At California State University, Long Beach, she is chair of the Lesbian, Gay, Bisexual, and Transgender Task Force and past-chair of the President's Commission on the Status of Women. Dr. Chun has served as cochair of the Committee on Racial and Ethnic Diversity of the Society for the Psychological Study of Lesbian, Gay, Bisexual, and Transgender Issues (APA Division 44), during which time the committee received the President's Award from the Asian American Psychological Association. She is currently the 2013 APA Division 44 representative to the National Multicultural Conference and Summit. She publishes and presents on intersections of racial, sexual, and other marginalized identities. Areas of clinical, scholarly, and advocacy interest include LGBT-affirmative counseling, bisexuality, multicultural and social justice issues, women's issues, clinical supervision and training, group therapy, and outreach and consultation.

Colleen M. Connolly, PhD, LPC-S, is an associate professor in the Professional Counseling Program and coordinator of the Marital, Couple, and Family Emphasis at Texas State University—San Marcos. She has focused her energies on LGBT-related areas, including serving on the editorial boards of numerous journals, cofounding a state division, and serving as past-president of the Association for Gay, Lesbian, and Bisexual Issues in Counseling (2004–2005). Her research and publication interests largely surround issues related to lesbian and gay couples, including clinical issues, created family, strength, resilience, stressors, and communication competence.

Shirley Cornett, PhD, LPCC, has practiced in and run clinics with some of the most diverse clientele in New Mexico. Practicing as an African American counselor has given her a unique view of family and comprehensive, diverse techniques for working with client and family problems. Her diversity research has focused on studying well-known leaders in diversity and analyzing characteristics of leadership.

Paul A. Datti, PhD, CRC, HS-BCP, is an assistant professor at the University of Scranton, where he directs the undergraduate Counseling and Human Services program. The author of scholarly publications relating to LGBT issues and counseling practice, Paul has given several national, regional, state, and local presentations related to this topic. In addition to assisting LGBT persons in practice, Paul has developed graduate and undergraduate coursework on counseling LGBT clients and is active in many service activities focusing on the population. Paul is also the current president of the Pennsylvania Association for Lesbian, Gay, Bisexual, and Transgender Issues in Counseling, a chapter of the Association for Lesbian, Gay, Bisexual and Transgender Issues in Counseling.

Brian J. Dew, PhD, LPC, is an associate professor in and chairperson of the Department of Counseling and Psychological Services at Georgia State University. Dr. Dew's research on addictive behaviors earned him the 2007 Outstanding Faculty Research Award from Georgia State University's Department of Education as well as the 2007 Outstanding Addictions and Offender Professional Award by the Association of Addictions and Offender Counseling. Dr. Dew has held numerous professional leadership roles, including president of the Association for Lesbian, Gay, Bisexual and Transgender Issues in Counseling; director of the Atlanta Meth Task Force; and board member for the Society for the Advancement of Sexual Health, formerly known as the National Council on Sexual Addiction and Compulsivity.

Suzanne M. Dugger, EdD, LPC, is a professor in the Department of Leadership and Counseling at Eastern Michigan University, where she also serves as the coordinator of the school counseling program. Prior to joining the faculty at Eastern Michigan University, she completed a bachelor's degree in psychology at Harvard University, a master's degree in counseling at Central Michigan University, and a doctorate in counseling psychology at Western Michigan University. Her counseling experience includes 5 years as an elementary school counselor, 3 years in university counseling centers, and 8 years of part-time private practice. A long-time advocate for the needs of sexual minority youth, Dr. Dugger has served as a trainer for the American Psychological Association's Healthy Lesbian, Gay, and Bisexual Students Project, as the human rights committee chair for both the American Counseling Association and the Michigan School Counselor Association, and as cochair of the American Counseling Association Task Force for the National Summit on Sexual Minority Youth in the Schools. In recognition of her research and service contributions related to the needs of sexual minority youth in K–12 schools, Dr. Dugger received the Michigan Counseling Association's Human Rights Award in 2002.

Randall D. Ehrbar, PsyD, is a clinical psychologist specializing in work with transgender clients. Dr. Ehrbar was elected a Fellow of the American Psychological Association (APA) in 2010 for his work in this area, and as far as he knows, he is the first out transgender Fellow of APA. Dr. Ehrbar has contributed to the area of transgender issues through his work with clients as well as through professional publications and service. Dr. Ehrbar participated in a 2-year postdoctoral fellowship during which he received intensive training and experience working with transgender people at the University of Minnesota Program in Human Sexuality. He then went on to work for several years at New Leaf Services for Our Community, an LGBT community mental health center in San Francisco. He is currently working at the University of Colorado Counseling and Psychological Services.

Beth A. Firestein, PhD, is a licensed psychologist in private practice in Loveland, Colorado. She has been a practicing psychologist for 25 years. She specializes in working with gay, lesbian, bisexual, and transgender populations and others with alternative sexualities or lifestyles. Dr. Firestein is the editor of two books on the topic of bisexuality written for researchers and clinicians in the field of psychology: *Bisexuality: The Psychology and Politics of an Invisible Minority* (Sage, 1996) and *Becoming Visible: Counseling Bisexuals Across the Life Span* (Columbia University Press, 2007).

S. Lenoir Gillam, PhD, LPC, NCC, is a professor in the Department of Counseling, Foundations, and Leadership at Columbus State University in Columbus, Georgia. She received her PhD in counseling psychology from The University of Georgia and has worked in school, community, and university settings. She is also a licensed professional counselor and a licensed psychologist in Georgia and a nationally certified counselor. Lenoir is a past-president and Fellow of the Association for Specialists in Group Work, a division of the American Counseling Association. Her research agenda and special interests include group work, supervision and training, multicultural issues, and school counseling.

Terry S. Gock, PhD, MPA, is a clinical and forensic psychologist. He is the director of the Pacific Clinics Asian Pacific Family Center in Los Angeles County, California, and is also in part-time private practice. In addition, he has served as an organizational consultant for more than 30 government and nonprofit entities across the nation in multicultural competency training, strategic planning, organizational development, and program planning. Dr. Gock is a past-president of the American Psychological Association (APA) Division 44 (the Society for the Psychological Study of Lesbian, Gay, Bisexual, and Transgender Issues). He is also a Fellow of both APA and the Asian American Psychological Association. He was honored with an APA 2011 Presidential Citation, in part for his "lifelong devotion to multiculturalism" in psychology.

Douglas C. Haldeman, PhD, has been a counseling psychologist in independent practice in Seattle for 27 years. He also serves as a clinical professor in the Department of Psychology at the University of Washington and an evaluator for the Federal Aviation Administration. His long publication record includes issues of ethics; practice guidelines for marginalized groups; and competent treatment of lesbian, gay, and bisexual individuals and families. This scholarship has won him a number of awards, including an APA Presidential Citation (2005) from the American Psychological Association and the John D. Black Award (2007) from the Society of Counseling Psychology. He has held a number of governance positions in the American Psychological Association, including a term on the Board of Directors (2006–2008). Presently he serves as chair of the Board for the Advancement of Psychology in the Public Interest and is a trustee on the Boards of the American Psychological Association Insurance Trust and the Association for the Advancement of Psychology.

Paul F. Hard, PhD, LPC, CS, NCC, is an assistant professor in the Department of Counselor, Leadership, and Special Education at Auburn University Montgomery in Montgomery, Alabama. He received his PhD in counselor education and supervision from The University of Alabama and has worked in community and university settings. He is also a supervising licensed professional counselor in Alabama and a nationally certified counselor. Dr. Hard is a past-chair of the Southern Region of the American Counseling Association and a past-president of the Alabama Counseling Association. He currently serves on the Alabama Board of Examiners in Counseling. He has more than 13 years of experience in community mental health work as well as 20 years of experience in ecclesiastical work. His research interests include ethics, best practice issues, supervision and training, multicultural issues, LGBT issues in therapy, complicated grieving, and spirituality in counseling.

David W. Hart, MS, is a doctoral student and research assistant at the University of Missouri—St. Louis and an adjunct faculty member at Southwestern Illinois College. He completed his master's degree in counseling at California State University, Fullerton, where he received the Faculty Award for potential as a counselor. For the first 7 years of his career, Hart worked for Gay and Lesbian Services Center of Orange County as both a mental health counselor and a program manager of HIV prevention services. His scholarly research interests are in the clinical integration of spirituality and professional counseling, gay identity development, and counseling the older adult client. He has a passion for promoting social justice through his clinical practice and scholarly research and is a member of the American Counseling Association and Counselors for Social Justice.

A. Michael Hutchins, PhD, is a licensed professional counselor in private practice in Tucson, Arizona. He works primarily in individual and experiential group settings with men who have histories of early childhood abuse and trauma, and he has been active in human rights and social justice advocacy endeavors throughout his career. He was the founding president of Counselors for Social Justice and is a past-president and Fellow of the Association for Specialists in Group Work. As an early cochair of the Association for Lesbian, Gay, Bisexual and Transgender Issues in Counseling, he received the American Counseling Association (ACA) Kitty Cole Award for his advocacy work. He has served on the board of Wingspan, the gay, lesbian, bisexual, and transgender community center in Tucson, and has been on the City of Tucson's Gay, Lesbian, Bisexual and Transgender Advisory Commission to the mayor and city council. Using the ACA Advocacy Competencies as a framework, he continues to be involved in advocacy to combat growing fear and oppression in the state of Arizona. Michael is an avid cyclist and can likely be found on one of the many bicycle paths in Tucson early in the morning before the desert heat scorches the pavement.

Susan Kashubeck-West, PhD, received her PhD in counseling psychology in 1989 from The Ohio State University. A licensed psychologist, she has been on the faculty of Drake University (1989–1993), Texas Tech University (1993–2001), and the University of Missouri–St. Louis (2001–present), where she currently holds the position of professor. Her research interests include LGBT issues, particularly internalized heterosexism and experiences of subtle discrimination. Dr. Kashubeck-West teaches courses in multicultural counseling and counseling sexual minorities. She is a member of the American Psychological Association task force charged with revising the *Guidelines for Psychological Practice With Lesbian, Gay, and Bisexual Clients.* She and her long-time partner are raising a son who they note was their 10th anniversary gift to each other.

Douglas Kimmel, PhD, is professor emeritus in the Department of Psychology, City College, City University of New York, and has an independent psychology practice in Hancock, Maine. He was chair of the Association of Gay Psychologists (1977); president of the Society for the Psychological Study of Lesbian, Gay, and Bisexual Issues (Division 44 of the American Psychological Association [APA]; 1987–1988); and served on APA's Committee on Gay, Lesbian, and Bisexual Concerns (1981–1983), the Board of Social and Ethical Responsibility (1984–1986), and the Board for Applications of Psychology in the Public Interest (2006–2008), focusing on aging issues. His textbook *Adulthood and Aging* (Wiley, 1974, 1980, 1990) included sexual orientation and an interview with a gay man. He is coeditor of *Psychological Perspectives on Lesbian, Gay, and Bisexual Experiences* (Columbia University Press, 1993, 2003) and coeditor of *Lesbian, Gay, Bisexual, and Transgender Aging: Research and Clinical Perspectives* (Columbia University Press, 2005). He was a cofounder of SAGE (Services and Advocacy for GLBT Elders) in New York City in 1977. His website is www.tamarackplace.com/kimmel.

Peggy Lorah, DEd, NCC, LPC, is the director of the Center for Women Students at The Pennsylvania State University, where she is also an affiliate faculty in Counselor Education, Women's Studies, and College Student Affairs. She has practiced as a clinician in community mental health, drug and alcohol, and domestic violence programs. She has done research in the area of affirmative services with lesbian, gay, and bisexual populations. She is a past-president of the Pennsylvania Association for Lesbian, Gay, Bisexual, and Transgender Issues in Counseling.

John F. Marszalek, PhD, LPC, NCC, is a program coordinator and core faculty for the MS in Mental Health Counseling Program at Walden University. He has been a counselor educator for more than 10 years, previously on the faculty of Barry University in Miami and Xavier University in New Orleans. He has been a counselor for more than 15 years, maintaining private practices in Fort Lauderdale; New Orleans; and Columbus, Missouri. Dr. Marszalek's research interests include gay, lesbian, and bisexual identity development theory and factors promoting and inhibiting long-term gay relationships.

Connie R. Matthews, PhD, NCC, LPC, is managing partner of New Perspectives, LLC. She does consulting and training around helping groups and organizations to be more culturally competent in working with their LGBT constituents. She is also a counselor educator as well as a researcher, with a focus on affirmative counseling with lesbian, gay, and bisexual clients. She has previously worked and volunteered in the substance abuse and domestic violence fields. She is an associate editor of the *Journal of Lesbian, Gay, Bisexual, and Transgender Issues in Counseling,* a past-president of the Pennsylvania Counseling Association, and a past-chair of the American Counseling Association North Atlantic Region.

Ron McLean, PhD, LPC, LMHC, is the director of McLean Counseling and Training Services in Metuchen, New Jersey. He is also the director of the university counseling center at the University of Maryland Eastern Shore in Princess Anne. He received his doctorate in counselor education and family therapy from Saint Louis University. His research and practice interests include sexual minorities, multiculturalism, spirituality, college student retention, and counselors' entrepreneurial competence. When he is not working he enjoys spending time with his partner and their four children.

Michael J. Potoczniak, PhD, attended the University of Miami for his PhD work and is currently working as a licensed psychologist at Student Health Services for the University of California at Berkeley. His work with clients currently focuses on gay men's health, transgender health, polysubstance dependence, posttraumatic stress disorder, attention-deficit/hyperactivity disorder, bipolar spectrum disorders, issues related to HIV/AIDS, motivational interviewing, and career issues. He is an adjunct faculty at the Graduate School of Education at Manhattan College in New York City and has a private practice in Berkeley, California.

Jeffrey P. Prince, PhD, is the Director of Counseling and Psychological Services at the University of California, Berkeley, and a past-president of the International Association of Counseling Services. He has worked in the field of college counseling and career development as a psychologist, teacher, and trainer for more than 25 years. He serves on a number of editorial boards and has held a range of leadership positions within the American Psychological Association, where he was elected a Fellow for his significant contributions to the field of psychology. He is the author of numerous publications pertaining to college student counseling, LGBT student career development, social justice, and international student mental health.

Ana Puig, PhD, NCC, LMHC, Qualified Supervisor (FL), is an associate scholar and research director in the Office of Educational Research, College of Education, at the University of Florida and an affiliate faculty in counselor education. Her research interests have focused on complementary therapies in breast cancer care, spirituality and health issues in counseling, religiosity and academic achievement, and multicultural spirituality. She has more than 20 years of clinical experience and has worked with LGBTQ individuals and couples in inpatient, outpatient, and private practice settings. Dr. Puig has conducted lectures on LGBTQ identity development nationally and internationally, including speaking on multicultural and spiritual considerations in working with this population.

Jane E. Rheineck, PhD, LCPC, NCC, is an assistant professor at Northern Illinois University. Dr. Rheineck's research and publications have focused primarily on women and the implications of counseling lesbian and gay individuals. Dr. Rheineck is a licensed clinical professional counselor in the state of Illinois and has a clinical background that reflects a broad range of experiences that include adolescent inpatient residential treatment, outpatient counseling with adults, and mental health counseling in the schools.

Kate Richmond, PhD, is an assistant professor of psychology and a contributing member of the Women's Studies Department at Muhlenberg College. In addition to teaching, she currently maintains an active private practice, in which she specializes in the treatment of trauma and issues related to gender. Dr. Richmond has produced more than 20 refereed publications and presentations in the area of gender, trauma, feminism, and multicultural and international psychology. Dr. Richmond has been honored on two separate occasions for outstanding teaching.

Kathleen Y. Ritter, PhD, MFT, NCC, CCMHC, is a professor of counseling psychology at California State University, Bakersfield. She and Dr. Anthony I. Terndrup coauthored the *Handbook of Affirmative Psychotherapy With Lesbians and Gay Men* (Guilford Press, 2002) and were awarded the Distinguished Book Award from Division 44 of the American Psychological Association in 2003. Dr. Ritter is a Fellow of Division 44 and was granted the Distinguished Professional Contribution Award from that division in 2008. Over the years, she has frequently published and presented on topics related to sexual minority concerns.

Catherine B. Roland, EdD, LPC, NCC, is a professor at Montclair State University and director of the Counselor Education PhD Program. Her research and national presentations have focused primarily on gender issues, women in transition, lesbian and gay mental health issues, and midlife and older adults. Dr. Roland has had a private therapy practice for 25 years, specializing in LGBT couples and individuals and women in transition. She edits *Adultspan*, a national journal specializing in developmental approaches to counseling adults.

Glenda M. Russell, PhD, is a psychologist both at Counseling and Psychological Services at the University of Colorado at Boulder and in private practice. She has conducted research on the psychological consequences of anti-LGBT politics, internalized homophobia, and outgroup activism. She is the author of *Voted Out: The Psychological Consequences of Anti-Gay Politics* and with Janis Bohan of *Conversations About Psychology and Sexual Orientation.*

Samuel Sanabria, PhD, LMHC, NCC, is an assistant professor of counselor education at Rollins College in Winter Park, Florida. His research interests include ethical practices in counseling, same-sex parenting, the development of homoprejudicial attitudes, LGBT issues, and Latino concerns. He has more than 15 years of experience counseling couples, families, adults, and adolescents regarding sexual and gender identity concerns.

He is an active member of the American Counseling Association (ACA), having served on both the Bylaws and Ethics Committees. Dr. Sanabria is also a member of the ACA divisions Counselors for Social Justice and the Association for Multicultural Counseling and Development and is currently a board trustee for the Association for Lesbian, Gay, Bisexual and Transgender Issues in Counseling.

Hemla D. Singaravelu, PhD, LPC, NCCC, is an associate professor in the Department of Counseling and Family Therapy at Saint Louis University. She is also the cochair and director of the master's program. Prior to teaching at Saint Louis University, she served as an assistant professor at Missouri State University and as the Coordinator of Career and Mentor Programs at Fitchburg State University in Massachusetts. She received her doctorate in educational psychology/counselor education from Southern Illinois University at Carbondale and specializes in career development and multicultural/diversity counseling. She has published and presented in the areas of multicultural counseling (including gay and lesbian) issues, the career development of diverse populations, and international students. She has been on the editorial board of the *Journal of Counseling & Development, The Career Development Quarterly,* and *Journal of LGBT Issues in Counseling.* She was born and raised in Malaysia.

Anneliese A. Singh, PhD, LPC, NCC, is an assistant professor in the Department of Counseling and Human Development Services at The University of Georgia. She received her doctorate in counseling psychology from Georgia State University in 2007. Her clinical, research, and advocacy interests include LGBTQ youth, Asian American/Pacific Islander counseling and psychology, multicultural counseling and social justice training, qualitative methodology with historically marginalized groups (e.g., people of color, LGBTQ, immigrants), feminist theory and practice, and empowerment interventions with survivors of trauma. Dr. Singh is a past-president of the Association for Lesbian, Gay, Bisexual and Transgender Issues in Counseling. She is the recipient of the 2007 Ramesh and Vijaya Bakshi Community Change Award and the 2008 Counselors for Social Justice 'Ohana Award for her organizing work to end child sexual abuse in South Asian communities and to increase the visibility of South Asian LGBTQ people.

Misti A. Storie, MS, is the education and training consultant for the National Association of Alcohol and Drug Abuse Counselors (NAADAC), the Association for Addiction Professionals. Storie is the technical writer for NAADAC's educational programs, including *Integrating Treatment for Co-Occurring Disorders: An Introduction to What Every Addiction Counselor Needs to Know* as well as the educational seminars *New Horizons: Integrating Motivational Styles, Strategies and Skills With Pharmacotherapy; Pharmacotherapy: Integrating New Tools Into Practice; New Innovations in Opioid Treatment: Buprenorphine;* and *Medication Management for Addiction Professionals: Campral Series* that toured across the United States from 2006 to 2009. She is also the primary author and editor of *The Basics of Addiction*

Counseling: Desk Reference and Study Guide, Tenth Edition, and numerous articles concerning addiction-related issues for *NAADAC News.* Storie holds a master of science degree in professional counseling from Georgia State University; a master of science degree in justice, law, and society from American University; and a bachelor of arts degree in psychology from Emory University, with minors in sociology and violence studies.

Anthony I. Terndrup, PhD, MA, LPC, LMFT, is the executive director of the Pastoral Counseling Center of the Mid-Willamette Valley in Corvallis, Oregon, where he practices pastoral psychotherapy and trains pastoral counselors. In addition to coauthoring their notable text *Handbook of Affirmative Psychotherapy With Lesbians and Gay Men,* he and Dr. Kathleen Ritter have presented more than three dozen continuing education workshops for several professional associations on counseling with lesbian, gay, and bisexual clients in numerous cities across North America. In 2009, Dr. Terndrup completed a master's degree in pastoral ministry at the Northwest Center for Catholic Graduate Theology (University of Portland–Gonzaga University). He is a certified Fellow in the American Association of Pastoral Counselors.

M. Carolyn Thomas, PhD, LPC, CS, LMFT, LBSW, is a professor of counselor education at Auburn University Montgomery. She is a Fellow of the Association for Specialists in Group Work (ASGW) and the National Career Development Association (NCDA) and has served on the boards of both the ASGW and NCDA. Dr. Thomas is currently the ASGW representative on the American Counseling Association Governing Council. She received the Point of Light Award for her work with family violence. Her publication and presentation interests have concentrated predominantly on counseling older persons, groups for victims of family violence, and career development with elementary school age children.

Joy S. Whitman, PhD, LCPC, is a licensed clinical professional counselor and associate professor of education in the Counseling Program at DePaul University. In addition to teaching at DePaul, she serves in the American Counseling Association as the Governing Council representative for the Association for Lesbian, Gay, Bisexual and Transgender Issues in Counseling and is a past-president of this division. Her research focus is on LGBT issues, specifically training counselors to provide affirmative therapeutic treatment to LGBT clients, and she has written and presented on this issue throughout her career. She also maintains a small private practice serving lesbian, bisexual, and gay clients.

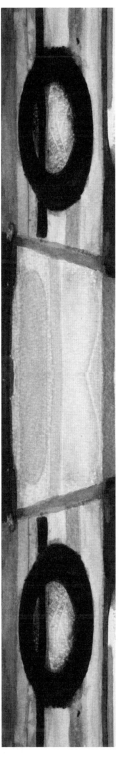

Section 1
Developmental Issues

Competent counselors will

- ◙ understand that biological, familial, and psychosocial factors influence the course of development of GLB orientations and transgendered identities.
- ◙ identify the heterosexist assumptions inherent in current life span development theories and account for this bias in assessment procedures and counseling practices.
- ◙ consider that, due to the coming out process, LGBT individuals often may experience a lag between their chronological ages and the developmental stages delineated by current theories.
- ◙ recognize that identity formation and stigma management are ongoing developmental tasks that span the lives of LGBT persons.
- ◙ know that the normative developmental tasks of LGBT adolescents frequently may be complicated or compromised by identity confusion; anxiety and depression; suicidal ideation and behavior; academic failure; substance abuse; physical, sexual, and verbal abuse; homelessness; prostitution; and STD/HIV infection.

Note. Each section introduction begins with the relevant competencies for working with lesbian, gay, bisexual, and transgender persons from the Association for Lesbian, Gay, Bisexual and Transgender Issues in Counseling.

1

In the chapters that compose this section, our authors look at the various developmental issues that face LGBT clients: counseling with lesbian, gay, bisexual, transgender, queer, questioning, and intersex (LGBTQQI) youth, coming out, counseling with intersex and transgender clients and their families, counseling across the life span, and career development. These developmental issues cut across the entire life span and the cases address those processes.

The first chapter, "Sexual Minority Youth: The Case of Donald Wilson," by Suzanne M. Dugger and Laurie A. Carlson, addresses the role of school counselors as advocates for LGBTQQI students. School counselors are a critical part of the delivery of mental health services in our society. They are at the front lines of this system and therefore are often the first to see problems as they arise in young people. They can then make effective referrals to community resources, because with 400 students to every one school counselor, counselors simply do not have the time to do individual or family counseling.

Drs. Dugger and Carlson present the case of Donald Wilson, a 15-year-old high school student who is questioning his sexual orientation. They address in a comprehensive way the resources, barriers (including professional, familial, legal, and confidentiality issues), and role of the school counselor in being an effective advocate for LGBTQQI students. Having a safe and understanding adult to talk to about same-sex feelings can make all the difference in the world to a young person, and Drs. Dugger and Carlson handle this in a sensitive, knowledgeable, and understanding way.

From children and adolescents the section moves on to adult gay men with John F. Marszalek and Edward P. Cannon's chapter "Coming Out for Gay Men." Coming out is one of the most important events in the life of an LGBTQQI person, and it may be fraught with peril. The process is composed of two different aspects: coming out to one's self and coming out to others. The first is the culmination of many years of consideration, and the latter is a series of events over a person's lifetime. Both are important.

Issues of "why" and "how to" form the foundation for this issue. Counselors can help their clients consider the advantages and disadvantages of coming out in the workplace or school as well as provide clients with opportunities for behavioral rehearsals directed toward developing strategies for informing others. Drs. Marszalek and Cannon discuss these issues in the context of the case of Jeremy. They also address the issues that flow from coming out, including the effects on opposite-sex spouses, families, and friends.

The next chapter addresses an issue rarely discussed in the literature: intersex clients. We include this chapter in this section because intersex is an issue that starts in infancy and impacts clients throughout their lives. Theodore R. Burnes and Kate Richmond write on "Counseling Strategies With Intersex Clients: A Process-Based Approach."

Intersex is the term given to babies born with ambiguous genitalia. Often it is the medical team that decides, with little guidance from the parents, the sex of the child. Frequently problems arise as intersex children grow up. Drs. Burnes and Richmond present a composite case using a process-oriented framework and combining the issues and experiences of many of their intersex clients. Becky, an intersex woman, feels betrayed by her parents and her physicians. Important to this case is providing truthful information about the client's body, naming "the pain," and giving the client the space to discuss feelings of shame around her body and embarrassing experiences with other people.

Similar to other chapters in this book, the authors use a feminist conceptualization in order to validate oppressions and traumas to Becky's body. Bibliotherapy is helpful for intersex clients because information about the condition and about others who deal with it is not readily available. Other therapeutic techniques in this case include cognitive therapy to counter thoughts such as "I'm a freak" and Gestalt techniques to help the client reconnect with what the body is saying. The chapter ends with a discussion about ethics for working with intersex clients.

From individuals the section moves on to family concerns throughout the life span. Stuart F. Chen-Hayes discusses "Counseling and Advocacy With a Gay Father, a Straight Mom, and a Transgender Adolescent." Dr. Chen-Hayes recommends two books for families with transsexual and gender variant persons: Boenke, Dudley, and Bowden's (2008) *Trans-Forming Families* and Brill and Pepper's (2008) *The Transgender Child*. Both books explain the issues facing children and youth and their families as they negotiate gender identity and gender expression. Dr. Chen-Hayes's chapter deals with numerous intersecting identities and complex issues. Maya is a multiracial African American and Mexican child of divorced parents who have joint custody of her. The father, Roberto, is a gay Chicano and has a Chinese American boyfriend. Maya was referred for counseling by a teacher who caught her drinking. Maya, who has a background of sexual abuse, ultimately comes out as transgender. Her internal image of herself is as a boy, not a girl. Using techniques from cognitive behavior therapy and narrative therapy with bibliotherapy, the counselor helps Maya and her two families cope with these complex issues.

This section then moves on to the last stage of development. Two chapters discuss the issues of gay older adults: Douglas Kimmel's "Counseling Older Gay Men" and M. Carolyn Thomas, S. Lenoir Gillam, and Paul F. Hard's "Counseling Older Lesbians: The Case of Pat and Selene."

Gay men face aging issues similar to those of their heterosexual counterparts; however, the stresses of aging experienced by gay men are compounded by society's stigmatization of their sexual orientation and the emphasis within gay culture on youth (Berger, 1980, 1996; Kelly, 1977; Kimmel, 1978; Pope, 1997; Pope & Schulz, 1990). Older gay men face issues of a stigmatized sexual orientation, invisibility related to their sexual orientation, and general negative stereotypes and discrimination regarding aging.

Berger and Kelly (1996) remarked on the need for counselors to be versed in LGBT issues, community, and resources in order to be effective in counseling aging LGBT individuals. Therapists should give particular consideration to both the usual aging issues and the specific problems faced by aging lesbians. Physicians and other caregivers are often reluctant to recognize or discuss matters of sexual orientation related to older adults (Pope, 1997). Berger and Kelly also noted that older clients may be more reticent about all forms of self-disclosure, which may compound problems establishing a therapeutic environment unless the therapist takes steps to create an open atmosphere. Counselors may therefore need to address their own personal ageism issues in order to facilitate disclosure as well as be prepared to advocate for their clients.

Issues of access to services may be magnified in more rural settings where LGBT-specific services may not exist. Berger and Kelly (1996) observed that the availability of positive LGBT referral resources may be limited. They noted that gerontological services are often homophobic or hold the heterosexist notion that older LGBT persons do not exist. Although some researchers have observed that the LGBT population is becoming less urban (Signorile, 1998), social services and support for LGBT persons continue to remain predominantly in urban environments (Robinson, 2005). The culturally sensitive counselor must therefore be prepared to advocate for gay and lesbian clients and assist them in accessing services.

In "Counseling Older Gay Men," Dr. Kimmel presents two cases that intertwine aging with cultural diversity and sexual issues and address the physiological, economic, emotional, and cultural aspects that older gay men face.

Many of the issues discussed here hold true for older lesbians as well as older gay men. Drs. Thomas, Gillam, and Hard use the 4 S Model—Situation, Self, Support, and Strategies (Thomas & Martin, 2010)—to present the case of Pat and Selene.

The final chapter of this section, "An Asian Indian Woman's Ethnic, Sexual, and Career Identity" by Hemla D. Singaravelu, addresses the developmental issue of career choice. Providing effective and culturally appropriate career counseling to gay and lesbian clients may appear at first glance to be largely the same as helping nongay or nonlesbian clients identify and pursue their career goals. Since 1990, a substantial body of literature has addressed career counseling with lesbian and gay persons, but very little of the past or recent career counseling literature regarding gay men and lesbian women has addressed the issues of nondominant racial or ethnic groups in the United States (Pope et al., 2004). Dr. Singaravelu presents the case of a young Asian Indian lesbian woman who is struggling with her career issues. Issues of multiple cultural identities and the intersection of lesbian and gay issues with race and ethnicity are central to this career development case.

References

Berger, R. M. (1980). Psychological adaptation of the older homosexual male. *Journal of Homosexuality, 5*(3), 161–175.

Berger, R. M. (1996). *Gay and gray: The older homosexual man* (2nd ed.). Boston, MA: Allyn & Bacon.

Berger, R. M., & Kelly, J. J. (1996). Gay men and lesbians grown older. In R. P. Cabaj & T. S. Stein (Eds.), *The textbook of homosexuality and mental health* (pp. 305–316). Alexandria, VA: American Psychiatric Association.

Boenke, M., Dudley, D., & Bowden, L. (Eds.). (2008). *Trans forming families: Real stories about transgendered loved ones* (3rd ed.). Washington, DC: PFLAG Transgender Network.

Brill, S., & Pepper, R. (2008). *The transgender child: A handbook for families and professionals.* Berkeley, CA: Cleis.

Kelly, J. (1977). The aging male homosexual. *The Gerontologist, 17,* 328–332.

Kimmel, D. C. (1978). Adult development and aging: A gay perspective. *Journal of Social Issues, 34,* 113–130.

Pope, M. (1997). Sexual issues for elderly lesbians and gays. *Topics in Geriatric Rehabilitation, 12*(4), 53–60.

Pope, M., Barret, B., Szymanski, D. M., Chung, Y. B., McLean, R., Singaravelu, H., & Sanabria, S. (2004). Culturally appropriate career counseling with gay and lesbian clients. *The Career Development Quarterly, 53,* 158–177.

Pope, M., & Schulz, R. (1990). Sexual behavior and attitudes in midlife and aging homosexual males. *Journal of Homosexuality, 20*(3/4), 169–178.

Robinson, P. A. (2005). *Queer wars: The new gay right and its critics.* Chicago, IL: University of Chicago Press.

Signorile, M. (1998). *Life outside.* Boston, MA: Harper Perennial.

Thomas, M. C., & Martin, V. (2010). Group work: Elderly people and their caregivers. In D. Capuzzi, D. R. Gross, & M. D. Stauffer (Eds.), *Introduction to group work* (5th ed., pp. 505–536). Denver, CO: Love.

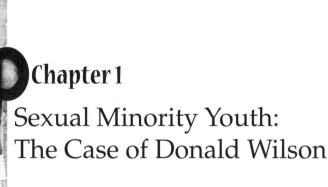

Chapter 1

Sexual Minority Youth: The Case of Donald Wilson

Suzanne M. Dugger and Laurie A. Carlson

This chapter presents the case of "Donald Wilson" and demonstrates the importance of recognizing developmental as well as diagnostic and cultural issues that might contribute to problems presented by sexual minority youth. In doing so, it describes counseling provided to a 15-year-old boy referred by his school counselor and concludes with recommendations for school personnel.

Introduction

Growing up in suburbia isn't always as easy as it seems. This was certainly the case for Donald Wilson. Poor Donald. As if having red hair and freckles weren't enough, Donald was also the only student in his school to regularly dress in cowboy boots and western-style shirts and to be a member of a 4-H club. The only extracurricular activity that interested him was horseback riding, but his school didn't have a club for this. Therefore, Donald had to travel to a more rural area, near an aunt's home, to join a 4-H equestrian club.

At 15, being "different" in these ways wasn't easy, and Donald knew he didn't fit in with any of the identifiable groups in his school. He wasn't part of the popular crowd, wasn't an athlete, wasn't known for academic achievements, wasn't an "emo," and wasn't a skater. Donald was . . . well, *nice*. He was one of the nicest young men in the school. Always polite and considerate, Donald was appreciated by his teachers despite his academic struggles. Although he mostly hated school, Donald clearly tried hard, cared about pleasing his teachers and about getting a good education, and didn't bother anyone. Fortunately, nobody really bothered Donald either. Instead they just left him alone. And that's how he felt. Alone. Alone and different.

These feelings were written all over his face when Donald met with his school counselor. Although the purpose of the meeting was simply to discuss and update his educational development plan, and similar meetings were being held with all 10th-grade students, the school counselor noticed what appeared to be Donald's sadness and decided to take some extra time with him. After asking Donald how things were going and getting the standard response of "fine," she chose to probe a bit more. When she commented that he didn't seem very happy and wondered aloud whether there was anything bothering him, Donald admitted that he didn't really like school and wished there were other kids who were more like him.

Educated not only in school counseling but also in the more clinical aspects of counseling, the school counselor decided to do a brief assessment for symptoms of depression. She was saddened but not surprised when Donald endorsed a number of depressive symptoms. Although she was well trained and able to provide counseling for such issues, she knew her role as a school counselor in a comprehensive guidance and counseling program didn't afford her the time needed to provide mental health counseling to students on an ongoing basis (Bowers & Hatch, 2005; Stone & Dahir, 2005). Therefore, with Donald's knowledge and consent, she called his mother and provided her with a list of several referral possibilities—including me (Suzanne M. Dugger), one of her former professors and a counseling psychologist working part time in private practice. This chapter details the clinical work I did with Donald and concludes by revisiting the school environment to make recommendations.

The Assessment Process

In developing an understanding of my clients, I strive for as complete a picture as possible. Therefore, I routinely begin my work with minors by first meeting with their parents (or guardians), and I ask that they not bring their child to this session. I find that such a meeting is quite helpful in a number of respects. First, it allows me to conduct a full clinical assessment from the parents' perspective. Especially when the child-client is not particularly forthcoming, the information I gain from that meeting can be immensely helpful. Second, the meeting allows the parents an opportunity to become acquainted with me and to determine whether they are comfortable allowing me to counsel their child. Finally, and very importantly, I use this meeting to discuss my approach to confidentiality and to explain to parents that I will honor their child's right to confidentiality and not reveal the nature of our conversations unless I have a serious concern about the child's safety or welfare.

Such was the case when I began working with Donald. In my initial meeting with his parents, I learned much about his family's constellation and about Donald's childhood history. They shared information about Donald's schooling, about his relationship with his two sisters, about his participation in their church, about his part-time job at a pet store, and about his lack of friends. I also invited each of them to respond to the Depression and Anxiety in Youth Scale (DAYS) Parent Rating Scale and asked them to arrange to have two of Donald's teachers complete the DAYS Teacher Rating Scale (Newcomer, Barenbaum, & Bryant, 1994).

It is not until the second session that I meet with the child. In this session, I invite the parents or guardians into the room at the very beginning to reiterate—this time in front of the child—that I will honor the child's right to confidentiality and not reveal information to the parents unless I have a concern about the child being seriously harmed by the parents or another adult (child abuse) or about the child seriously harming him or herself (suicide) or others (homicide). I find that providing informed consent with both the child and the parents in the room at the same time is quite useful, especially as children get older and attribute greater importance to privacy issues. After the informed consent part of this session, I ask the parents to leave so that the child and I can talk privately.

Not surprisingly, the adults' perceptions of the situation and issues at hand do not always match the child's perceptions. Therefore, it is essential that the counselor (whether in the school or community setting) remain open to each party's perspectives. Especially when working with minors, it is also essential that the counselor create a trusting atmosphere in which the child may feel safe enough to share what is really going on for him or her.

As with Mr. and Mrs. Wilson, I used the first session to get to know Donald and understand issues of concern to him. Although much of what Donald shared coincided with what I had learned from his parents, some of it didn't. Based on our session and his completion of the DAYS Student Self-Report (Newcomer et al., 1994), I learned that Donald was indeed experiencing a number of depressive symptoms—but not enough, in fact, to meet the diagnostic criteria for any mood episodes or disorder. In addition, Donald disclosed some feelings of generalized anxiety. Again, though, his symptoms were subthreshold, meaning that they did not meet the diagnostic criteria for him to be diagnosed with any specific anxiety disorder. I also learned that Donald didn't like church as much as his parents thought and that he found some of the parishioners to be "narrow minded and judgmental."

I also asked Donald about other social supports using age-appropriate language. After asking about his friends, I asked, "What about romantically? Are there any girls or guys you like? Is there anyone special?" Donald looked horrified and, in a decidedly huffy voice, responded, "Well *girls*, of course!" Acknowledging his dismay, I apologized to Donald and explained that, in my line of work, I never like to make assumptions about people. I expressed my awareness that sometimes guys like guys and sometimes guys like girls—that either way was okay with me and I just didn't want to make any assumptions.

In Donald's case, this was a critical moment in the development of a therapeutic alliance. Had I not asked about romantic relationships in an inclusive manner, I am confident the conversation that ensued would not have happened in that first session, and am not certain it ever would have. In response to my explanation, Donald simply murmured an awkward "oh" and we moved on to talk a little bit more about his friends at school. Suddenly, though, he interjected, "Well, maybe . . ." I looked up and waited for him to continue, and it seemed to take an eternity for Donald to complete his next sentence: "Well, maybe I like guys. I'm not sure." Donald's face was as bright red as his hair, and he seemed to appreciate my response. Looking him straight in the eyes and holding his gaze, I softly thanked him for taking the risk to share his uncertainty with me and said that, if he wanted, we could use some of our time together to help him figure things out.

As our sessions progressed, I learned that this was the first time Donald had ever acknowledged to anyone else that he was uncertain about his sexual orientation. I learned that one of the reasons he experienced some people in his church as narrow minded and judgmental was that they sometimes expressed homophobic beliefs. I also learned that Donald's feelings of depression and anxiety were related in large part to his internal struggles about sexual orientation.

Cultural and Contextual Considerations

In approaching work with all clients, it is essential to understand their presenting concerns in context. Donald was a Caucasian whose family heralded mostly from England and Scotland and had immigrated to the United States in the late 1600s. Donald was raised by God-fearing parents who believed wholeheartedly in the literal meaning of the Bible. As members of a conservative Methodist church, the family rarely missed church services on Sundays, and Mr. and Mrs. Wilson's social circle was composed entirely of other church members. Consistent with Church teachings, Donald's parents considered homosexuality a "perversion of God's created order" (*Book of Discipline* of the Free Methodist Church, as cited in "Homosexuality and Methodism," 2010) and believed that marriage should be restricted to heterosexual couples.

Socioeconomically speaking, Donald's family was considered working middle class. Both of his parents held high school diplomas and working-class jobs. His father worked on an assembly line producing auto parts, and his mother worked part time as an orderly in a local assisted-living facility. Geographically speaking, Donald's family lived in a suburb of Ann Arbor, Michigan. Although this particular suburb was noted for its conservatism and lack of diversity, Ann Arbor itself offers considerable diversity, particularly with regard to race, national origin, religion, and sexual orientation.

Developmental Considerations

A hallmark difference between counseling and psychology is that counselors tend to think more developmentally. Rather than specializing in diagnosis and the identification and treatment of mental disorders, counselors have special training in, and give great attention to the role of, normal developmental processes in creating and/or maintaining client difficulties. In approaching the assessment and diagnosis of any client, regardless of age, I therefore consider the presenting concerns from two perspectives: developmental and diagnostic.

My work with Donald was illustrative of this two-pronged approach. In addition to exhibiting subthreshold symptoms of both depression and anxiety, Donald was struggling with several developmental issues. Indeed, as those who regularly work with adolescents can attest, this stage of life is marked by a confluence of major developmental shifts. Table 1.1 identifies several shifts relevant to Donald's case.

Diagnostic Considerations

In addition to thinking developmentally about client concerns and the impact of various types of development on clients, it can also be useful to conceptualize cases from a diagnostic perspective. This is particularly important when clients seek to use insurance or managed care benefits to cover the cost of counseling, as payment for services is then dependent on medical necessity (Poynter, 1998). The multiaxial diagnosis I offered in Donald's case was as follows:

Axis I   309.28   Adjustment Disorder With Mixed Anxiety
              and Depressed Mood
              V62.89   Phase of Life Problem
Axis II   V71.09   No Diagnosis on Axis II
Axis III   None
Axis IV   Academic struggles
              Inadequate social support
Axis V   61

In arriving at this diagnosis, I considered substituting 313.82 Identity Problem for V62.89 Phase of Life Problem. Ultimately, though, I decided on Phase of Life Problem for three primary reasons. First and most important, from a conceptual framework, I viewed any identity problems Donald may have been experiencing (including problems with sexual orientation and religious values) as stemming from the developmental phase of adolescence, in which the emergence of sexual attractions is commonplace. Second, I believed that his struggle with clarifying his sexual orientation and his growing discomfort with his past religious teachings stemmed not so much from not knowing himself as from confusion regarding his own inner experiences contrasted with the contextual messages regarding sexual orientation with which he was raised. Third, in addition to being more clinically accurate, the diagnosis of Phase of Life Problem had the added benefit of being more ambiguous and less likely to signal to others (his parents or their managed care company) the nature of Donald's concerns.

Treatment Process

When I approached the treatment process with Donald, several key considerations informed my clinical work. Most important was the perspective that this was Donald's process, not mine, and that it was essential that I

Table 1.1   Developmental Shifts Affecting Donald Wilson

Developmental Type	Shift Occurring During Adolescence	Donald's Probable Experience of This Shift
Physical	Growth spurts Hormonal changes • Body odor • Moodiness • Hair growth • Spontaneous erections	In the past year, Donald had grown 4 inches, was definitely in need of daily use of deodorant, and was likely experiencing growth of hair in his armpits and pubic region. He wouldn't want anyone to know, but he sometimes had wet dreams and worried about getting an erection in the locker room after gym class.
Psychosocial	Struggles with solidifying sense of self (identity) Increased autonomy from parents Increased valuing of peer relationships Increased interest in romantic relationships	Like many adolescents, Donald was struggling to develop a solid sense of who he was. His level of self-confidence fluctuated quite a bit, and he became much more self-conscious than he had been as a child. Donald was feeling more isolated and different from his peers at school. Even so, Donald exhibited tendencies toward autonomy at home, and this was sometimes reflected in not wanting to be told what to do by his parents (and even being rude to them at times).
Sexual orientation	Increasing awareness of romantic attractions Increasing awareness of sexual attractions Acceptance of attractions varies by individual	Although Donald had experienced a feeling of attraction to other boys for about 3 years, he had only admitted this to himself within the past year. His family's involvement in the church and social messages that he received in school deeply affected his level of self-acceptance. At this point, he was just starting to conceptualize the nuances regarding the physical, emotional, and spiritual characteristics of attraction.
Academic and career	Increased emphasis in schools on content knowledge and skills Increasing emphasis on connection between school and career More attention to postsecondary options	Because of Donald's uncertainty about his sexual orientation and the related depression, he found it very hard to be successful in school. His grades were slipping, and this worried him because he recognized that, as a freshman in high school, his academic success would play an ever-increasing role in his postsecondary options.

(Continued on next page)

12

Table 1.1   **Developmental Shifts Affecting Donald Wilson** *(Continued)*

Developmental Type	*Shift Occurring During Adolescence*	*Donald's Probable Experience of This Shift*
Cognitive	Increased brain functioning, especially in the frontal lobe, associated with stronger abilities to reason, plan, and control impulses Greater understanding of complexities and nuances Improved decision-making capacity	Donald demonstrated strong reasoning ability through his dialogue and interactions with others. He certainly knew how to identify and navigate the social expectations within multiple aspects of his life. He understood that he "felt different" than others and also recognized when it was safe in counseling to share his doubts about his sexuality.
Moral	Increased sense of right and wrong Improved cognitive decision-making capacity may conflict with increased interest in peer approval	Although adolescence is typically marked by a stronger sense of right and wrong, Donald was struggling with his reactions to some of the teachings of his church, specifically as they related to homosexuality. In many ways, Donald presented within the post-conventional stage of Kohlberg's (1981) moral development theory in that he was struggling to navigate from seeking the approval of others to asserting his personal rights.

facilitate a process for Donald to arrive at his own conclusions rather than use the therapeutic process to promote my personal values or beliefs. Indeed, the *ACA Code of Ethics* (American Counseling Association, 2005) prohibits counselors from imposing their values on clients and requires that we honor our clients' autonomy. Therefore, it was important for me to help Donald explore *his* feelings, *his* attractions, *his* values, and *his* options.

It was also important for me to allow Donald to decide what we talked about in any given session—whether it be feelings of depression, feelings of anxiety, school-related concerns, irritating sisters, isolation at school, loneliness, or confusion about sexual orientation—rather than deciding for him what we needed to discuss. In addition to being ethically sound, this nondirective approach was clinically essential for Donald. It was, to be sure, a very scary experience for Donald to even acknowledge that he was experiencing some confusion about his sexual orientation. As counselors well trained in diversity issues and accepting of all sexual orientations, we can sometimes forget how difficult these issues may be for our clients. Whether they are young like Donald or considerably older when they begin to struggle with the possibility of same-sex attractions, clients are generally apprehensive, even scared, of the insights they might gain through the counseling process. A well-meaning "Congratulations" or "Yay, gay!" type of response to a client's disclosure can be too much, too soon. It can scare them away from you, away from the counseling process, and even away from the self-exploration process. It could also have the effect of steering or guiding them toward or away from where they ultimately need to be.

Therefore, I took a decidedly nondirective approach when working with Donald. From session to session, we discussed what *he* wanted to discuss. However, this does not suggest that I was using a person-centered theoretical orientation with him. Such an approach is based on the premise that the therapeutic relationship is both necessary *and* sufficient and that the counselor therefore needs only to provide the therapeutic conditions of growth: unconditional positive regard, empathy, and genuineness (Patterson, 1985). In contrast, though I certainly believe in the importance of the therapeutic relationship, I do not believe it is both necessary and sufficient. Instead, I believe that the therapeutic process is greatly enhanced by the addition of other elements. For me, these additional elements include psychoeducation as well as psychological interventions. In order to integrate these into the therapeutic process in a nondirective manner, it was essential that I do so *in response* to issues Donald raised. Consistent with treatment recommendations for adjustment disorders (Seligman, 2004), our counseling focused on helping Donald cope with the life stressors to which he was adjusting rather than on symptom reduction, and it was up to him which stressors we discussed in any given session.

In essence, he led the way and I responded therapeutically—sometimes with empathic responses, sometimes with educational responses, and sometimes with theory-based interventions. This blend of empathic listening, psychoeducation, and interventions permeated most of my sessions with Donald. Regardless of whether Donald chose to talk about school or family or religion or sexual orientation, it was common for me to listen empathically, facilitate Donald's exploration of the topic at hand, and incorporate psychoeducation or interventions as appropriate.

Interventions Specific to Sexual Orientation

Perhaps the most important intervention specific to Donald's confusion regarding his sexual orientation was the provision of a holding environment (Cashdan, 1988; Trembley, 1996) in which Donald could safely be uncertain. Rather than encouraging him to resolve his uncertainty as quickly as possible, I assured Donald that it was okay to be unsure and communicated a confidence that he would figure it out over time. We talked about what he experienced (thoughts, feelings, fantasies) that prompted him to be uncertain and what it was like for him to question the direction(s) of his sexual attractions and romantic interests. We discussed his increased awareness of how many others in his life seemed to assume heterosexuality—like when his grandma asked him whether he had a girlfriend yet. We laughed about his initial reaction to me *not* assuming he was heterosexual.

I provided psychoeducation about the various dimensions of sexual orientation: sexual attraction, sexual behavior, and sexual identity (Bostwick, Boyd, Hughes, & McCabe, 2010). This can be particularly important when working with school-age youth who may not yet be interested in or ready for becoming sexually active. Donald, for example, didn't have any history of sexual behavior, as he had never even been kissed, certainly didn't know how he identified, and was in the process of trying to understand his pattern of sexual attraction.

We brainstormed various types of clues that can signify sexual attraction and talked about how this might help him clarify whether he was sexually attracted solely to males, solely to females, or to both. In the context of how the human body might react when thinking about someone to whom one is attracted, we talked about autonomic responses such as sweaty palms, flushed cheeks, racing heart, dry mouth, breathlessness, butterflies in the stomach, and sexual arousal. I explained that these sensations are automatic responses rather than conscious decisions. We talked about how people don't really get to decide who they find attractive, that it "just happens."

This led, naturally, to a discussion about whether sexual orientation is a choice. Donald expressed great interest in this particular topic and began noticing how many messages from his church seemed to suggest that it was a choice. After he borrowed my copy of *Is It a Choice? Answers to the Most Frequently Asked Questions About Gay and Lesbian People* (Marcus, 2005), we talked about sexual attraction not being a choice and sexual behavior involving choice. I also showed Donald a handout illustrating the typical stages of a coming out process (Cass, 1979), and we talked about choice in the context of these stages.

Donald also struggled to reconcile what he considered conflicting messages from his religion: that God creates all people in His image and likeness but that homosexuality is a sin. After Donald revealed his increasing irritation with going to church and being subjected to homophobic teachings, I shared with him that people sometimes feel that they must choose either their religion or their sexual orientation but that others find a way to keep both parts of their identity. We looked online and found a group called Affirmation: United Methodists for Lesbian, Gay, Bisexual and Transgender Concerns and a resource called *Whosoever: An Online Magazine for Gay, Lesbian, Bisexual and Transgender Christians*. I also shared with him a book titled *Coming Out of Shame* (Kaufman & Raphael, 1996), which is particularly helpful with regard to reconciling internalized religious messages with the coming out process.

Outcomes

With regard to outcomes, Donald's initial presenting concerns included feelings of depression and anxiety, a lack of an adequate support group (friends) and concomitant loneliness, and frustration related to academic struggles. What is interesting is that none of these complaints became the consistent focus of our sessions. Although we certainly discussed these issues frequently, it became apparent that Donald's deeper concerns were related to his uncertainty regarding sexual orientation.

Donald and I worked together for approximately 2 years, with sessions in the first year generally occurring on a weekly or bimonthly basis and sessions in the second year occurring less frequently—bimonthly or monthly. Over this period, Donald came to the conclusion that he was indeed gay. He used the early counseling process to resolve his confusion about his sexual orientation and the later counseling process to assist him with integrating his sexual orientation into his identity. As described previously, this included attempts to resolve perceived conflict between his sexual orientation and his religious beliefs. In terms of the Cass (1979) model of gay identity development, Donald arrived at counseling either late in the Identity Confusion stage or early in the Identity Comparison stage and left counseling early in the Identity Acceptance stage.

As he worked through the process of coming out to himself and began to accept himself as he was, Donald began having fewer and fewer complaints of anxiety or depression. In fact, within approximately 8 months, those symptoms had largely subsided. However, he continued to feel rather isolated, and his grades improved only slightly. Part of Donald's continued sense of isolation was that he still had yet to come out to anyone in his family, church, or school. Donald had, however, begun participating in a coming out group in the Ann Arbor area and described this as a very positive, albeit scary, experience. As a result, Donald felt that he was "living two lives"—one in which he could be himself and one in which everyone assumed he was heterosexual and he was willing to play the part. This was becoming increasingly difficult, though, and Donald began avoiding church activities in which he anticipated hearing homophobic statements.

Although our counseling relationship ended before Donald's work did, I was pleased with the progress he made. It appeared to me that Donald would soon begin coming out to select individuals. He had, for example, told me about conversations he had with his mother after seeing something on TV or hearing something on the radio about gay issues. In these instances, Donald seemed compelled to explain to his mother that it was acceptable for "those people" to be gay and to point out the contradictions he perceived in their church's teachings. It is unclear whether his mother began to wonder whether Donald might be gay, but this seemed to be a way in which Donald could talk to her about gay issues without directly coming out to her and in which he could begin to gauge her receptivity should he decide to come out to her.

Sexual Minority Youth in the Schools: Recommendations for School Personnel

Like many young men and women, Donald Wilson began the process of coming out while a student in secondary school. Indeed, researchers have found that the average age of coming out to oneself and to others has declined significantly in the past decades, with the average age of coming out to oneself now being approximately 15 for young men and 16 for young women regardless of race or ethnicity (Grov, Bimbi, Nanin, & Parsons,

2006). Therefore, those working in middle and high schools should be cognizant that their students may be approaching or experiencing the coming out process. Lesbian, gay, bisexual, and transgender (LGBT) students in American schools continue to suffer invisibility, misunderstanding, verbal persecution, and often physical violence, leading to an increased need for understanding and advocacy from caring adults within the school community (Goodrich & Luke, 2009; Whitman, Horn, & Boyd, 2007). It is also important for educators to understand that these issues deeply affect the experience of students who have significant others in their lives who identify as gay, lesbian, bisexual, transgender, queer, or so forth.

Although their personal values and professional obligations may at times be at odds, adults in the school understand the critical nature of inclusivity and safety for all students, and they must accept responsibility for maintaining an environment in which all can achieve to their fullest potential. Regardless of where they stand personally on the issue of sexual orientation, it is the professional responsibility of educators to provide a safe learning environment for all students. School counselors in particular have a legal obligation to protect lesbian and gay students in schools (McFarland & Dupuis, 2001; Stone, 2003). School counselors can promote a safe and inclusive environment through a five-faceted approach: (a) self-reflection and professional development, (b) policy examination and revision, (c) physical environment inventory and adaptation, (d) faculty training and support, and (e) student education and advocacy.

Self-Reflection and Professional Development

It is essential that educators engage in an honest and open examination of their own personal values and that they identify various points of congruence or incongruence between their own values and the positions espoused by the profession. When there are conflicts or points of incongruence, it is incumbent upon educators to behave in accordance with their profession's position whenever acting in a professional capacity. This means that educators who personally disapprove of gay, lesbian, or bisexual "lifestyles" must nonetheless protect the right of such students to a learning environment safe from ridicule, judgment, and physical danger.

School counselors are called to go beyond ensuring safety by also demonstrating commitment to the affirmation of lesbian, gay, and bisexual youth. Specifically, the official position statement of the American School Counselor Association (ASCA) communicates a clear mandate that school counselors

> are aware of their own beliefs about sexual orientation and gender identity, are knowledgeable of the negative effects that result from stereotyping individuals into rigid gender roles, and are committed to the affirmation of youth of all sexual orientations and identities. (ASCA, 2007, p. 28)

This position statement highlights the importance of an honest examination of oneself. Indeed, "a counselor's individual belief or behavioral system, which goes unchecked for bias or prejudice, may result in unethical practices which alienate students before advocacy, or even counseling intervention, can take place" (Field & Baker, 2004, p. 59). This self-examination typically begins during training and continues throughout one's professional career. Several self-assessment tools are available to help gain insight into one's multicultural awareness, knowledge, and skill (Pope-Davis & Dings, 1995).

In order to increase awareness of the "negative effects that result from stereotyping" and in order to develop skills for the "affirmation of youth of all sexual orientations and identities," professional development is crucial (ASCA, 2007, p. 28). Many professional resources are available for increasing such awareness and skills. In addition to professional development initiatives within the school, there are numerous journals, workshops, and conferences available through professional associations such as the American Counseling Association, ASCA, and the Association for Lesbian, Gay, Bisexual and Transgender Issues in Counseling. Finally, a number of organizations with a strong online presence focus on safety and inclusion issues in the school. Two such organizations are the Gay, Lesbian, & Straight Education Network (GLSEN; www.glsen.org) and the Safe Schools Coalition (www.safeschoolscoalition.org).

Policy Examination and Revision

School policies are important for creating a culture of respect. Policies are most effective when they are clearly articulated, strongly stated, and well publicized. Consider the antiharassment and antidiscrimination policies in place at your school. Are LGBT students specifically identified within the language of these policies? Are all faculty, staff, and students educated about these school policies? If you find that written policies need revision, one very helpful resource for composing a strong and inclusive policy can be found at the American Civil Liberties Union website (http://www.aclu.org/lgbt-rights_hiv-aids/model-policy-schools).

Closely related to articulated policy is an appropriate process and set of procedures for responding to policy violations. The way in which administrators and decision makers respond to a breach of policy can make a significant difference in continued adherence to and support of that policy. An expedient and decisive response is critical to policy support; all too often policies are followed discriminately, with certain infractions (e.g., race-related harassment) being dealt with much more sufficiently than others (e.g., sexual or gender harassment). Therefore, your school should also have written procedures regarding how staff members should respond to policy violations, such as those involving antigay slurs (by students or staff members), harassment in the hallways, and physical altercations. The Safe Schools Coalition provides a number of resources to help in the articulation of such policies and procedures, including *An Administrator's Guide to Handling Anti-Gay (LGBTQ) Harassment* (http://www.safeschoolscoalition.org/guide_administrator_handleharass2005.pdf).

Physical Environment Inventory and Adaptation

Invitational theory is one framework that school counselors can use to evaluate and improve the larger environment of the school (Stanley, Juhnke, & Purkey, 2004). The basic premise behind invitational theory is that an environment falls on a continuum from intentionally disinviting to intentionally inviting. More specifically, this theory addresses a multitude of factors that affect the extent to which an environment is experienced as inviting, welcoming, and inclusive of all.

According to invitational theory, the physical environment is one important element that deeply affects how inviting or disinviting an environment is. Stanley et al. (2004) suggested that because the physical environment is much easier to observe than other forms of internal biases, it is a key element to consider when assessing whether an environment is inviting, welcoming, and inclusive of all. This is especially important to consider in schools because, depending on the observable artifacts present in the school building, the environment may be experienced as more or less inviting by various groups of students. For example, a school in which the hallways are decorated with Christmas trees and Santa Claus every December will likely feel more inviting to students who observe Christmas than to students who do not.

Therefore, in an effort to be more intentionally inviting toward many groups of students, schools should take great care to ensure a wide range of welcoming artifacts within their physical environment. This concept applies easily to artifacts that may communicate a welcoming message to students who do not (or eventually will not) identify solely with heterosexuality, whether this is because of their own sexual orientation or the sexual orientation of a family member. Examples of inviting environmental artifacts for LGBT students and students from LGBT families include safe zone stickers, rainbow stickers, posters with inclusive language and images, and LGBT-related literature in the library. The one caution here is that these items should always be used in a manner consistent with respect and inclusion. I am aware of at least one instance when a school official used a safe zone sticker to attract LGBT students to his office so that he could "pray for their healing." Such a practice is obviously in conflict with the ASCA position statement, the *ACA Code of Ethics,* and our professional responsibilities as educators.

Faculty Training and Support

As a school counselor involved in professional development for colleagues, it is important to recognize that you are not alone. A number of quality programs and materials are available for carrying out this work. As mentioned earlier, one national organization that provides extensive, quality resources is GLSEN. In addition to being useful for counselors' own professional development, the GLSEN materials are quite useful for providing professional development to fellow educators. One entire area of the GLSEN website is devoted to materials for educators (http://www.

glsen.org/cgi-bin/iowa/all/educator/index.html? state=tools&type=tools).
Another very professional and valuable publication that can be used to raise
awareness and understanding among faculty is the small booklet *Just the
Facts About Sexual Orientation and Youth: A Primer for Principals, Educators,
and School Personnel* (Just the Facts Coalition, 2008).

Student Education and Advocacy

In addition to helping increase the awareness of staff members regarding
the importance of recognizing and intervening to ensure a safe learning
environment for LGBT students, education geared toward students is also
necessary. One effective approach is to integrate LGBT issues into wider
antibullying and/or diversity awareness programs. Such programs teach
students about many forms of difference (including sex, race, religion,
sexual orientation, learning abilities, physical abilities) and discourage
bullying in any form. Another approach is to integrate lessons specifically
about LGBT issues into a wider curriculum.

Useful with either approach is the fact that a number of organizations
offer information and resources to help school counselors support LGBT
youth and their families. Some of the more familiar organizations include
GLSEN and Parents, Families, and Friends of Lesbians and Gays (PFLAG).
Both organizations offer material for youth as well as for adults who wish
to provide support. PFLAG's primary initiative for youth is the Safe Schools
for All program (http://community.pflag.org/Page.aspx?pid=1011). Other
initiatives that provide resources and advocacy materials include Project
10 (http://www.project10.org/) and the Mix It Up program within the
Southern Poverty Law Center's Teaching Tolerance initiative (http://www.
tolerance.org/mix-it-up?source=redirect&url=mixitup). Also, gay/straight
alliances have been shown to produce positive social and psychological
outcomes for LGBT students and allies (Friedman-Nimz et al., 2006). School
counselors can find valuable information regarding the formation and
facilitation of gay/straight alliances through GLSEN and the Gay Straight
Alliance (www.gaystraightalliance.org).

Conclusion

The case of Donald Wilson illustrates the experiences of a high school
student with the coming out process. Although the school counselor was
accurate in recognizing that the provision of ongoing mental health counseling for Donald was inappropriate in the wider context of a comprehensive
guidance and counseling program, one might wonder how the school environment contributed to Donald's need for such counseling. In his case,
he happened to have a school counselor who was very self-aware and well
trained in advocacy efforts. Had Donald taken the risk of coming out to
her, he would have found her to be very accepting and helpful. That being
said, one wonders about the other elements of this five-faceted approach.
How inviting was the school environment? Were physical indicators, such
as rainbow stickers, visible to signal an environment affirming of all sexual

orientations? Were educators well trained in how to intervene immediately and effectively when witnessing an antigay slur or harassment in the hallways? Were they supported in doing so by written policies and procedures? Did any of the classroom guidance lessons on bullying ever integrate and specifically include antigay bullying? And was there a gay/straight alliance within the school? If so, was it included in the list of extracurricular clubs in the student handbook?

Although we'll never know the answers to these questions, thinking about such issues offers hope for the future. By attending to each element of the five-faceted approach outlined here, you can provide better service to the Donald Wilsons in all of our schools. It is our hope that as you work to create a safe and inclusive environment for all students, this case study and discussion will be of use to you.

References

American Counseling Association. (2005). *ACA code of ethics.* Alexandria, VA: Author.

American School Counselor Association. (2007). *The professional school counselor and LGBTQ youth. Retrieved* from http://asca2.timberlakepublishing.com//files/PS_LGBTQ.pdf

Bostwick, W. B., Boyd, C. J., Hughes, T. L., & McCabe, S. E. (2010). Dimensions of sexual orientation and the prevalence of mood and anxiety disorders in the United States. *American Journal of Public Health, 100,* 468–475.

Bowers, J., & Hatch, P. A. (2005). *The ASCA national model: A framework for school counseling programs* (2nd ed.). Alexandria, VA: American School Counselor Association.

Cashdan, S. (1988). *Object relations therapy: Using the relationship.* New York, NY: Norton.

Cass, V. C. (1979). Homosexual identity formation: A theoretical model. *Journal of Homosexuality, 4*(3), 219–235.

Field, J. E., & Baker, S. (2004). Defining and examining school counselor advocacy. *Professional School Counseling, 8*(1), 56–63.

Friedman-Nimz, R., Altman, J., Cain, S., Kom, S., Karger, M. J., Witsch, M. J., . . . Weiss, M. (2006). Blending support and social action: The power of a Gay-Straight Alliance and PrideWorks conference. *Journal of Secondary Gifted Education, 17,* 258–264.

Goodrich, K. M., & Luke, M. (2009). LGBTQ responsive school counseling. *Journal of LGBT Issues in Counseling, 3*(2), 113–127.

Grov, C., Bimbi, D. S., Nanin, J. E., & Parsons, J. T. (2006). Race, ethnicity, gender, and generational factors associated with the coming-out process among gay, lesbian, and bisexual individuals. *Journal of Sex Research, 43,* 115–121.

Homosexuality and Methodism. (2010). Retrieved from http://en.wikipedia.org/wiki/Homosexuality_and_Methodism

Just the Facts Coalition. (2008). *Just the facts about sexual orientation and youth: A primer for principals, educators, and school personnel.* Retrieved from http://www.apa.org/pi/lgbt/resources/just-the-facts.aspx

Kaufman, G., & Raphael, L. (1996). *Coming out of shame: Transforming gay and lesbian lives.* New York, NY: Doubleday.

Kohlberg, L. (1981). *Essays on moral development.* San Francisco, CA: Harper & Row.

Marcus, E. (2005). *Is it a choice? Answers to the most frequently asked questions about gay and lesbian people* (3rd ed.). San Francisco, CA: Harper & Row.

McFarland, W. P., & Dupuis, M. (2001). The legal duty to protect gay and lesbian students from violence in schools. *Professional School Counseling, 4*(3), 171–179.

Newcomer, P. L., Barenbaum, E. M., & Bryant, B. R. (1994). *Depression and Anxiety in Youth Scale: Examiner's manual.* Austin, TX: PRO-ED.

Patterson, C. H. (1985). *The therapeutic relationship: Foundations for an eclectic psychotherapy.* Monterey, CA: Brooks/Cole.

Pope-Davis, D., & Dings, J. (1995). The assessment of multicultural counseling competencies. In J. G. Ponterotto, J. M. Casas, L. A. Suzuki, & C. M. Alexander (Eds.), *Handbook of multicultural counseling* (pp. 287–311). Thousand Oaks, CA: Sage.

Poynter, W. L. (1998). *The textbook of behavioral managed care: From concept through management to treatment.* Bristol, PA: Brunner/Mazel.

Seligman, L. (2004). *Diagnosis and treatment planning in counseling* (3rd ed.). New York, NY: Springer.

Stanley, P., Juhnke, G., & Purkey, W. (2004). Using an invitational theory of practice to create safe and successful schools. *Journal of Counseling & Development, 82,* 302–309.

Stone, C. B. (2003). Counselors as advocates for gay, lesbian, and bisexual youth: A call for equity and action. *Journal of Multicultural Counseling and Development, 31,* 143–155.

Stone, C. B., & Dahir, C. A. (2005). *The transformed school counselor.* Boston, MA: Lahaska Press.

Trembley, E. L. (1996). *Relational therapy concepts.* Kalamazoo, MI: Author.

Whitman, J. S., Horn, S. S., & Boyd, C. J. (2007). Activism in the schools: Providing LGBTQ affirmative training to school counselors. *Journal of Gay & Lesbian Psychotherapy, 11*(3–4), 143–154.

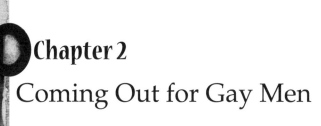

Chapter 2
Coming Out for Gay Men

John F. Marszalek and Edward P. Cannon

Identifying Data and Background Information

Jeremy Miller, a 26-year-old Caucasian man, had come to counseling as a result of his fiancée's discovery of male pornography on his computer. He had felt same-sex attractions since adolescence and had come to the decision that he must now find a way to be honest with himself as well as with the people in his life. He had been raised in a strict Christian denomination in which homosexuality was rarely discussed; if it was brought up, it was only in a negative light. Jeremy was the youngest of three sons and had been raised in a working-class suburb of a large midwestern city. He had excelled in athletics from the time he was in middle school and received a soccer scholarship to a major university. He currently lived with his fiancée Amy and worked as an account representative for a large insurance company. Jeremy stated, "When I was 15 I knew I was gay, but knowing and accepting are two very different things."

In high school and college, Jeremy would bond with his soccer team-mates by sharing fictitious tales of sexual conquests and would flirt with women in order to deflect attention away from his true feelings. He would even go so far as to taunt boys who appeared effeminate or who "acted gay." In his mind, Jeremy believed that being happy as an openly gay person was simply not possible, so he developed a heterosexual persona and compartmentalized his attractions to other boys. That secret, Jeremy now said, was like a tight knot in his stomach, always threatening to seep out. He lived in almost constant fear of rejection from his brothers, his parents, his teammates, his friends at school, and his church.

In order to blunt the reality of his same-sex attractions, and to fit in with the other jocks, Jeremy began drinking alcohol socially in high school. He joined a fraternity in college, and his drinking only escalated. He discovered that although drinking alcohol allowed him to numb his feelings, it also made him susceptible to inappropriate expressions of his bottled-up emotions. On at least one occasion, Jeremy made an advance toward a fraternity brother. The young men were so inebriated from alcohol that each could dismiss the encounter as experimentation, but Jeremy knew otherwise. Also during college, Jeremy would occasionally visit the gay bars in the city near his university. There, after a few drinks, he would summon the courage to talk to another man he found attractive. He had several sexual encounters during this time but would always tell himself that he was just letting off steam and that these encounters didn't mean anything.

Looking back on this period in his life, Jeremy recalled, "I was like a ticking bomb; I thought I could suppress it, keep it locked away in some dark corner of myself, but I couldn't." Jeremy reported feeling demoralized during most of the past 5 years and often used alcohol to numb his feelings. Jeremy found that alcohol could be a relaxant that would temporarily take away the loneliness, but the feelings would later come back stronger than ever. According to Jeremy, "You wake up one morning thinking 'I can handle it, everything is fine,' and the next morning you don't want anybody to see your face, because you think that if people look at you they will know." Suffering in silence seemed to be Jeremy's coping mechanism, but clearly this was no longer working for him.

During his senior year in college, Jeremy sought the advice of the campus minister, who advised him to "seek strength through his faith" to fight his same-sex attractions. Because he wanted to please his family and church community, Jeremy devoted many hours to praying and attending faith services in order to suppress his true feelings. Jeremy reported that during this time he went through "all sorts of emotions, tears, anger and despair." At one of the church services held on campus, Jeremy met Amy, and he began to believe that he could actually be heterosexual. Despite his unequivocal attraction to men, Jeremy found a deep friendship with Amy and told himself that if he prayed hard enough, his feelings for Amy would become romantic ones. Unfortunately, this did not happen, but nevertheless Jeremy let Amy believe that he was sexually attracted to her. In their faith, sex should not happen until marriage, so Jeremy felt secure in remaining abstinent with Amy. Jeremy recalled, "I became a master of disguise and could play the straight man down to a tee, sometimes overcompensating by getting into fights or by being overly aggressive because I didn't want the real me to be found out. As hard as I prayed for those feelings to go away, over time they only got stronger. I used to ask God, 'What is the answer?' but there wasn't one."

Presenting Issues

As mentioned earlier, Jeremy's fiancée discovered male pornography on his computer and demanded an explanation. Jeremy denied everything, telling Amy that a hacker must have gotten control of his computer. Amy also confronted Jeremy about his excessive drinking, but he only told her that entertaining was a major part of his job and he couldn't help that fact that he had to meet with clients in bars and restaurants. This confrontation with Amy brought up feelings of guilt and shame for Jeremy, as well as feelings of confusion and hopelessness. "It's so difficult to be so close to someone, and every day tell them that you love them and hear them say they love you, know the words were true, but also knowing the real me wanted to take over." He even briefly considered suicide.

It was during this time that Jeremy's strong faith helped him see that God must have a plan for him and that it must be to be his true self. Jeremy summoned the courage to seek out a counselor, and despite canceling three times, he finally brought himself to an intake appointment. Jeremy's presenting issues included his feelings of anxiety and depression, his search for a coherent identity, and his abuse of alcohol. He would need to develop a personal identity that included his sexuality and would also need to resolve the shame and fear around having a socially stigmatized self. Transforming Jeremy's self-hatred into a love of self would be a major goal of counseling. His natural internal resistance to accepting that he was a member of a despised minority, coupled with a lack of information and role models, would make identity formation a complex challenge for Jeremy.

Diagnoses

Axis I	Identity Problem (313.82). This is the least stigmatizing diagnosis (a V code, or problem in living). Jeremy reports feelings of depression and even a past suicidal ideation (which on further exploration is a passive wish to no longer live a lie). This diagnosis reflects Jeremy's struggle to accept his true identity. He does not meet the criteria for major depressive disorder.
	Alcohol Abuse (305.00). This diagnosis is a result of Jeremy's reporting that on numerous occasions he drove his car home after consuming several alcoholic beverages (recurrent substance use in situations in which it is physically hazardous).
Axis II	No diagnosis
Axis III	No diagnosis
Axis IV	Raised in a culture not accepting of homosexuality
Axis V	Global Assessment of Functioning = 80 (current)

Theoretical Framework

I (John F. Marszalek) conceptualized Jeremy's case using object relations theory and integrating it with Teyber's (2006) interpersonal process approach, person-centered theory, and cognitive behavior theory. Although it may seem odd to use a psychoanalytic theory in working with a sexual minority—or anyone who is not a White Euro-American, for that matter—I agree with Sommers-Flanagan and Hutz (2008) that the focus is on the individual and how he or she makes meaning of his or her experiences regardless of his or her diverse background. In addition, whereas in the past most psychoanalytic organizations viewed homosexuality as a mental disorder, today reputable psychoanalytic organizations such as the American Psychoanalytic Association no longer hold that view. The American Psychoanalytic Association Committee on Lesbian, Gay, Bisexual, and Transgender Issues (2010) has stated that "same-gender sexual orientation cannot be assumed to represent a deficit in personality development or the expression of psychopathology" ("Position Statements," Para. 2) and that "a psychoanalytic frame of reference [e.g., conscious and unconscious factors] is very useful in trying to understand why it is difficult to achieve attitudinal changes" (Para. 1). In addition, the American Psychoanalytic Association has made resolutions in support of legal recognition of same-sex marriage, in opposition to the U.S. military policy prohibiting service based on sexual orientation and in opposition to "public or private discrimination" (Para. 5).

It was obvious to me that Jeremy was struggling with true-self/false-self issues. Winnicott (1960/1996) described the true self as comprising the spontaneous, creative, real person, whereas he described the false self as having the function of hiding and protecting the true self and the part that interacts with the outside world. Problems occur when the true self is too deeply hidden and when the false self becomes what the individual knows as his or her real self. Winnicott spoke of the "good enough mother" to describe the mother who provides enough affirming experiences to enable the formation of a true self that is not completely buried. In today's world, I think it's fair to say that this could be referred to as "good enough parenting." In addition, I conceptualized this case considering the concepts of good and bad objects. Objects are internalized representations of one's relationships. Object relations theorists (e.g., Fairbairn, 1958/1996; Scharff, 1996; Winnicott, 1960/1996) focus on the importance of attachments, especially the early attachments with parents, one's internalization of these attachments, and one's drive to maintain those attachments. No parent is perfect, so there will obviously be times when a child feels neglected or rejected and internalizes the neglecting aspects of the parent; however, there will be other times when the child feels nurtured and internalizes the loving aspects of the parent. As children internalize these experiences with their parents, they use the defense of splitting to dichotomize the frustrating, rejecting aspects of the parent into a "rejecting object" and the nurturing, affirming aspects of the parent into an "ideal object" (Scharff, 1996, p. 16). With good enough parenting, in which the relationship is characterized more by nurturing and loving,

> gradually the child will be able to increasingly integrate her ambivalent feelings toward the sometimes frustrating and sometimes responsive parents into a stable and affirming relational schema of self and other, which becomes the basis of self-esteem and identity. Under greater attachment threats, however, the child cannot do this without resorting to splitting defenses. These splitting defenses preserve the image of an idealized, "all good," responsive, parent with whom the child

is internally connected. But the price is high; Reality is distorted, the self is fragmented, and the child becomes the one who is "bad." The frustrating parent is no longer "bad," which allows the child to view the external world as safe. The price, however, is inner conflict. The child believes that, if only he were different, parental love would be forthcoming. (Teyber, 2006, pp. 10–11)

Treatment Goals and Interventions

In sum, I hypothesized that Jeremy had a strong rejecting object that was composed of internalized messages (e.g., internalized homophobia) rejecting his true self and a weaker, affirming ideal object. The rejecting object was composed of messages in support of the false self and seeking substitutes (e.g., alcohol, pornography) for true self–to–true self attachments.

Establishing a Holding Environment

One goal of treatment was for me to provide what object relations theorist D. W. Winnicott (1960/1996) described as a holding environment by providing good enough parenting. This holding environment is a nurturing environment in which Jeremy could explore his true self, including his sexual orientation identity, and feel safe enough to be vulnerable in relaxing his protective, false self. This would thus fulfill the following of the Competencies for Counseling Gay, Lesbian, Bisexual and Transgendered (LGBT) Clients: "Competent counselors will acknowledge the societal prejudice and discrimination experienced by LGBT [lesbian, gay, bisexual, and transgender] persons and assist them in overcoming internalized negative attitudes toward their sexual orientations and gender identities" (Association for Lesbian, Gay, Bisexual and Transgender Issues in Counseling [ALGBTIC], 1997, "Helping Relationships," Competency 1).

Often also described as the therapeutic alliance, the development of this environment is an ongoing goal of treatment. It begins the day the client first enters the counselor's office and continues up until and possibly beyond (through internalizations) the final session. As our therapeutic relationship strengthened, I hoped that Jeremy would be able to internalize our relationship as an ally of his true self (i.e., an ideal object) so that he could hold onto our relationship when he left our sessions.

As I strove to provide a holding environment, I also wanted to observe patterns in both his past and present relationships to determine how they had been internalized as rejecting and ideal objects. I sought to observe these patterns in his discussions of current relationships, past relationships, dreams, and fantasies. I also wanted to begin to observe how these patterns emerged in our interactions through transference and countertransference, which I address in the next section.

In our initial sessions I conducted an intake interview, worked at establishing the beginning of a therapeutic alliance, formed initial hypotheses, and discussed a plan of action with Jeremy. One of his initial questions was whether he could be gay and still live a "traditional heterosexual lifestyle," and I explained that we could figure that out together; however, my task would be to help him figure that out, not tell him who he should be or how he should live. *(Helping Relationships Competency 4: Competent counselors will understand that attempts to alter or change the sexual orientations or gender identities of LGBT clients may be detrimental or even life-threatening, and, further, are not supported by the research and therefore should not be undertaken; ALGBTIC, 1997.)*

My response to this question seemed surprising to him, because he said he was accustomed to being told what to do by important people in his life (i.e., parents and minister). This discussion provided a nice segue for me to explain that in order to understand him better, I wanted to first conduct a thorough history of his life, including important experiences and relationships. I led him through this history by saying things such as "Tell me about your childhood," "What was school like for you?" and "Describe your parents for me." He painted a picture for me of a "normal, happy childhood"; however, as I inquired further I learned that his response was indicative of an unspoken family rule: "Don't rock the boat; be normal." He described his parents as being concerned about appearances and making sure that they were always among the best dressed, drove the right cars, and so on. Using an Adlerian technique, I asked him to describe his earliest recollections of his childhood: He recalled being on stage for a Christmas play at his church and his mother fussing about his outfit before he walked on stage with the other children. The picture of his mother in my mind was of one of the *Stepford Wives,* a woman who was concerned about appearances above everything and who had difficulty expressing her affection to her family outside of words. Jeremy described his father as very religious, heavily involved in the church as a deacon, and more apt than his mother to demonstrate his affection of his sons; however, it usually related to their accomplishments. He recalled the pride he saw in his father's eyes when he excelled in school and soccer. Jeremy stated that he was viewed as a "star" at his church, a leader in the church youth group, and an ideal son. Jeremy said his younger brother did not do as well in school and was more likely to embarrass his family, such as by being caught drinking on a church youth retreat. Jeremy said that seeing the disappointment in his parents' faces toward his brother made him not want to fail in their eyes.

Promoting Identity Development and Self-Esteem

Another goal of treatment was to actively work with Jeremy in promoting his sexual orientation identity development, which I knew generally correlated with an increase in self-esteem. *(Human Growth and Development Competency 7: Competent counselors will affirm that sexual minority persons have the potential to integrate their GLB orientations and transgendered identities into fully functioning and emotionally healthy lives; ALGBTIC, 1997.)*

Understanding Relationship Patterns and Internalized Objects

I first wanted to help Jeremy develop an understanding of his pattern of relationships and how they were related to his internalized object relations. Jeremy had developed attachments with his parents and most others based on his false self, in effect protecting and hiding his true self. He had learned at an early age to be what others expected him to be. I hypothesized to him that it was as if he had antennae on his head that enabled him to know what was acceptable and what was not acceptable of him to others. Jeremy readily agreed with this hypothesis, describing how he was good at his job because he could be whatever he needed to be to make a sale. He also described relationships with friends in which he felt he was acting. I also hypothesized to him that he had a "critical self" that told him that it was not okay to be himself and that he should hide himself from others. I suggested that the critical self comprised all the ways we've been told (nonverbally or verbally) that we're not okay. The concept of a critical self made sense to him, and he often used that term when describing the conflict he felt inside between his "critical self" and "true self."

Processing the Here and Now

Developing an understanding of his own critical self and patterns of rela-tionships went hand in hand with developing the therapeutic alliance. The more comfortable Jeremy felt with me, the safer he felt discussing his criti-cal thoughts of himself and the ways in which he hid himself from others. It also provided me with an opportunity to consider how his relationship pattern entered into our relationship, another means I used to promote his identity development and self-esteem. I used an interpersonal process approach (Teyber, 2006) to focus on what happened in our relationship. As Yalom (2002) described, I used my "here-and-now rabbit ears" (p. 50) to observe Jeremy's verbal and nonverbal reactions to me, my office, and anything else related to our work together.

For example, sometimes I would notice that Jeremy seemed uncom-fortable, and I would inquire about it. He would generally say that he had imagined that I was judging something he was saying or that he was considering discussing something that he imagined I would judge. These became opportunities to consider how he projected his critical self onto me and others, assuming that he would be judged critically. They also became opportunities to use cognitive–behavioral strategies to challenge the notion that *everyone* would judge him. I should note that in challenging his internalized critical messages, I would not be unrealistic and I would acknowledge that there are people who would judge him (i.e., I would acknowledge that prejudice and hatred do exist and that one does need to protect oneself).

Another example of using an interpersonal therapy approach was when I was aware of my own countertransference reactions to him. For example, prior to one of our sessions, I was showing a colleague out of my office around the same time Jeremy entered the waiting area. When we entered my office, I noticed that he seemed a little distant and that I was experienc-ing countertransferential feelings of being small compared to him. I asked him what it was like for him to see me talking to someone else, and after quite a bit of processing he acknowledged that I had sounded very "gay" to him when he had heard me speaking to my colleague. (Note that this was after I had disclosed to him that I am gay.) I encouraged him to talk about how it made him feel for me to "sound gay." This here-and-now moment led to a discussion of what it meant to "sound gay" and his fear that other people would see him that way. He recalled a time when he was a child and his father told him to "stop acting like a fag" when he was dancing to a song on the radio. Jeremy said the look in his father's eyes was of extreme disapproval, and he had never forgotten that look. The memories of others' disapproval were clues to his internalized rejecting object that reinforced the distancing of his true self in relationships.

Self-disclosure is an important interpersonal process issue that can impact both the therapeutic environment and the client's internalization of the counselor as an ideal object. As Isay (1996) discussed, the self-disclosure issue for gay counselors is whether to disclose their sexual orientation to their clients. Like Isay, I believe that I can be a positive model for gay clients struggling with identity issues; at the same time, I do not immediately tell clients that I am gay unless they ask or appear to be wondering about it (e.g., based on their dreams or frequent discussions of people they know who are gay). *(Helping Relationships Competency 2: Competent counselors will recognize that their own sexual orientations and gender identities are relevant to the helping relationship and influence the counseling process; ALGBTIC, 1997.)* Although most of my clients know that I am in a gay relationship through colleagues of mine that have referred them or because of my involvement in the gay community, Jeremy said that he did not know that I was gay. This fact was most obvious in the fear he had during our first session in telling me that he "had a secret" that was difficult for him to discuss. During our subsequent sessions he did not ask me anything about my life outside of the office and often worried that I judged him for being gay. Because I tell clients that we can discuss their dreams as a means to further explore their unconscious, Jeremy entered counseling around the tenth week with a dream about me in gay bar. I responded by asking Jeremy whether he wondered if I was gay. He replied that he had been wondering for awhile but did not feel comfortable asking me. I acknowledged that I was gay and asked him how he felt about knowing that. He expressed relief and stated that he felt it would be easier to be open with me. He also stated that he felt I was like him and not stereotypically effeminate. After this disclosure, he became more open about his fantasies, both sexual and nonsexual, and he seemed less defended in our sessions. At the same time, as in the example when he heard me talking in the waiting room, there were times when we would process here-and-now moments in which I became the rejected gay person and he became the critical parent.

The processing of these here-and-now moments proved to be valuable in providing Jeremy with a different type of relationship in which he could process his feelings about the relationship, relax his false self, learn about the ways in which he had projected aspects of internalized objects onto others, and experience a relationship in which he could be himself. As he internalized our relationship, evidenced by his dreams of me and imagining what I might say to him when he was struggling with something between sessions, he gradually progressed through the stages of gay identity development (see Marszalek & Pope, 2008).

Decreasing Substance Abuse

Another treatment goal was to help Jeremy consider how his abuse of alcohol could be viewed as unsatisfying attempts to satiate his emptiness—emptiness due to a lack of attachments (external and internal) that enabled him to relax his false self and that provided real true self–to–true self connections. I suggested to him that the alcohol provided a substitute for the feeling of connection one can have in a relationship in which the false self is relaxed. He related to this idea because he recounted the times he had "let out [his] gayness" when he was drunk. He did not report any alcoholism in his family, and I was unsure whether he had a genetic predisposition to alcoholism. I did provide him with material on high-risk drinking and groups in the area such as Alcoholics Anonymous (including the gay Alcoholics Anonymous meeting at the nearby LGBT community center). I also expressed my concern that he was playing with fire by drinking and driving, endangering both himself and others. I was extremely careful to express my concern in a tone and manner that was not critical and also encouraged him to call me between sessions if he considered bingeing.

Outcomes

Jeremy and I met regularly for approximately a year and a half. In the beginning he met with me twice weekly and transitioned to once weekly as he began to feel more comfortable with himself. I encouraged him to meet with me as frequently as we were able in the beginning in order to form the therapeutic relationship and to provide a holding environment that could be internalized more rapidly. Jeremy was able to afford twice-weekly sessions, which is not the case for many clients. I also encouraged him to call me between sessions if he felt suicidal, if he thought he was going to binge on alcohol, or if he just needed to check in. Jeremy rarely called because he was concerned that he would be bothering me (which was another here-and-now moment to process) but stated that knowing that he could helped him feel less alone.

Many of our sessions revolved around Jeremy's eventual decision to end his relationship with Amy, his concerns about his coworkers discovering that he was gay, and whether he should disclose his sexuality (i.e., come out) to his parents. Jeremy went back and forth for several months on whether to stay with Amy. As he became more accepting of himself, it became more difficult for him to have a romantic relationship with Amy, and he eventually ended the relationship. Amy was understandably angry and refused to have any contact with him, believing even after he came out to her that his homosexuality was a choice. The ending of one of the few close relationships in his life was difficult for him and led to a period of mourning during which we processed his guilt, doubts, and sadness.

Jeremy had hoped that Amy could still be his friend, and her refusal to have contact with him was very difficult for him. His ending of the relationship also constituted making a commitment in his mind to a gay identity. He began to discuss his desire to meet other gay people and to someday be in a relationship. He recounted a dream in which he was sitting on the porch of a cabin in the woods with another man and experiencing a sense of connection, spiritually and emotionally. Jeremy had told me in an earlier session that one of the times he felt he was most in touch with himself was when he was in nature. This dream seemed to spark an acknowledgment to himself of his yearning for relationships. It also led to discussions on his evolving spirituality and how it was different from the religion in which he had been raised.

Sometime around our ninth month of meeting, Jeremy accepted my referral to a gay men's coming out group led by a colleague at the city's LGBT community center. The group had mixed effects in terms of our work together. He related to other men's coming out stories, which affirmed his own experience. He also met a few other men who worked in business-related jobs and who he felt could relate to his fear of losing his job if others discovered he was gay. However, men whom he described as being "effeminate" triggered his own internalized homophobia, and we would sometimes revisit his fears that he could not fit into the gay community and that if people knew he was gay, they would see him as he saw these men. Over time he became less fearful but could still be judgmental about gay men who were what he described as "stereotypical."

Jeremy's substance abuse decreased over time and he became less apt to drink and drive; however, he continued to drink when he socialized with his new friends. The gay bar scene became very alluring to him, and during this time I found myself attempting to balance my concerns about his drinking and frequent sex with my understanding that he was reliving his adolescence. I provided him with information on safe sex and also made interpretations on casual sex, like alcohol, sometimes being a substitute for real attachments. I had to be careful that I made such interpretations in a tone and manner that did not sound critical. I also noticed out loud that his "party" self seemed to be different from the self in his dream. He acknowledged that the sex felt empty to him when it was a one-night stand but that for the first time he could remember he was having fun.

Around the time of our 14th month working together, Jeremy began dating someone he had met through the coming out group. He continued to meet with me for the next 3 months, although less frequently, and brought his new boyfriend to meet me at one point. When the two of them decided to move in together, Jeremy decided he was ready to "leave the therapy nest," as he described it. He asked to be able to return in the future if he ever wanted, and I assured him that as long as I was here my door was open to him. At the time of our final session, Jeremy was living two lives: an open gay man among his social contacts and a closeted gay man with his coworkers and family. He stated that he felt comfortable with himself but did not want to risk his job and did not feel ready to come out to his parents.

Multi- and Cross-Cultural Issues

Jeremy and I were Caucasian men, both born in the United States and both of a middle-class socioeconomic status. I was about 10 years older than Jeremy, although that did not appear to lead to any issues other than my own countertransferential feelings at times of being a big brother to Jeremy. If Jeremy had been of a different ethnicity or socioeconomic status, it would have been important to be aware of how our differences impacted the transference and countertransference and to openly discuss our differences in here-and-now processing. In addition, if Jeremy had been from another minority group in addition to being a sexual minority, it would have been important to consider how his sexual orientation identity intersected with his other identities (e.g., his racial identity). *(Social and Cultural Foundations Competency 4: Competent counselors will know that the developmental tasks of LGBT women and people of color include the formation and integration of their gender, racial, and sexual identities; AL-GBTIC, 1997.)* Finally, Jeremy's religion had been an important aspect of his overall identity, and it was important to acknowledge this identity and provide support as he developed a spiritual identity separate from the religion of his childhood.

Conclusion

Jeremy came to counseling with true-self/false-self issues. Through counseling, Jeremy became aware of how he had hidden his true self behind a false self composed of his perceptions of who others thought he should be. He became more accepting of himself, although he continued to live a double life in order to protect himself. Although Jeremy's fear of being openly gay with his family and coworkers may have been based on the internalized homonegativity that he projected onto others, it is also possible that Jeremy's concerns were valid and that he would face discrimination based on his sexual orientation. Consequently, it was important that he not feel pressured to come out to his family or coworkers during counseling. In an ideal world, Jeremy would be able to live openly as a gay man; however, the reality is that in most locations gay men are not considered a protected class by local and state governments.

Jeremy's experience is not unlike what other gay men, and any other clients for that matter, experience when they have learned to relax their false selves enough to learn who they really are. We have found object relations and interpersonal therapies to be effective in helping clients understand how internalized critical aspects of relationships can lead to a strengthening of a false self at the expense of true self–to–true self attachments. Creating a strong therapeutic alliance and using immediacy to process what happens in that relationship is imperative for enabling clients to feel safe enough to explore who really are. In addition, this is especially crucial when working with gay men who have experienced judgment not only in their relationships but from society as a whole.

References

American Psychoanalytic Association, Committee on Lesbian, Gay, Bisexual, and Transgender Issues. (2010). *Position statements: Psychoanalytic discussion points on homophobia.* Retrieved from http://www.apsa.org/Member_Section/Committee_Resources_and_Work_Rooms/Lesbian_Gay_Bisexual_and_Transgender_Issues.aspx

Association for Lesbian, Gay, Bisexual and Transgender Issues in Counseling. (1997). *Competencies for counseling gay, lesbian, bisexual and transgendered (LGBT) clients.* Alexandria, VA: Author.

Fairbairn, W. R. D. (1996). The nature and aims of psychoanalytic treatment. In D. E. Scharff (Ed.), *Object relations theory and practice* (pp. 98–109). Northvale, NJ: Jason Aronson. (Original work published 1958)

Isay, R. A. (1996). *Becoming gay: The journey to self-acceptance.* New York, NY: Owl Books.

Marszalek, J. F., III, & Pope, M. (2008). Gay male identity development. In K. L. Kraus (Ed.), *Lifespan development theories in action: A case study approach for counseling professions* (pp. 294–327). Boston, MA: Lahaska Press.

Scharff, D. E. (Ed.). (1996). *Object relations theory and practice.* Northvale, NJ: Jason Aronson.

Sommers-Flanagan, J., & Hutz, A. (2008). Psychoanalytic theory in action. In K. L. Kraus (Ed.), *Lifespan development theories in action: A case study approach for counseling professions* (pp. 163–198). Boston, MA: Lahaska Press.

Teyber, E. (2006). *Interpersonal process in therapy: An integrative model* (5th ed.). Belmont, CA: Thomson.

Winnicott, D. W. (1996). Ego distortion in terms of true and false self. In D. E. Scharff (Ed.), *Object relations theory and practice* (pp. 236–247). Northvale, NJ: Jason Aronson. (Original work published 1960)

Yalom, I. D. (2002). *The gift of therapy: An open letter to a new generation of therapists and their patients.* New York, NY: Harper.

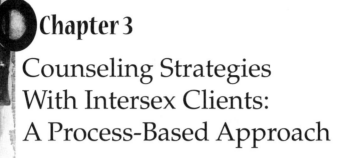

Chapter 3

Counseling Strategies With Intersex Clients: A Process-Based Approach

Theodore R. Burnes and Kate Richmond

Intersex—often referred to as a "condition"—is an umbrella term used to describe any individual born with atypical genital or reproductive anatomy. Consistent with the *Clinical Guidelines for the Management of Disorders of Sex Development in Childhood* (Intersex Society of North America, 2006), we advocate a patient-centered approach when using psychological interventions with intersex clients. In an ideal scenario, intersex clients would have the option to pursue patient-centered psychological support early in their lives; however, given the lack of accessible mental health providers and the reality that the decision to engage in therapy is often made by the client's parents, some intersex clients do not seek therapy until later in life. As feminist psychologists, we have been privileged with the opportunity to receive training and to work clinically with adult intersex clients. In order to promote therapeutic care and to advocate for the needs of intersex clients, we have formulated a composite case to address some of the clinically relevant issues that may arise when one is working with adult intersex clients. In providing this case study, which combines the experiences of several of our clients, we hope to give voice to many of the concerns that are often ignored or minimized among intersex adults while ensuring the anonymity of those involved. For clarity, we present this case from the perspective of one therapist working with one client.

Intake and Initial Diagnostic Data and Demographic Information

Rebekkah ("Becky") was a 23-year-old Jewish American woman who worked for a local advertising firm as a junior account executive. On her intake form, Becky reported, "My employer told me I have problems concentrating and

I should get some help." She reported no suicidality and no homicidality and denied a history of physical or sexual abuse. Becky indicated that she had had one previous experience with counseling for 2 months when she was 5 years old because of her parents' divorce.

When asked more about her difficulties focusing on her work, Becky reported that she had started dating a young man 1 month ago and stated, "It was a big mistake to get involved with him." She reported that her romantic interest, Michael, had been a friend for about 5 years, and the two had begun dating as their friendship strengthened. Becky cried during the intake and mentioned, "I've never told him, but I have some . . . issues with who I am." She reported having "a time when I was about 12 that I felt different for the first time . . . I just didn't feel like the other girls." Becky remembered that her mother and father often argued after she went to bed: "I could hear them yelling things in their room, like, 'I don't know how to tell her what happened!'" She also reported that she and her mother had had a conversation when she was 13 and Becky had asked her mother about certain sexual organs; her mother's response was, "All boys and girls grow up with all types of sexual feelings; however, the doctor that took care of you when you were born said that you might be different in terms of how you develop." When Becky asked her about these differences, Becky's mom noted, "I think that the doctors weren't sure if you were a boy or a girl, so they said you would develop differently . . . but you were born a beautiful girl, and so everything is fine, just a little different in terms of development." Becky reported that as she matured into adolescence and throughout this time, her mother would often accompany her to doctor's appointments, during which Becky routinely had genital examinations. Following such examinations, her mother and the doctor would ask Becky to wait in the waiting room while they talked to each other. "I never had a conversation with a doctor that my mother wasn't involved in until I went to college."

Becky denied any history of being sexually active. She noted that she had had scars around her genital area since birth, and she often felt that she "needed to wait to find the right person to have sex with who would be okay with the scars." Becky noted that she had not been sexually active but had started to think about having sex with Michael, another potential prompt for her to enter counseling. Becky noted that there had been times in her history when she had had sexual feelings and desires for men and for women, but she had only wanted emotional and physical relationships with men. When asked whether those feelings were ever acted on, Becky noted, "No. I was just . . . scared." Although she had not dated other men before Michael, Becky stated that nothing had been a problem with their relationship until now. Her boyfriend was a consultant and lived in a large West Coast city.

When asked about her family, Becky revealed that her mother, father, and aunt all lived in a large suburb of the West Coast city in which she and Michael both lived. Becky reported feeling very connected to her religion and had been for quite some time. Becky noted that the Jewish community was "a big piece of my life . . . although I have never really felt close to them. In fact, I haven't felt close to a lot of people." She identified her sources of social support as her boyfriend Michael and her good friend Chantal, a young woman with whom she worked. She had not told any of her roommates about her thoughts surrounding her gender history or her relationships issues. Becky reported being unable to concentrate on work, as "I'm sure Michael will leave me if he finds out . . . I think I like him . . . although knowing some of my issues, I am worried about what sex with him will be like."

Standardized Assessment

In addition to a clinical interview, Becky agreed to complete several standardized psychological tests so that I could more fully understand her presenting concerns. These psychological tests were the Beck Depression Inventory–II, the Beck Anxiety Inventory, and the Personality Assessment Inventory. The Beck Depression Inventory–II (Beck, Steer, & Brown, 1996) is a 21-item self-report instrument intended to assess the existence and severity of symptoms of depression as listed in the American Psychiatric Association's (1994) *Diagnostic and Statistical Manual of Mental Disorders* (4th ed.). Becky scored an 11 on this assessment, marking her within the mild-to-moderate depression range (10–18). The Beck Anxiety Inventory (Leyfer, Ruberg, & Woodruff-Borden, 2006) is a 21-question multiple-choice self-report inventory that is used to measure the severity of an individual's anxiety. Becky scored an 18 on this assessment, placing her within the moderate-to-severe anxiety range (16–25). The Personality Assessment Inventory (Morey, 2007) is a multiscale test of psychological functioning that assesses constructs relevant to personality and psychopathology in various contexts. Becky produced a valid profile, with significant elevations on the anxiety-related disorders (ARD), depression (DEP), and anxiety (ANX) scales. Specifically, the ARD scale was the most elevated scale. ARD subscale configurations included average scores on the Obsessive-Compulsive subscale (ARD-O), high scores on the Phobias subscale (ARD-P), and high scores on the Traumatic Stress subscale (ARD-T). These scores indicate a pattern of responses that suggests that the respondent experienced a traumatic event in the past that produces recurrent episodes of anxiety that includes interpersonal withdrawal from relationships. Becky's codetype was ARD-DEP, characterized by an inability to make decisions and common to respondents who meet diagnostic criteria for trauma-related histories and depression-based mood disorders.

Diagnostic Conceptualization

Following the formal assessment process, I synthesized the information gathered within the framework of Becky's life and considered a diagnosis. We discussed how best "to name the pain," and I explained that a diagnosis could offer a powerful source of self-knowledge (Brown, 1994). This initial discussion was crucial for Becky, and it became a critical therapeutic moment for her. When intersex clients receive truthful information about their bodies and are given the opportunity to openly talk about their experiences, shame is notably reduced and identity formation can begin (Colapinto, 2000; Williams, 2002). By verbalizing that throughout her life Becky had experienced countless shameful and embarrassing interactions with people whom she should have been able to trust—namely, her parents (and also her physicians)—and that these events had occurred because of the medical community's overreliance on a limiting and oppressive binary sex structure, she could at least begin to consider an alternative explanation for her presenting problem and reduce self-blame.

Another part of this initial diagnosis discussion was an exploration of Becky's strengths, which was also an essential part of the therapeutic process. Becky's resilience, despite the assault on her body and self, was astounding. Becky was bright, verbal, emotionally expressive, and motivated to work in therapy. In addition, although she had not shared her identity concerns with Michael or Chantal, she had established a strong bond with both of them. Furthermore, Becky's strong religious ties were an important source of support and strength. Becky reported that she often relied on her faith in God to get through difficult times.

This intake assessment resulted in the following principal diagnosis using the *Diagnostic and Statistical Manual of Mental Disorders* (4th ed., text rev.; American Psychiatric Association, 2000):

Axis I	313.82	Identity Problem
	309.81	Anxiety Not Otherwise Specified
Axis II	V71.09	No Diagnosis on Axis II
Axis III	Surgery at infancy (without informed consent)	
Axis IV	Parent relational concerns	
	Intimacy concerns	
	Partner relational concerns	
Axis V	70 (Current); 65 (Past Year)	

Case Process and Interventions

With Becky, I used a conceptual framework that integrated both relational-cultural (Jordan, 2000) and feminist (Worell & Remer, 2003) theories, a knowledge of trauma therapy (Briere & Scott, 2006), and the importance of identity development and integration for individuals who have experienced cultural oppression (Brown, 2008). With this framework, the plan for counseling utilized both short-term and long-term goals, and I applied interventions that would help to achieve these different types of goals.

The feminist conceptualization assumes that symptoms serve as a communicative function and reflect learned strategies for coping with environmental stresses (Brown, 1994). Thus, Becky's current symptoms were viewed as specialized coping behaviors rather than manifestations of pathology (Worell & Remer, 2003). One of my short-term goals was to decrease some of Becky's symptoms of anxiety and depression. I began by continually revisiting and validating Becky's feelings and helping her to relabel these symptoms as coping mechanisms for dealing with an oppressive history in which she was often not the authority on her own experience. An additional goal was to have an open discussion about how her previous experience with the medical community would influence the therapeutic alliance. Becky had been betrayed by the medical community, and as a psychologist it was important for me to acknowledge and openly discuss my relationship to the medical model. For example, I posed questions such as "It is not uncommon for people who have been hurt by a health care provider to question their trust in other providers. Have you ever felt that way?" and stated, "Becky, I wonder if you have any concerns because I am part of the medical community." Naming and acknowledging the power structures that exist outside the therapeutic relationship is an effective way to deflate some of its authority (Ballou, Hill, & West, 2008). In recognizing the role of power within the therapeutic relationship, the aim was to develop a strong alliance, which is a crucial component of a successful therapeutic outcome (Brown, 2008; Pearlman & Courtois, 2005).

Another short-term goal was to have Becky explore and learn about the difficult histories of other intersex-identified individuals. The use of bibliotherapy also aimed to demystify the role of the therapist (Worell & Remer, 2003). By providing Becky with access to knowledge about the therapeutic process, bibliotherapy aimed to minimize the likelihood that I was the only possessor of critical therapeutic information. Bibliotherapy also encouraged transparency, an important interpersonal dynamic between Becky and me. It reinforced the message that "I trust your own power in this process" and that power would be shared. This significantly helped Becky to feel validated in her own experience and continually helped her form a trusting relationship with me. I encouraged Becky to visit the website of Accord Alliance (www.accordalliance.org) and to read books such as *Hermaphrodites and the Medical Invention of Sex* (Dreger, 1998), *As Nature Made Him* (Colapinto, 2000), *Lessons From the Intersexed* (Kessler, 1998), *Sexing the Body* (Fausto-Sterling, 2000), and *Surgically Shaping Children* (Parens, 2008).

Another short-term goal was to help Becky establish healthy boundaries with other people in her life and to help her recognize that she had authority over the level of intensity to which these relationships progressed. Using the counseling process as a way to speak about Becky's relationships with people such as her mother and Michael and displaying alternatives to specific relational patterns through gentle and supportive questioning helped her to gain insight into and utilize specific relational strategies. For example, I asked Becky, "It sounds as though you have had difficulty with your mother speaking to professionals on your behalf. If you had the chance to speak to professionals without your mother, what questions would you ask, and what information would you want?" Becky agreed with these hypotheses and said that she would want to know more about her biological development, about specific physical and biosocial milestones that she believed (but was not sure) she had reached. Becky began to see herself as an authority who could competently interface with doctors on her own behalf, despite her own developmental history of feeling silenced about her own medical care. This process also helped to minimize the extent to which Becky felt helpless when thinking about her future interactions with doctors.

One of our long-term goals was to help Becky deal with many of the symptoms associated with the early assault on her body. These symptoms included mistrust, learned helplessness, hopelessness, and fear. Brown (2008) described the importance of trauma survivors writing their own narratives and then telling their stories in therapy. In doing this important work, Becky could reflect on her experiences, explore the meaning ascribed to those experiences, and acknowledge intersections between what had happened to her and how she coped (Brown, 2008). Prior to reprocessing, we practiced progressive relaxation and deep breathing in session together. These techniques allowed Becky to regulate difficult emotions (such as fear, anxiety, and anger) as they occurred during the retelling of her experiences (Briere & Scott, 2006). This was especially useful when Becky recounted the invasive genital examinations she had received as an adolescent.

When reprocessing, I gently asked Becky to describe her feelings and thoughts as if they were occurring in the present. Becky explained that she felt tremendous fear and hopelessness. She described thoughts such as "I can't escape," "I must be a freak," and "This is all my fault." We discussed the accuracy of these thoughts, where they may have come from, and how to counter such disruptive thinking patterns (Briere & Scott, 2006). Becky agreed that many of her thinking patterns were due to the fact that her parents and doctors did not appropriately explain what was happening to her, nor did they provide an opportunity for informed consent. And because she was essentially ignored in this process, Becky could not trust her own feelings about the situation. By sharing her story, Becky began to gain insight into the context behind her surgery as an infant and her subsequent medical examinations as an adolescent. She could heal from shame and her own self-doubt about her thoughts and feelings.

Another long-term goal was to recognize, express, and address the anger Becky experienced toward significant people in her life, especially her mother. Becky's anger emerged during the reprocessing of her medical examinations. During this time, Becky's anxiety increased so much that she decided to call out of work; she reported having difficulty sleeping, experiencing painful stomach pains after eating, and dealing with significant disruptions in concentration and memory. Because of the severity of her symptoms, I suggested consulting with a psychiatrist. This enraged Becky, who stated, "I knew you would send me for a medical evaluation eventually!" As she spoke, she clenched her fist and began lightly pounding it against her lap as she emphasized certain words and phrases. Using certain techniques that integrated relational-cultural and Gestalt techniques (Yontef, 2005), I asked Becky about her hand movements. Specifically, I asked, "I notice your hand movements as you are getting angry in our work together. If the anger in your hand movement had a voice, what would it say?" This discussion led to her expressing anger directly at me. Using cultural-relational reprocessing

(Jordan, 2000), Becky and I used her anger as a framework to investigate how our process could be used as an example for how she could open a discussion with her mother about her anger and consequently begin to help her gain trust in herself and with her mother.

Another long-term goal was for Becky to explore and develop a positive identity. Lev (2004) noted that many intersex individuals may choose to identify with an intersex identity, whereas others may identify with a specific gender (male or female). Thus, it was crucial that Becky feel encouraged to consider many gender options, allowing for the expression of curiosity, excitement, fear, and ambivalence (Williams, 2002). By again relying on supportive bibliotherapeutic resources such as *My Gender Workbook* (Bornstein, 1997), I used therapy to explore Becky's reactions to a variety of intersex identities. I also encouraged her to reflect on how her intersex identity may intersect with other identities in her life that were important to her, especially her Jewish identity (Brown, 2008). Furthermore, I continuously affirmed, believed, and helped to relabel shaming experiences while encouraging Becky to acknowledge her strengths and resilience throughout her developmental experience. Not only will this intervention aid in the short-term goal of decreasing symptoms of anxiety and depression, but a long-term outcome will help Becky to approach her current relationships with Michael and other people in her life with more authority over her own engagement in relationships, activities, and functioning.

Assessment and Case Process Outcomes

Assessment Outcomes

As a result of my 15 sessions with Becky, I saw a decline in her symptoms as marked by assessment data collected during her last session, 15 weeks after her initial intake assessment. Becky scored a 9 on the Beck Depression Inventory–II (Beck et al., 1996), marking her within the not depressed range (0–9). Becky scored a 16 on the Beck Anxiety Inventory (Leyfer et al., 2006), a lower score in the moderate-to-severe anxiety range (16–25) than her score at intake. On the Personality Assessment Inventory (Morey, 2007), Becky endorsed scale elevations on the ARD and ANX scales but had elevated scores on the DEP scale within the normal range. The ARD scale was again the most elevated scale but was just above the normal range for a respondent of her age.

Process-Based Outcomes

My work with Becky resulted in different process-based case outcomes that showed Becky's progression throughout her work in counseling. I found that our various short-term goals (a decrease in symptoms, open discussions about her experiences, learning about experiences and stories of intersex-identified individuals) were met in our 15-session process, with Becky being able to openly process some of her history with me throughout our work and identifying through virtual and in-person channels specific individuals with whom to communicate. Our case process resulted in all three of our long-term goals progressing. Specifically, Becky was able to recognize her anger outside of session and used the last sessions of our work to process incidents in which she identified anger, was able to recognize the cause, and was able to remove self-blame. I also noted that by the end of our work together, Becky noted that she wanted to explore a possible sexual encounter with Michael. She and I processed this portion as part of our termination work together, noting possible outcomes and how she would be able to seek and gain support from within the intersex community regardless of the outcome. Becky was able to connect with other intersex community members through support groups that she found at http://www.isna.org/support. These various assessment and process-based outcomes demonstrate that this framework did work with Becky and produced positive changes in her overall functioning.

Implications, Reactions, and Conclusion

This case study is one example of how our process-oriented framework, which includes tenets of trauma-based, feminist, and relational-cultural practice, can be used with intersex clients. We believe that this composite case exemplifies the importance of acknowledging the trauma and shame many intersex individuals experience as a result of living in gender-dichotomized cultures. Although this framework is applicable to counseling with many intersex individuals, it is important to recognize and attend to the unique characteristics of every client.

Issues of Ethics and Professional Integrity

Consistent with the *Clinical Guidelines for the Management of Disorders of Sex Development in Childhood* (Intersex Society of North America, 2006), we believe that there is a critical need for therapists to evaluate issues of ethics when working with intersex clients. The fact that surgeries to "fix" the bodies of intersex individuals happen without the consent of the infant and often without the consent of parents directly violates the ethical code of the counseling profession (e.g., American Counseling Association, 2005), which supports individuals' autonomy (Dreger, 1999). Furthermore, issues surrounding mental health professionals' competence in working with intersex individuals and the divergent concepts of "relieve pain and suffering" and "first do no harm" are often apparent in work with intersex clients. We urge individuals to utilize ethical decision-making models that are grounded in the current knowledge, attitudes, and skills pertinent to working with intersex clients.

Implications for Counseling

In addition to ethics, we believe that this case study has several implications for feelings of transference, or common human experience (Brown, 2008), that come up as a result of working with intersex clients. Initially therapists may experience a sense of helplessness due to the pressure of working within a medical model for diagnostic purposes but feeling forced to use a medical, diagnostic-focused framework for reimbursement purposes. Specifically, therapists may feel angry about using diagnostics when so many environmental and contextual factors exist, as in the case of Becky. Furthermore, therapists may experience some form of vicarious traumatization (Pearlman & Saakvitne, 1995) as they listen to the experiences of intersex clients, resulting in a need to seek their own support, supervision, or personal therapy to work through their own stress and reactions. Given all of these issues, we urge providers to engage in appropriate and ethical consultation with colleagues as often as needed. As with all cases, professionals and trainees who provide mental health services should be sure that they are constantly evaluating their own reactions and biases through their own reflection and their own engagement with other professionals in an appropriate manner. By engaging in such reflection, clinicians can also use these feelings in their process with clients to help model the act of trusting one's own feelings and being genuine about one's own feelings in relationships.

Finally, we also believe that Becky's case has strong implications for therapists in their roles as advocates for intersex individuals and communities. Becky's case exemplifies the importance of therapists helping to train medical physicians and other clinicians and advocate with medical administrators about the importance of intersex identities and helping to support families in their decisions about sex assignment, surgery, and hormones as they cope with unresolved grief, fear, and confusion. With such social justice efforts aimed at multiple levels of systemic change, we hope that the treatment of intersex individuals inside the therapy room and the hospital room will improve dramatically.

References

American Counseling Association. (2005). *ACA code of ethics.* Alexandria, VA: Author.

American Psychiatric Association. (1994). *Diagnostic and statistical manual of mental disorders* (4th ed.). Washington, DC: Author.

American Psychiatric Association. (2000). *Diagnostic and statistical manual of mental disorders* (4th ed., text rev.). Washington, DC: Author.

Ballou, M., Hill, M., & West, C. (Eds.). (2008). *Feminist therapy theory and practice: A contemporary perspective.* New York, NY: Springer.

Beck, A. T., Steer, R. A., & Brown, G. K. (1996). *Manual for the Beck Depression Inventory–II.* San Antonio, TX: Psychological Corporation.

Bornstein, K. (1997). *My gender workbook: How to become a real man, a real woman, the real you, or something else entirely.* New York, NY: Routledge.

Briere, J., & Scott, C. (2006). *Principles of trauma therapy: A guide to symptoms, evaluation, and treatment.* Thousand Oaks, CA: Sage.

Brown, L. S. (1994). *Subversive dialogues: Theory in feminist therapy.* New York, NY: Basic Books.

Brown, L. S. (2008). *Cultural competence in trauma therapy: Beyond the flashback.* Washington, DC: American Psychological Association.

Colapinto, J. (2000). *As nature made him: The boy who was raised a girl.* New York, NY: HarperCollins.

Dreger, A. D. (1998). *Hermaphrodites and the medical invention of sex.* Boston, MA: Harvard University Press.

Dreger, A. D. (Ed.). (1999). *Intersex in the age of ethics.* Hagerstown, MD: University Publishing Group.

Fausto-Sterling, A. (2000). *Sexing the body.* New York, NY: Basic Books.

Intersex Society of North America. (2006). *Clinical guidelines for the management of disorders of sex development in childhood.* Rohnert Park, CA: Author.

Jordan, J. V. (2000). The role of mutual empathy in relational/cultural therapy. *Journal of Clinical Psychology, 56,* 1005–1016.

Kessler, S. J. (1998). *Lessons from the intersexed.* Piscataway, NJ: Rutgers University Press.

Lev, A. I. (2004). *Therapeutic guidelines for working with gender-variant people and their families.* Binghamton, NY: Haworth Clinical Practice Press.

Leyfer, O. T., Ruberg, J. L., & Woodruff-Borden, J. (2006). Examination of the utility of the Beck Anxiety Inventory and its factors as a screener for anxiety disorders. *Journal of Anxiety Disorders, 20,* 444–458.

Morey, L. C. (2007). *The Personality Assessment Inventory professional manual.* Lutz, FL: Psychological Assessment Resources.

Parens, E. (2008). *Surgically shaping children: Technology, ethics and the pursuit of normality.* Baltimore, MD: Johns Hopkins University Press.

Pearlman, L. A., & Courtois, C. A. (2005). Clinical applications of the attachment framework: Relational treatment of complex trauma. *Journal of Traumatic Stress, 18,* 449–459.

Pearlman, L. A., & Saakvitne, K. W. (1995). *Trauma and the therapist: Countertransference and vicarious traumatization in psychotherapy with incest survivors.* New York, NY: Norton.

Williams, N. (2002). The imposition of gender: Psychoanalytic encounters with genital atypicality. *Psychoanalytic Psychology, 19,* 455–474.

Worell, J., & Remer, P. (2003). *Feminist perspectives in therapy: Empowering diverse women* (2nd ed.). Hoboken, NJ: Wiley.

Yontef, G. (2005). The relational attitude in Gestalt therapy theory and practice. *Gestalt!, 9*(2). Retrieved from http://www.g-gej.org/9-2/relationalgestalt.html

Chapter 4

Counseling and Advocacy With a Gay Father, a Straight Mom, and a Transgender Adolescent

Stuart F. Chen-Hayes

Background

Roberto was a 52-year-old gay divorced Chicano with joint custody of his 13-year-old multiracial African American and Mexican daughter Maya, who lived with him and his new boyfriend Conrad, a Chinese American from Hong Kong who had recently moved in. Roberto had identified as gay ever since he had left his 20-year marriage and come out at age 42. He was on good terms with his ex-wife Shaniqua; they had joint custody of Maya and lived one neighborhood away from each other. Both Roberto and Shaniqua were recovering alcoholics. Roberto and Shaniqua both agreed that counseling would be helpful and signed the consent form for 13-year-old Maya to receive treatment.

Presenting Issues

The presenting issue was that a teacher had called Roberto stating that she had caught Maya drinking at an eighth-grade dance party. Roberto talked to Shaniqua, Conrad, and Shaniqua's husband Ray to brainstorm what they should do and to present a united front to Maya. Everyone agreed that it would be important to go to counseling to support Maya and "nip this in the bud," as Roberto framed it. The adults were all concerned that Maya could repeat her parents' alcoholism patterns, and they sought counseling for her to ensure that this would not occur. They sought a family counselor with a background in addictions.

In the first session, Maya was angry and sullen and did not want to talk to any of the four adults in her life. The counselor asked that all four of the adults in her life come in for the initial session with Maya. They didn't understand why they needed to do so, but they agreed to support Maya.

The counselor had explained that he would be working from a family systems perspective, so the key persons in Maya's life needed to be present to help her work through the issues. The counselor also said that research indicated a greater likelihood of a successful outcome from counseling with parental participation.

The counselor asked for time alone with Maya in a second session after they had met as a group with her father and mother to build trust and join with her, as she was the most reluctant of the three family members to engage in dialogue. In the family session, Maya sat with a look of anger the entire time and did not say a word other than "hello" until her parents left the room. As the counselor and Maya talked, it became clear that Maya did not feel safe sharing with her parents in the room. She quizzed the counselor on what would happen. The counselor said that he did not keep secrets, but depending on the information that she shared, he would reserve the right to share if there was a danger to herself or others. Maya slowly warmed to the counselor, but it took a number of individual sessions over several months before she was ready to disclose her core issues. In the meantime, the counselor asked to work with Maya's parents in one session and with Maya in separate sessions to reinforce the parents' collective support of Maya and to give Maya the chance to work on issues separately and lessen the intergenerational conflict. He complimented Maya's parents on their ability to focus on what was best for her and to act as a team. Initial goals included the use of drug screens for Maya to ensure that there was no subsequent misuse of alcohol or other drugs, and her parents agreed to this, although Maya was furious. No one wanted to be put in the place of having to play investigator over Maya's use of alcohol and other drugs, and the drug screens allowed the focus of counseling to be on counseling instead of truth seeking. The counselor used empathy, support, and microskills (Ivey, Ivey, & Zalaquett, 2009) to build a therapeutic relationship with Maya and her parents from the initial sessions. The most challenging issues were Maya's pace in trusting counseling and allowing all of her concerns to come forward. Trust issues were key for her, but as the drug screens showed that she was clean, she was able to let go of her resentment about that challenge to her integrity and began to open up more to the counselor.

Diagnosis

Although a family systems perspective sees issues as relational, most of the *Diagnostic and Statistical Manual of Mental Disorders* (4th ed., text rev.; American Psychiatric Association, 2000) is focused on individual diagnoses, even though a family systems approach to counseling *was* used in part to work on interrelationships between family members for problem resolution.

Axis I issues for Maya included parent/child issues and alcohol abuse. Axis II issues for Roberto included parent/child issues. There were no Axis II issues for either family member. Axis III issues for Roberto were liver disease and asthma. The Axis III issue for Maya was alcohol abuse. The Axis IV issue for Roberto was a new relationship; Axis IV issues for Maya were loneliness, alcohol abuse, and declining grades. The Axis V Global Assessment of Functioning (GAF) for Maya was 65, and the Axis V GAF for Roberto was 80.

Subsequent Sessions

The counselor asked to see everyone in both households for the first session, as Maya split her time between the two. During the intake, it emerged that Maya had been a very good student until sixth grade, when her grades started to decline and she developed an attitude with the adults in her life. She got into verbal fights, rarely wanted to spend time at home, and instead wanted to hang with her friends. Both her mom and dad shared that she often tried to play them against each other but that they worked hard to coordinate as best they could the parenting in the two households. Roberto, until recently single, had relied on family and friends to watch Maya after school when he was working, which usually worked out well. Shaniqua and her husband also relied on some of Shaniqua's family members to watch Maya during the day when she was staying with them. Shaniqua hated to do that but didn't have a choice.

Goals

Goals for counseling treatment were established as the counselor asked the family what their hopes and dreams were for Maya. Every adult agreed that they wanted Maya to graduate from college—something none of the adults in the family had yet to do, although Roberto and Shaniqua had both had some prior college. Maya stated that she just wanted to be left alone and to get out of her family as soon as she could be independent. She expressed no interest in the future other than spending time with friends. Initial goals for the family were to focus on ensuring Maya's alcohol use ended, improving Maya's grades and increasing her interest connected to school activities and her future career or college plans, as well as lessening her anger/attitude toward the adults in her life. In addition, parent–child communication and monitoring of Maya's whereabouts in this blended family were also needed, particularly in balancing Roberto's new relationship with his live-in boyfriend and her mom's current marriage.

From a family systems perspective, Roberto and Shaniqua coparented well, yet both reported extreme frustration and guilt at their daughter's drinking. They feared that she could repeat their bad choices with a family history of alcoholism on both sides. Both parents continued in Alcoholics Anonymous and had been sober for more than a decade. Their journey to sobriety came about as Roberto owned being gay and came out in the marriage. Both recognized how they had used alcohol to avoid feelings of pain, loss, hurt, and anger. The focus for the parents in counseling was initially on how to better monitor Maya's behavior and set limits when custody was shared between two households. Roberto reported feeling like an adolescent again with his new boyfriend and readily admitted that he was not supervising his daughter as well as he had when he was single, in part because she was now almost a teenager. The counselor explored family-of-origin parenting styles and found that both Roberto and Shaniqua had grown up in rigid, authoritarian homes and had rebelled by being the opposite—permissive—as young adults and that they both needed to work on setting strong limits and consistent rules with Maya.

As weeks of counseling continued for Maya individually, she began to open up to the counselor about what had changed for her in sixth grade when her grades started going downhill. The counselor used a number of cognitive–behavioral techniques (antecedent, behavior, consequence) as well as narrative questioning to attempt to figure out what had happened at that time for Maya's grades to drop, but he did so in a gentle and collaborative way so as not to push the envelope too fast or too far. The counselor's interventions included questions such as "What was happening in your life at that time that started to go in a different direction?" and "How did teachers and your family and friends experience you differently at that time?"

Maya was wary of sharing her secret but instead told the counselor, "I have a friend, Anita. She's having a hard time. Something really bad happened to her and I don't know how to help her out. The counselor said, "What was it?" Maya responded, "Anita told me her uncle was forcing her to have sex with him and didn't know what would happen if she told." The counselor said, "Wow, Anita really trusts you to share such painful information. What did you tell her?" Maya said, "I said you just don't know who you can trust with your personal business." The counselor said, "Well, if it is a counselor, and someone discloses that kind of abuse, they are mandated to report it to the state." Maya replied, "Really? I thought counseling was confidential." The counselor said, "It is, but if you share something that is harming you or others, then confidentiality has to be broken. It's like when the teacher caught you drinking. That was a danger to you, and she called your dad to make sure you were safe." Maya said, "I was so mad at her for doing that." The counselor affirmed that Maya was a great friend to be able to help out Anita with something so painful.

All of a sudden, Maya burst out sobbing in tears and said, "I can't take it anymore. I'm Anita. It's my uncle. He said he'd kill me if I told anyone about his having sex with me." The counselor remembered that in the intake she had denied that anyone had abused her, but he knew it was not uncommon to find that young people used alcohol to dull the pain when an adult they had expected to keep them safe was doing the opposite. The counselor affirmed her courage for being honest and telling the truth and asked who in the family she felt she could trust with the information. Maya said she'd thought about telling her dad's boyfriend because he was the only one who didn't know this uncle well, but she was afraid what would happen if she did. The counselor asked which side of the family the uncle was on, and Maya shared that it was one of her mom's brothers who was supposed to be watching out for her after school. The counselor shared that he would need to report the incident and discussed with her a plan for safety and asked to convene a meeting with Roberto, Shaniqua, and Maya as soon as possible so that he could be there to support Maya when she delivered the news to her parents. Maya really didn't want to be there but eventually she agreed. Maya shared that he had not attacked her for several weeks and that she had pleaded repeatedly with her mom and stepdad to go somewhere else after school other than her uncle's house.

The counselor made the report and asked Maya to share with her parents what she had told him. Maya's dad was furious, and Maya's mom was in total shock. Shaniqua couldn't believe that her baby was in danger with her brother. Both parents rallied to Maya's defense and agreed that she could have absolutely no further contact with that uncle until the allegations were investigated. For the first time in counseling, Maya ran to her mom and jumped in her lap and said, "I was so scared that you wouldn't believe me. He said he'd kill me if I told you." A new goal was negotiated—the three of them working on keeping Maya safe and recovering from the sexual abuse and the feelings of guilt and shame both in Maya and in her parents.

The uncle eventually was arrested and jailed on Maya's allegation. The rest of the extended family came down hard on Shaniqua, but she knew that she had to stand by her daughter. Shaniqua said that most of her brothers were heavy drinkers and that she had thought this brother was the safest one for her daughter to be with. She said that she was incredibly angry and full of guilt for having placed her daughter in his home, but she had no other alternative. This was one of two major turning points in the counseling process. Maya's sharing of the abuse and the subsequent learning by her mom, dad, and herself about the dynamics of incest and how to recover from the abuse and become a survivor became the centerpiece of the counseling. Her parents' unwavering support of Maya and their belief in her story indicated the greatest likelihood for a successful outcome of healing from the sexual abuse.

Maya's parents continued their strong commitment to ensuring that their daughter was safe at all times, and her drug screens came back consistently negative over the next few months. Maya shared that she had started drinking to numb the pain she had felt at being violated. She had told a friend (Anita) who had encouraged her to tell the counselor the truth. Over the next several months, Maya joined a group for other middle school survivors of sexual abuse. She became her old self again, according to her parents, and dove back into her studies, refusing to allow her uncle's threats to get in the way of the life she wished to live. The counselor had introduced the idea of narrative counseling and attempted to help the family find a way to externalize the issue of alcohol getting in the way of relationships between multiple family members. Roberto and Maya named the problem that kept lurking between Maya and her parents "shadows." But as Maya returned to her former self, deep down she realized that the alcohol and the abuse had been keeping her distracted from another shadow.

Roberto was an extremely masculine gay man, the type of man that most men would never assume was gay. Shaniqua was feminine and girly. Maya had always been a tomboy on the inside, but on the outside looked very femme until the last couple of years when she had cut her hair, stopped wearing dresses, and only wanted to hang out with boys. Maya was mom's girl in some ways and had been femme when she was younger, but in the past 2 years she resented her mom and only wanted to hang out at her dad's house. Deep down she hated who she was—her uncle had attacked her in part to make her "act more like a girl," she said. She so hated what he had done to her. But one day she shared in counseling that she had always wanted to be a boy. Having a gay dad was in some ways comforting to her, but he was so macho that she really worried about telling him that she felt her life was a lie and that she was really a he.

The counselor appreciated Maya's trust in him once again and shared that he was honored that she was able to be so honest with herself and with him. He asked what she would like most. She shared that she'd like to be a boy and that she wanted her parents to accept her as a boy. The counselor asked how Maya wanted to proceed. She shared that she wanted to do a session with her mom first and then strategize how to tell her dad. The counselor agreed. Shaniqua's jaw dropped when Maya shared her latest revelation. Shaniqua said, "Well, I thought it was bad enough when your *papi* came out as gay on me, and now you are telling me you are really a boy?"

It took her a couple of months of supportive counseling and a number of individual sessions to help Shaniqua lessen her fears and hold on to that place of love she had for her child no matter what, but with time Shaniqua was able to come around and, looking back, see that this made a lot of sense. Her daughter had never liked dresses, had always played with boys, was great at sports, and in many ways was the mirror image of her dad. But Shaniqua and Maya both worried what Roberto's response would be when he found out that Maya was transgender. Maya shared that she was ready to tell her dad if her mom could be in the room. The counselor agreed, and in the next session Maya told her dad about who she really was. The silence in the room was deafening. Roberto didn't speak for 5 minutes.

When he opened his mouth he said, "Baby, I love you no matter who you are." Shaniqua and Maya exchanged the biggest smiles they'd ever shown. Roberto was in shock, but he said, "I've been through one coming out already, and if I made it through 10 years clean and sober I can make it through two coming outs and another 10 years." Roberto also shared that he hadn't come out to his parents before they had died. With the alcohol abuse ended, the parent–child communication greatly improved, and the sexual abuse recovery work ongoing, the counselor now negotiated a new goal. The final goal was to explore Maya's transgender identity development and what she needed and wanted to have happen.

Coming Out Process

The counselor used a modified version of D'Augelli's (1994) identity development model stages but included transgender persons and a focus on family systems. The model included framing how to help the two generations move across the lesbian, gay, bisexual, and transgender (LGBT) family developmental issues. The initial focus was on Maya's *coming out internally* as transgender. She had always been gender nonconforming, and her parents had assumed that they had a tomboy. However, Maya had always felt male and stuck with a body, family, and Chicana/Black cultural expectations that never matched her real self in terms of gender—that girls are to be feminine and boys are to be masculine, and that's the way it is traditionally. Getting caught drinking and having to admit to the prior sexual abuse gave her courage, over time, to be honest about the other shadow in her life that was keeping her from the others around her.

In addition, *coming out externally* was another focus of the developmental process. Maya was initially mortified about how everyone would respond to her coming out and coped by withdrawing and hiding from others, especially in middle school. Now that her parents knew and were accepting of their soon-to-be son, they could plan the transition process both at school and in terms of medical procedures.

The next area of development was becoming an *LGBT offspring*, which was Maya's parents' work in recognizing that they had a transgender child. Maya had known that Roberto was gay from early on and had grown up with an out gay dad but did not disclose this at school for fear of being teased and for cultural reasons of keeping quiet about one's personal and family business. Yet Maya was always proud of her dad and from a distance had admired his struggles of being a gay divorced parent. Roberto's journey had some parallels for his new son to emulate. Roberto and Shaniqua both struggled with the idea of their daughter becoming their son, but they had gotten through Roberto's coming out as gay over time too. Shaniqua felt pretty cut off from the rest of her family after the disclosure of abuse by her brother and chose not to share any information about Maya's transition. Roberto's parents were both deceased, but his boyfriend Conrad's family had a transman in it in Hong Kong. When Maya learned about this, there was an instant bond between her and Conrad, whom she previously had had little time for and saw as an interloper in the house. Hearing that Conrad's nephew was out as a transman in a conservative family gave Maya great optimism and hope.

Maya's parents realized that they needed to learn a lot more about what being transgender was all about. The counselor recommended a number of trans-affirming websites for Maya and her parents. In addition, bibliotherapy included Brill and Pepper's (2008) *The Transgender Child*, Boenke's (2008) *Trans-Forming Families,* and Bornstein's (1997) *My Gender Workbook* to read about other trans youth and families and Bornstein's journey through "genderland." Maya was encouraged to attend a support group for genderqueer youth at the local LGBT center, to meet other genderqueer youth, and to notice her feelings and thoughts about being transgender with feedback from peers and the group facilitator. Ultimately, the support group confirmed and affirmed her transgender identity and she sought to become a boy. However, she didn't want to cut up her body or take hormones yet. It was too scary for her, and her dad's insurance didn't cover the costs. She decided that she would rather simply dress as a boy full time and take on a male name and gender identity/expression. It took several more months, but eventually Marcus emerged.

The counseling continued, with Marcus's parents coming for sessions periodically to discuss their loss of Maya their daughter and their support for Marcus their son. Marcus ended counseling with the knowledge that one day he might choose to do sex reassignment surgery, but he felt that he had a group of great friends now in the high school he would be attending. He now felt that he could officially and legally transition from female to male even if he didn't go under the knife. He and his parents agreed that they would return to counseling if any of the survivor or alcohol issues emerged. In the meantime, they felt that although they'd lost a daughter, they'd gained a son who was happy, who was healthy, who was doing well in school, and, for the first time in their lives, who was all he was meant to be.

Conclusion

In sum, counseling was successful for the presenting issue with this family and for the goals that emerged as counseling exposed the deeper issues at play for the family. From a family systems perspective, transference and countertransference are psychodynamic constructs not useful in postmodern family theory conceptualization. The issues for the professional counselor are adequate training and/or supervision for working with alcohol abuse, gender identity/expression, divorce, same-gender couples, and affirmation of diverse ethnic/racial identities and how to work effectively with gender variation in a sexist, genderist, and heterosexist climate.

With the initial crisis of alcohol abuse disclosed and managed successfully, the midpoint of counseling shifted to sexual abuse allegations and recovery as a survivor of incest. As Marcus's trust in the counselor grew, he was able to share his greatest shadow, that of being transgender. With the eventual support of both birth parents and a transman connection in Conrad's family, as well as a supportive group of genderqueer youth at the local LGBT center, Marcus and his parents were able to end counseling having weathered three major life transition issues prior to the start of high school. The counselor also shared that he would be happy to do check-up appointments for any of them if relapse became an issue and/or if Marcus decided to move toward altering his body with hormones or surgery.

References

American Psychiatric Association. (2000). *Diagnostic and statistical manual of mental disorders* (4th ed., text rev.). Washington, DC: Author.

Boenke, M. (Ed.). (2008). *Trans-forming families: Real stories about transgendered loved ones* (3rd ed.). Washington, DC: PFLAG Transgender Network.

Bornstein, K. (1997). *My gender workbook: How to become a real man, a real woman, the real you, or something else entirely.* New York, NY: Routledge.

Brill, S. A., & Pepper, R. (2008). *The transgender child: A handbook for families and professionals.* Berkeley, CA: Cleis.

D'Augelli, A. R. (1994). Identity development and sexual orientation: Toward a model of lesbian, gay, and bisexual development. In E. J. Trickett, R. J. Watts, & D. Birman (Eds.), *Human diversity: Perspectives on people in context* (pp. 312–333). San Francisco, CA: Jossey-Bass.

Ivey, A. E., Ivey, M. B., & Zalaquett, C. P. (2009). *Intentional interviewing and counseling* (7th ed.). Belmont, CA: Cengage.

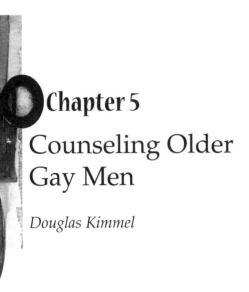

Chapter 5

Counseling Older Gay Men

Douglas Kimmel

For many counselors the idea of working with older adults can be a window into assorted stereotypes, myths, and fears about aging. At first, one's own dread of aging may emerge and there can be reactions such as unreasonable negative expectations and a reluctance to become involved. There may be an unconscious association of aging with death as well as a conscious connection of aging with disability and decline. Moreover, older clients may bring out emotional reactions to the counselor's own past experiences with parents or grandparents and evoke unfamiliar transference, including deference, pity, and solicitude. With older gay men there is an additional myth: Gay man do not grow older, and if they do they are lonely and depressed.

Elders are a cross-section of the population who have nothing in common except age. In that way they are parallel to lesbians and gay men, who are a cross-section of individuals who have sexual orientation in common. Knowing only a person's age or sexual orientation gives very little information about the person as an individual. In fact lesbian, gay, bisexual, and transgender elders are an extremely diverse cohort of survivors who have experienced aspects of history that may be unfamiliar to younger counselors (Kimmel, Rose, & David, 2006).

This chapter presents two clients who provide a glimpse into the diversity of gay male aging and the interesting range of pragmatic issues that it can present to a counselor. These cases are an amalgam of several individuals and do not include confidential information from any clients.

Identification, Background, and Presenting Issues

David, a White 70-year-old man, had been accepting of being gay since college in the 1960s, although he had been discrete and not open about

53

his sexuality except with close friends until after completing his graduate work with a doctorate. Actively seeking progressive supportive groups, individuals, and mentors, David dated men during college and graduate school and began a career as a college professor in which he was able to be openly gay with both faculty and students. He began a long-term relationship that continued after more than 40 years of shared living and extensive community involvement. His concern was of failing health, especially for himself but also for his husband (they were married in Canada). They currently had a multistory home that required physical ability to climb multiple flights of stairs for all daily activities and wondered whether it was time to move, perhaps to a retirement community. He was finding that dietary restrictions, relationship issues arising from spending much more time together than before retirement, and growing feelings of depression had led him to seek professional help.

Jonathan, a 70-year-old White man, began by noting that he had been in therapy frequently throughout his adult life trying to cope with being bisexual. He had experienced all types of therapy from a variety of mainly supportive analysts and counselors; however, given the historical period and the pathological view of homosexuality at the time, they had focused on helping him to "adjust" rather than to affirm his sexual orientation and explore what gay life existed at the time. As was typical in the 1960s, he married and was able to suppress his same-sex attractions through a busy career and family activities. Unlike many of this period, he did not seek outside encounters with men and lived in a mostly asexual relationship with his wife, having only enough sexual interest to father two children who were now adult parents living in a different part of the country. A year after he had retired his wife died after a prolonged illness; he had been the primary caregiver. Since then he had begun to explore gay life, which had become far more accessible through the Internet and subsequent social contacts. In particular, he had discovered the gay male BDSM (bondage, discipline/dominance, submission/slave–master, or sadomasochism) community and had begun to develop a friendship network as well as a set of new skills and attitudes about sexuality. He had also met a somewhat younger man with whom he had thoughts of developing a long-term relationship, but he was concerned that this may not be feasible because he was reluctant to come out to his children and extended family and feared that they would not accept a committed same-sex relationship.

Interventions With David

The first session is usually very important, as sometimes it is the only therapy session that takes place, and it usually brings the current issues into focus. Once the informed consent process is done, I usually ask, "How can I help?" David's reply was essentially a request for information, referral, and experienced guidance about issues he had given a lot of thought already. He described his health concerns and the recent hip replacement surgery for his husband that made the plan of aging in their present home problematic. He wondered about gay-friendly retirement housing options, clearly not wiling to consider "going back into the closet" in old age because of the need for assisted living or nursing care. They had pets that also had to be taken into consideration in housing options. Then, turning to broader health care issues, he wondered about end-of-life issues and how his marriage in Canada would affect decisions about health care and last wishes in his home state. Finally, he had begun the process of writing a will but did not know how to proceed in a way that would ensure that his wishes would be carried out, especially if his husband outlived him, or if his siblings were to contest the provisions of the will, as had happened with several of his friends. My intervention at this point was to offer the names of two gay-friendly lawyers who specialized in life-planning issues.

Turning to his daily life at present, he noted how he and his husband had tended to get in each other's way during the day since he had retired from the college last year. Also, the days now tended to flow together, so he found it hard to keep track of the days of the week and felt that things that used to take just a few minutes now seemed to take hours to finish. He went to the gym most days to swim and work out but seldom saw any friends and missed the casual interaction he used to have at school. Increasingly his life had begun to feel empty and his primary social contact was his husband, who had spent most of his day working from home for several years since his semiretirement. Hearing this, I pulled out my Geriatric Depression Index and went through the quick 20 questions to gauge the extent of his depression. Because the index is transparent, his moderately high score indicated that he wanted me to know that his mood was a serious problem. He was not on any antidepressant medication and said that he did not want to lose his sexual responses, as that would be especially depressing. He had not discussed his depressed mood with his physician but was willing for me to do so and signed the release of information statement. He also asked whether I knew of any gay male physicians who might provide services to both he and his husband now that they were both on Medicare and no longer needed to restrict their medical choices to the physicians in the college health program. Only one doctor on my list accepted Medicare, but he was well trained in geriatric issues, so I suggested that David visit him to see if he felt comfortable. We decided to wait until that connection was made before I contacted the physician, but I gave him the name of one standard antidepressant that typically does not affect male erection for him to think about.

At the end of the first session David was pleased that I was not just a passive listener, as he feared a therapist would be, thanked me for the referrals, and agreed to continue working with me on the three themes: issues of daily living, depressed mood, and the process of thinking though future living arrangements. We agreed that a regular weekly time would help him know which day of the week it was and begin to give some help with daily scheduling. I suggested that he keep an informal diary of his daily activities by time and record his level of enjoyment in each activity and mood level.

In the next several sessions we focused equally on the three themes. The diary exercise helped him gain more control over his daily schedule, find better times to do specific tasks, and pay attention to doing things that gave him enjoyment at least once each day. It also brought out his dependence on alcohol after dark every day, a routine that his husband did not share but tolerated. We examined his depressed thinking habits, especially his tendency toward catastrophizing, usually triggered by a pain or memory lapse, that made him think his life was going "downhill fast." I gave him some standard cognitive behavior therapy (CBT) exercises to focus on his negative thinking habits and suggested some ways of stopping the negative thoughts that led him to spiral down into a depressed mood. As a former teacher, he readily saw the value in reading a book on CBT and was amused at the exercise book that went with it. Although I have not been trained in the protocol of CBT for depression, David developed much expertise on his own. I also emphasized the interpersonal theoretical orientation of doing enjoyable activities, avoiding unpleasant interactions, and paying attention to daily experiences that trigger anger or aggravation. We discussed ways in which he did and did not release anger appropriately, the use of exercise as a way of relieving the fight-or-flight response to aggravation, and the risk of turning anger inward instead of using it to motivate constructive action. Finally, we spent some portion of each session problem solving the home living situation. The first step was to encourage David and his husband to each create some separate private space where they could retreat for work or some enjoyable activity. The second step was to encourage the use of "I" language when a disagreeable interaction was beginning instead of the "you" language of attacking each other. We considered a conjoint session, but David's husband was not interested, so I suggested that David note some typical disputes that led to disagreeable interactions. It turned out that these often involved issues of territoriality or privacy—such as David feeling the kitchen was his husband's territory and he was excluded, or David feeling that his partner invaded his private space without permission when David was chatting on the Internet.

This latter issue led me to ask about their sexual relations and how each of them dealt with sexuality inside and outside the relationship. It turned out that they had ceased sexual relations several years ago and David's primary outlet was now masturbation, usually while viewing Web cam interactions with Internet chat buddies, watching porn, or just fantasizing when alone. He assumed that his husband's sexual life was similar but was not sure. They had agreed during the onset of the AIDS epidemic to avoid any sexual activity that might involve a risk of HIV infection, and this eventually eliminated any sexual contact between them or with others outside the relationship. They had both been tested for HIV and were negative, but the loss of several close friends during the first two decades of the epidemic gave sexuality a grim aspect that David had not been able to shake since.

Recognizing that these issues were unlikely to be fully resolved in individual therapy, I asked whether he wanted to work on any of the three key issues in relationships: money, power, and sex. He agreed that they had concerns about all three and that the first two had come out clearly when they had met with the lawyer to draft the wills, power of attorney, and health care directives and to consider establishing living trust documents. At present, however, David was reluctant to upset their established relationship. He wanted to continue being sexually active but did not expect their sexual relationship to resume.

We therefore decided to focus on working out a living situation that would provide opportunities for privacy as well as for shared space. They had investigated the existing gay-friendly retirement communities and felt that such a limited group of residents would be potentially as uninteresting as a straight retirement community would be unpleasant. Thus, they were investigating finding an apartment in a building with an elevator and wheelchair accessible doors, bath, and kitchen cabinets. In searching for this apartment they contacted their local SAGE (Services and Advocacy for GLBT Elders; www.sageusa.org) group for assistance and recommendations. In this contact with SAGE they began to find some new interests, such as a monthly brunch club, some discussion groups, and social activities. Soon David had become a "friendly visitor" to a SAGE client about his age, and through SAGE some new friendships developed.

The combination of medication provided by the new gay physician, CBT and interpersonal therapy for depression, and a more conscious use of exercise to relieve aggravation—as well as more enjoyment in life through SAGE activities—led to a reduction in David's depressed mood and less need for alcohol in the evening. At this point therapy ended, with David and his husband still looking for new housing and still disputing territoriality, but more frequently discussing their issues instead of blaming each other.

Transference Issues

As an older gay man in a long-term relationship, it was often too easy for me to empathize with David. Now and then I could use a generic example from things I had learned in my relationship in the therapy, but I always had to check myself first to be sure it would be a helpful analogy or suggestion rather than an interfering focus on me instead of David. In our final session he noted that these personal examples were often helpful, but not always. As a helping professional, I also felt reluctant to ignore the relationship issues about power, money, and sex, but I had to remind myself that it was their relationship and they needed to deal with those issues in their own ways. In fact, their work with the lawyer on the trusts they eventually did set up provided a concrete format for this discussion with a helpful outside person who was also sensitive and understanding.

Interventions With Jonathan

As with David, the first session with Jonathan was very important, because he was testing me to see how comfortable I was with his bisexual history,

BDSM interests, and exuberant joy in diving into the gay scene at the age of 70. In response to my question "How can I help?" he became thoughtful and told me of this new relationship he had stumbled into that was both limiting and also very inviting because it provided a sense of stability and intimacy he missed greatly after his wife died. This ambivalence led him back into therapy after many years without any professional counseling. It turned out that he had met a younger Asian man at a party and that they had been dating and enjoying the "most wonderful mutual sex" he had ever experienced. However, he was unfamiliar with the man's cultural background, knew nothing of his family or living circumstances, and felt he did not share any interest in BDSM. One reason he chose to see me was because of my interest in Asia, which he discovered on my professional website. I told him I had visited several Asian countries, with extended visits to Japan; had published research on gay Asian men; and had had several Asian friends over the years. I also indicated through some questions about his BDSM experiences that I was not upset by these activities and had some knowledge about them (Nichols, 2006). For example, I asked whether his practices were "safe, sane, and consensual." These terms are standard descriptors for all types of activities in the BDSM community, which includes men and women with heterosexual, bisexual, and same-sex sexual orientations. I also offered that a session with his Asian partner would be possible if they wished at some point.

In general, the first session went well and we decided to focus on some of the unprocessed aspects of his transition from a monogamous heterosexual lifestyle to an adventurous journey into the contemporary world of gay life. Some of the issues that I thought would be relevant included HIV and other sexually transmitted diseases, appropriate sources of information about BDSM practices, development of basic dating skills, and gaps in information about gay male sex practices. He agreed that these topics were important, assured me that he had been tested for HIV (and was negative) and knew about safer sex practices, but said that he had not thought about other sexually transmitted diseases. He also felt a need to spend some time on his wife's death and his continued grieving her, as well as on his relationships with his adult children and their families. He was unsure how to integrate his past and present lives and did not want to waste his limited future lifetime floundering in ambivalence or overindulgence in the temptations of the moment.

I made a note to inquire in future sessions about his end-of-life planning, financial planning, and will because these issues would be very complicated, especially if he were to begin a long-term relationship. I also wanted to find out more regarding his previous therapy and his medical history, especially as some BDSM practices are more physically stressful than regular sexual behavior. It also seemed appropriate to limit the initial contract to six additional sessions to focus our attention on the issues at hand and avoid the sessions becoming weekly reports of his new sexual adventures.

The following four sessions were fairly task-oriented ones, focusing on his grief and a review of the long marriage and parenthood chapters of his life, his end-of-life planning, and steps to take for arranging the appropriate documents and deciding who would be best to make health and financial decisions now that his life had changed so dramatically. We also spent considerable time thinking about strategies for talking with his family about his new life, whether it was truly necessary and appropriate, and when to begin and with whom. In general, we concluded that if a significant relationship emerged that would definitely affect financial plans, his children would need to be told; but until then, his private life would be protected, as would the sensitivities of his children regarding their mother. We did identify one close family member, Jonathan's cousin, who had been openly gay for many years and was well regarded by the family, as one person Jonathan would confide in, because we thought there should be someone in the know should there be a health emergency with which the family needed to cope.

Jonathon's health was good, but he was interested in finding a "kink-friendly" doctor he could confide in regarding his interest in medication for erectile concerns and the physical risks of various sexual practices he wanted to try. Fortunately, he lived in an urban area where I could help him locate such a medical doctor. He also was able to find a knowledgeable lawyer to develop the necessary documents for end-of-life planning and to discuss their ramifications for his biological family. His previous therapy had been decades earlier, and he reported no emotional problems apart from the acute transition in his life. His use of alcohol was limited to wine with meals and an occasional glass of wine in social settings. He had no medications except the typical cholesterol medication and multivitamins. He exercised by walking the dog daily, and his weight was appropriate. His age was obvious in his appearance, but he was astonished to find that his younger Asian friend found him attractive and that the BDSM friends valued expertise in their activities more than physical attractiveness. His mood was generally good, and I saw no signs of personality or mood abnormalities that required attention at that time.

He did invite his friend Ken to the fifth session, and I was relieved to find that he had U.S. citizenship, so immigration issues would not be a concern if they did begin a long-term relationship. Ken was of Japanese ancestry but had been born in Hawaii, where he had been educated through college. His parents did not know he was gay and kept constant pressure on him to get married and have children. Jonathan had been urging him to come out to them, so we discussed this issue in some detail, as it had become a matter of considerable dispute: Jonathan wanted to visit Ken's family, and Ken resisted the possible exposure that would be inevitable. I reminded Jonathan of the issues that would be raised if Ken were to visit Jonathan's family and also pointed out the difficulty new couples sometimes have when they travel together anywhere; it might be best to take their first trip to a neutral location so both would be unfamiliar with the country and culture and they could practice traveling together as equals.

One of the issues Jonathan had raised in previous sessions was whether Ken was genuinely interested in him or had some monetary goals. My first response was whether Jonathan would ask the same question if Ken were female. Was this a reflection of some negative attitudes about gay men, or was it a reflection of age bias in the sense of distrust of a younger person's motives? Even if it were one of Ken's motivations, would this be a negative point, as Jonathan might be gaining many valuable intangible benefits from a relationship with someone younger who might wind up caring for him just as he had for his late wife? With this concern in mind, I facilitated their discussion of the rewards and benefits of their potential relationship. This gave me a chance to observe their interaction, note body language, and note the extent to which Jonathan used his age or status to put Ken down. It all seemed to be appropriate in terms of body language and a lack of interruptions or dominating conversation, and they agreed at the end that each of them could benefit in both tangible and intangible ways from each other.

Although we did not specifically discuss BDSM at Jonathan's request, I pointed out that each person's sexuality is as unique as his or her fingerprint: If two people match more than 70%, so to speak, they are likely to be pretty compatible sexually. I also noted two aspects of male same-sex relationships that are not common sense. First, when two people "make love" very well their bodies are very likely to feel the emotion of love; this is a natural biological response and should not be interpreted as *love*, which involves knowing and trusting the other person in many aspects of life. Thus, two men making love are well advised to avoid "the L-word" until they have come to know and like each other in many other ways. Second, most male couples eventually want to explore sex outside their relationship and need to work out some sort of mutual agreement that is comfortable for both of them. Ideally this need does not occur until after an initial period of monogamy that allows the relationship to be firmly established. But whenever it happens, it is better if it can be discussed first, even if the decision is to keep it secret from each other so that it does not damage the primary relationship. They nodded and accepted a reference to a book on gay couple relationships written by a couple with a considerable age difference between them (McWhirter & Mattison, 1984).

Jonathan and I did make the sixth session our last one but left open the opportunity to meet again if things came up. As usual, I facilitated a review of our sessions together and recalled the theme from one of our early sessions about Jonathan beginning a journey, as if he were going to a place he had not visited before. He may find many things there that he likes, or that are new and exciting, and some that are not to his taste. There may be many stations on the journey, and he may get off at some and skip others. Part of the journey may be with Ken, part of it alone. This image of a *journey* is useful because it allows for some bad times that are seen as part of the journey, a temporary situation that need not affect the next part of the journey. It also points out the experimental nature of the adventure. The model applies, of course, both to Jonathan and Ken as well as to Jonathan's exploration of BDSM.

The only follow-up I received from them was a wedding announcement with a photograph of the two of them both dressed in black leather at the marriage ceremony in Amsterdam a year later.

Transference Issues

The issues for me with this client focused on the explicitly sexual nature of many of our discussions. It was important that Jonathan's adolescent-like excitement of exploring BDSM and his exciting love making with Ken not be a voyeuristic experience for me in a way that distracted from the difficult work we had to do with regard to Jonathan's transition from the heterosexual universe to contemporary gay male life. It was primarily for this reason that I suggested we limit and compress our work into six sessions. I also kept a close guard on my use of personal experiences in order to maintain sufficient distance to be objective about what Jonathan was experiencing, what BDSM meant to him, and how he, as a White man, was thinking about Ken as a Japanese man. Stereotypes and deeply buried issues of power, control, and submission are important to consider when working through issues such as those presented by Jonathan's journey.

Conclusion

Counseling older gay men can be an interesting and challenging experience. Often they bring years of competent coping skills, pragmatic issues, and unique individuality into the sessions that can make stereotypes of aging disappear quickly, as these two cases demonstrated. Of course, they can also bring the misconceptions of aging we foster in our culture, as if it has to be lonely, depressing, and disabled. These despairing cases are the most difficult to deal with because the narcissism ("no one has ever suffered as much as poor me") and the life-long self-defeating stance has been perfected. I throw up my hands with such clients and am consoled with the observation that although some appear to have perfected misery to an art form, they nevertheless seem to have accommodated to it and survive.

References

Kimmel, D., Rose, T., & David, S. (Eds.). (2006). *Lesbian, gay, bisexual, and transgender aging: Research and clinical perspectives.* New York, NY: Columbia University Press.

McWhirter, D. P., & Mattison, A. M. (1984). *The male couple: How relationships develop.* Englewood Cliffs, NJ: Prentice Hall.

Nichols, M. (2006). Psychotherapeutic issues with "kinky" clients: Clinical problems, yours and theirs. *Journal of Homosexuality, 50*(2/3), 281–300.

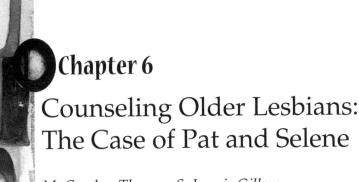

Chapter 6

Counseling Older Lesbians: The Case of Pat and Selene

M. Carolyn Thomas, S. Lenoir Gillam, and Paul F. Hard

Pat and Selene

Pat and Selene are in their late 60s and have been life partners for 27 years. Pat is a biology professor and Selene taught art in the public school system for 30 years. Selene has been experiencing health problems due to Parkinson's disease (PD) but has continued working. However, the disease has progressed and she has had difficulty using her art skills, so she has decided to retire. Pat had intended to work a few more years but is also considering retirement to help care for Selene and do some things they have both always wanted to do.

Although the families of both women acknowledge the significance of their relationship and are supportive to a large extent, the specific nature of their relationship has never been discussed openly. Selene has two grown children with their own families, and her children are pressuring Pat to seriously consider an assisted care facility for Selene in the near future. Selene is a great lover of animals, has always enjoyed her beloved pets, and is definitely upset about the prospect of being away from those pets. Caring for Selene is the only area of conflict between the couple and Selene's family, but it is a serious issue with Selene and also Pat, who does not want to be separated from Selene.

Presenting Issues

Pat and Selene go to a licensed professional counselor to ask for help in resolving their issues, which include (a) retirement planning for both Pat and Selene; (b) preparation for the progression of PD symptoms; (c) support for Pat, who will be the major caregiver for Selene; (d) coping strategies for dealing with PD; and (e) decision making with the couple and Selene's family about Selene's future care.

Many of the challenges faced by Pat and Selene are the same as those faced by any aging person or couple. However, combining the usual aging issues with specific problems faced by aging lesbians requires special attention and competency with regard to assessment, treatment goals, and treatment modalities (Association for Lesbian, Gay, Bisexual and Transgender Issues in Counseling [ALGBTIC], 1997). Any planning about such concerns as legal issues involving medical care requires an exploration of advantages and disadvantages of decisions made within the context of social and attitudinal barriers that create unique challenges for this couple (ALGBTIC, 1997). Heterosexism impacting lesbians can add unexpected disadvantages when one is considering options, and many privileges afforded older heterosexual couples are not equally applied to same-sex couples.

Assessment and Diagnosis

After two initial sessions of general assessment and a review of Selene's medical records, the counselor should concentrate first on (a) helping Pat and Selene plan for a retirement that is meaningful and continues a productive quality of life and (b) involving all concerned in a group decision model to plan for Selene's future care. Neither Pat nor Selene meet diagnostic criteria for an Axis I or Axis II disorder, but Selene's PD and the psychosocial and environmental stressors that accompany her health concerns are impacting decisions about retirement and are significant focal points of counseling. The first assessment need is education about the possible effects of PD and the current status of Selene's symptoms.

Possible Effects of PD

Selene has experienced several of the initial symptoms of PD, but the disease was diagnosed early and her treatment to date has been effective. She has a resting tremor, which means she experiences a tremor when not doing work or painting. This tremor has spread to both sides of her body. She experiences fatigue and must rest more than previously required. She has minor balance and coordination problems, and she encounters increased difficulty with fine motor tasks. She reports that she experiences occasional mild depressed moods, which she attributes to not being able to do the art work she so enjoys. At present, both medical reports from Selene's physician and her self-report suggest that there is no evidence that the depressed moods are the direct result of PD. Furthermore, Pat agrees with Selene's assessment of the depression.

Selene has not experienced rigidity, stooped posture, significant slow movement, loss of facial expression, difficulty swallowing, slurred speech, behavioral problems, or cognitive impairment (Parkinson's Disease Foundation, 2010). Symptoms vary for persons with PD, but nearly all persons with PD eventually experience some degree of cognitive dysfunction (Marsh, 2008). Impaired cognitive symptoms can range from mild memory disturbances and attention difficulties that are merely a nuisance to more severe executive dysfunction, short- and long-term memory problems, and language dysfunctions that severely influence performance.

In assessing Selene's symptoms and prognosis for preparing for a continuing productive life, Pat, Selene, and the therapist initiate retirement planning for the couple. The couple is also referred to a PD psychoeducation self-help group to teach them about possible future symptoms of PD, develop coping skills for dealing with the possible disease effects, and learn solutions and strategies from other patients with PD and their caregivers. Although the self-help group can provide some adjunctive support for addressing these issues associated with Selene's PD, the couple and therapist make a point to discuss potential benefits, limitations, and risks of group participation. For example, the women may not want to disclose the specific nature of their relationship with the group. They cite concerns about prejudice or discrimination regardless of their degree of openness about their relationship.

Factors Affecting Retirement Possibilities

Pat and Selene have a positive attitude about aging and seem to have avoided common stereotypes of aging as a time for inactivity, dependency, living in the past, loneliness, decline, disengagement, and incapacitating physical and mental limitations. Instead they seem to view aging as another developmental period of opportunities for achievement, positive balance, and achievement of ego integrity. The couple wants to concentrate on preparing for this new stage of development.

Pat and Selene have a history of continuous professional, community, and social involvement. The positive assessment of their attitudes about aging is influential in retirement planning, which will obviously need to include continued involvement in their professions, community, and support systems. Retirement plans will also need to include continued intellectual and spiritual growth.

Because both Pat and Selene have good retirement programs, their retirement plans will probably not be greatly limited by insufficient funds, although living on a fixed income might require careful consideration, especially considering Selene's health issues. Travel and activities will need to reflect Selene's need for rest, her limited mobility, and the need to simplify daily activities (Rosner & Henchcliffe, 2003).

Assessing the Family's Willingness to Make Joint Decisions About Selene's Future Care

The only conflict about plans for Selene and Pat is centered around Selene's future care. Her children seem adamant about exploring an assisted care facility; Selene is even more adamant about living at home, no matter how the PD progresses; and Pat is willing to support Selene's wishes. Rather than engage in traditional conflict resolution, the counselor may want to use a model of shared decision making that involves identifying resources, planning alternatives, securing support, and including input from all concerned parties while hopefully leaving the decision to Selene. Pat and Selene plan to consult with their attorney early in this process to ensure that they are legally protected to make decisions in the event of ongoing or unanticipated familial conflicts centered around Selene's future health care.

With Pat and Selene's informed consent, the counselor arranges a session with Selene's children to explain the Schlossberg, Waters, and Goodman (1995) 4 S model of decision making. Such a meeting will also serve as a screening session to see whether the children are appropriate candidates for cooperative family decision making.

Theoretical Framework and Treatment Modalities

Existential philosophy is the underlying framework for all of the suggested treatment modalities and models. Even with some serious health concerns, Pat and Selene are viewing aging as a positive developmental period of growth and attainment of ego integrity. They both want to plan for continued productive, meaningful, and worthwhile lives, and they want to jointly approach this period of ego integrity.

Treatment Model for Retirement Planning

The 1989 Riker and Myers model for retirement planning, adapted by Thomas, Martin, Alexander, Cooley, and Loague (2003), would be useful in working with Pat and Selene. With the considerations needed to accommodate the PD, Thomas et al. would recommend retirement planning in the areas of (a) professional involvement, (b) community involvement, (c) social involvement, (d) intellectual stimulation, and (e) spiritual growth. Some of this planning can be accomplished in couples counseling. If Pat or Selene wishes to address separate needs regarding retirement or any other issue via individual counseling at some point during the process, then referrals will be made as appropriate.

Group Counseling for Pat and Selene

As previously noted, a PD support group will provide both Pat and Selene with support from other patients and caregivers. The group will also relieve isolation, give valuable information about coping skills, and provide a safe place to express feelings associated with experiencing PD. Actually, Pat and Selene may benefit from three different kinds of PD groups. A separate caregivers group might help Pat through difficult times when she may not want to burden Selene with her caregiving difficulties. Likewise, a separate PD group for patients would benefit Selene at times when she may not want to express fears and anxieties to Pat. Both could benefit from a PD self-help group, which is different from a counseling or psychoeducation group. Support groups are small therapeutic groups led by professional counselors with the goal of healing, support, and growth in a confidential environment. A self-help group, in contrast, resembles more of an organization that is open to the public, is led by members who are probably not counselors, and has the primary objective of providing information and advocacy (Riordan & Beggs, 1988). Although each of these group modalities may benefit Pat and Selene, the therapist processes with them how to realistically make informed decisions about adjunctive services in the likelihood that resources such as time and energy make these modalities more overwhelming than helpful.

The 4 S Model for a Solution-Focused Family Group

Thomas and Martin's (2010) adaptation of the Schlossberg et al.'s (1995) 4 S model provides a viable strategy for a decision-making family group. The model includes exploring the factors of (a) situation, (b) self, (c) support, and (d) strategies. Families are often torn or experience conflict when older people face the decision about leaving their home, community, and personal support system and either moving to live with children or entering a care facility. Using the 4 S model adapted to a family group experience is helpful when such changes in living arrangements are being considered. Pat and Selene, Selene's children, and any grandchildren or other concerned family members join for four to six sessions to (a) identify resources and deficits in the existing living arrangement, (b) explore the advantages and disadvantages of Selene's remaining at home or eventually moving to a care facility, (c) assess Pat, Selene, and input from Selene's family of origin to balance the strengths and liabilities of either decision, (d) learn new strategies for the success of either choice, (e) allow Selene to choose from among the alternative plans and strategies, and finally (f) develop tentative alternatives if Selene's choice is not successful.

The counselor serves as the facilitator for the family group, fostering cooperative decision making and maximum empowerment of Selene with input from Pat and Selene's family of origin. This model can be reused from time to time, depending on Selene's symptoms and Pat's continued health. The use of this group adaptation of the 4 S model allows decisions to be based on information, strategies, and possibilities rather than on fear and helplessness.

Goals of Treatment

The goals of counseling are listed here separately for Pat and Selene as a couple, Pat, Selene, and Selene and her children.

Goals for Pat and Selene as a Couple

At the end of counseling Pat and Selene will

1. Be better educated about the possible effects of PD on Selene, with knowledge that every patient experiences symptoms in a different manner.
2. Have support from other patients with PD and caregivers of persons with PD.
3. Maintain an existential attitude about aging together.
4. Have a completed mutual retirement plan and alternative plans based on an assessment of all areas of their lives.
5. Possess legally binding documents that facilitate their rights to make a wide range of decisions for each other in anticipation of Selene's future health care needs.

Goals for Pat

In addition to the mutual goals for Pat and Selene, at the conclusion of treatment Pat will

1. Have a retirement plan that enables her to continue in a productive, meaningful life.
2. Have a support system in place for caregivers of people with PD.
3. Know coping strategies for addressing the current and possible future effects of Selene's PD.
4. Have a realistic plan for her own life combined with caregiving.

Goals for Selene

In addition to the mutual goals for Pat and Selene, Selene will

1. Have a retirement plan that enables her to continue in a productive, meaningful life based on her own needs, talents, and capabilities.
2. Have a support system in place for dealing with her PD.
3. Know coping strategies for dealing with PD symptoms.
4. Maintain a close relationship with her children and their families.
5. Have a plan with alternatives for her future care based on cooperative decision making and the consensus of her family.

Goals for Selene and Her Children

The main goals for Selene and her family of origin are to

1. Maintain their current, mutually supportive relationship.
2. Have a plan with alternatives for Selene's future care that satisfies Selene's children's needs to know that Selene will have satisfactory care.
3. Preserve the involvement, cooperation, and support of Selene's children for Selene and her relationship with Pat.
4. Maintain Selene's empowerment over her life without excluding her children or Pat.

Application of Interventions

Individual and group counseling interventions already recommended for Pat and Selene are fairly generic, but specific descriptions of the application of the Riker and Myers (1989) retirement decision model and the Schlossberg et al. (1995) 4 S model of decision making will explain how the models are used for Pat and Selene. Because Pat and Selene are older lesbians, specific considerations are warranted.

Retirement Counseling Model

The counselor should include the five life arenas identified by Riker and Myers (1989) and adapted by Thomas et al. (2003) for planning Pat's and Selene's later years. Specifically, counseling will help Pat and Selene identify ways to promote meaningful professional, community, and social involvement in addition to ongoing intellectual stimulation and spiritual growth.

Professional Involvement

Pat and Selene were both active in their respective professional organizations and will choose to continue their involvement, but with modified intensity. Ongoing, needed, specific tasks that maintain continued, meaningful involvement can replace demanding leadership positions.

Community Involvement

Previous intense volunteer and consulting activities can also be replaced with less rigorous tasks. Pat and Selene may wish to change the focus of past energies that were strictly associated with their biology and art professions to community needs they have always wanted to address. For example, they might want to help provide healthy resources for lesbian, gay, bisexual, or transgender (LGBT) youth. Selene may want to start LGBT art groups with a local therapist.

Social Involvement

During assessment sessions, Pat and Selene were found to be in the Identity Synthesis stage of the Cass (1979) identity development model. They built and maintained a support system that consisted of an admixture of both heterosexual and LGBT supportive persons. Pat and Selene may want to expand their social environment to more older persons or persons who travel more frequently. Developing new relationships and social support networks may require a second coming out phase when meeting new persons from other communities with whom they feel comfortable.

Intellectual Stimulation

Pat and Selene have probably spent their working years learning mainly within their individual professions. Retirement can be an exciting period of being able to choose areas of growth not directly associated with past work requirements. Although Selene's art work is restricted by PD, she may find other art-related areas to explore. Pat may satisfy a desire to snorkel or scuba dive among reefs while traveling or pursue some other nonbiological interest. Furthermore, universities offer many educational opportunities for older persons, elderhostels are available to provide travel-related programs and services, and education-focused tours and cruises are abundant. Because their work will no longer restrict areas of learning, the gamut and modes from which to choose shared or individual intellectual stimulation are limitless.

Spiritual Growth

During assessment, the counselor found that Pat and Selene both had histories of religious involvement but in different churches. Both women tended to ignore conservative elements of their faiths and associate with the more accepting congregations or parts of congregations. Aging might present added existential issues for both women, and they might wish to find a supportive group of older LGBT persons who are exploring the meaning and spiritual issues in aging.

The 4 S Decision Model

To resolve the issue of Selene's current and future care, the counselor will involve Pat, Selene, and Selene's family in a group using the Thomas and Martin (2010) adaptation of the Schlossberg et al. (1995) 4 S model of decision making.

Situation

After jointly examining the current need for Selene's care, Pat, Selene, and Selene's family find no current need for any assisted care. Selene can function very effectively in her home with her pets. Selene's family is able to express their fears that Selene's symptoms will later require care that neither they nor Pat can provide. In looking at the advantages and disadvantages of a care facility, Pat and Selene point out that same-sex couples are often discriminated against in such facilities by both staff and residents. Pat and Selene might be separated, Pat may have few rights to be involved in Selene's treatment decisions, and possible prejudice and discrimination may create an environment in which Pat and Selene feel it is unsafe to maintain the affectionate and physical aspects of their relationship (Bauman, 2008; Friend, 1990). The most devastating disadvantage for Selene is separation from her pets and Pat. The group mode provides opportunities for Pat and Selene to voice their feelings about separation and for Selene's family to share their fears that Selene will not have sufficient care.

Self

Given the advantages and disadvantages of the choices discussed in the situation, the counselor invites Pat, Selene, and Selene's family to explore their own personal and demographic characteristics that will influence decisions about Selene's care. Members honestly explore their values, willingness to cooperate in Selene's care, personal strengths and coping skills in difficult situations, health, and financial capabilities. Each member also honestly expresses any biases about aging and older lesbians so that myths can be removed as barriers to healthy development. Decisions can be made about which persons will assume certain caregiving tasks whether Selene stays at home or enters a care facility.

Support

The counselor assigns each member the task of exploring possible support in the community. Friendships, community networks, PD self-help groups, institutional programs, and health providers are all explored to identify ways in which Pat and Selene can stay together and Selene can receive sufficient care should her symptoms become more debilitating.

Strategies

The support researched and identified is assessed by Pat, Selene, and Selene's family. Once the resources are identified, the group can balance the assets and liabilities and be able to reach a workable decision. Areas of missing or weak resources can be remedied, and alternative resources can be developed.

This 4 S group may meet over a period of weeks or months. The final decision about current and future care should rest with Selene, but alternative plans can be made to accommodate anyone's residual concerns. The counselor should invite the group to request another round of group sessions if the situation changes radically because of an unexpected factor.

Outcomes

Repeating the specific goals for Pat and Selene as a couple, Pat, Selene, and Selene and her children is not necessary to predict the outcomes of the counseling. The individual and group counseling with the counselor, combined with the support and self-help groups in the community, are adequate to accomplish all the specified goals.

Recommendations

The main counseling recommendation is to provide intermittent individual, couple, and family sessions to assess the effectiveness of the plans, all within the context of an affirming counseling process that addresses the unique issues facing this couple. Occasional monthly or bimonthly sessions allow the counselor to reinforce previous counseling, add resources, modify goals because of changed circumstances, and resume concentrated counseling should drastic chance factors occur.

Clinical Considerations

Berger and Kelly (1996) remarked on the need for counselors to be versed in LGBT issues, community, and resources in order to be effective in counseling individuals such as those described in this case study. Therapists should give particular consideration to both the usual aging issues and the specific problems faced by aging lesbians (ALGBTIC, 1997). Physicians and other caregivers are often reluctant to recognize or discuss matters of sexual orientation related to older adults (National Association on HIV Over Fifty, n.d.). Berger and Kelly also noted that older clients may be more reticent to engage in self-disclosure, which may compound problems establishing a therapeutic environment unless the therapist takes steps to create an open atmosphere. Counselors may therefore need to address personal ageism issues in order to facilitate disclosure as well as be prepared to advocate for their clients.

Issues of access to services may be magnified in more rural settings where LGBT-specific services may not exist. Berger and Kelly (1996) observed that the availability of positive LGBT referral resources may be limited. They noted that gerontological services are often homophobic or hold the heterosexist notion that older LGBT persons do not exist. Although some commentators have observed that the LGBT population is becoming less urban (Signorile, 1998), social services and support for LGBT persons continue to remain predominantly in urban environments (Robinson, 2005). The culturally sensitive counselor must therefore be prepared to advocate for lesbian clients and assist them in accessing services.

References

Association for Lesbian, Gay, Bisexual and Transgender Issues in Counseling. (1997). *Competencies for counseling gay, lesbian, bisexual and transgendered (LGBT) clients.* Alexandria, VA: Author.

Bauman, S. (2008). *Essential topics for the helping professional.* Boston, MA: Pearson.

Berger, R. M., & Kelly, J. J. (1996). Gay men and lesbians grown older. In R. P. Cabaj & T. S. Stein (Eds.), *The textbook of homosexuality and mental health* (pp. 305–316). Alexandria, VA: American Psychiatric Association.

Cass, V. C. (1979). Homosexual identity formation: A theoretical model. *Journal of Homosexuality, 4*(3), 219–235.

Friend, R. (1990). Older lesbian and gay people: A theory of successful aging. *Journal of Homosexuality, 20*(3/4), 99–118.

Marsh, L. (2008). *Not just a movement disorder: Cognitive changes in PD.* Retrieved from http://www.apfeldorffoundation.org/uploads/6/0/3/9/6039876/251_cognitive_changes_in_pd.pdf

National Association on HIV Over Fifty. (n.d.). *Educational tip sheet: HIV/AIDS and older adults.* Retrieved from http://www.hivoverfifty.org/

Parkinson's Disease Foundation. (2010). *Symptoms.* Retrieved from http://www.pdf.org/en/symptoms

Riker, H. C., & Myers, J. E. (1989). *Retirement counseling: A handbook for action.* New York, NY: Hemisphere.

Riordan, R. J., & Beggs, M. S. (1988). Some critical differences between self-help and therapy groups. *Journal for Specialists in Group Work, 13,* 24–29.

Robinson, P. A. (2005). *Queer wars: The new gay right and its critics.* Chicago, IL: University of Chicago Press.

Rosner, J. & Henchcliffe, C. (2003). *Coping with dementia: Advice for caregivers.* Retrieved from http://www.pdf.org/pdf/fs_coping_dementia.pdf

Schlossberg, N. K., Waters, E. B., & Goodman, J. (1995). *Counseling adults in transition* (2nd ed.). New York, NY: Springer.

Signorile, M. (1998). *Life outside.* Boston, MA: Harper Perennial.

Thomas, M. C., & Martin, V. (2010). Group work: Elderly people and their caregivers. In D. Capuzzi, D. R. Gross, & M. D. Stauffer (Eds.), *Introduction to group work* (5th ed., pp. 505–536). Denver, CO: Love.

Thomas, M. C., Martin, V., Alexander, J. J., Cooley, F. R., & Loague, A. M. (2003). Using new attitudes and technology to change the developmental counseling focus for older populations. *Counseling and Human Development, 35*(8), 1–8.

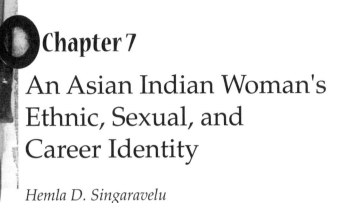

Chapter 7

An Asian Indian Woman's Ethnic, Sexual, and Career Identity

Hemla D. Singaravelu

Lakshmi, who is 37 years of age, is an attorney at a law firm and is experiencing extreme dissatisfaction with her career and workplace. As a woman and an Asian Indian, she does not feel like there is an opportunity for advancement in her Caucasian male–dominated conservative firm. She feels like many of the cases are not given to her, and she spends time doing paperwork and attending to smaller cases. She is fearful of bringing this up with her supervisor, as it might be viewed negatively against her. She does not even feel connected with her colleagues and finds that she is very different from them. Getting up every morning to go to work seems like drudgery, and 6 years after having passed the bar examination, she wonders whether she has chosen the right profession. She constantly looks forward to the weekend, when she can spend some quiet time reading and writing.

Lakshmi's parents are very proud of her accomplishments, particularly her being hired by a high-profile corporate law firm. Her parents, who identify as Hindus, migrated from India when she was 16 years old. Her father had accepted a position as a researcher and physician at a university medical school. Her father is retired now, and her mother works as a pharmacist. Lakshmi is the youngest of four children. She has two brothers who are physicians and one sister who is an attorney. During her teenage years, Lakshmi wanted to be a writer but was discouraged by her parents. They expressed that she would be wasting her time and that she should follow in the footsteps of her siblings. Lakshmi has always been loyal to her family; however, in the past few years she has been somewhat reserved with them. They have been pressuring her to get married now that she is established. They have also expressed their fear that Lakshmi might be too old to find a husband or have children. Unbeknownst to her family, Lakshmi has been in an intimate partnership with Tina for 4 years.

Tina, who is 42 years of age, is a professor of economics at a state university. She has come out at work as a lesbian, has successfully established herself, and is happy in her profession. However, she has been worried about Lakshmi, who has not been sleeping or eating well and has been feeling generally unhappy. Lakshmi complains about work constantly, and when Tina brings up moving, Lakshmi gets upset, tells Tina that she does not understand that it is not easy to just move or make a change, and they end up arguing. Tina wonders whether Lakshmi is unhappy with their relationship. There are times when Tina has difficulty talking to Lakshmi about work or their future and finds that their communication styles are different as well. She has met Lakshmi's family on only five occasions in 4 years, and Lakshmi typically introduces her as her "friend." Tina wishes that Lakshmi would tell them about their relationship. Tina has brought this up several times in the past, but it only causes them arguments. Lakshmi feels that her family, especially her parents, will not accept their relationship because they may be concerned about how it might impact the family, and she does not want to be ostracized by them. Tina wonders whether moving might resolve some of their problems and even help their relationship. At the urging of her partner Tina, Lakshmi comes in for counseling.

Introduction

There seem to be several layers impinging on Lakshmi's life. Clearly her work life and career identity are very much intertwined with her personal life. The following paragraphs address the multiple layers of Lakshmi's life by first conceptualizing Lakshmi based on her cultural background and relationship and then addressing issues counselors need to keep in mind when working with clients like Lakshmi. The term *counseling* is used to describe both career and personal counseling, as neither can be separated in addressing a person's life, especially Lakshmi's.

Conceptualizing Lakshmi

Cultural Heritage and Career Development Implications

Being an Asian Indian itself brings a multitude of issues to the surface. Lakshmi's parents are immigrants to the United States and as such may still hold values and belief systems similar to those of their country of origin, India. It is quite common in collectivist cultures to regard education as paramount to the development of children; however, this emphasis on education is heightened in the Indian culture. As young adults, individuals of Indian descent are cognizant of how their career decisions will impact the family name and the family's reputation. Certain occupations are associated with prestige, and it is possible that this is the case for Lakshmi as well. Lakshmi may have chosen the field of law to follow in the footsteps of her sister and to fulfill an expectation of her family, particularly her parents. Focusing on a career in the arts or writing could have negative connotations with regard to livelihood, her family's stature in the community, and maybe even her stature in the community.

Also inherent in typical collectivist cultures is the importance of emotional interdependence as well as obligations and welfare to the group. Other values, such as respect and reverence for elders; family loyalty and obligation; placing a high value on education, self-discipline, and morality; shame; order; and familial and gender hierarchy (Ho, 1987; Triandis, 1995) are prominent. India's strong sense of community and group-defined orientation means a greater acceptance of hierarchical settings both within the family and in society at large (Almeida, 2005). In the family structure, three prominent familial relationship roles are father/son, husband/wife, and elder siblings/younger siblings. The family structure is customarily hierarchical and patriarchal, with the father assuming leadership over the household. Respect and power are afforded to Asian parents and increase as they age. Parents usually live with their children or may retain their own residence as they get older. Deviating from most of these traditional values can mean that the whole family will lose face. Despite the elimination of the traditional caste system, attitudes still remain with respect to social class and status in the community. Career choices impact and reflect social status and family background. However, these cultural nuances may not totally apply to Lakshmi because of her acculturation into her new country, the United States. Unlike her parents, Lakshmi may not have these same values and belief systems and may not adhere to traditional roles. Her parents, however, may see their parental authority weakening, thus creating a greater generation gap between them and their children.

Based on the information provided, there seems to be a theme that all of Lakshmi's family members are employed in prestigious medical and legal professions. Furthermore, given the statement not to "waste her time" with a career as a writer but to pursue a degree similar to that of her siblings, it is likely that Lakshmi herself sees a high level of educational attainment and professional achievement as an important pursuit, as evidenced by her career choice. This is not only a theme but an expectation within her family. Even her romantic partner Tina has achieved success in her career as a professor.

Furthermore, Lakshmi's gender and ethnic representation may be influencing her success and comfort level at work. It is possible that her current boss is taking her work for granted, seeing her as less capable than her male counterparts. Although she is in a high-profile law firm it is likely that she is making less money than her male coworkers as well.

Identity

Central to a person's sense of self and esteem/confidence is the development and state of his or her personal identity. Identity commitment is important for emotional adjustment, well-being, and satisfaction. For Lakshmi, identity can be a convergence of her ethnic identity (Greene, 1994), sexual identity, and career identity. Ethnically speaking, she is an Asian Indian woman who has lived in India for 15 years and in the United States for 22 years and thus is minimally bicultural. Given that much of her adolescent years and young adulthood was spent in the United States, it is uncertain to what extent Lakshmi identifies with her culture of origin and how this impacts her relationship with her family and her career decisions.

It is clear, however, that she is not as comfortable with her sexual identity/ orientation based on that fact that she has kept it a secret from her family and possibly her coworkers too. Coming out is a process that entails a recognition of an individual's sexual orientation and the integration of an identity as a gay man or lesbian into the individual's personal and social worlds. It usually takes several years for someone to realize and fully accept that he or she is gay or lesbian. Once someone has come out to oneself, it may take several more years to come out to others. In the Hindu culture, in which sexuality is rarely discussed, homosexuality is considered an improper behavior or life path in spite of the representation of same-sex relationships and gender variance in Hinduism. So it is understandable if Lakshmi's difficulty in coming out to her family is based on internalized homophobia and fears about being ostracized by her family. In line with Vivienne Cass's (1979) identity formation model, it is possible that Lakshmi is between tolerating her sexual identity and accepting it, in that she maintains two separate identities, a public one (straight) and a private one (lesbian), and discloses her sexual orientation selectively. She may be trying to fit into society, particularly at work, by continuing to pass (pretend to be heterosexual) at pertinent times. This strategy effectively prevents her from being faced with others' reactions (anticipated to be negative) toward same-sex attraction.

In the present day, a person's sense of self-worth and identity is tied to his or her profession and career identity. It is clear that Lakshmi is questioning her career choice and is dissatisfied with her current work environment. Work is highly important to psychological health, as it can promote connections to the broader social world, enhance well-being, and provide a means for satisfaction and accomplishment. Disruptions in work can lead to anxiety, depression, and other serious conditions in addition to creating rifts in relationships. One wonders how Lakshmi would describe her self-worth. In addition, being an Asian in a predominantly Caucasian male workplace may not be comfortable; however, this can be compounded by her sexual minority status, causing Lakshmi much distress. So it is not surprising that she is unable to relate to her colleagues. However, it is unknown how Lakshmi would describe her identity and whether there is any form of integration of her work, home, and family life.

Intervention

It is uncertain whether Lakshmi is familiar with the counseling process, so it is important that the first session be spent describing the counseling process with her and gauging her attitude toward and perception of counseling. Her presenting problem must be addressed during the first session. Some of her symptoms that mimic depression, like her general unhappiness, lack of appetite, and lack of sleep, must be addressed to assist her in her daily functioning, if needed.

In terms of an approach to counseling, Lakshmi may prefer a more directive form of counseling like solution-focused or a cognitive–behavioral approach and may even expect solutions from the counselor. Lakshmi must be made aware of the counselor's approach to counseling, the client–counselor role, and the fact that counseling is a collaborative effort and requires a process of exploration. It is also possible that Lakshmi would be comfortable with narrative approaches to counseling (Savickas, 2000). Narrative approaches do lend themselves easily to taking a nonknowing and open stance, thus allowing the client to share his or her story and, in this instance, his or her cultural background and experiences. Whichever approach is used with Lakshmi, it is important to remember that her values and belief system have been influenced by her cultural heritage and upbringing, and these can differ greatly from the counselor's beliefs. Counselors also need to be aware that many counseling approaches (career theories included) are based on Western values and beliefs, and thus some of the constructs in the approaches may not directly apply to someone like Lakshmi or to understanding her family functioning. Hence, some adjustments to these approaches will need to be made.

Using certain tools like the career lifeline and her family genogram will help create a platform for conversation and getting more information about Lakshmi. The career lifeline, which represents a chronological life span, will allow Lakshmi to trace all experiences and events, both positive and negative, that have influenced her career development and decisions from her earliest memory to the present day. This includes important milestones in her life. This exercise will get Lakshmi to think about what her career means to her and the various elements and issues that are involved. Her family genogram, in contrast, will provide a visual representation of multigenerational themes with regard to at least three generations of her family's careers; ideas about acceptable career choice, achievement, and success; relationship dynamics; gender roles, expectations; and so forth. Values and beliefs and how family relationships, emotional relationships, and social relationships are defined can all be discovered using a genogram (McGoldrick & Gerson, 1985). Also, assessments and activities that elicit Lakshmi's interests, abilities (like the Strong Interest Inventory), and personality (e.g., the Myers–Briggs Type Indicator) may help clarify Lakshmi's likes and dislikes.

An important point for discussion with Lakshmi is her sexual identity development and her career development and how both are interactive; hence, her sexual orientation and occupational choice must be blended on some level in order for her to achieve career satisfaction. As people move through phases of identity development, issues of vocation choice will resurface and must be reevaluated.

It is also important to address Lakshmi's relationship with her partner and how it might be impacting her career decisions. Lakshmi and Tina are in an interracial or cross-cultural relationship. It might be important to address possible cultural discrepancies in communication, how each defines what relationship means, messages they have received about career development and decision making, how achievement and success are defined, and their overall differences in values and beliefs.

Managing and maintaining a committed relationship can be difficult for opposite-sex couples, but this task is compounded in same-sex relationships when there are no models to follow or when there is no acceptance or recognition of one's commitment to each other (Ritter & Terndrup, 2002). This might be the case with Lakshmi and Tina. Furthermore, struggling between the pressures to marry and retain family support or to leave their communities and choose an alternative life path adds to the stress on the relationship and career decisions. There might be a point in counseling when Lakshmi may want to bring Tina in with her to address some of these issues.

There are several questions that need to be asked of Lakshmi. For example, Is she comfortable with her sexual identity? To what extent are her values and beliefs similar to her parents'? Why did she choose law as a profession? Have Tina and Lakshmi had this type of tension in their relationship in the past?

Conclusion

In the case of Lakshmi, the 37-year-old Asian Indian lesbian attorney, the intersection of career, ethnicity, and sexual orientation provides the context for her life decisions. Her work life and career identity are very intertwined with her personal life. It is therefore critical to understand Lakshmi based on her cultural backgrounds and relationship, and it would be inappropriate to try to separate her many identities. Instead, the counselor should approach her as a rich tapestry to be appreciated in order to aid the resolution of the issues she brings to counseling.

References

Almeida, R. (2005). Asian Indian families: An overview. In M. McGoldrick, J. Giordano, & N. Garcia-Preto (Eds.), *Ethnicity and family therapy* (pp. 377–394). New York, NY: Guilford Press.

Cass, V. C. (1979). Homosexual identity formation: A theoretical model. *Journal of Homosexuality, 4*(3), 219–235.

Greene, B. (1994). Lesbian women of color: Triple jeopardy. In L. Comas-Diaz & B. Greene (Eds.), *Women of color: Integrating ethnic and gender identities in psychotherapy* (pp. 389–427). New York, NY: Guilford Press.

Ho, M. K. (1987). *Family therapy with ethnic minorities.* Newbury Park, CA: Sage.

McGoldrick, M., & Gerson, R. (1985). *Genograms: Assessment and intervention.* New York, NY: Sage.

Ritter, K., & Terndrup, A. (2002). *Handbook of affirmative psychotherapy with lesbians and gay men.* New York, NY: Guilford Press.

Savickas, M. (2000). Renovating the psychology of careers for the twenty-first century. In A. Collin & R. Young (Eds.), *The future of career* (pp. 53–68). Cambridge, England: Cambridge University Press.

Triandis, H. C. (1995). *Individualism & collectivism: New directions in social psychology.* Boulder, CO: Westview Press.

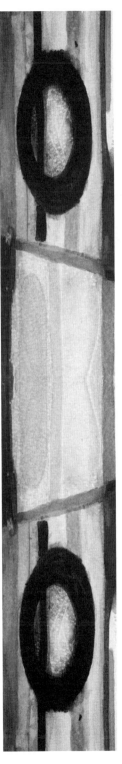

Section 2
Relationship Issues

Competent counselors will

o acknowledge the societal prejudice and discrimination experienced by LGBT persons and assist them in overcoming internalized negative attitudes toward their sexual orientations and gender identities.
o understand that heterosexism pervades the social and cultural foundations of many institutions and traditions and may foster negative attitudes toward LGBT persons.
o understand that biological, familial, and psychosocial factors influence the course of development of GLB orientations and transgendered identities.
o use professional development opportunities to enhance their attitudes, knowledge, and skills specific to counseling LGBT persons and their families.

The relationships we have play an important part in our life satisfaction. LGBT persons in particular relationships face many challenges. This section illustrates the challenges inherent in these relationships and the ways in which therapists can help their LGBT clients meet these challenges.

The first chapter in this section is "Lesbian Couples and Marriage Counseling" by Colleen M. Connolly.

Competent couples and marriage counseling, which is an integral part of working with the LGBT population, requires unique assessments and interventions. LGBT couples are faced with abundant challenges. Having to shield oneself, sometimes on a daily basis, can lead to relational fatigue and relational unrest and can ultimately cause or contribute to such issues as depression, anxiety, sexual intimacy issues, drug and alcohol abuse, and suicidality. These challenges and stressors, which all occur within the context of pervasive societal oppression, can go not only unnoticed and unnamed but even unclaimed by those within the population. Unaddressed stressors can worsen into an internalized couple dynamic and result in chronic stressor overload and relational fracture. Here, Dr. Connolly presents the case of Chris and Jackie and describes both effective and ineffective counseling methods and interventions.

Sometimes couples issues are dealt with in the context of individual counseling. Armand R. Cerbone discusses just that in "Desire, Love, and Shame in Gay Male Relationships: The Case of Tyler." Shame is a key component of gay male relationships (Downs, 2005). According to Downs (2005), shame has three stages: People move from being overwhelmed by their shame, to compensating for their shame, and then to discovering authenticity. The shame that most gay men have grown up with impacts them throughout their lives in all of their developmental tasks (Cerbone, 1990). For some, shame impacts the ability for sexual intimacy. Yet gay men are resilient and do overcome these challenges to have fulfilling relationships and lives. In his chapter, Dr. Cerbone discusses work he did with Tyler on relationship issues in individual therapy. Tyler is negotiating a long-term relationship. Dr. Cerbone shows how he helped him navigate individual conflicts around relationships and sexual intimacy in the context of a homophobic and heterocentric culture.

Parenting is difficult for most people. And again, being part of an LGBT couple creates unique challenges, which Dr. Susan Kashubeck-West discusses in her chapter "Parenting Issues for Lesbian Couples." Using a multicultural, feminist approach, Dr. Kashubeck-West presents the case of Diana and Jasmine and their 4-year-old son Theo. Such an approach focuses on striving to understand clients in terms of their multiple and intersecting identities—identities that lead to varied experiences of privilege and oppression as clients move through their social environments.

The case described by Dr. Kashubeck-West moves through teaching communication skills, teaching the women to validate each other's experiences with their respective families, and teaching them to work as a team. Dr. Kashubeck-West also tried to help this family connect to an accepting social network. This did not happen.

The next chapter in this section uses a systems approach. It also addresses the very difficult situation of when one of an assumed heterosexual couple comes out as gay. Connie Callahan and Shirley Cornett write on this in a "A Reluctant Husband and Troubled Family."

Families are best understood from a systems approach. Drs. Callahan and Cornett tapped into the following systems for their case study: individual, interactional, intergenerational, and community (Breen-Ruddy & McDaniel, 2008; Weeks, 1989). They also relied on the Marital Status Inventory (Crane, Newfield, & Armstrong, 1984) for formal assessment and Satir (1972) for informal assessment. In their case study, the presenting problem for each family member provided the clues for unraveling the distorted projections that were impairing healthy functioning (Satir, 1982). This case involves a husband coming out; combines issues of ethnicity (Hispanic ethnicity), religion (Catholicism), and the psychiatric illness of the wife; and describes the impact of all of these on the family.

LGBT couples and families sometimes are international in scope. Stuart F. Chen-Hayes writes on this in "Counseling and Advocacy With An International/Dual National Same-Gender Couple and Family." The case described by Dr. Chen-Hayes illustrates the concepts of immigrationism and familyism, concepts he introduced in 2009 (Chen-Hayes, 2009). These concepts describe the prejudice caused by the power differentials of citizens in a dominant culture restricting the resources of noncitizens in their country. The case involves a multiracial, multilingual, multinational gay-headed family as it navigates two different countries. It touches on career decisions, parenting, and couple stressors. As in other case studies in this book, family systems and cognitive therapy theories are used. Family systems theories examine relationship interactions rather than individual pathology (Goldberg, 2010) and do not usually include a diagnosis.

Nonmonogamy impacts many couples. Most therapy training looks at nonmonogamy in a negative way, as infidelity. However, this is not always the case. Sari H. Dworkin deals with this issue in her chapter "A Therapist Expands Her Ideas About Relationships." Therapists must recognize that issues of nonmonogamy or polyamory may come up in work with bisexual clients (Dworkin, 2002; Gustavson, 2009). Many therapists have difficulty with the idea of nonmonogamous committed relationships and must explore their own biases so as not to foreclose exploration. In addition, many bisexual clients are in marriages with partners who identify as heterosexual, and this can create problems, especially when the bisexual partner wishes to express his or her bisexuality (Dworkin, in press). Dr. Dworkin explores a case in which she had to expand her own ideas and ensure that her countertransference was not getting in the way. In this case, a client in a heterosexual marriage who defines herself as heterosexual falls in love with a woman and expands her sexual identity to include bisexuality and her marriage to include the woman and the man she loves.

The final chapter in this section deals with the metamorphosis of issues from grief counseling to bisexuality. Beth A. Firestein addresses this metamorphosis in "Counseling Bisexual Clients: More Than the Sum of the Parts." All therapists see clients who come in with one presenting issue or series of issues and, during the course of therapy, find that other issues become salient. Dr. Firestein's first case begins with grief counseling and ends with issues of bisexuality at the forefront. Dr. Firestein begins with grief and trauma work and moves to a discussion of bisexual sexual identity issues. This case also explores ways to balance the needs of one's partner with an ongoing relationship with the client's family. The second case is a fascinating story of a woman who identifies as bisexual and her husband, who transitions from male to female. Dr. Firestein emphasizes a feminist approach to therapy and notes that this particular client sought her out because she both used this approach and had experience with LGBT populations. Dr. Firestein's client was very supportive of her partner's transitioning, but emotional issues on the part of the partner impacted the relationship. These emotional issues led the client to consider opening up the relationship. This second case is another instance of a therapist needing to help a client explore the possibilities of nonmonogamy.

References

Breen-Ruddy, N., & McDaniel, S. H. (2008). Couple therapy and medical issues: Working with couples facing illness. In A. S. Gurman (Ed.), *Clinical handbook of couple therapy* (4th ed., pp. 618–640). New York, NY: Guilford Press.

Cerbone, A. R. (1990, August). *Coming out as a lifelong developmental issue: Erik Erikson rethought.* Poster session presented at the 97th Annual Meeting of the American Psychological Association, Boston, MA.

Chen-Hayes, S. F. (2009). Types of oppression. In American Counseling Association (Ed.), *The ACA encyclopedia of counseling* (pp. 383–384). Alexandria, VA: American Counseling Association.

Crane, D., Newfield, N., & Armstrong, D. (1984). Predicting divorce at marital therapy intake: Wives' distress and the Marital Status Inventory. *Journal of Marital and Family Therapy, 10,* 305–312.

Downs, A. (2005). *The velvet rage: Overcoming the pain of growing up gay in a straight man's world.* Cambridge, MA: DaCapo Press.

Dworkin, S. H. (2002). Biracial, bicultural, bisexual: Bisexuality and multiple identities. *Journal of Bisexuality, 2*(4), 93–107.

Dworkin, S. H. D. (in press). Bisexual identities: Current research and future directions. In C. J. Peterson & A. R. D'Augelli (Eds.), *Handbook of psychology and sexual orientation.* New York, NY: Oxford University Press.

Goldberg, A. E. (2010). *Lesbian and gay parents and their children: Research on the family life cycle.* Washington, DC: American Psychological Association.

Gustavson, M. (2009). Bisexuals in relationships: Uncoupling intimacy from gender ontology. *Journal of Bisexuality, 9,* 407–429.

Satir, V. (1972). *Peoplemaking.* Palo Alto, CA: Science and Behavioral Books.

Satir, V. M. (1982). The therapist and family therapy: Process model. In A. M. Horne & M. M. Ohlsen (Eds.), *Family counseling and therapy* (pp. 73–94). Itasca, IL: Peacock.

Weeks, G. R. (1989). *Treating couples: The intersystem model of the Marriage Council of Philadelphia.* New York, NY: Brunner/Mazel.

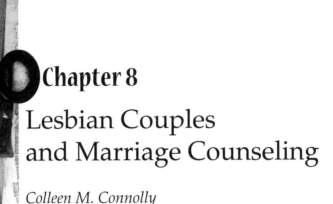

Chapter 8

Lesbian Couples and Marriage Counseling

Colleen M. Connolly

Competent couples and marriage counseling, which is an integral part of working with the lesbian, gay, bisexual, and transgender (LGBT) population, requires unique assessments and interventions. This chapter describes both effective and ineffective counseling methods and interventions using a case study example of a couple, Chris and Jackie. In this chapter, I describe the counseling process this couple engaged in not only to highlight their story but also to identify the broader challenges and inherent strengths of most, if not all, LGBT couples.

LGBT couples are faced with abundant challenges. Assaults can range from the close and covert, such as an automatic question of "Are you married?" in a state and country that largely disenfranchises that right and responsibility, to the overt but distanced news coverage of picket signs bearing the hate-filled words "God Hates Fags." Having to shield oneself, sometimes on a daily basis, can lead to relational fatigue and relational unrest and can ultimately cause or contribute to such issues as depression, anxiety, sexual intimacy issues, drug and alcohol abuse, and suicidality. These challenges and stressors, which all occur within the context of pervasive societal oppression, can go not only unnoticed and unnamed but even unclaimed by those within the population.

This clinical scenario shows three different phases of counseling. This tripartite example helps to demonstrate the underlying issues inherent in U.S. society, provides examples of when to engage in individual work versus couples counseling, and shows the flow of counseling through these arenas. The names in this case example are intentionally gender ambiguous. Whether it is Jacqueline and Christine, Jack and Christopher, or Jacqueline and Christopher, the issues affecting couples must be addressed initially, thoroughly, and within the context of the multicultural and cross-cultural issues. These issues impact the individuals within the dyad, the couple's surrounding support system, and the therapist–client interrelationship. Although Jackie and Chris's first attempt at couples counseling proved to be unsatisfying and unsuccessful, they ultimately discovered appropriately matched, competent counselors to help them in their individual and relational journeys.

Clinical Vignette

Chris and Jackie approached couples counseling with hesitation. They had sought couples counseling several years earlier, and when asked what their experience was, there was an audible groan. The couple reported that during that time they had unusual struggles in their relationship; distancing, with the accompanying reduction in emotional, sexual, and intellectual intimacy, had felt commonplace. Their relational rules always included monogamy, but Jackie had had a year-long affair that caused great disconnection in their relationship. During that time there was an awful distance, and when they did try to talk things out, the conversation often quickly became heated, which led to more hurt and disconnection.

They sought couples counseling from someone strongly recommended within the community. Issues with how to communicate about the affair, how to set boundaries, and how both might focus on their autonomous presence within the relationship were at the forefront of this initial clinical work. Fights escalated within the counseling room and frequently spilled out into the couple's home space. The stress and strain continued, and the couple stopped living together.

Jackie and Chris never really wanted to completely end their relationship, yet they had difficulty coming back together in a way that felt safe and was mutually satisfying. For approximately 2 years they were in a transition phase; they became close friends and occasional lovers and for a time developed other romantic relationships. However, they always remained a part of each other's primary "family." The second part of their work was what seemed to be unrelated individual counseling. However, at the base of this work was each person processing loss and grief—not of the affair, not of the fights, but of the unthinkable loss that precipitated the couple's tumble.

What was that tumble? As one lives disenfranchised in a society, as when one is LGBT in this society, tumbles can come in many forms: the loss of job or career, being cut off from parents, self-harm. For Jackie and Chris it came in the form of a loss of children and ultimately family.

Chris and Jackie, ages 49 and 42, respectively, had enjoyed a decade of close interfamilial relationships. Jackie's brother and sister-in-law were open and accepting of their relationship and actively encouraged the couple to be secondary parental figures to their children. This encouragement began largely because the brother and his wife lacked sufficient time to parent after receiving her diagnosis of breast cancer. Close and loving relationships with the children were fostered, and as Chris and Jackie stepped in during round after round of chemotherapy, the children became a central part of the couple's life.

One day that ended. Suddenly Jackie's brother and sister-in-law announced that Chris and Jackie could no longer be with the children unsupervised. Jackie and Chris were told they were not good enough, that their relationship was not valid, that it was "wrong." A newfound religious conviction was at the root of this family's decision. After all of the years of love and care, Jackie and Chris's relationship with the children ended abruptly. For the couple it led to a growing sense of vulnerability, a lack of trust, and ultimately isolation. Chris and Jackie's disconnection and disruption as a result of the injury, and the emotional violence associated with that rupture, caused what seemed like an endless reverberation. Most friends were unaware of their struggle or even that they lived apart for a couple of years, which limited additional support.

Their own level of internalized homophobia surprised Jackie and Chris, as not only were they highly educated in this area, but each worked rigorously in different ways with social justice issues. However, the external homoprejudice contributed to an abundance of shame, and the couple was unable to unpack that shame from their relationship; they internalized that something was wrong with *them.*

During their second attempt at counseling, which occurred individually while they were not living together, Chris and Jackie were able to unravel the underlying issues. Jackie entered counseling because of significant suicidal ideations at the end of an interim relationship. Before long Jackie shared with the counselor the loss of the niece and nephew and brother and sister-in-law and ultimately the disintegration of the larger family connection. The counselor then explored how that loss was so deep, so devastating. Jackie's counselor quickly and efficiently encapsulated the problem and honored not only the significance of the couple's relationship but also the connection with the children and what those children represented to this couple in their 40s.

In separate individual counseling Chris expressed the continued loneliness, isolation, and struggle with mounting life stressors. Chris's counselor, working from the growth-fostering, mutually empathic Relational-Cultural Theory, noticed how Chris continued to reference Jackie and their continuing and strong bond. When this counselor asked, "Why are you two not together?" Chris responded, "That is complicated and complex." That fourth session began the process of unleashing the pain and grief of losing the children, the fear of being erased from their lives, and the familial and social ostracism. Toward the end of that session, the heterosexual counselor efficiently and empathically named her prevalent feeling after hearing the story: She felt outrage.

Within a few months of beginning individual counseling, Jackie and Chris reconnected and began living together again, but they had difficulties making relational sense of the past, the present, and what the future might hold. The third part of the counseling process involved a return to couples counseling to process the mutual injury, to explore the dynamics that impeded them as a couple, and to strengthen their resilient processes. Spirituality, and how this loss affected each individual and the relationship, emerged. A discussion about monogamy and its meaning to both parties ensued. Self-limits—what one can and cannot do, what one will and will not tolerate—rather than limits set upon the other were an important part of this phase. Family of choice became an essential part of their discussions, as did discovering alternative forms of familial and social support. This counseling process was pivotal for Chris and Jackie in regaining self and relational health and vibrancy.

Retrospection

Counseling is not always contained but certainly can vary in its configuration and come in sections over time. Phase 1, the initial couples counseling, was unsuccessful and unrewarding. The first couples counselor did not work from a theoretically solid base and did not inquire about family history or external stressors affecting the couple. Moreover, the focus on communication issues and developing a solid sense of self contributed to a deeper sense of isolation for the partners.

The absence of a theoretical orientation and therapeutic relationship contributed greatly to the counseling's lack of success. More important, though, is that the disenfranchised grief went unnoticed, unnamed, and untamed. Looking back, the loss was but a footnote in that first encounter with couples counseling, a passed-over "Oh, yes, that's so hard." Also, focusing on the present and surface issues unrelated to the stressors did not serve the couple well and actually exacerbated their problems. In terms of a diagnosis, during the initial couples counseling the focus of attention was the Partner Relational Problem (V61.10). When Jackie and Chris began counseling, their Global Assessment of Relational Functioning (GARF) would have been rated at 42. Ineffective arguments interfered with their daily routines, decision making was impeded, and the couple reported a generally unsatisfying relationship.

The individual work of Phase 2 of counseling was a critical part of the couple's process because the grief at that point was too profound to hold within the dyad. Both partners had their own reaction based on their own experiences of living and loving in their family of origin and in life. A diagnostic assessment of Jackie and Chris as individuals showed that Jackie demonstrated symptoms of Major Depressive Disorder (296.33) and Alcohol Abuse (305.00) and had a Global Assessment of Functioning (GAF) of 50 largely because of the suicidal ideation; Chris showed symptoms that equated to a diagnosis of Generalized Anxiety Disorder (300.02) and a GAF of 62.

Phase 3 of counseling was vital for Chris and Jackie. The individual counseling allowed for a solidification of the self within the relationship and an ability to create a renewed and mutual vision of a future together. The final couples counseling process began with the couple functioning at a moderate GARF of 65. The couple still experienced pain and reactivity when nonroutine issues presented, and this feeling intensified when related to the loss. After 10 more sessions of couples counseling the GARF was 81, and Chris and Jackie showed better problem solving and organization and experienced an enhanced emotional and relational climate.

A more effective and direct counseling approach would have been to inquire during the initial intake and assessment phase about any external stressors that might be affecting the relationship. Integrating individual counseling within the couples work or, based on the counselor's theoretical perspective, referring to other counselors for that work would have provided stabilization and continuity for the couple. For Chris and Jackie those external stressors were at the core of their struggle as a couple and as individuals. In other words, the couple would have benefited from the couples and individual counseling occurring concurrently rather than in a step-by-step fashion.

Clinical Implications

Homoprejudice can be subtle, and issues often lie beneath the surface waiting to be invited into therapeutic conversation. Clients rely on our expertise as counselors to begin this dialogue. When counselors do not address such issues, stressors that are external, nonnormative, and ambiguous can turn into an acute relational crisis. Counselors can help couples significantly by assessing for the pervasive societal stressors associated with homoprejudice and heterosexism at the outset and naming them when present. It's important to assess broadly before setting goals and to renegotiate goals when stressors come to the forefront. It is imperative to recognize injuries to the self and to the relationship that are societally induced and then attend to the grief, fear, and vigilance that the individual developed to cope. We must not only attend to the physical risk of harm to self and others but also assess for emotional and spiritual risk and injuries.

For Chris and Jackie, unaddressed stressors worsened into an internalized couple dynamic and resulted in chronic stressor overload and relational fracture. Assessing at the outset and then actively and continuously examining our own preconceptions and assumptions helps to guard against a heterocentric bias. Continually using transference issues to a therapeutic advantage and closely monitoring our own countertransference is imperative, lest our own life experiences overshadow the clinical work. We must resist the assumption that presenting issues are related to the couple being LGBT. However, if we ignore, minimize, or dismiss small micro- or macrostressors and societal, cultural, and familial injuries, we might not be helping a couple, and, moreover, we risk causing harm.

On a positive note, despite all of the stressors and strains associated with living marginalized in U.S. society, LGBT couples continue to bond, endure, and thrive. This combined strength and resilience amid pervasive and ongoing stressors is remarkable. The counseling process benefits from recognizing and honoring the flexibility, adaptability, and creativity LGBT couples show in forming, maintaining, and sustaining their relationships. Marginalized couples often use an us-against-the-world approach and form a united front against challenges. Successful couples typically show great determination to move beyond adversity and to thrive.

LGBT couple relationships also are affiliative, affectional, and typically sexual. Counselors would do well to continually assess for a variety of processes that are integral to this population. For example, LGBT couples can and do create unique relationships based on their mutual needs versus tradition. What are their relational rules? Are they explicit, mutual, and matched for each partner's unique needs? They also expand family to include family of choice, which must be added to our assessment of family of origin. In addition, whether it is out of fear, lack of knowledge, or overcompensating so as not to overly focus on the sexual component, counselors often err by omitting the sexual intimacy assessment, which can rob clients of effective counseling.

Furthermore, in a community in which family can be lost and new family created, being cognizant of the fact that not all unions "end" but can transform and continue in a close, affiliative, and interreliant way can help our clients and the therapeutic process. Although these relationships might look different from or similar to the heterosexual norm, the tenacity, endurance, and ability to transform in LGBT relationships can be considered not only a strength but a unique and often necessary part of the culture.

Identity formation and disclosure also greatly impact relational growth and development and should be considered in the counseling process. Counselors must consider the identity development stage of each individual and how the partners' stages interact with each other. Societal constraints can be daunting regardless of one's stage of LGBT identity development or disclosure. Personal disclosure—to whom, when, and how one discloses—is a personal choice but one that often needs to be negotiated within relationships. Partners often are not matched in this respect and need help negotiating this terrain.

Although it is important to assess clients without presuming that orientation is directly related to the presenting problems, it is also imperative to remain aware that familial, social, and societal injustices occur and that a global assessment is necessary. The shared sense of community outrage that Chris's individual counselor expressed helped her client heal and move from resignation to action steps for both self and the relationship. Because that counselor was speaking as a heterosexual woman, it helped Chris generate a sense of the power of heterosexual allies: "I am not in this alone; we are not in this alone." For change to occur, we must all hold and express personal, professional, and cultural outrage at such social injustices.

Rather than following a heterosexual norm and script, counselors must remain abreast of the literature and counseling trends and keep current with deeper understandings of how LGBT couples negotiate their environment and relationships. Doing so will strengthen their ability to see, hear, and experience each couple as unique. Not assessing for external impediments can further harm the system. As Chris and Jackie's vignette shows, this couple's healing began only when those external societal and familial stressors were allowed to come to the forefront and the loss, grief, and subsequent vigilance and fear were addressed on the level of the individual and couple.

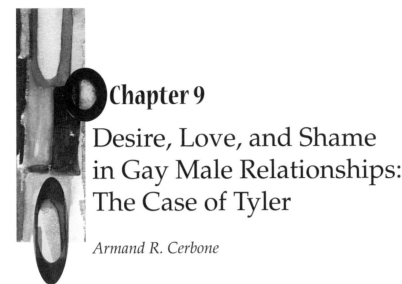

Chapter 9

Desire, Love, and Shame in Gay Male Relationships: The Case of Tyler

Armand R. Cerbone

> *Better the trouble that follows death than*
> *the trouble that follows shame.*
>
> —Irish saying

Tyler: A Case Study in Gay Male Relationships

It may not be customary to explore the issues of couples in the context of individual psychotherapy. However, it is quite common for clients working individually with a psychotherapist to present relationship issues. The case of Tyler illustrates in vivid fashion the three factors of gay relationships I wish to explore. Those are, first and foremost, that the effects of the stigma against same-sex relationships are still grossly underestimated; second, that maintaining deep and satisfying emotional and sexual bonds is more challenging than is customarily understood, regardless of sexual orientation; and third, that the underlying dynamic of stigmatized relationships is shame, particularly in its internalized form.

The case of Tyler is notable for the number of conflicts and challenges that can arise when gay men negotiate a long-term romantic relationship. These are both individual and shared in character. Individual conflicts include personal history prior to the relationship, values, and beliefs about relationships and sexuality and adjustments made to a gay identity in a homophobic and heterocentrist culture. These adjustments, often referred to as *coming out,* can be understood as an extra developmental step gay men must undertake as a direct consequence of cultural bias and discrimination (Cerbone, 1990). It is a task that affects every other developmental task throughout the life span, particularly establishing and maintaining intimacy. Shared conflicts are those that result from the interaction of two gay men, each with his unique developmental patterns, relationship history, and integration of sexual identity and behavior.

Presenting Issues and Referral

Tyler entered psychotherapy to deal with longstanding depression and anxiety. He also complained of a bad relationship he could not conclude. Desire had died, and differences in personalities had exacerbated the loss of sexual desire to the point of complete incompatibility and tolerance. Despite an agreement that their relationship had ended, his former partner still lived in Tyler's home and continued to be supported by Tyler. "I feel responsible for him. If I force him to leave, I don't know how he will make it on his own," he would say. Only Tyler's guilt kept them under the same roof.

Tyler had been referred by his primary care physician for depression and anxiety. The physician, who had prescribed an antidepressant for his mood disorder, also monitored Tyler's HIV status. Though positive for a number of years, Tyler kept to a regimen of medications that had kept him in good health. Although HIV was acknowledged as a relevant subtext influencing his life, Tyler's infection rarely became a significant focus of psychotherapy. He stated that he had adjusted to his health status and that it presented few barriers in his life. Only when in later sessions he began exploring life expectancy issues related to growing older did HIV require direct attention. As he reported, "Except for having to inform dates of my status, I haven't felt any negative effects or interferences. And my health has always been really good." For his mood disorder, the physician had prescribed an antidepressant.

Tyler reported guilt and anxiety associated with sexual behavior. "I experience a lot of anxiety and guilt after casual sexual encounters. I usually go to a bar with a back room, drink more than I should, and find someone who wants to have sex." He reported that this behavior conflicted greatly with his Catholic beliefs about homosexuality. He admitted he carried a heavy burden of shame as a result, with ambivalence about his sexual orientation deriving from his strong religious convictions. Yet he enjoyed an active and satisfying social life among a circle of friends who were almost exclusively gay. He never entertained any heterosexual fantasies or mentioned a history of dating women. He reported one instance of falling deeply in love with another man that had ended painfully. Nonetheless, embracing a homosexual identity would mean abandoning the traditions of his faith and of his staunchly Catholic family. Being loyal and true to the Church and its traditions were important values he did not want to change. An examination of these beliefs over months revealed a deep spirituality that was an enduring bulwark in his life. Tyler struggled to reconcile his spirituality with the sinfulness of his sexual behavior.

Embedded in these issues were internalized homophobia that inhibited positive integration of his sexual identity and behavior, an externalized locus of evaluation that kept him in thrall to ecclesiastical norms of sexuality that damned him to hell if he pursued a gay life, and an ambivalent self-esteem that acknowledged his intellectual and professional achievements while berating him for not adhering to his Catholic values. Resolving these issues was pivotal to his capacity for satisfying attachments to another man, for they constituted moral barriers to the intimacy and attachments he longed for.

In many ways these problems seemed out of character for a very bright, thoughtful, and introspective lawyer in his mid-40s who enjoyed considerable professional success and the respect of his colleagues and friends. They also flew in the face of his self-confidence as a sexually attractive man. He would often report, "I get hit on quite a lot." Yet the barriers to the gay relationships and intimacy he desired evidenced gaps in his psychosexual development. As could be expected, these lacunas showed up in his behavior (e.g., Saturday night drinking and casual sexual encounters followed by Sunday morning guilt and self-recrimination).

I hypothesized the following diagnoses: Axis I: dysthymia; anxiety; no Axis II disorders; Axis III: HIV; Axis IV: relationship conflicts with family and intimate partners; Global Assessment of Functioning: 70–85. Axis I included posttraumatic stress disorder (PTSD), because Tyler's symptoms (e.g., excessive drinking, acting out sexually, episodic anger and agitation, self-esteem issues) can be consistent with PTSD. I concur with those psychologists who consider adjusting to being gay in a hostile culture a type of PTSD. From the time that a gay person becomes aware that he is different and that this difference is dangerous, his sense of self is under attack. As therapy with Tyler revealed other symptoms (e.g., physical and sexual abuse), this secondary diagnosis proved appropriate. Early in the counseling, I referred Tyler for a psychiatric evaluation that resulted in a new regimen of medications for anxiety and depression.

Transference/Countertransference

The potential for countertransference was considerable. Both of us were raised in Catholic families for whom the Church was a significant influence. Both had found in the Church a nurturing harbor from the chaos of family dynamics (e.g., both had alcoholic fathers who abandoned us emotionally). Both found in the Church the promise of safety and happiness—if not in this life then in the next—if only we were true to each and every of its teachings. Both recognized the constraints the Church placed on our psychosexual development. Both had attended Notre Dame (though at different times, and he as an undergrad and I as a graduate student) and were steeped in its Catholic ivy traditions.

As all therapists are with their clients, I was invested in the resolution of his conflicts and in his growth as a gay man. I was equally aware of his deepening trust and confidence in me, based on his perception of me as someone who faced and resolved similar conflicts. How was I to help him find a route to integration of sexual identity that was his own and not a mirror image of mine? How was I to help him transform the spirituality that anchored his values and gave meaning to his actions without undue influence from me? To our mutual advantage, Tyler had a longstanding relationship with a spiritual director, a priest for whom Tyler had great respect and with whom he had found helpful guidance. Whenever there arose an overlap of the psychological and the spiritual or a conflict between the two, I could and did refer him to the expertise of his director. That the priest accepted and supported Tyler's sexual orientation meant that there were never occasions when Tyler felt forced to choose between the relationships but could grapple more confidently with the tensions between integrating his sexual and religious identities.

I had the benefit of having consulted weekly with two colleagues for more than 30 years. They know my vulnerabilities and me well. They proved helpful and wise in my work with Tyler. I also had the guidance of the American Psychological Association's (2007) policy on religion, which encourages respect for religious values and beliefs while recognizing the effects of religion-derived prejudice.

There remained another potential for countertransference. I have spent most of my career fighting antigay prejudice and advancing an understanding of lesbian, gay, bisexual, and transgender people based on accurate information. My activism has on occasion infiltrated my work with some clients. On one occasion, early in my professional coming out when I had felt particularly vulnerable, a closeted client objecting to the pressure he felt to come out terminated therapy with the comment "Your politics are fine but your therapy sucks" (Cerbone, 1991). Keeping my wishes for Tyler's growth from becoming an inordinate need required constant monitoring.

The Initial Stages of Psychotherapy

During the initial stages we explored Tyler's understanding of his faith and the values that gave him meaning, particularly the ways in which they competed with his abiding hopes for intimacy with men. We also examined festering childhood and adult conflicts with his family that absorbed considerable psychic energy and complicated his attempts to establish successful intimate relationships. Together these conflicts left him with shame and guilt and failure. The conflicts overlapped, and consequently therapy moved back and forth among them, particularly after Tyler met a man with whom he fell in love.

I would usually find Tyler reading nonfiction books in the waiting room. I used his interests to suggest other readings on the effects of antigay stigma (e.g., Downs's, 2005, book on shame in gay men). Tyler also found helpful occasional psychoeducational discussions, such as ones on the developmental stages of relationships that helped him to normalize his conflicts and circumvent further shame of failure.

Family History and Conflicts

The fifth of six children (three sisters and two brothers), Tyler reported an intensely passionate alienation from most of his family. At the heart of this were his accounts of repeated beatings from an older brother that he believed were known but ignored by his parents. Only later during treatment did he reference obliquely and then reveal directly that the abuse was also sexual. When he spoke of it initially, his voice lowered and he looked away from me. During the years of abuse, his fear of nighttime thrashings led him to seek safety by sleeping on the family's porch. Again, he believed his parents overlooked what he felt they knew. "How could they not have noticed I was sleeping with the dog on an unheated porch? They must have heard the noise from the bedroom!"

With time Tyler came to speak directly and painfully about the years of abuse and could identify his feelings as both shame and anger. His anger provided a healing antidote to the shame and discomfort the memories stirred, affording him more compassion for his younger self. Yet strikingly he could not be angry with his father. Though willing to examine this, he could not explain the pass he gave his father but centered his anger on his mother and brother.

During the period Tyler was exploring his issues with his family and his new relationship, which is the subject of this chapter, his father fell terminally ill. Despite the expression of pain caused by his father's overlooking the abuse Tyler had experienced at the hands of his older brother, Tyler resolved that his father's death should be as peaceful as possible. He repeatedly set aside any suggestion in psychotherapy that his plan deserved deeper exploration and understanding. Rather than risk an empathic break, I framed his stance as an understandable moral and ethical choice that underscored the importance of his father to him and of his self-esteem as a dutiful son. During this time Tyler reported that he was greatly consoled and supported by his new partner.

His resistance to reaching some resolution while his father was still living revealed the complexity of his ambivalence about that relationship and his deep longing for his father's love and respect. It also exposed the need to find some resolution to the sexual and physical abuse he had endured. The threat of further abuse stopped when he was physically mature enough to threaten his brother with a worse beating. Each time he talked about it, his distress was palpable. Not until his father died did his anger with his father find expression. "How could he [i.e., his father] not know? How could he ignore my sleeping on the porch? What did he think was going on?" Today Tyler remains burdened by the responsibility he feels to his mother and resentful of her encouraging him to care for his abusive brother, who has remained dependent on his family. Although he bears much less of the guilt he formerly felt, his anger will flare at suggestions that he should be more caring toward either. He himself likened the sharp anger and his intolerance even to be in their presence to PTSD.

A Measure of Healing

Within a few months of counseling, Tyler pressured his former partner to move out of his home. I had asked him, "What would you feel if you didn't feel guilty?" Stunned at first, he was thoughtful and responded with some surprise, "Anger!" The anger not only clarified the limits of his responsibility, it powered his confrontation with his former partner. Time and again in therapy, his anger would dissipate immobilizing guilt and shame, clarifying conflicts, and freeing him to act.

Also important to note is that his rigid adherence to the Church's position on homosexuality softened enough for him to examine the Church's antigay teachings and their impact on his life and behavior. He sought monthly counsel from a priest who supported his coming to accept his sexuality and help him temper his self-punitive conscience. This dovetailed favorably with his psychotherapy. He adopted an independence from the institutional magisterium while maintaining a vibrant spirituality. Notably missing was the shame he had formerly felt in not conforming to the Church's antigay teachings. As he loosened the grip of the Church on him, he accepted his sexuality more firmly. As he accepted his sexuality, his depression lifted notably and his anxiety abated. Both had the salubrious effect of making him more disposed to dating and relationships. The allure of casual sex faded. These improvements in turn enhanced his capacity for sexual attachments that would meet his needs for emotional intimacy.

As his independence from the institutional church and other teachings developed, the value he drew from spiritual direction attenuated. In recent months he has yearned to find a spirituality to replace the one he feels he had to abandon in order to accept his sexual identity. Needing to keep within my role as a psychologist, I supported his consultations with his priest as an important longstanding and meaningful relationship, and I encouraged him to work on his changing relationship with his church in the context of spiritual direction. Never in our work together have the two relationships conflicted.

The Relationship

Sexuality and Early Ambivalences

At the point our exploration of his relationship begins, Tyler had met and fallen in love with a man unlike other men he had dated or pursued, one who had also fallen in love with Tyler.

"I met Iggy [Ignacio] at a Halsted Street bar on a night for HIV-positives. He is not at all my usual type. Usually, I am attracted to bigger guys. This guy is smaller and Latin. Very different for me." Yet the attraction grew as they got to know each other. They enjoyed long daily talks together and often shared lunches near their downtown offices. The easy nature of their communication complimented and intensified their sexual relationship. Tyler felt their being HIV positive facilitated their bonding because it removed a possible barrier to intimacy that discordant couples often face.

"Iggy is different. There is something very different about this relationship. I don't know what it is, but I feel close in ways I never have, and he feels the same. We seem to have connected at a very deep level that neither of us understands completely." We considered that the difference may be not just in Iggy but in him too. Perhaps Tyler was experiencing a greater readiness for a different relationship as a result of the work he had been doing in therapy. The obstacles to a relationship with another man appeared to have attenuated sufficiently to allow his serious pursuit of a lover.

Yet even in their early days together, Iggy made it clear that he was not satisfied sexually. He stressed that sexual satisfaction was *the* criterion by which he would judge the viability of any relationship. Tyler reported that Iggy had warned him that, because he doubted Tyler could satisfy him, he should not expect their relationship to last or to be exclusive. The tenuous character of Iggy's commitment dismayed and frustrated Tyler; Tyler had thought Iggy enjoyed their sex. It introduced performance anxiety that compromised Tyler's sexual functioning and made work of sexual play. Tyler grew impatient and bitter with Iggy's arbitrary conditions. "I spend most of the time trying to get him off. He never gives me what I want. Even when it seems we are both really into it and I am ready to give him the sex he says he wants, he becomes very passive and just lies there. Or he moves to stop me from the very thing he says he wants. I get angry and lose my erection."

This scenario persisted across the multiple separations. When Tyler would lose his erection he feared and resented that Iggy took this as proof positive that this was not the relationship for him. Fearing that he might be impotent, Tyler consulted a urologist who found nothing wrong and suggested that the difficulty was psychological. With that reassurance, Tyler's performance anxiety abated while his anger with Iggy intensified. The medical opinion corroborated and justified his concern that Iggy was the problem. He expressed growing doubts that Iggy could sustain emotional intimacy because of immaturity. They began a pattern of breaking up only to reunite weeks later, convinced their connection was too deep and meaningful to abandon. "I can't explain it," Tyler would say. "There is something good that draws us together that I can't let go of."

Iggy's behavior and ambivalence became the focus of Tyler's attention as a major deterrent to the relationship's growth. Tyler entertained finding a relationship with another and even took overtures from other men more seriously. I noted that it appeared that his ambivalence too was contributing to their seesawing. I suggested that perhaps the ambivalence existed on both their parts to protect each from a deeper commitment and fears of loss. In addition, I asked him to reflect on the feelings a deeper commitment to Iggy would engender. He responded by saying, "Well, it would feel like I was more committed than he was."

I responded with a challenge. "Isn't it more important to know what you want independent of what Iggy wants or fears?" Then I asked him to think of the feelings that being more committed than Iggy might stir. His first response was to say that it made him angry. It took a session or two more for Tyler to recognize that his anger sprang from his vulnerability to being abandoned. That awareness led him to consider how much vulnerability he could tolerate. I supported this direction for two reasons. Knowing the threshold beyond which he could manage his anxiety effectively, Tyler could be clearer with Iggy that being threatened with the ending of the relationship if Tyler could not fulfill his sexual needs angered and frightened him. The other reason was to allow Tyler to evaluate how he might better manage his ambivalence without withdrawing, only to seek the relationship again. Separating again became less attractive an option for responding to his anger and the fears behind it.

Considering that his fears of abandonment may have roots in his history, I encouraged Tyler to consider how his relationship with his family, particularly with his father, might play out in his relationship with Iggy. Tyler resisted at first, preferring to attribute the impasse to Iggy's ambivalence, but admitted that understanding his own feelings would ultimately be more productive. He came to perceive parallels he had not considered. He identified anxiety arising in both his vulnerability to abuse within his family and the constant threat of abandonment from Iggy. He saw too his subsequent rejection of and withdrawal from his family as similar to his seesawing with Iggy. The insight removed withdrawal as a first option and strengthened his commitment to finding other ways to resolve their stalemate. I made a recommendation that he and Iggy seek couples counseling, which the couple did.

Couples Counseling

While the couples counseling had limited success in resolving sexual vulnerabilities, it allowed Tyler and Iggy to set monogamous boundaries around the relationship. They accepted monogamy as much to protect themselves from mutual fears of abandonment as to determine whether the relationship could grow in the face of continuing disappointments. What is significant is that Tyler reported with obvious pleasure and relief that Iggy had said in a counseling session that he loved him. Iggy also added paradoxically that he hated Tyler because he loved him. Tyler intuitively understood the paradox because to some extent he shared it; loving bound them as much as it relieved persistent anxieties. In our individual sessions Tyler consistently voiced dissatisfaction with the joint counseling, feeling he was not understood and that the therapist was more supportive of Iggy's right and need for sexual fulfillment than for Tyler's issues. Despite reported attempts to correct this with the couples counselor, Tyler stated the therapist stood by his support for Iggy's rights to sexual fulfillment. Tyler terminated the counseling in frustration and with no resistance from Iggy and wondered once again whether the relationship was viable. "Could it be different with someone else?"

However, their overt statements of love and commitment in front of a witness marked an important passage the couple had been working toward. The commitment allowed for, even mandated, a deeper examination of the anxieties provoked by their attachment and the unexplored meanings of their sexual frustrations. Moreover, it provided a safety net in which their feelings and resentments could be addressed. It was possible then to shift Tyler's attention to his own ambivalence and away from the distress he experienced from Iggy's ambivalence and the criticism he felt under Iggy's sexual standards. Even while recognizing that he contributed to the instability, Tyler continued to report his and Iggy's mutual frustrations and disappointments as grounds for questioning the merits of their relationship. Again the question of the possibility of a better relationship with someone more compatible arose. While respecting his doubts, I encouraged him to attend more to how his ambivalence might protect him from loss and how his fantasies of leaving Iggy for a better relationship might represent more a preemptive strike and less the desired resolution to their difficulties. Did he believe he would not face other, equally challenging problems with another man? Hadn't he elected several times to quit the relationship for the same causes, only to return? What made this time different? Perhaps, I suggested, the problems they faced were endemic to committed intimate relationships.

At the same time we considered how he might better understand Iggy's ambivalence. Perhaps both were anxious about attachment. Perhaps Iggy coped with his anxieties by seeking safety in setting a sexual bar that was impossible to meet. My objective was not to redeem Iggy but to arouse Tyler's compassion in hopes that empathy might lead to a more productive outcome than separation to avoid anxiety. I reminded him too of the importance of considering what commitment meant, citing his unwavering commitment to nursing his dying father despite his anger and hurt. How was his commitment to Iggy different? After reflecting, Tyler responded with feeling, "Relationships are hard!" To which I queried, "Why would you expect them to be easy?"

Tyler and Iggy Today

With the commitment firmly established before their counselor, we could distinguish among those issues that were typical of all couples regardless of sexual orientation, those that were the result of stigma and prejudice against same-sex relationships, those that were shaped by individual histories and idiosyncratic traits and habits, and those that derived from the interactions of all three. For instance, in the early stages of their relationship Tyler frequently cited Iggy's lingering loyalties to his former partner as a dependency that competed with his relationship to Tyler. Making the distinctions and identifying their likely sources in Iggy's history provided signposts that guided the exploration of issues and dynamics. The distinctions had the additional benefit of mitigating any incipient guilt and fear of inadequacy. They also facilitated Tyler's tolerance for Iggy's approach–avoidance swings.

The mutuality of the commitment also established a contract that neither could break without reflection. It reduced the probability of separation as a way of managing their anxieties and frustrations. It required too that they consider how threatening separation undercut the commitment they had pledged and threatened their partner.

At this writing Tyler and Iggy are more grounded in their love and commitment. Although questions of Iggy's sexual gratification have not been laid to rest, Iggy's commitment to Tyler remains strong; Tyler reports that he enjoys sex with Iggy more. Arguments that arise between them are circumstantial and do not threaten the relationship. Psychotherapy has turned to resolving persistent issues with family, to finding a meaningful spirituality that can inform life as Tyler moves through middle age, and to assessing career directions.

Discussion

Most of the gay couples I see complain of disappointing sexuality or the death of sex in the relationship. Couples will often understand this as the natural course of a relationship (i.e., sexual desire diminishes over time). Couples opine that this is due to beliefs that libido decreases with age, that a man needs a variety of sexual partners, or that gay men are not meant to be monogamous. Still others will cite the effects of familiarity and emotional intimacy that makes sex with lovers feel like incest or sex with a best friend. For example, one man in a 20-year relationship who yearned for the excitement and validation he believed would come with sex outside the relationship opined that "having sex with him would be like having sex with my brother." In contrast, his partner sought sex for the intimacy and bonding he could not imagine finding with another.

Usually these explanations are accepted without much reflection, supported instead by the reports and tales of other gay couples or accepted as a norm of the gay male subculture.[1] Often this has led the couple to support one partner or both seeking sexual gratification and fulfillment outside the relationship, again as a common measure endorsed by the subculture. A complaint heard frequently in counseling is that the decline in eroticism has attenuated the attachment and reduced its value; the couple may express love for each other but no longer feel "in love." Never do couples consider without prompting the effects of discrimination. I work from the assumption that such explanations should be treated as hypotheses to be examined deeply and critically, much as our training as scientist–practitioners would recommend. My intent is not to assume that the norms or explanations in the subculture are false but to recognize that other hypotheses may be equally relevant to the issues the couple presents.

I also believe that the effects of stigma on the lives and loves of gay men need to be examined deeply when one is treating foundering relationships. I have found repeatedly that what may be the effects of stigma are often accepted as the results of one's own bad habits and failures or those of one's partner's rather than the effects of a noxious environment, much as fish accept their polluted waters as normal. Exploring the effects of stigma can normalize the couple's difficulties, attune them to subtle manifestations of shame, reduce their anxieties and fears of humiliation or abandonment, and create options for conflict resolution that they might not otherwise

---

[1]There is no judgment, positive or negative, implied in a couple's electing to open the relationship to sex with other partners. Just as with other actions the couple chooses, the motivations and process by which these actions are determined and the effects of the implementation are important to examine.

consider. It further alerts them to consider the effects of stigma that may arise in any long-term relationship.

Another assumption I make is that the vulnerabilities intrinsic to emotional and sexual intimacy in enduring relationships are more daunting than is commonly understood or assessed, regardless of one's sexual orientation. Those vulnerabilities, as this case has demonstrated, are essentially the risks of emotional injury, particularly rejection, abandonment, or shaming. What distinguishes gay couples in this regard is that the very behavior that makes all individuals vulnerable in intimate relationships is stigmatized. Stigmatizing sex between persons of the same gender complicates establishing intimacy and intensifies the risks associated with maintaining it.

Finally, I believe strongly that in the climate of homophobia that still characterizes contemporary American culture and politics, every same-sex relationship is an achievement regardless of its form or length of duration. It represents a will to be whole, a need for emotional and sexual attachment that cannot and will not succumb to oppression, and a triumph of indomitable human spirits.

References

American Psychological Association. (2007). *Resolution on religious, religion-based and/or religion-derived prejudice.* Retrieved from http://www.apa.org/about/governance/council/policy/religious-discrimination.pdf

Cerbone, A. R. (1990, August). *Coming out as a lifelong developmental issue: Erik Erikson rethought.* Poster session presented at the 97th Annual Convention of the American Psychological Association, Boston, MA.

Cerbone, A. R. (1991). The effects of political activism on psychotherapy: A case study. In C. Silverstein (Ed.), *Gays, lesbians, and their therapists: Studies in psychotherapy* (pp. 40–51). New York, NY: Norton.

Downs, A. (2005). *The velvet rage: Overcoming the pain of growing up gay in a straight man's world.* Cambridge, MA: DaCapo Press.

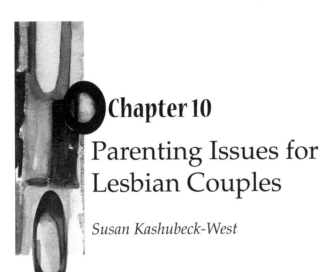

Chapter 10

Parenting Issues for Lesbian Couples

Susan Kashubeck-West

Identifying Data

Jasmine is a 34-year-old middle-class African American woman who identifies as a lesbian. She has a master's degree in nursing and has been employed as a nurse practitioner in a medical practice for 6 years. She has been with her current partner, Diane, for 8 years. Diane is 32, is White, identifies as a lesbian, comes from a working-class background, and is an attorney for a medium-size law firm in town. The couple lives in St. Louis. They were married (legally) in 2008 in a small ceremony in California. Both women were raised by parents who identify as Christian; however, neither woman identifies as religious. Jasmine and Diane are the parents of Theo, a 4-year-old boy to whom Jasmine gave birth.

Background

Jasmine and her two younger siblings (one brother and one sister) were raised by her mother and father in a middle-class neighborhood in St. Louis. Jasmine grew up attending public schools that were racially diverse, and she went to college at a public university in the same city. Both of her parents are still alive and recently celebrated their 40th wedding anniversary. Jasmine's parents were raised in St. Louis, and both came from large families. Hence, Jasmine has a very large extended family, most of which lives in the area. Jasmine's father is retired from his job of 40 years working for the railroad, and Jasmine's mother works as a hairdresser in a salon. After graduating from college, Jasmine went to work at one of the large hospitals in town. Her favorite shifts were weekend nights in the emergency room, as that was when it was the busiest and her job was very fast paced. Jasmine earned her master's degree in family nursing practice 6 years ago and since then has been working in a medium-size medical practice.

Diane grew up with two older siblings (both sisters) in a large city on the East Coast. Her mother worked inside the home caring for Diane and her siblings. Diane's father had steady employment as a truck driver on long-haul routes, which meant he was frequently away during Diane's childhood. When Diane was 16, her father took a new job driving for a firm headquartered in St. Louis and the family moved there. Diane's parents are still married. One of her older sisters married a man and moved to California; the other sister and her husband have two children and live in the St. Louis area. Diane's parents live in a small house in a working-class neighborhood and typically experience money pressures at the end of each month. Diane was a straight-*A* student in high school, completed college at a public university in St. Louis, and graduated from law school from a prestigious private university in the area. After graduation, Diane was hired by a large law firm that required new associates to work approximately 80–90 hours a week. Diane worked there for 3 years and then moved to a smaller firm, where she typically works about 50 hours a week.

Jasmine and Diane met 8 years ago in a lesbian softball league. Each had been out as a lesbian since college, and each had dated other women. Diane was the first White woman Jasmine had been involved with, whereas Diane had dated women from a variety of ethnic backgrounds before getting involved with Jasmine. After dating about 6 months, they moved in together into an apartment in a diverse neighborhood. During the first few years of their relationship they both were quite busy, as Diane was working long hours at her new job as a lawyer and Jasmine was working full time and completing her nurse practitioner degree at night. When Jasmine had finished her degree and Diane had moved to the smaller law firm, they began to talk about having children. Their plan is for each of them to have a child and for both children to be biracial, with one biological parent who is White and one who is African American. Their son Theo just turned 4, and Diane is currently trying to get pregnant via artificial insemination. Jasmine and Diane bought a house in the same neighborhood as their apartment, and they both very much enjoy where they live. Other than their mortgage and Diane's student loans, they report having no outstanding debt and living on a budget that enables them to save money each month and pay ahead on Diane's student loans.

Jasmine and Diane have a fairly good support system consisting of friends and relatives. However, they report not having as much contact with their friends as they used to, as their friends (none of whom have children) have quit calling them as regularly. Apparently these friends tend to do many activities on the spur of the moment, and typically Jasmine and Diane cannot find a babysitter that quickly. With both of their families in town, they regularly attend family dinners and other family events.

Presenting Issues

Jasmine came to see me on the recommendation of one of her nursing colleagues, with whom I had worked several years ago. Jasmine reported feeling tired and experiencing a lot of stress in her relationships: her relationship with Diane, her relationship with Diane's parents, and her relationship with her own parents. Jasmine said that she thought she was mildly depressed. My questioning during the initial session revealed that Jasmine also experienced occasional bouts of anxiety. These most often occurred when she was drifting off to sleep, and they tended to revolve around something terrible happening to Theo or Diane.

Jasmine reported that the stress in her relationship with Diane seemed to stem from her difficulty with Diane's family. In contrast to how they treated Diane's brothers-in-law, Diane's parents did not include Jasmine as a full member of the family. They often introduced the husbands as sons-in-law, whereas they simply introduced Jasmine by name and did not indicate her relationship to Diane. Similarly, when Diane's parents sent out their annual Christmas letter, the husbands of Diane's sisters were included, whereas Jasmine was never mentioned. More painful for Jasmine was the inequitable treatment she perceived Theo receiving. Diane's parents always remembered to celebrate his birthday and buy him Christmas presents, as they did for their other grandchildren. However, it was common for Diane's mom to buy "little things" for her two other grandchildren, and she regularly called their parents and offered to babysit or to take the children out to the zoo or other fun places. She rarely made such offers to Diane and Jasmine, and she almost never bought Theo things. Consequently, both Jasmine and Diane believed that Diane's parents saw their other grandchildren as their real grandchildren and saw Theo as something less than that. Diane believed that her parents were being heterosexist, whereas Jasmine perceived racism as also playing a role. Jasmine believed that if she were White and male that Diane's parents would see her relationship with Diane as just as important and valid as that of Diane's sisters and that they would treat Theo equally. Diane did not think racism played a part in her parents' treatment of Jasmine or Theo.

Another couple issue reported by Jasmine was that Diane struggled with Jasmine's family, primarily around being perceived as a true mother to Theo. Diane felt that Jasmine's family saw Jasmine as Theo's real mother and Diane as more of a stepmother. They regularly talked to Jasmine about parenting Theo but typically left Diane out of those conversations. Legal issues were also a mild stressor for the couple, as Diane did not have legal parental rights in Missouri. Although they were legally wed in California, their marriage was not recognized in Missouri. Consequently, for Diane to be seen as a legal parent to Theo, a second-parent adoption needed to take place. Although Diane and Jasmine had talked several times about doing this, neither of them had taken the initiative to begin the legal proceedings. The lack of legal parental recognition tended to be experienced as a stressor when minor emergencies occurred, such as when Theo broke his wrist and Diane had to take him to the emergency room, or when Diane worried that if Jasmine were to die Jasmine's parents would try to gain custody of Theo. Finally, the demands of work and parenting had reduced the time that Jasmine and Diane spent together as a couple. Most of their free time was spent with their son and in doing all of the routine maintenance activities of life, such as cooking, cleaning, grocery shopping, and so on. Their social activities usually included their son and typically involved spending time with relatives.

Diagnosis and Rationale

Because Jasmine was the initial client, I gave her a diagnosis after the first two sessions. The diagnosis was given to satisfy insurance requirements and, as diagnoses often are, was focused only on one individual. Prior to formulating the *Diagnostic and Statistical Manual of Mental Disorders* (4th ed., text rev.; American Psychiatric Association, 2000) diagnosis, I considered Jasmine's life context using Hays's (2001) ADDRESSING model (Age and generational influences, Developmental and acquired Disabilities, Religion and spiritual orientation, Ethnicity, Socioeconomic status, Sexual orientation, Indigenous heritage, National origin, and Gender).

Axis I	309.28	Adjustment Disorder With Mixed Anxiety and Depressed Mood
Axis II	V71.09	No Diagnosis
Axis III	None	
Axis IV	Problems with primary support group	
Axis V	Global Assessment of Functioning = 70 (current)	
	Global Assessment of Relational Functioning = 75 (current)	

Theoretical Framework and Goals

The underlying theoretical approach I use with all clients is a multicultural feminist approach. I strive to understand my clients in terms of their multiple and intersecting identities, and I see these identities leading to varied experiences of privilege and oppression as clients move through their social environments. Thus, I see the difficulties that clients report as resulting from an interaction with people and institutions in their lives. With multiculturalism and feminism as a foundation, I also utilize theoretical assumptions and strategies primarily from humanistic and cognitive perspectives.

The initial goals of treatment that Jasmine and I formulated included reducing her symptoms of depression and anxiety and increasing her relationship satisfaction. After five sessions of individual work and a concomitant reduction in Jasmine's symptoms of anxiety and depression, we negotiated a more intentional focus on Jasmine's relationship. Diane was invited to join Jasmine in couples counseling with me. The three of us negotiated a focus on improved communication in the relationship, a greater sense of commitment on the part of each partner to the relationship, and their empowerment as a couple for dealing with oppression from their families and society.

Interventions

My initial work with Jasmine focused on hearing her story and understanding her experiences within the context of her position in a particular cultural environment. The initial session focused on letting Jasmine tell me about her life, the issues that brought her to counseling, and what her hopes and expectations were for our work together. As we worked together, I concentrated on understanding Jasmine's experiences, validating her perceptions, and asking questions that invited her to explore potential intrapersonal, interpersonal, and larger systemic influences in her life. After several sessions, Jasmine reported that feeling understood by me led her to no longer doubt her own experience of racism from Diane's family. Feeling validated reduced her sense of isolation and self-doubt, resulting in an improvement in her mood. During these initial sessions, I also asked Jasmine whether she wanted to explore where her anxiety at night might be coming from or whether she wanted to focus simply on reducing it. Jasmine felt that the anxiety was less pressing than other issues and that she would rather try strategies to eliminate it instead of exploring it in depth. Therefore, I taught Jasmine the thought-stopping method to use when she found herself getting anxious in bed at night. Jasmine reported that with practice she found it easier and easier to shift herself out of a negative spiral in her thoughts and into more pleasing images and thoughts about fun activities in which the family might engage. Finally, we also discussed the issue of self-care as a strategy for improving Jasmine's mood. She reported that she had used to exercise regularly and had found that helpful in a variety of ways but had stopped after the birth of Theo. I encouraged her to start exercising again as part of an overall goal to improve her wellness.

With her symptoms of anxiety and depressed mood easing, Jasmine stated that she wanted to work on her relationship with Diane. We both felt that having Diane be a part of this process was integral to improving the relationship. Prior to asking Diane to join Jasmine for couples counseling with me, I discussed how a shift to couples counseling would mean that I could no longer see Jasmine as an individual client. Jasmine stated that her main priority at this point was improving her relationship with Diane and that she both understood why I could not see her individually at the same time and felt that she did not need individual counseling anymore.

Couples counseling with Jasmine and Diane initially focused on helping each partner really hear the other person's experience. We focused on communication skills such as speaking from one's own experience, listening without interrupting, and communicating one's understanding of the other's statements. Starting from the premise that this relationship was strong and that they as a couple had many assets that could be used to help alleviate their difficulties gave them room to relax and not worry that their current problems meant that they could not succeed as a couple. Important work occurred around Diane and Jasmine really hearing and understanding each other's experience with regard to their families. For example, helping Diane to hear and understand Jasmine's experience of Diane's family as engaging in racist, heterosexist, and unfair treatment of Jasmine and Theo created a new level of understanding and trust between Jasmine and Diane. Instead of dismissing Jasmine's pain because validating it meant seeing her own family as racist, Diane was able to sit with and acknowledge the racism demonstrated by her family and also see how denying Jasmine's experience was racist behavior on Diane's own part. Dealing with such awareness was very painful for both partners, and it resulted in a new level of shared experience and understanding of each other that felt to both partners as a deepening of the relationship bond. Similarly, Jasmine was able to take a hard look at how her own family interacted with Diane, saw her own privilege as the biological parent of Theo, and saw how Jasmine's parents frequently negated Diane's role as an equal parent. Understanding how both society and Jasmine's family treated Diane as a second-class parent was eye opening for Jasmine, especially as she could see that her silence on this issue meant that she was colluding in the oppression experienced by Diane.

During couples counseling we also worked on brainstorming strategies for approaching their families to change the patterns of interaction the couple had with them. For example, with regard to Jasmine's family, the couple planned to (a) increase Diane's caregiving role with Theo when they were around Jasmine's family to highlight her role as a parent; (b) have Jasmine and Diane talk about joint parenting decisions they had made when they were with Jasmine's family; and (c) involve Jasmine's family in planning for their next child, which would be conceived and carried by Diane. In addressing how Diane's family interacted with Jasmine and Theo, the couple decided that the first step would be for Diane to confront her family about how she felt about their inequitable treatment of Theo and Jasmine and the consequences of that treatment for her, Jasmine, and Theo. Depending on how this confrontation went, more strategies would be decided on by the couple in consultation with me.

Couples counseling also involved paying attention to building the importance of the couple unit within the family. More specifically, Jasmine and Diane became aware of how they functioned together primarily as parents to Theo rather than as a romantic, intimate couple. Parenting is very demanding, and many couples struggle with how to give attention to themselves as a couple in the face of ongoing time pressures. Diane and Jasmine came to understand that others in their lives (primarily their families of origin but also many of their coworkers) were more comfortable seeing them primarily as parents rather than as a loving couple (a consequence of heterosexism). They also saw how their own internalized heterosexism interfered with their interactions with each other in romantic, intimate ways. These understandings led to a desire on the part of the couple to reinvigorate the romantic aspect of their relationship. We explored what had attracted them to each other in the first place, what kinds of activities they enjoyed doing together, and what new things they had learned about each other over the years. I encouraged them to carve out time and space in their lives to focus on each other. Date nights once a month, lunch together once a week, and enrollment in a couples massage course were identified by Diane and Jasmine as activities they felt would improve their relationship as a couple within a family.

Outcomes

Couples counseling initially focused on teaching each partner how to communicate her feelings and experiences to the other person and working with each woman on listening carefully to what her partner had to say. As they were able to be open to and validate the other partner's experiences with their families, an increasingly strong sense of trust and commitment to the relationship developed. Rather than seeing each other as the problem, Jasmine and Diane were able to see themselves as a team that could interact as a united front with their families. Pursuing the strategies they identified for improving their interaction with Jasmine's family, especially with regard to her family's perception of Diane as an equal parent with Jasmine, resulted in some significant improvement. For example, Jasmine's mom started talking about pregnancy with Diane and about how different it is to raise two children compared with one child. When Diane announced her pregnancy at a family gathering, Jasmine's family celebrated enthusiastically.

When Diane confronted her own parents about their treatment of Jasmine and Theo, they responded initially with defensiveness and denied any differences in how they treated Diane's child versus their other grandchildren. We had discussed this possibility in therapy, and Diane was able to gently point out instances of inequitable treatment and focus on how painful this was for her and Jasmine. Several weeks later, Diane's parents surprised Theo with a special day at the zoo for just him, and they bought him a stuffed animal while there. Diane's mother acknowledged to her that it was difficult to admit but that they did seem to treat Theo more as a "step-grandchild rather than as a real grandchild" and that they felt embarrassment when telling friends and acquaintances about Jasmine and Theo. Diane talked with them about how everyone in U.S. society has internalized to some extent negative feelings about same-sex relationships and how important it was to her that they work on overcoming their heterosexism, as she and Jasmine did not want their children getting messages from their grandparents that there was something wrong with their family composition. Diane also encouraged her parents to examine whether discomfort with Jasmine being African American might also be a factor in how they treated her. Learning about Diane's pregnancy created more opportunities for her parents to see how they had not celebrated Jasmine's pregnancy to the same extent that they wanted to celebrate with Diane. A further nudge toward change occurred when Diane told her parents that she and Jasmine and the children would not spend time with them if Jasmine and Diane perceived that they treated the two children differently because the second child was their biological grandchild. After some bristling by Diane's father about not liking threats, Diane's parents appeared to make significant efforts to include Jasmine and Theo as important members of their family.

Another therapeutic outcome was a decision by Jasmine and Diane to focus on spending less time with their large extended families and more time creating quality relationships with individual members of their families. In addition, they were successful in creating more couple time through occasional lunches, date night once a month, and joining the couples massage class. An added benefit was an increase in their frequency and enjoyment of love making, something that had gradually declined after Theo's birth.

I had hoped that Jasmine and Diane would build a network of friends who either had children or were supportive of including children in social activities. Although they had talked about joining a lesbian and gay parenting group in town, this never happened. Likewise, they had strategized about other ways in which to meet same-sex couples with children but did not pursue any of these avenues. Thus, Jasmine and Diane did not improve the quality of their social support network outside of their families. Similarly, although they voiced on several occasions the importance of doing a second-parent adoption of Theo, they did not make progress on this issue.

Countertransference Issues

During my work with Jasmine and Diane, I endeavored to keep several issues in mind regarding potential countertransference issues. First, I paid attention to how my own experiences as a member of a lesbian couple raising a child could affect how I understood the experiences of this couple and how I might encourage (or fail to encourage) them in their pursuit of specific goals. Second, I checked to see how my identity as a White woman might create barriers or challenges to my understanding of, and relationship with, Jasmine. Third, I monitored my behavior toward both Jasmine and Diane as mothers, given that my role as the biological mother of a child could lead me to identify more with Jasmine and cause unintentional slighting of Diane's role as a parent.

Conclusion

This case illustrates some of the issues that may arise in working with lesbian parents. Jasmine and Diane experienced stressors common to many parents regardless of sexual orientation, and they experienced specific issues related to being a lesbian couple. For example, many couples with children report experiencing a lack of time and energy for focusing on the couple relationship, and it is not uncommon to hear parents complain about how their own parents or in-laws judge or comment on their parenting abilities. Issues that may arise in lesbian parent couples include a nonbiological parent not being perceived as an equal parent in the eyes of family, friends, and society; a lack of social support from friends and family; and a lack of legal rights for both parents. Focusing on strengths, intersections of identity, and ways in which privilege and oppression affect individuals, the couple, and the family unit as a whole are important strategies to consider in working with lesbian parents.

References

American Psychiatric Association. (2000). *Diagnostic and statistical manual of mental disorders* (4th ed., text rev.). Washington, DC: Author.

Hays, P. A. (2001). *Addressing cultural complexities in practice: A framework for clinicians and counselors.* Washington, DC: American Psychological Association.

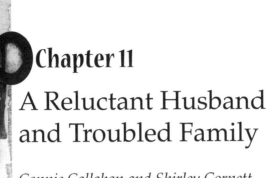

Chapter 11

A Reluctant Husband and Troubled Family

Connie Callahan and Shirley Cornett

Introduction

A 44-year-old Hispanic man sought counseling for his wife, a 43-year-old Hispanic woman, and for his two sons, ages 16 and 17. Samuel came to the first session by himself. The onset of problems in this family supposedly began with a coming out process for the husband, who surprised his wife of 22 years by confessing the beginning of a homosexual affair. Worried about himself and his entire family, Samuel agreed to family counseling after the first session. The wife, A.J., who became the identified patient, presented with major depressive disorder. The psychiatric nurse practitioner at Southwestern Counseling Services diagnosed major depressive disorder after two intake sessions before referring A.J. to Dr. Connie Callahan as a primary counselor. A.J. displayed the symptoms of unipolar depression.

Five years before seeking treatment for the fourth time, A.J. acknowledged that her husband turned out to be "a gay man who stepped out of his marriage vows." Her husband, a good Catholic soul (by his own description), felt guilty about his infidelity and confessed to his wife that he was in love with another man. His coming out process left A.J. angry and depressed, caused concern in his oldest son that he himself might have homosexual tendencies, and turned the youngest son into a parentified child.

Background Information

At the time of her husband's confession, A.J. immediately "took to her bed" and refused to eat, talk, or contribute to the household in any way except on Sundays, when she went to Mass and stayed afterward to meet with her priest for counseling. Her first attempt at counseling was with her priest.

She wanted him to castigate her husband. From her own description she would mainly rant and rave about Samuel's betrayal of her marriage and her sense of being a woman. The reaction of her priest did not satisfy her, and she would return home to bed after her Sunday afternoon counseling sessions. According to her, the priest explained to her that her husband was the head of the household, that men did sin, and that forgiveness was the motto of the Catholic Church. As she became more and more incapacitated, her husband pursued his love interests and became an infrequent visitor to his home. A.J. tried her best to indoctrinate her sons against their father. Then the oldest son turned 18 and moved out of the house and away from the family to attend college. The youngest son, 16, began to take care of his mother, cleaning the house, doing the grocery shopping, cooking, and spending all of his time when not in school at home. These dynamics had been in play in this family for 5 years before they sought counseling with Dr. Callahan.

A.J., in the course of her 5-year depression, had sought individual counseling two other times with poor results. None of the counselors supported her expectations of changing her husband. Samuel insisted that his family come to counseling because he was considering divorcing his wife, he was worried about his oldest son's withdrawal from the family, and he was worried about his youngest son's development (i.e., his lack of friends, his lack of appropriate social interaction, and his growing desperation). During the first session with A.J. and the entire family, a biopsychosocial systems conceptual model was presented to help explain the multiple systems active in this family's life. In particular, it was necessary for the family to understand how the individual system, the interactional system, the intergenerational system, and the community system simultaneously affected one another (Breen-Ruddy & McDaniel, 2008; Weeks, 1989).

Diagnosis

For three sessions, the biopsychosocial systems were explored. In determining hot spots in the individual system, A.J. was found to meet the criteria for a specific mental health diagnosis. In fact, her multiaxial evaluation included the following:

Axis I	296.32	Major Depressive Disorder
	302.79	Sexual Aversion Disorder
Axis II	None	
Axis III	Symptoms, Signs, and Ill-Defined Conditions	
Axis IV	Problems with support group: estrangement from husband; oldest son moved to college	
	Problems related to the social environment: inadequate social support	
	Occupational problems: unemployment	
	Economic problems: inadequate finances	
Axis V	Global Assessment of Relational Functioning = 65 (continuous for 5 years): major impairment in work, family relations, judgment, and thinking	

Presenting Issues

Conjointly with engaging in family counseling sessions, A.J. agreed to enter counseling on an individual basis with a psychiatric nurse practitioner who could prescribe and monitor medications and work on her depression and sexual aversion. Dr. Callahan spent 3 months convincing A.J. that depression was a biological condition as much as a psychological problem. Being ill contributed to both the family dysfunction and the depression. The payoff for being in bed all the time was that the youngest son took over the household chores and basic living functions, leaving A.J. in her misery and producing an unbalanced family. In a family meeting in session, round-robin questions were asked of each family member and the answers discussed in detail, highlighting how parenting roles had been abandoned and how each family member had assumed the chores and activities normally performed by A.J. Each member completed a chart noting what they did in 30-minute increments for a 7-day period to illustrate the shift in function and roles in the family. The men in the family were surprised at how much work they were doing and how little interaction with life there was for A.J.

Besides discussing A.J.'s and her youngest son's dysfunction, the family expressed emotions that were contributing to the presenting problem. A.J. remained angry, sad, and hopeless. A.J. stated that she could not forgive her husband for having an affair. She would often cry during sessions and state that she did not know what she was going to do. Samuel wavered between joy in his homosexual relationship to despair that he had "caused [his] wife's depression" and anxiety that he would lose contact with both sons. The oldest son was sad that he had had to withdraw from the family but sought peace in the university. He said that he felt a little guilty about spending all of his time at the university but that he would rather be there than at home. The youngest son became despairing at the demands of his mother and his lack of a social life. He stated that he could not sleep and that he was afraid to leave his mother alone because she might not get enough to eat and might just sleep all the time. He also stated that his friends had gotten tired of listening to him complain about his mother and that he was so busy trying to clean the house and cook that he had no time to spend with his friends. He also noted that many of his friends were spending more time with girlfriends, and he was mystified about that process. Such individual factors affected the whole family.

Theoretical Frameworks

The family communication style and family roles (Satir, 1972) contributed to the family stress. A.J., the family *blamer,* dominated the family, found fault with Samuel, and self-righteously accused the husband. The youngest son adopted the role of the *placater* by always agreeing with the blamer, by apologizing, and by trying to please. The oldest son, as the *super-reasonable* family member, remained detached and robot-like and maintained intellectual control by not becoming emotionally involved in the family drama. Samuel partially played the role of the *irrelevant* by trying not to relate, by being afraid to offend or hurt others, by being "sorry" about everything, by refusing to take any responsibility for anything, and by distracting by deflecting to the other family members.

In terms of the interactional system of the family, the youngest son and mother were enmeshed with diffuse boundaries, and the oldest son was too disengaged. The youngest son took complete care of A.J. and got upset because he could not meet all of his mother's emotional needs. The disengaged son stayed at college, refused to come home, and avoided most contact with others because he was afraid that he had inherited his father's homosexual tendencies. The oldest son stated that he spent most of his time with male students and male friends. In a counseling session he said, "You don't suppose I am really gay like my dad, do you? I would be afraid of going to hell if I were gay." His upbringing cast homosexuality as a sin.

The mother's depression kept her in a position of power. The youngest son waited on her hand and foot. Samuel was afraid to engage her because she would always become enraged and rant for hours about his homosexuality. This would cause him to disengage, to seek solace from his lover, and then to feel terribly guilty about being away from his family.

A.J.'s sexual aversion had kept her from having sex with her husband for more than 16 years. This contributed to Samuel's infidelity and to his pattern of coming and going in the household. He would divide most of his money between his family and his lover and would feel guilty about that. He would feel guilty for enjoying himself and for not spending enough time with his sons. He volunteered these types of feelings on several occasions during sessions.

The intergenerational system had an interesting history. A.J. had lost her mother in an accident when she was 6 years old. Her maternal grandmother reluctantly raised her and a younger sibling. When both girls reached puberty, the grandmother wrapped their breasts with tape in an attempt to keep them from growing. This and a script about sex being dirty, bad, and undesirable contributed to A.J.'s sexual aversion. A.J. stated that she had done her duty by bearing two sons and had no intention of ever having sexual relations with anyone again. Her grandmother had made it clear that raising A.J. and her sister was a burden she did not want, and her main pattern of childrearing involved distancing and emotional and physical cutoff. Samuel's family of origin held him to the life script that "once you are married, you stay married, no matter what." This produced feelings of guilt and helplessness that needed to be addressed in counseling. A sexual history with just A.J. and Samuel in session revealed A.J.'s ideas about sex. A.J.'s husband directly told her that without sex, he felt agitated and lonely and that his needs had not been met. A.J. never told him she was sorry for not having sex with him. She just indicated that sex was dirty and that she could not change her feelings. A.J.'s affect remained flat during all of these interactions. Given the information about A.J.'s early conditioning and her unwillingness to try to change, Samuel was asked what he could have done differently in dealing with his needs and sense of loneliness. He stated that he had waited way too long for sex, that he had tried to discuss these issues with his wife on numerous occasions, that maybe he had no other options except to remain celibate, and that his hunger for human affection had led to his affair.

Goals of Treatment

The biopsychosocial system model also addresses the community system. The husband and A.J. believed that their community failed them. Samuel indicated that he was afraid to stand as a gay man because that was just not accepted in the Hispanic world, and he turned away from his faith when the Church condemned his actions and wanted to work on his unacceptable, sinful homosexual behavior. A.J. turned to the Church for help but would not accept the doctrine that she simply forgive her husband and submit to him (after the church reclaimed him and returned him to a heterosexual state). It must have been devastating to both A.J. and her husband to recognize that their communities would not be of any help or solace. The community systems that could improve functioning in the family were the educational systems in the boys' lives.

Addressing the oldest son's fears of becoming homosexual like his father and addressing the need of the youngest son to become active in school and to develop a social life became shared family goals. Dr. Callahan asked the oldest son about attraction to and fantasies of males and females. She asked him to differentiate between friendships and romantic interests. He reviewed his past relationships and interests with the whole family present and decided for himself that having male friends was fine, that he was attracted to and interested in females (but needed help figuring out how to develop a long-lasting relationship with one), and that he didn't think he was gay. The youngest son filled out an activity schedule on which he slowly began to add activities outside the home. He considered roadblocks to carrying out the activities and developed contingency plans if things did not work out the way he anticipated they would. Both Dr. Callahan and Samuel reinforced all behaviors that took him out into world away from his mother. Helping A.J. overcome her depression became another family goal, along with the husband taking definitive action about his homosexuality. The question of divorce loomed.

Interventions

The interventions used in family counseling varied as each family member sat in the hot seat. The first intervention involved a family genogram, used to gather the intergenerational history of the family and to capture the family structure. Questions asked and statements made about the genogram included the following:

1. Describe your current "family" composition, including people and pets (e.g., names, ages, gender, relationship).

2. Describe how the parents met and what led each of them to choose to be with the other.
3. What are the 10 most important communication rules in your family (e.g., "Adults are to be listened to first," "Everyone has a right to share feelings and opinions," "Sexual information is not to be discussed")?
4. What "blueprint" have the parents made for the sons (e.g., goals for career, family, lifestyle, personality traits, values)?
5. How do the parents teach the sons (e.g., modeling, directives, rewards, punishment)?
6. What are the basic jobs that are required to maintain your family (e.g., grocery shopping, cooking, paying bills)?
7. Who is responsible for each job, and how is responsibility determined (e.g., gender, age, size, interest, ability)?
8. How is "job performance" (or nonperformance) dealt with (e.g., appreciation, money, privileges, withholding)?
9. What three areas would you work on to make your family a "happier place to live"?

This provided background clues to the distress in the family.

Depression ran in A.J.'s family, and her grandmother's role in distorting normal sexual activity in the marriage subsystem was uncovered in the analysis of the genogram. In reviewing the genogram with the family Dr. Callahan administered the Marital Status Inventory (Crane, Newfield, & Armstrong, 1984), which provided a good indication that the couple was likely to divorce. The family's answers about problems in communication, jobs required to maintain the family, and family responsibility led Dr. Callahan to administer the Marital Status Inventory.

An analysis of Samuel's involvement in his homosexual relationship indicated an impacted commitment to the couple's relationship. Issues of control and responsibility were also assessed, and it was found that the husband abdicated responsibility and A.J. controlled their sons; this led to a good discussion of the results of those behaviors. In that discussion, both sons expressed reactions of hurt and stress to the breakdown of the marital subsystem. The genogram also allowed for an analysis of the bonds among the family members, such that the parent–child dyad created the parentified behavior in the youngest son.

Several sessions were devoted to family structure, and these were informative for the family. Colapinto (2000) pointed out that families form an internal organization that dictates how, when, and to whom each member relates. Dr. Callahan presented these internal maps as hunches and had the family confirm or deny them. Structural family therapy alignments, power, and coalitions were exposed. A.J. and her sons had joined together against the father. The power in the family belonged to A.J., because she exerted the most influence on the family's daily operations. Triangulation was evident. Both sons agreed that A.J. insisted that the boys adopt her hurt and outrage at her husband's homosexual affair. Samuel agreed that he felt betrayed by that alignment and explained that this sense of betrayal and A.J.'s continued outrage caused him to disengage from the family. In family sessions, each person would present a problem. Dr. Callahan asked family members to sit directly across from each other when dyads were involved. A problem-solving model with four steps was used: (a) Define the problem as specifically as possible, (b) generate possible solutions to the problem asking the questions "Will the solution help?" "How will this solution make others feel?" and "Will this solution harm anyone?" (c) try the solutions, and (d) analyze the effectiveness of the solution chosen. During each step, the members of the dyad changed places and stated their own views and ideas about the problem. These dialogues, with different family members taking on each other's roles, helped each family member understand that instead of working on any problem, they were stuck in a process in which no change was possible. A.J. had the most difficult time playing the role of her husband, but the sons had no problems being enraged like A.J., feeling hurt like their father, and acting upset as each other. Once the family members could see the role each of them played, and once they began to understand their family patterns, cognitive–behavioral interventions such as a problem-solving model, the positive data log, activity scheduling, and goal setting were used in therapy.

Outcomes

After 16 months of therapy some issues were resolved. The older son moved into university housing and quit taking his mother's side. He decided that if his father wanted to be gay that was okay, and he worked through his sense of homophobia by spending some time with his father and his father's "friend." He did not resolve his feelings about himself. The younger son quit taking care of the mother, started dating, and became active in some school activities. He would talk to his father but still had unresolved issues about his father's sexuality. He talked a lot to a Catholic priest about his father. A.J. became increasingly angry as therapy progressed because her sons quit taking care of the house, the shopping, and the food. She had to begin to stand on her own two feet. As she became angrier, the husband removed himself from the home but did continue to support her financially. He worked through his identity as a gay man in therapy and spent a lot of time with his new partner. He decided to file for divorce and to engage with his sons as much as he could. At termination, all family members were left with the message that any of them could resume therapy if they felt the need.

This challenging family responded well to many of the family therapy interventions. Sixteen months is longer than most families we have seen spend in counseling, but the deep family issues and the willingness of most of the family members to engage in therapy and to try to resolve issues kept everyone busy. Life changes provided evidence of the success of therapy with this family.

References

Breen-Ruddy, N., & McDaniel, S. H. (2008). Couple therapy and medical issues: Working with couples facing illness. In A. S. Gurman (Ed.), *Clinical handbook of couple therapy* (4th ed., pp. 618–640). New York, NY: Guilford Press.

Colapinto, J. (2000). Structural family therapy. In A. M. Horne (Ed.), *Family counseling and therapy* (pp. 80–95). Itasca, IL: Peacock.

Crane, D., Newfield, N., & Armstrong, D. (1984). Predicting divorce at marital therapy intake: Wives' distress and the Marital Status Inventory. *Journal of Marital and Family Therapy, 10,* 305–312.

Satir, V. M. (1972). *Peoplemaking: How understanding your family can make you a better parent.* Palo Alto, CA: Science and Behavioral Books.

Weeks, G. R. (1989). *Treating couples: The intersystem model of the Marriage Council of Philadelphia.* New York, NY: Brunner/Mazel.

Chapter 12

Counseling and Advocacy With An International/ Dual National Same-Gender Couple and Family

Stuart F. Chen-Hayes

The counseling literature has developed a small but growing amount of work specific to lesbian, gay, bisexual, and transgender (LGBT) couples and families with multiple cultural identities, but most of the focus has been on heterosexism, sexism, and challenging racism. For some clients, issues of citizenship and immigration are more salient, yet there is little counseling literature devoted to the issues of immigrationism (i.e., prejudice multiplied by power that is used by persons of dominant citizenship statuses to restrict access to individual, cultural, and systemic resources by noncitizens in a particular country; Chen-Hayes, 2009). Counselors can use additional information in working with same-gender couples and families facing issues of migration and immigration in a world in which only 12 nations currently offer same-gender marriage at the federal level and several dozen others offer some form of either civil union or domestic partnership status in all or part of their nations. The present case study highlights the issues facing a multiracial, multilingual, multinational gay-headed family as they seek counseling for help with important parenting, couple, and career decisions across two countries.

Background

Yibin, a 35-year-old dad, and Jeremy, a 28-year-old dad, had twin 3-year-olds (Mei-Hsiang/May and Tzu-Chun/Ethan) with a surrogate from Vancouver, Canada. The couple had residency in New York State, where their Massachusetts marriage was a recognized gay marriage. They had started dating 7 years ago. Yibin (called *baba*, the Mandarin word for *father*, by his children) was a first-generation immigrant from Taiwan with dual citizenship in the United States. He was of Han Chinese ethnicity and had come to the United States to study in Boston as a graduate student in business. He was fluent in English, Mandarin, and Taiwanese.

Jeremy was a U.S. citizen adopted by parents of Norwegian and French ethnicities. He was White in terms of his racial identity but did not know his specific ethnicities. He had a master's degree in teaching English as a second language and had decided to put his career on hold to be a stay-at-home dad for the first years of the twins' lives. The presenting issue for couples and family counseling was that Yibin had been offered and wanted to accept a career-advancing job as a senior vice president for a top company in Shanghai. Both men recognized the importance of the career move for the family but wondered how well they would transition to life in Shanghai given that only one of them was fluent in Chinese and there were few other out, gay-parented families in the country. The tension revolved around how they would balance Yibin's likely 80-hour work weeks for the 3-year period of the employment contract with Jeremy as a "trailing spouse." After an initial counseling session with the parents and children, the counselor requested that subsequent sessions focus only on the parents.

Goals

Initial goals for counseling were to help the couple work through couples issues related to the transition abroad, support networks, family expectations, family resources, career differences, the imbalance of work and family responsibilities versus traditional gender role expectations, reducing the stress of Jeremy's greater parenting responsibilities, and increasing Yibin's time for parenting and the relationship both now and in China. Negotiated goals included making time for the couple to focus on their needs and issues; looking at issues of being out in the family, at work, and in different ethnic/cultural/national settings (Chen-Hayes, 2003a); and engaging in some brief sex therapy work to deal with the emotional fallout of the move and partner resentment. Finding unique outcomes and strengths for Jeremy in challenging his fears would allow him to branch out into other interests and eventually return to part-time work because the visa requirements in China would require his doing so as a single man.

Yibin had friends in China, but Jeremy's friends were all in the United States. The couple's friends were excited for them but wished they could stay in the United States. Yibin's family lived in Taiwan and was excited to be able to see the grandchildren much more often. Jeremy's family was in the metropolitan New York City area, and although they were supportive of the move, his parents wished they could have as much time with the grandchildren as they had had in the past 3 years. The couple had issues around which career to prioritize and whose needs were more important— the dads' or the kids'. There was also a discrepancy in how the men felt in terms of comfort with being out as gay. Jeremy was more open as a gay man and had been politically active in undergraduate and graduate school professional associations for LGBT persons. Jeremy was very social but missed adult friendship because of the daily demands of parenting twin

3-year-olds. Opposites attract, however, and Yibin was more conservative, was more introverted, and was not active in LGBT issues at work. Jeremy had been out to his parents since a teenager with complete support; Yibin had come out to his parents and siblings after he had immigrated to the United States, but they had not been supportive until the twins had arrived. The twins' birth had brought Yibin closer with his siblings and mother, but his father was still distant and didn't acknowledge their marriage overtly.

Interventions

Yibin was excited for the move. Jeremy initiated the counseling, as he wanted to be supportive but expressed fear and resentment that his career was on hold and that China would be a place where he would be an outsider culturally and linguistically. The counselor said, "Tell me more specifics about your concerns about being an outsider." Jeremy said, "I have a lot of fears about how I would even be able to remain in the country for an extended period of time since our relationship is not recognized in China." He continued, "How could we even go if I can't even stay in the country for more than a few months at a time as a nonworking spouse?" Jeremy felt that he needed to remain the primary parent for the twins at home. Yibin heard these fears but had been so busy with work that he hadn't had much time for parenting or being a husband. Both men recognized that their relationship needed to be more of a priority after 3 years of parenting. The counselor asked, "How do you maintain your couple relationship when one is so busy with work outside the home and the other so busy with work inside the home?" Yibin said, "We try to have some date nights, but getting a regular sitter is a problem. The drive between our home and Jeremy's parents' home is 60 miles one way, so it doesn't make for easy transitions for a quick night out or a long weekend away when I'm working 70-hour weeks."

Jeremy joked, "I can't wait for the twins to turn six, because then it will be *my* turn to return to the work world outside of home, too." The counselor found this a key point in the counseling and asked, "What can the two of you do now to start the process rolling for Jeremy to explore his greater roles outside the home in a few years and Yibin's supporting Jeremy in this process?" But Jeremy stated that he felt a growing loss of having been away from his career for 3 years—more than he had expected. Yibin reasoned that the fact that his company would pay for live-in help should ease Jeremy's concerns. Jeremy stated, "Intellectually I know that will be good, but there is no guarantee that that woman will speak any English." They debated putting the children in an immersion school so that they could learn Chinese. Jeremy was also open to learning Mandarin, but he worried about having few social outlets and filling his time beyond being a stay-at-home dad. The prospect of living in a country where he had no friends, gay contacts, or connection to the language caused him to lose sleep and feel distanced from Yibin sexually.

Facebook is not allowed in China, so a major connection to his friends and family would be lost by going overseas. Jeremy added, "Not that I have much time for Facebook with the twins, but it is a social outlet once they've gone to bed."

In addition, as an English-as-a-second-language teacher, Jeremy knew he could find part-time work in Shanghai if a cram school was willing to sponsor him. He'd rather be working in a more legitimate educational institution, but he would work in the cram school if he had to. He hoped he wouldn't have to teach after-school intensive English, but staying in China for a longer period of time would mean securing an extended visa as an unmarried man because their marriage was not recognized. This dilemma would likely require that he teach at least part time. Yibin said, "Fortunately, we have academic backgrounds that allow us varied opportunities in China even if the government is repressive and doesn't recognize our family."

Jeremy took the lead in terms of parenting because of Yibin's long work hours. Jeremy's father was nontraditional and very involved in raising him, and Jeremy found that parenting came easily to him. Yibin was more traditional and wasn't close to his father; he had no problem with Jeremy taking the lead. He said, "It is a huge relief that Jeremy is so good with the kids because I can focus more on my work. We're about to open a new office in Shanghai and I will need to take the lead on it." He understood, though, that Jeremy needed more support in parenting than the corporate world allows. Yibin thought that adding household help in Shanghai would resolve these issues, at least in part. Jeremy wanted Yibin to have more family time and to share more of the parenting, even though they both knew that their family time would likely decrease given the expectations of Chinese corporate culture—a big part of Jeremy's concerns. He wanted Yibin more involved in parenting, not less. Yibin said he would like to be more involved, but he knew it wouldn't be likely for the time that they would be in Shanghai. Jeremy relied on his parents at times when he felt overwhelmed or needed a weekend break, and he wouldn't have access to them in Shanghai.

Yibin's parents were excited to fill in this gap and spend long periods of time in Shanghai, but they didn't speak much English, so Jeremy was concerned about communication issues and how everyone would adjust. They both worried about the realities of the Chinese workplace culture, which has killer days and nights and little time off. The husbands would see less of each other, and their roles would change significantly. Jeremy was unsure how he would make connections with other parents when he didn't speak Mandarin; this was particularly true of his making connections with other gay men, most of whom were without kids or closeted to family. He resented that their marriage would have even less validity than in the United States and worried about the long-term prospects for both the relationship and his happiness with an impending "imbalance only growing" overseas. Even though he was close to his adoptive parents, he stated that he "felt abandoned in some ways," which paralleled his quest (so far unsuccessful) to find his birth parent(s) and learn why he had had been put up for adoption. Lastly, the kids were excited to see a different country, sad about leaving behind one set of grandparents, but happy to see more of their *A-ma* and *A-gong* (Taiwanese for *grandmother* and *grandfather*). May proudly announced to brother Ethan in the first counseling session, "We're going to see them all the time now when we move!"

Diagnosis

A family systems perspective looks at the interpersonal relationships between couples and family members as one key to eliminating unhelpful interactions. This gay couple and gay-parented family dealt with normative family life cycle transition issues as they sought to strengthen their couple skills and parenting skills and manage the most stressful part of the family life cycle—parenting young children (Goldberg, 2010; McGoldrick, Carter, & Garcia-Prieto, 2010). They recognized their stress and sought help for challenging elements of immigrationism, familyism, and heterosexism as they negotiated marriage and parenting across two national boundaries (Chen-Hayes, 2009). Jeremy shared his persistent fears, and an Axis I diagnosis of anxiety was used for Jeremy, with both men having V-codes including employment issues, couple issues, parenting issues, and phase-of-life issues. There was no Axis II diagnosis for either man. In terms of Axis III, Yibin had rheumatoid arthritis and Jeremy was a survivor of skin cancer and had insomnia. Axis IV issues included employment, parenting, and acculturation concerns. Axis V was a General Assessment of Functioning (GAF) of 85 for Yibin and 75 for Jeremy. Yibin was shocked to see the 10-point difference on the GAF. That set off a lightbulb in his head that he "really needed to figure out ways to be more supportive of Jeremy." Jeremy was delighted to hear Yibin talk in this way, because prior to coming to counseling Yibin had dismissed his concerns because he was "too sensitive."

Subsequent Sessions

It was great to meet the children and see the family in action, but the counselor recommended, and Jeremy and Yibin agreed, that sessions would be more beneficial if they could work as adults alone on parenting and couple issues. The counselor negotiated a child care arrangement so that the kids could play in the next room with a professional caregiver during sessions. Yibin and Jeremy appreciated such accommodations so that they could focus on themselves and not worry about the kids. They also appreciated that the counselor was able to do Sunday sessions—the only day of the week that Yibin consistently could participate given his 6-day work schedule.

The counselor shared that in addition to working from a family systems perspective, in subsequent sessions he would use evidence-based cognitive–behavioral techniques to assist Jeremy with his fears (assigning Burns's, 1999, self-help cognitive therapy chapters on anxiety in the first session, including the specific written exercises of keeping a daily mood log and performing cost–benefit analyses) and evidence-based couples work to focus on strengthening the men's relationship (using Gottman et al.'s research predicting which heterosexual and same-gender relationships would be successful and which would not; Driver, Tabares, Shapiro, Nam, & Gottman, 2003; Gottman et al., 2003). Finally, the counselor shared his commitment to working with the couples' strengths and helping them find a new narrative that externalized the "problem" (White & Epston, 1990), focusing on solutions to strengthen them individually, as a couple, and as a family. The couple worked with the counselor and came up with the concept of "busi-ness" as getting in the way of their time together—too much work outside the home for Yibin and too much work at home for Jeremy made for two tired, stressed gay dads with little time or energy for themselves or their relationship. They were experiencing a decline in relationship satisfaction typical of many couples of all sexual orientations with young children (Goldberg, 2010; McGoldrick et al., 2010). The counselor normalized this and said, "Just like heterosexual parents with young children, gay men and lesbians with young children, according to the research, end up feeling pretty similar to where you guys are at right now—all work and not much play makes for stressed-out parents and kids." The men laughed when they heard this, and Jeremy joked about Yibin's straight-acting "fetish." Subsequent goal setting included helping the couple make the decision about whether to take Yibin's employment offer and move to Shanghai for 3 years. In addition, the couple agreed to focus on how Yibin could be more supportive of Jeremy as the lead parent prior to moving to Shanghai, including by developing more couple's time in preparation for a move and finding a better balance of both men's career, parenting, and couple goals.

The first task in counseling was to quickly decide on the offer to move to Shanghai. In an early session, there was a terrific crash followed by crying in the room next door, and for once Jeremy stayed in place and Yibin went running to see what was wrong with the kids. It turned out that Ethan had accidentally knocked over a lamp—no one was hurt, but the lamp sustained mortal wounds. Yibin was used to letting Jeremy take the lead in parenting at home and elsewhere, and Jeremy was amazed to see him spring into action. This metaphor was used to show the importance and power of Yibin taking more responsibility and time for parenting to ease the stress and frustration that had been building in Jeremy's life. In subsequent sessions the couple was asked to continue looking at how they could interrupt the "busi-ness" from their lives to make more time for themselves as a couple and relieve the parenting burdens on Jeremy. Yibin agreed to set better limits at work and to return to being the primary cook for the family. Jeremy felt that his time was never his own and that all he did was work for the kids and Yibin. He welcomed Yibin's offer to cook on Sundays for the week so that he could focus on some much needed personal time, such as taking yoga classes while the kids were at preschool. Jeremy said, "And those will be *hot* yoga classes!" Jeremy saw Yibin making big efforts to reconnect with him, and in turn he agreed that they should take the job offer in Shanghai. They eventually agreed that "corporate culture vultures" had swooped in way too many times to affect both their relationship and their parenting and that they needed to figure out specific ways to tame those birds if they were going to head overseas.

Jeremy found *The Feeling Good Handbook* (Burns, 1999) helpful; the teacher in him found it easy to focus a few minutes each day on his moods and thoughts, and after a few weeks he really got into the idea that he could start to change his feelings with his thoughts. He also asked Yibin to be home by 7 p.m. two nights a week and cook so that he could start yoga classes on Tuesdays and Thursdays; Yibin agreed. Jeremy felt that Yibin making clear changes in his work patterns to help him around the house was the biggest factor in motivating him to consider the move. In addition, the counselor picked up a lot of criticism going both directions between the two men and shared his concerns about how that could be harming the relationship. He introduced Gottman's Four Horses of the Apocalypse: Stonewalling, Defensiveness, Criticism, Contempt (Driver et al., 2003). He shared how Gottman was one of only a few researchers who have compared research with heterosexual and lesbian and gay couples to predict successfully which couples would break up and which ones would stay together (Gottman et al., 2003).

The men had not heard of Gottman's work and were curious about it. They saw that each of them was vocal in criticizing the other, but rarely did they use contempt, which matched findings that heterosexual couples were more likely than same-gender couples to use coercion (Gottman et al., 2003). Yibin was much more likely to stonewall and avoid arguments, and Jeremy was much more likely to be defensive. They worked with the counselor to lessen their use of criticism with each other and to lessen the other "horsemen" in their subsequent counseling sessions. They also worked on the concept of "bidding," what Gottman referred to as playful verbal or nonverbal ways of inviting one's partner to be involved with the other partner. They surprised each other with sexy notes during the week and a range of other creative ideas that brought back much of the playfulness of their dating in graduate school. This playfulness helped greatly when they neared the time to go abroad to China to secure a school for the twins and to see where they would be living. At this point their travel agent told them that they were refused a visa and had to go to the Chinese consulate directly.

This affront united the couple in outrage at why they were being singled out—was it because they were gay, was it because they had kids via surrogacy, or was it something related to Yibin's dual citizenship with Taiwan and the United States? What is interesting is that even though Jeremy was the more politically active of the two around LGBT issues, Yibin became incensed at this affront. Jeremy saw a side of Yibin that had not previously emerged and really admired his partner's righteous anger and courage. They went to the consulate, and although they will never know the reason why they had to appear in person, visas were secured. In the remaining months before leaving for Shanghai, counseling continued with work and family balance issues and the need for the couple to help Jeremy transition effectively. The counselor also focused on how the couple interacted, including time for romance and sex. Yibin and Jeremy agreed that they'd really decreased their romantic and sexual time because of the work and parenting realities of their lives. Both made strides in ensuring at least 1 hour a week for sexual time, when they would lock their door and not answer any calls or kids' requests unless the apartment was burning down.

Yibin and Jeremy left counseling a few weeks prior to their move to China and were told that the counselor would send them a 6-month follow-up e-mail to check in, see whether they had continued making gains, and gain feedback on the counseling process. In their e-mail response, Yibin shared that they had found a place to live, hired help, and found a part-time Chinese language school for their twins in Shanghai. They were able to find a large expatriate community in which to develop friendships with other parents, although most of the parents they met were heterosexual, to neither man's surprise. They also made some gay friends who were single and quite in awe of how the men had been able to transition to being gay dads in Asia. They both expressed an interest in returning to the United States eventually; Jeremy's bottom line had been to go for a maximum of 3 years and then return to the United States. Yibin was okay with that as long as the job market held out for him. The global recession had them concerned, but they reported a fairly smooth transition to Asia, one that Yibin had expected but that Jeremy felt much better about as he met other gay folks who spoke English, which lessened his feelings of isolation. They wrote in a follow-up e-mail about some funny experiences that they had had with the kids as others tried to figure out where "the mom was" on a regular basis. Yibin's company paid for a live-in cook/household assistant fluent in Mandarin, and she became the doting "aunt" to "her kids." Jeremy had multiple offers to teach English as a second language but hadn't taken one, although they knew he would have to do so soon to remain in the country on a work visa. Jeremy felt that the twins were doing well enough that he could work part time while they were in school, although he was not happy about it. Mei and Ethan loved learning Chinese and enjoyed spending time with *A-ma* and *A-gong*, who had been visiting for a month from Taiwan. Jeremy and Yibin's major resentment was that their marriage was not recognized in China.

In the meantime, Jeremy had met some gay activists in China online to try to figure out ways that he could support other couples (both native and international) who were seeking to raise children in China. Yibin declared two nights a week as "home-at-a-decent-hour nights" and refused to work past 6 p.m. on Tuesdays and Thursdays. Initially he was worried about how his company would deal with it, but the men reported having one date night a week on one of those nights, and having in-home help allowed them more time to connect as a couple. Although they continued to be in different places with outness and with being political as LGBT (Chen-Hayes, 2003a, 2003b), Jeremy reported that his fears had lessened and that he was now doing yoga on his own at home when the kids were at school, which helped him focus. The couple reported that their sex life improved overseas, especially with Yibin home two nights earlier than even in the States, having let the "corporate culture vultures" fly the coop at least twice a week.

Conclusion

In sum, counseling was successful at assisting Yibin and Jeremy through normative life cycle issues; Jeremy's anxiety; and the challenges of heterosexism, familyism, and immigrationism. Although a family systems approach doesn't focus on transference/countertransference, the counselor had extensive experience with male couples, gay parents, and dual national couples and families and worked collaboratively with the couple and family throughout the counseling. The couple chose this counselor because of his perceived competence in working with dual-career couples, LGBT-headed families, parenting, relationship issues, Asian and Euro-American worldviews, and immigration issues. The counselor was able to join successfully with both men in the initial session of counseling and build on that bond as counseling progressed. In summary, the counselor supported the couple as a team parenting twins and what was best for both individuals at the same time. In additionn, the counselor used brief, culturally affirming interventions that focused on couples' strengths and specific cognitive techniques for reducing anxiety and the use of narrative to help the couple restory its narrative for success as a team, as a gay couple, and as a gay-parented family with multiple ethnic, racial, national, gender, and sexual orientation identities.

References

Burns, D. D. (1999). *The feeling good handbook.* New York, NY: Plume.

Chen-Hayes, S. F. (2003a). Assimilation, queer pride, or in between: Personalizing GLBT relationships, sexual practices, and politics. In J. S. Whitman & C. J. Boyd (Eds.), *The therapist's notebook for lesbian, gay, and bisexual clients: Homework, handouts, and activities for use in psychotherapy* (pp. 85–91). Binghamton, NY: Haworth Clinical Practice Press.

Chen-Hayes, S. F. (2003b). Challenging multiple oppressions with GLBT clients. In J. S. Whitman & C. J. Boyd (Eds.), *The therapist's notebook for lesbian, gay, and bisexual clients: Homework, handouts, and activities for use in psychotherapy* (pp. 174–178). Binghamton, NY: Haworth Clinical Practice Press.

Chen-Hayes, S. F. (2009). Types of oppression. In American Counseling Association (Ed.), *The ACA encyclopedia of counseling* (pp. 383–384). Alexandria, VA: American Counseling Association.

Driver, J., Tabares, A., Shapiro, A., Nam, E. Y., & Gottman, J. M. (2003). Interactional patterns in marital success and failure: Gottman laboratory studies. In F. Walsh (Ed.), *Normal family processes: Growing diversity and complexity* (pp. 493–513). New York, NY: Guilford Press.

Goldberg, A. E. (2010). *Lesbian and gay parents and their children: Research on the family life cycle.* Washington, DC: American Psychological Association.

Gottman, J. M., Levenson, R. W., Swanson, C., Swanson, K., Tyson, R. K., & Yoshimoto, D. (2003). Observing gay, lesbian, and heterosexual couples' relationships: Mathematical modeling of conflict interaction. *Journal of Homosexuality, 45*(1), 65–91.

McGoldrick, M., Carter, B., & Garcia-Prieto, N. (Eds.). (2010). *The expanded family life cycle* (4th ed.). Boston, MA: Pearson.

White, M., & Epston, D. (1990). *Narrative means to therapeutic ends.* New York, NY: Norton.

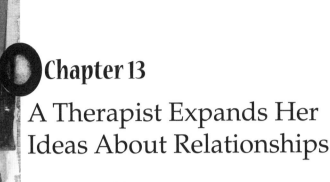

Chapter 13

A Therapist Expands Her Ideas About Relationships

Sari H. Dworkin

Bisexuality requires that therapists expand their ideas about many dimensions of sexual identity and how it manifests. Therapists must move beyond dichotomous thinking about sexual orientation and identity. Dichotomous thinking implies that sexual orientation/identity is either heterosexual or homosexual. Bisexuality implies another complete orientation/identity and also brings more into focus the idea of a continuum of orientation/identity (Firestein, 2007). People may fall in different places along the continuum depending on context. In addition, many bisexuals (although not all) are open to *polyamorous* relationships, or relationships that involve more than one partner at a time (Dworkin, 2002). This openness sometimes feeds into the myth that bisexual people are unable to develop stable, committed relationships. Some believe that this myth stems from many factors, but one factor is that the culture is sex-phobic and unable to move beyond traditional sexuality and traditional definitions of relationships. Therapists are susceptible to the myths and stereotypes of the culture. The case presented here forced me to examine many of my beliefs about relationships. This case is a composite case, with identifying data changed to protect the client and significant others.

Happily Heterosexually Married

Connie was referred to me by her family physician. She complained about stress on the job, depression, and anxiety. Her primary care physician prescribed Prozac and Xanax, and these medications were helping, but Connie wanted some strategies for coping. Connie was middle aged, female, Hispanic, middle class, and college educated. She had been happily heterosexually married for 30 years, had three adult children (two daughters and one son) who were all married with children of their own, and had an extensive extended family all living nearby. She had been at the same company in various positions for more than 20 years and liked where she worked and what she did. Recently, because of budget cuts, her workload had increased and she was feeling overwhelmed. Her confidence was starting to waver, as more pressure meant less time on tasks, and Connie was worried about making mistakes. Diagnoses included dysthymic disorder (Connie reported that beginning in childhood she had often had bouts of sadness) and generalized anxiety disorder. There wasn't any indication of an Axis II diagnosis. On Axis III she complained about headaches from the stress. Psychosocial and environmental issues (Axis IV) focused on occupational problems; her Global Assessment of Functioning (Axis V) was 70, minor symptoms. Our work focused on identifying stress reduction techniques, disputing irrational beliefs about needing to be perfect, and finding other ways to handle work situations. After a few sessions, and after a good rapport and therapeutic alliance had developed, Connie dropped a bombshell. A major part of her stress was that she was "very attracted, more than friends" to a female employee who had recently been transferred to her section.

Enter Ann

Ann had been assigned to Connie for orientation and training. Connie found Ann to be a quick learner and easy to talk to. Connie liked Ann, often had lunch and coffee breaks with Ann, and had started to socialize with Ann outside of work. Ann often came over to Connie's house on weekends and got along well with Tomas, Connie's husband. They both enjoyed fixing trucks and cars. During one of their lunches together Ann came out as a lesbian to Connie. This was something new for Connie. She wasn't ignorant about lesbianism but had never known a lesbian before. The lesbian identity added to Ann's allure for Connie. Connie admitted she was struggling not only with her respect and admiration for Ann but with her feelings of arousal around Ann. Connie asked Ann not to discuss her lesbian identity in front of her extended family or her husband Tomas, as Tomas often made disparaging remarks about homosexuals. Connie explained to Ann that her Hispanic family (Ann identified as a Caucasian, "mainstream American"), all of whom were Roman Catholic, would never be able to accept Ann as a lesbian. Ann was fairly closeted, so this didn't create any problems for her.

I asked Connie about her own beliefs about homosexuality given her religious and ethnic upbringing. This was all very confusing to Connie. Connie loved her husband; was happily married; had always been attracted to the other gender; believed that homosexuality was "against God and unnatural"; and believed that homosexuality was part of White culture, certainly not Hispanic culture. Obviously these were all important issues to explore. I suggested that we begin with the last one—that homosexuality was part of White culture—because that was the easiest one to dispute.

Then we could move on to the others. At this point I began to consider the following diagnoses on Axis I in addition to the ones noted earlier: partner relational problem, identity problem, and phase-of-life problem.

Exploring Beliefs About Homosexuality

I asked Connie what made her believe that homosexuality was only in White culture. She stated that she had never met a Latino or Latina who identified as gay or lesbian, and her brother always said that there are no Hispanic gay people. This was an opportunity to educate Connie about the fact that homosexuality has occurred in every culture and every historical time period. I directed her to some books about Hispanic gays and lesbians and told her about Dignity, the lesbian, gay, bisexual, and transgender (LGBT) group of the Catholic Church. (This was a shocking revelation to Connie, that Catholics could be gay and gays could be Catholic.)

In addition, I wondered whether Connie would be willing to speak to a gay-affirmative Catholic priest about scripture and Catholicism. This is outside of my competence, but I always have names of LGBT-affirmative clergy in the community where I practice because religion and spirituality often come up with clients. Connie was open to this.

Identity and Heterosexual Marriage

The most important issues were also the most complex. What did Connie's attraction to Ann mean about Connie's understanding of herself and her marriage? Of course it might not mean anything about her identity, and it didn't have to impact her marriage, because attractions do not necessarily lead to actions. This could just be exciting information that could expand Connie's knowledge about and understanding of the world. Connie said, "I understand this but I think I want to act on my attraction to Ann." Ah—this statement changed our discussion.

One of the questions I had for Connie was whether she had discussed her new attraction with her primary care physician and was then referred to me because of my expertise working with LGBT issues. Connie admitted that she had worked up the courage to bring this into the discussion with her female physician. Another question I had for Connie at this time was this: On a scale of 1 to 10, how much of your current anxiety and depression is due to your confusion about your attractions, your desires, and your current marriage? Her response was a 9. I use scaling questions frequently with clients as a way to get a quick assessment of where the client is. My next scaling question was this: On a scale of 1 to 10, how important is it to preserve your heterosexual marriage? Her response was a 10. Even though my primary theoretical orientation is cognitive behavior therapy, like most therapists I use techniques from a variety of approaches. Following the scaling question I used the miracle question: If a miracle happened overnight and everything was the way you wanted it to be, how would you know that the miracle happened? What would be different? Connie responded, "I would be living with Ann and Tomas in a committed relationship. Tomas and Ann would get along well. My [adult] children and extended family would accept all of us."

Given Connie's background I was surprised to hear this. Obviously Connie had given much thought to this, even though we were just beginning to explore the issues in therapy. She was also clearer and more open to operating outside of the traditional in terms of her relationship than I would have expected.

Countertransference

I became aware of my own anxiety. Was this anxiety coming from the realization of how difficult this situation might be to resolve in a good way? Was my anxiety due to what I considered some unrealistic hopes? Was my anxiety due to my own feelings regarding polyamorous relationships? Intellectually I had no problems with how consenting adults arrange their lives. Emotionally I had a hard time accepting that this was even a realistic possibility. For myself I couldn't imagine arranging an open polyamorous relationship because of jealousy, time, and energy. Did I buy into the myth that bisexual people (even though Connie had not identified herself as bisexual, she was considering bisexual behavior) cannot have committed relationships? It was important for me to recognize my countertransference and remain aware of my own thoughts and feelings so they didn't interfere with my work with Connie. Connie needed a safe space to explore all possibilities free from any blinders or biases from her therapist.

Critical Events

Tomas left on a fishing trip and Ann stayed over at Connie's house. That weekend they had sex. "What was that like for you?" I asked. "Terrifying, wonderful; I'm in love, I feel so guilty." We explored all of these feelings in depth. Tomas was back home and Connie was anxious and confused. Ann wasn't helping. When Tomas wasn't around she pressured Connie about making a decision, choosing one or the other. "I'm not leaving my husband, but I can't bear the thought of giving up Ann." I brought up the possibility of a polyamorous relationship, recognizing how out of the box this would be for a Catholic Hispanic woman. Surprisingly, after I defined what a polyamorous relationship might look like, Connie did not immediately reject this idea. Neither Connie nor I could envision Tomas or Ann agreeing to this even if Connie was open to it, and that wasn't a given at this point. Connie said, "What am I going to do? Maybe I just need to disappear." Given Connie's tendencies toward depression I explored this further. She admitted being depressed, even having some suicidal thoughts but no plan. "How do I get out of this?" I reminded Connie how new this situation was and that it was too early to make any decisions. I offered couples counseling for a session or two with her and Tomas, or her and Ann, or even at some point all three of them. Connie was not ready to consider this.

Over the next few months Ann and Connie managed to find more opportunities to be together and to have sexual relations. At the same time Connie was still sleeping with Tomas. Tomas seemed oblivious, even though Ann had practically moved into Tomas and Connie's home. Connie was surreptitiously reading books about lesbianism and bisexuality. She had started to consider a bisexual identity for herself. All this was difficult for Ann, who wanted Connie to herself and wanted Connie to adopt a lesbian identity. Connie was not about to discount her heterosexual attractions, her love for her husband, and her heterosexual marriage history. She also worried about being rejected by her children and grandchildren. Currently they were very accepting of Ann, seeing her as a close friend of Connie. The extended family accepted Ann into the family.

One day Connie called me in crisis. She was distraught. Tomas had asked her if she loved Ann, and without thinking she had said yes. Tomas stormed out of the house. After I assessed for suicide and determined that Connie was not at risk, we brainstormed how she could handle this until our next appointment. A few sessions later Connie was distraught again. Tomas had informed their children (all adults) about this new development. Their two daughters were confused but not ready to abandon either their mother or their father. With their son it was a different story. He immediately took his dad's side and said he wanted nothing to do with his mom again. Connie and her daughters had many discussions. Her daughters had had conflicted relationships with their dad and often wondered why their mom stayed with him, so even though they had never imagined their mother in a relationship with a woman, they were not totally opposed to this.

When I next saw Connie she was calmer. Tomas had come back and told her he loved her and didn't want to lose her. She didn't want to lose him either, but neither did she want to lose Ann. Connie was now open to bringing Tomas into the session, and we scheduled that.

Negotiating a Marriage/Relationship

The couple's sessions were stormy. Tomas, who hadn't attended church or confession since the kids had left the house, shouted Catholic proscriptions against divorce and homosexuality and shouted about the sanctity of marriage. Connie assured Tomas that she loved him, used to believe the same religious tenets, and never in her wildest dreams could imagine falling in love with a woman or acting on it. When I suggested that the three of them might be able to work something out, Tomas attacked me for putting these ideas into his wife's head. Internally I checked my own feelings about what I was saying. It felt genuine.

It was obvious that a great deal of work would need to be done in session with Tomas and Connie and eventually Ann. Because I had seen Connie individually for close to a year, I knew I couldn't do that work. She was my client. Finding a therapist open to helping these individuals explore a potentially polyamorous relationship with lesbian and heterosexual aspects in the context of a traditional, Hispanic, Catholic background was not easy.

I felt it was my responsibility to find someone I thought would be appropriate for them (actually for Connie, my client). I did find someone, a female therapist, LGB affirmative and open to exploring different relationship patterns. Connie continued to see me individually. She reported that the sessions involving the three of them were difficult but that she was hopeful.

Update

About 1 year later, Connie, Tomas, and Ann were living together. Connie and Ann shared a bedroom and Tomas slept in another room. Connie spent most of her time with Ann. The extended family continued to include Ann in events, and nothing was ever explicitly discussed. Connie grieved that her son had become estranged from her and her husband, although the daughters had come to love Ann and accept the strange (to them) situation. Tomas and Ann tolerated each other. Through our sessions together Connie began to define herself as bisexual and actually started to engage in the LGB community with Ann. Work remained stressful but not because of Ann. Mild depression and anxiety continued to be a focus of therapy while therapy continued. Connie did finally decide to terminate therapy but occasionally sent me a letter letting me know how things were going.

Analysis

It's not unusual for clients to come in with one set of issues, only to have others emerge once trust and rapport have been established. This certainly was the case with Connie. Her new issues brought her into a world she knew little about. Her case is an example of the fluid sexual identity that many women report. Connie never questioned her heterosexual identity until she became attracted to a woman. Even then, Connie did not look back at her history to find occasions where this heterosexual identity might have been questioned. Although she had some knowledge of lesbianism, her identity moved from heterosexuality to bisexuality, an identity that had never been on her radar screen. At middle age not only did her sense of sexual identity change but so too did her ideas about marriage and relationships. These ideas moved from the traditional to an examination of wider possibilities. This led to struggles with her religious and cultural beliefs and assumptions. There were losses to grieve, the worst being the estrangement of her son. Her husband did remain with her, but that relationship showed strain under the new arrangement.

For me, this case forced me to examine my own beliefs and biases about different relationship arrangements. I had to acknowledge that it wasn't accurate to assume, on either a conscious or an unconscious basis, that what works or doesn't work for me models what will work or not work for others. Granted, this case doesn't illustrate the most successful polyamorous relationship (another bias of mine?) because the persons involved were tolerating one another rather than truly embracing their polyamorous arrangement. Some research I have engaged in gave me examples of more successful polyamorous relationships.

Attempting to get a better understanding about how women manifest their bisexual identity I interviewed women throughout the United States and in Israel (Dworkin, 1996). Through that qualitative study I met a woman who was in a committed relationship with another woman and a man, a woman who was in a committed relationship with two men, and a woman in a monogamous heterosexual marriage who missed the emotional and sexual bonds with women she had had prior to her marriage and who had discussed with her husband having a female lover. This last woman found that her husband (who had known she was bisexual before they married) was not averse to exploring this (although he had no desire to be sexually involved with either another woman or a man). The case described in this chapter also gave me a window into the complexities that ethnicity and religion add to considerations for change in how a relationship manifests.

Conclusion

It is important that therapists get trained in the different issues affecting bisexuals and also people who change their sexual identity in midlife or later. The concept of sexual fluidity is still controversial. Too often bisexuals are grouped with lesbians and gays as though they are exactly the same. In addition, although it has become almost a cliché to say this, therapists have to examine their biases and stereotypes. The myths and stereotypes about bisexuals are different from those about lesbians and gays and include relationship and commitment issues. No matter what a therapist calls it (countertransference, self-awareness), these biases can affect the therapeutic relationship. It is also important that therapists are trained to recognize and understand how the intersection of various beliefs and contexts will impact a client's life and may impact the choices the client makes. The case described in this chapter illustrates all of these points.

References

Dworkin, S. H. (1996). *Bisexual women, understanding sexual identity: Research in progress.* Unpublished manuscript, Department of Counseling, Special Education and Rehabilitation, California State University, Fresno.

Dworkin, S. H. (2002). Biracial, bicultural, bisexual: Bisexuality and multiple identities. *Journal of Bisexuality, 2*(4), 93–107.

Firestein, B. (2007). Cultural and relational contexts of bisexual women: Implications for therapy. In K. J. Bieschke, R. M. Perez, & K. A. DeBord (Eds.), *Handbook of counseling and psychotherapy with lesbian, gay, bisexual, and transgender clients* (pp. 91–117). Washington, DC: American Psychological Association.

Chapter 14

Counseling Bisexual Clients: More Than the Sum of the Parts

Beth A. Firestein

Counseling bisexual clients provides the therapist with opportunities to apply foundational knowledge about sexual orientation, identity development, and relationship dynamics to a wide range of clients with diverse life situations. It is an incredible opportunity for growth as a therapist and as a person. Although there will certainly be repetition of themes in our work with clients of various sexual orientations, the configuration of relationship possibilities involving queer-identified and bisexual clients is truly vast in number and variety. In this chapter I share two case studies involving bisexual clients or bisexuality as a theme of importance in the therapeutic work. Each case represents a composite of several individual cases, and details have been altered to protect the confidentiality of all individuals and their life situations.

Falling in Love and Coming Out Bisexual: One Woman's Journey

Background Information and Initial Diagnosis

Serena was a 32-year-old Caucasian woman with a 6-year-old son, Bryce. Serena was referred to me by her physician for posttraumatic stress related to her husband's death in a single-car accident 2 years before. Serena's presenting complaints were persistent depression and anxiety accompanied by recurring intrusive thoughts about her husband's traumatic death. Her initial presenting concerns were not related to issues of sexual orientation. She identified as heterosexual and had never questioned her sexual orientation or given it much consideration.

My initial assessment was that Serena was experiencing a delayed grief reaction and posttraumatic stress disorder triggered by the abrupt and unexpected death of her husband. She and her husband had been married for 10 years and had one son, who was 4 years old at the time of his father's death. In exploring Serena's relationship with her deceased husband, it came to light that the marriage had been loving but also conflict ridden and that his death had occurred within hours of his storming out of the house following an argument between the two of them.

Our initial focus was grief counseling and utilization of eye-movement desensitization and reprocessing (EMDR) to reduce traumatic symptoms. In the grief work, we discussed the incident in detail and worked through the specific feelings that haunted her relating to the accident: among these were guilt, shame, shock, and a deep feeling of loss. The EMDR functioned to diffuse the intensity of her startle response and the easily triggered emotional and physiological reactions that she still suffered around this incident.

Therapy gradually reduced her symptoms and brought Serena greater acceptance and less reactivity to reminders of her loss. As we worked together in therapy her immediate trauma reactions receded and safety and trust within the therapist–client relationship developed and deepened. Serena began discussing other parts of her life, including her family of origin and her social support network. In the context of this discussion, she repeatedly referred to a particular special friendship with a female coworker with whom she had become very close over the past year.

Over a period of weeks, Serena hinted at the romantic and sexual nature of her close friendship with Carrie, her coworker. Tentatively she began to discuss the evolution of their relationship, a close friendship that had gradually become an intimate romantic involvement over the past year. She was not aware that I work extensively with lesbian, gay, bisexual, and transgender (LGBT) clients, and this was not the reason for Serena's initial referral for counseling.

From Grief to Sexual Identity Exploration: An Evolving Conceptualization

While the grief and trauma work continued, the focus of our sessions turned increasingly toward Serena's conflicted thoughts and feelings relating to her intimate relationship with Carrie. For example, Serena would talk about the fun and joy they shared and the development of meaningful friendships with several lesbian couples, but in the same session she would also discuss waking up in the morning next to Carrie feeling that their relationship was "wrong" and that she could not envision herself in a long-term relationship with a woman.

Serena did not identify her relationship with Carrie as a true romantic involvement, stating that it was impossible for her to think of the relationship in those terms because she was heterosexual and continued to identify this way.

She had never consciously entertained the possibility that she might be lesbian or bisexual because she had never had an experience that stimulated her to consider this option. She participated in the relationship for many months without altering her sense of identity or precisely naming her relationship with Carrie. She simply lived it. It was only in the context of therapy that she began discussing the conflicting feelings and questions about herself raised by her involvement with Carrie. In therapy I validated her sexual and romantic history with men while simultaneously validating her present relationship with Carrie. I did not challenge her self-definition, but I did introduce her to the concept of bisexuality and how that concept might allow her to think about herself in a way that validated all of her feelings, past and present, in a single, integrated identity. Eventually Serena began to tentatively play with the idea of bisexuality as a way to characterize herself and her relationship, but there was never any pressure from me for her to change the way she labeled her sexual orientation.

Coming to Terms With a New Sexual Identity

Serena's sexual identity and her deepening relationship with Carrie increasingly became the focus of our therapy sessions. Serena continued to struggle with internal conflict relating to her involvement with Carrie, including the implications of this involvement for her view of herself and her position in the mainstream worlds of work and family. Her primary concerns were how to conceptualize her own sexual identity; fear that her relationship with Carrie might be publicly exposed (e.g., in the workplace); and great worry about the reactions of her parents, siblings, and long-time heterosexual friends.

In therapy I provided a safe space to discuss the positive and problematic aspects of her relationship. Serena also talked about her ongoing attractions to men and her surprise at having fallen deeply in love with a woman for the first time. We further explored the possibility that she might be bisexual and her increasing engagement with the lesbian community. As therapy progressed, Serena's lived experience of the relationship replaced her stereotypes of what it meant to be homosexual.

Serena came out to her family very gradually and met with considerable resistance from various family members, especially her very religious grandparents, who were of an older generation. Her mother went through a long period of alternating reactions, including rejection, denial, criticism, acceptance, and emotionally embracing Serena's partner. Dealing with her mother through this process was quite emotionally difficult for Serena. I affirmed Serena's ability to value her own experience of loving and worked actively with her to confront her internalized homonegativity and binegativity. Fortunately, her partner Carrie was supportive, understanding, and flexible in the face of the reactions of Serena's family. Eventually Serena also came out to the majority of her friends.

Redefining the Vision of "Family"

Although Serena was very much in love with Carrie and very happy with their relationship, it was very difficult for her to reconcile her feelings for Carrie with her ongoing attraction to men and her vision of herself as someday remarrying and once again having a heterosexual family lifestyle. As the relationship with Carrie continued to grow and blossom, this possibility seemed to recede more and more in Serena's mind and she had to move through feelings of loss over it. In therapy I assisted Serena in developing a new vision of family that included her partnership with a woman. It was helpful to reflect in therapy on couple relationships with lesbian friends, including some who had children.

Serena also worried about how her relationship with a woman might impact her 6-year-old son and how he might be treated in school: possibly teased by peers or not allowed into their homes because he had two female parents. To her great relief, her son Bryce and her partner Carrie formed a strong, warm bond with one each other, and Bryce fully accepted Carrie's role in their lives. Initially they did not explain the nature of their relationship to Bryce. When they did finally disclose this to him, he had already integrated an experiential sense of the three of them as "family," and the disclosure, although quite difficult for Serena, turned out to be anticlimactic for Bryce. The family went on as usual.

Serena gradually came to view herself as "probably bisexual" and later as a bisexual woman who felt no need for confining labels. She did not perceive herself as a lesbian. She and her partner have maintained a monogamous relationship, and Serena's self-identification (or lack of self-labeling) has presented no problem for her partner. Carrie continues to be very accepting of Serena with or without a clear lesbian or bisexual identity. Carrie and Serena have also developed a supportive circle of lesbian friends.

Outcome

Although my initial work with Serena occurred over about a year, she has returned to therapy occasionally for help with specific issues involving her partner and her parents and grandparents. Inevitably there have been some problems and relationship challenges in the 8 years that Serena and Carrie have been a couple. Most of these have been fairly ordinary developmental and relational challenges, but other challenges have threatened the stability of the relationship and their status as a committed couple. Serena and Carrie have continued to remain in a committed partner relationship, and for the most part their relationship and their family have thrived.

Serena's family of origin continues to present difficulties from time to time, sometimes excluding Carrie from family gatherings held at the grandparents' home because of their complete lack of acceptance of Serena's new sexual identity and her relationship with her female partner. Serena's parents and Carrie's parents are accepting and inclusive around holidays and other family events. Serena has worked through the majority of her internalized homophobia and now has a sense of pride in her identity. Though it is not her personal style to stand up as an activist on gay issues, she is sensitive to issues of social justice about same-sex relationships. She now stands up for herself and her partner in various situations and does not feel that she must "hide." This year she and her partner attended the gay and bisexual pride march in a nearby urban community. With respect to coming to terms with her new sexual identity, Serena's therapeutic journey has been quite successful.

Transference and Countertransference

Initially I found it challenging to be patient with Serena's fear and resistance to considering a bisexual or lesbian identity. I had to let go of my notions about the primary importance of self-identification and immediately connecting with a queer-, same-sex-relationship-affirming community. I could empathize with Serena's early confusion about integrating her history of satisfying heterosexual involvement and ongoing attractions to men with the strength of her romantic feelings for this particular woman. I had to be very conscious not to project my own life story onto hers or to judge her journey of self-discovery by comparing it to my own journey of recognizing and embracing myself as a bisexual woman.

Overall the experience greatly broadened my understanding of the range of expressions that may manifest in same-sex and other-sex relationships. I learned a great deal about how another bisexual woman balances her relationships with her family of origin and her partner, finding ways to validate her partner while still feeling a sense of belonging with most members of her family. Serena values Carrie as her lover and partner, and their own family relationship includes her partner's very healthy relationship with Bryce, who is now almost 11 years old. The family structure has provided a consistent and loving environment for Bryce in the years following his father's death, and Carrie has now parented Bryce longer than he was parented by his biological father. The prospects for this family's future seem quite promising.

A Bisexual Woman and Her Transgender Spouse: A Matrix of Challenges and Possibilities

Background Information

Lindsey was a 43-year-old woman who lived with her life partner, to whom she was legally married. She also had one young adult son, 26, who lived on his own. Lindsey self-identified as a bisexual woman. Her childhood and family background included a significant amount of physical, verbal, and emotional abuse; poverty; and a mother who was severely mentally ill. Lindsey became pregnant at a very young age and her life was filled with difficulty. Eventually she escaped her circumstances and utilized her intelligence and resourcefulness to obtain an undergraduate college degree and establish a productive and engaging work life and personal life.

At the time of our initial consultation, Lindsey was employed in a mid-level professional position. Her partner Kathryn came from a very successful, established family and worked in a high-paying technical position. They had been together for 6 years and had been living together in an attractive urban neighborhood.

Presenting Concerns

Lindsey located me through her research on the Internet. She was seeking a feminist therapist who specialized in working with LGBT populations, polyamory, and alternative lifestyle issues. Lindsey explained that her partner Kathryn, 46, was a male-to-female transsexual who had mostly completed her transition. She had known of Kathryn's identity and transgender status from the beginning of their relationship. In fact, they met through the queer community. At the time they met, Kathryn was moving into her transition more fully. Over the course of their relationship, Kathryn fulfilled requirements for living full time in her preferred gender role and sought and obtained sex reassignment surgery.

Lindsey was seeking therapy to sort out her feelings about her relationship with Kathryn and to make some lifestyle decisions. The most accurate diagnosis seemed to be adjustment disorder with mixed emotional features. She was seeking individual therapy at this point in time. Lindsey shared that she was fully supportive of her partner's transition and that her own identity as a bisexual woman contributed to her comfort with loving her partner regardless of her partner's gender. They had married when Kathryn was still legally a man and still living part time in a male gender role. According to state law, they remained legally married at that time.

The couple had a healthy sex life and worked well as a team. Each brought different resources and talents to their partnership. Lindsey reported that she had assisted and supported Kathryn throughout her process of gender transition and that this had been a stressful but largely rewarding process for both of them. Lindsey's current reason for seeking therapy concerned problems that had developed in their partnership since Kathryn's sex reassignment surgery.

Both partners had been looking forward with great anticipation to the completion of Kathryn's physical transition via sex reassignment surgery. Kathryn underwent the surgery but developed postsurgical complications, primarily chronic pain that had a major adverse impact on the couple's sexual life. At the time Lindsey sought counseling she was concerned because her partner had fallen into a significant depression, and their inability to have a sexual life was becoming extremely problematic for Lindsey. She had a healthy, higher sex drive and had no outlet within the confines of their monogamous—now asexual—relationship.

Kathryn had suggested the possibility of opening up the partnership to allow Lindsey to have other sexual partners to meet her sexual needs. Lindsey had come to counseling in part to explore her feelings and examine how she felt about acting on this option.

Objectives and Course of Treatment

The initial objectives of therapy with Lindsey included understanding the complex background of her marriage/partnership with Kathryn and how elements of her own individual history had affected her relationship choices. Another early objective was to understand the history of Lindsey's relationship with Kathryn and how Kathryn's formal gender transition had affected the relationship dynamics and the nature and quality of the intimacy in their relationship.

A major part of the work in therapy consisted of helping Lindsey sort through her feelings of loss and disappointment about Kathryn's deterioration in mood and functioning following her unsuccessful surgical procedure. Another key element of the work involved examining fully the proposed option of expanding the relationship beyond monogamy. Kathryn had raised the idea in several of their candid discussions about their sex life and about Lindsey's disclosure about the ways in which her sexual needs were not being met. Initially Lindsey responded to the suggestion with surprise and feelings of uncertainty. She wondered whether it would be "disloyal" to open the relationship to other sexual partners. In therapy we explored the positive and risky elements of making the decision to open up the relationship. Although I considered bringing Kathryn into a couple of the sessions, it seemed unnecessary given her complete support of Lindsey in this regard and Lindsey's stated desire to have a private place to sort out her individual feelings.

This exploration led to Lindsey's decision to try the open relationship, and she decided to initiate action to find one or more outside lovers to share sexual experience with while remaining committed to the primacy of her partnership/marriage with Kathryn. Kathryn was remarkably open and supportive toward Lindsey as she moved into the open pursuit of auxiliary sexual friendships and sexual relationships. We worked to refine Lindsey's vision of what she was seeking and processed individual options for connection as they arose for her in the course of our therapy work.

Challenges and Interventions

Several challenges arose during the course of our work together. Initially Lindsey had to address issues of apprehension over initiating contact with new potential sexual partners. We explored the specific internal and external barriers she perceived to initiating this course of action. We discussed issues of safety and anonymity involved in meeting people online, which seemed to be the easiest way to meet potential lovers. Lindsey also struggled with feelings of guilt over whether she was betraying vows made to Kathryn by choosing to move into an open relationship. This required work in therapy and work between the couple to redefine what commitment meant to the two of them in the context of their newly fashioned relationship. Lindsey was quite successful in moving through these initial challenges.

Larger issues arose relating to the deterioration in Kathryn's personal and professional functioning relating to her descent into depression. This was actually a more problematic issue for the couple than the opening of the relationship. Kathryn's depression was starting to affect virtually every aspect of their relationship. In this context, childhood issues of abandonment, codependency, and caregiving arose for Lindsey, and this became a primary focus of our individual therapy work.

The focus of therapy shifted to the larger question of whether the partnership could survive the confluence of the multiple stressors that were occurring and the destructive effect they were having on Lindsey's psychological well-being and the relationship. In the meantime, Lindsey initiated a sexual relationship with a new male lover who shared many of her sexual interests. The relationship was sexually fulfilling but emotionally limited, and Lindsey struggled with her own desire for greater emotional involvement in her relationship with her male lover.

Kathryn's struggles with depression and the adjustment issues associated with the initiation of Lindsey's new love relationship created issues that I felt would best be addressed through couples therapy. Lindsey and Kathryn were both open to this idea. I referred the couple to a very expert LGBT- and poly-aware practitioner for relationship counseling. The initiation of this auxiliary therapy modality has been very beneficial for the couple. I coordinated care with the couple counselor to ensure that we cooperated in our efforts to assist both the individual members of the couple and the couple as an entity with their own developmental hurdles.

Outcome

Lindsey has gained a great deal of clarity about her own needs and feelings and has successfully worked through most of the psychological and internal emotional barriers to opening up the relationship in a consensual manner supported by her partner Kathryn. Kathryn's layoff from her high-level professional job led to more depression and created a greater strain on the couple. The couples therapist recommended that Kathryn be evaluated for medication for her depression. Kathryn began taking antidepressants, and her depression has improved dramatically.

Lindsey succeeded in having several sexual experiences and developing a significant emotional/sexual relationship outside of the partnership. However, this relationship has come with its own complications and struggles that have also become a focus of our therapeutic work. Most important, this series of challenges and decisions has opened the door to deeper issues for Lindsey to address. These issues concern self-esteem, posttraumatic stress related to earlier childhood abuse, and other personal psychological issues requiring individually focused therapeutic attention. The couple also continues to pursue couple counseling to address relational issues and the treatment of Kathryn's depression.

Transference and Countertransference

Transference issues have been largely invisible in my therapeutic relationship with Lindsey. This does not mean that such issues haven't arisen or may not arise in the future; rather, they have not been prominent in our work to date. With regard to countertransference, I have had to struggle with my intense empathy for this bisexual woman who is operating in uncharted territory with access to minimal social support.

I have also struggled with my own opinions regarding various courses of action Lindsey is considering with respect to her primary partner and her current lover. It is challenging to keep my opinions separate from my more objective conceptual analysis of the case and my therapeutic interventions. It is helpful to talk to other professionals and receive consultation on these matters from therapist peers, particularly those with experience with LGBT issues and counseling individuals and couples around issues of alternative lifestyles. Lindsey and I continue to meet every 1–2 months to continue this work. This therapeutic story is a work in progress.

Conclusion

These two cases represent only a very small slice of the range of potential clients therapists may encounter as they move more deeply into working with LGBT individuals and families. The work is deeply challenging and also deeply rewarding. Just as there is an absence of roadmaps for our sexual minority clients, there is also an absence of roadmaps for therapists seeking to assist such clients.

Heterosexual, bisexual, gay, lesbian, and transgender therapists each face different challenges in working with LGBT and other sexually alternative clients. Biases, fears, and stereotypes emerge for therapists of every orientation and sexual identity arising from their own positionality with respect to the dominant culture and their own experiences of their sexual identity and personal relationship history. It is important for therapists of every orientation to remain cognizant of their own identity and life experiences and how these affect their work with various clients. Perhaps these case examples can provide a bit of guidance and inspiration to the therapist seeking to learn how to serve sexually diverse clients.

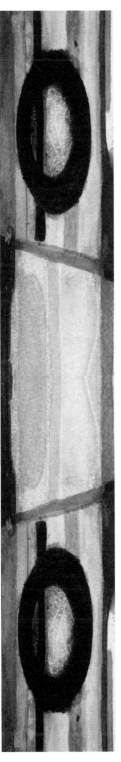

Section 3
Contextual Issues

Competent counselors will

- acknowledge that heterosexism is a worldview and value-system that may undermine the healthy functioning of the sexual orientations, gender identities, and behaviors of LGBT persons.
- understand that heterosexism pervades the social and cultural foundations of many institutions and traditions and may foster negative attitudes toward LGBT persons.
- recognize how internalized prejudice, including heterosexism, racism, and sexism, may influence the counselor's own attitudes as well as those of their LGBT clients.
- know that the developmental tasks of LGBT women and people of color include the formation and integration of their gender, racial, and sexual identities.
- familiarize themselves with the cultural traditions, rituals, and rites of passage specific to LGBT populations.

This section begins with Ron McLean's chapter "Working With African American Lesbian, Gay, Bisexual, Transgender, and Queer People." African Americans who identify as lesbian, gay, bisexual, transgender, and queer (LGBTQ) are still invisible and still face oppres-

147

sion from both within and outside of the LGBTQ community. Dr. McLean attempts to help therapists better understand how cultural oppression promotes depression in same-gender-loving Black men. Relying on Vontress, Woodland, and Epp (2007), Dr. McLean considers the concept of cultural dysthymia, which occurs when cultural institutional practices impose social discontent in a manner that fosters a condition called *dysthymia*. Whereas Vontress and his colleagues use the concept of cultural dysthymia in terms of race, Dr. McLean asserts that it is applicable to sexual orientation as well. Also, Dr. McLean shares a brief synopsis of theoretical concepts that have influenced his counseling process. Finally, after presenting a case history, he offers some ideas and methods for helping same-gender-loving Black men work through a process of overcoming cultural dysthymia, primarily through the use of narrative counseling and other therapeutic concepts.

The second chapter in this section is Mark Pope's "Native American and Gay: Two Spirits in One Human Being." The history of Native Americans in the United States is important to understanding the experiences of clients who are Native American and gay. Dr. Pope begins his chapter with a moving quote from Wilma Mankiller regarding the roles that Christian missionaries and the federal government played in attempting to eliminate the Native culture. He then describes the positive ways in which Native peoples often dealt with those who were different ("two spirited"). This provides the context for the case of Erik, a 32-year-old Cherokee man. When Erik seems stuck, Dr. Pope uses a Native American story (or *guided visualization*, as mainstream cultural therapists would call it) with him. This story helps Erik get in touch with his feelings of closeness to his tribe. Dr. Pope is able to establish a close relationship with Erik by disclosing his own Cherokee background and understanding of the issues Erik was dealing with. Dr. Pope also successfully uses the Native American story technique to help Erik work on other issues, such as his HIV status. In this chapter readers are also exposed to the use of Native American history and customs as therapeutic interventions. The chapter concludes with a review of critical issues for therapeutic work with Native American LGBT clients.

The section continues with Terry S. Gock's "'Why Did God Make Me This Way?' The Case of a Chinese American Gay Christian Man." Sam's case involves many intersecting factors: a Chinese American identity (though Sam was not born in the United States and as a youth he was considered "fresh off the boat"), sexual orientation, and religion. Dr. Gock works with Sam from a strength-based approach that integrates cognitive behavior therapy, psychodynamic therapy, and social–ecological elements. In describing how he uses these integrated theories, Dr. Gock expands on the psychological constructs he considers critical in this case. The issues are similar to those most clients bring to therapy but are described within the context of growing up Chinese, gay, and Christian. This includes the experience of microaggressions, a lack of community resources, and the social conformity expected within Asian culture. It also includes strengths from cultural values such as harmony and self-improvement. This chapter provides another example of the positive impact of the therapist's self-disclosure (Dr. Gock is Chinese American) on the therapeutic process. The fact that both Dr. Gock and his client are Chinese American also invites challenges that Dr. Gock discusses in the chapter.

Samuel Sanabria and Ana Puig continue exploring the intersection of race, ethnicity, and sexual orientation in their chapter "Counseling Latin Gays and Lesbians." Any study of gays and lesbians in the context of Latino culture can be complex because Latinos are not a homogenous population. Yet within the diversity of national backgrounds, social ideals, and distinct cultural histories that make up the vibrant Latino community there are some general themes. It is important to keep this in mind when counseling gay and lesbian Latinos. In general, the ideals of familial duty, gender roles, and religious observance are strongly emphasized, although not every Latino/a may bring these issues to counseling. These principles can lead to less tolerance of lesbian and gay individuals within the Latino population. Thus, it is also important to note the challenge that gay and lesbian Latinos face in integrating their ethnic identity with their sexual orientation.

Latino societal pressures may come with many homophobic messages from family and community, and the gay and lesbian culture may not reflect the fundamental ideals of the Latino culture. Gay and lesbian Latinos may be afraid, therefore, to disappoint their families. They hide their true selves to avoid this but may also separate themselves from other gays and lesbians and the support that they could provide. These stressors can lead to depression, anxiety, substance abuse, and in some cases suicidal ideations.

Drs. Sanabria and Puig present two cases—those of Hector and Sofia—to illustrate these issues. The goal of counseling with Latin gays and lesbians should be to recognize and respect the individual's ethnicity and, within that context, to reduce the effects of homophobia, integrate cultural identities, encourage positive social relationships, and promote self-acceptance.

The next chapter, "Multiracial/Multiethnic Queer and Transgender Clients: Intersections of Identity and Resilience" by Anneliese A. Singh and Kirstyn Yuk Sim Chun, considers the added dimension of transgender. Drs. Singh and Chun discuss two cases that integrate the intersections of racial/ethnic diversity with queer and transgender identities. In the first case they use cognitive behavior therapy, which encourages clients to understand how their thoughts, moods, behaviors, and physical reactions interact in response to their environments (Greenberger & Padesky, 1995). The second case is discussed through a narrative therapy lens. Narrative therapy asserts that clients make meaning of their lives through the "stories" they tell themselves (Combs & Freedman, 1996). Presenting issues are viewed as the result of a "dominant" storyline becoming dissatisfying or unfulfilling to clients' current lives (White, 2007). Drs. Singh and Chun also bring feminist and social justice emphases into their second case (that of Jeremy). This means that they pay attention to the power differential in the counselor–client relationship and issues of societal privilege and oppression that are influencing Jeremy's well-being as a multiracial/multiethnic transgender person.

Drs. Singh and Chun include a diagnosis of gender identity disorder on Axis I for Jeremy to enable discussion in the goals of treatment and to acknowledge the societal stressors that transgender people encounter, but they made it clear to the editors of this book that they do not endorse the inclusion of gender identity disorder in the *DSM*.

Continuing the discussion of transgender and transsexual persons is Randall D. Ehrbar's chapter "Transsexual Case Studies: Transition Is Not the End of the Road." In the *International Statistical Classification of Disease and Related Health Problems*, transsexualism is defined as the

> desire to live and be accepted as a member of the opposite sex, usually accompanied by a sense of discomfort with or inappropriateness of one's anatomic sex, and a wish to have surgery and hormonal treatment to make one's body as congruent as possible with one's preferred sex. (World Health Organization, 1992, p. 365)

This definition is consistent with how some people who identify as transsexual use the term; however, as with other identity terms, there can be disagreements about the term.

Dr. Ehrbar presents two cases. Both are discussed from a trans-affirmative therapy perspective informed by feminist and client-centered therapies. Therapists working with this client population must be familiar with the requirements of the World Professional Association for Transgender Health Standards of Care (Meyer et al., 2001). These standards are flexible guidelines regarding the transition process that establish eligibility and readiness criteria for client access to medical aspects of transition. This takes the form of a letter documenting a client's gender identity, gender history, and mental health. Having a reality-based understanding of the transition process on both a medical and social level is an important part of being ready. Thus, therapists are the gatekeepers to medical transition. Both clients described by Dr. Ehrbar face trauma issues along with transsexual issues. RF also faces issues of aging. Other issues therapists should be aware of when working with transsexual clients is substance abuse and sexual orientation.

The special problems faced by clients who live in rural areas are often ignored. Paul A. Datti addresses the needs of rural LGBT individuals in his chapter "Counseling With Rural Lesbian, Gay, Bisexual, and Transgender Persons." In urban areas, there are often many signs that an LGBT community exists. LGBT bookstores, community centers, bars, and LGBT-owned and -operated businesses proudly display affiliations and rainbow flags. All of this evokes an air of common and normalized culture in which LGBT persons may easily exist among a larger population. This perceived ease of city living is part of what Weston (1995) portrayed in her essay on rural-to-urban migration among lesbian and gay persons. She contrasted the benefits of communities and acceptance in cities with the absence of communities and the abundant persecution in rural areas and suggested these as reasons why many rural persons relocate to big cities.

However, many LGBT persons stay in rural areas (Lindhorst, 1997; Oswald & Culton, 2003). And whether or not they choose to migrate, their experiences and worldviews may be very different from those of LGBT persons from urban or suburban areas. Dr. Datti presents the case of a rural LGBT client that addresses issues encountered by these individuals, presents a counseling approach, and presents recommendations for better serving this population.

The last chapter in this section focuses on religious and spiritual concerns. In "Mario's Journey of Faith," Kathleen Y. Ritter and Anthony I. Terndrup discuss the case of a man who is conflicted about his religious beliefs (Catholicism) and his attractions to men. Drs. Ritter and Terndrup rely on the following theoretical frameworks: cognitive–behavioral, existential, psychodynamic, family-of-origin, and psychoeducational. They want therapists to know that in order to assist clients like Mario in resolving religious issues, they must become familiar with the ideas of James Fowler. Fowler describes the phases individuals go through when developing an authentic and personal faith. Mario's counselor uses Fowler's ideas to conceptualize the case and to help Mario reframe his religious struggles. Another helpful framework for use with this population is that of grief and loss.

References

Combs, G., & Freedman, J. (1996). *Narrative therapy: The social construction of preferred realities.* New York, NY: Norton.

Greenberger, D., & Padesky, C. A. (1995). *Mind over mood: Change how you feel by changing the way you think.* New York, NY: Guilford Press.

Lindhorst, T. (1997). Foundation knowledge for work with rural gays and lesbians: Lesbian and gay men in the country; practice implications for rural social work. In J. Smith & R. Mancoske (Eds.), *Rural gays and lesbians: Building on the strengths of communities* (pp. 1–12). Binghamton, NY: Hawthorne.

Meyer, W., III, Bockting, W., Cohen-Kettenis, P., Coleman, E., DiCeglie, D., Devor, H., . . . Wheeler, C. (2001). *The Harry Benjamin International Gender Dysphoria Association's standards of care for gender identity disorders, sixth version.* Retrieved from http://www.wpath.org/documents2/socv6.pdf

Oswald, R. F., & Culton, L. S. (2003). Under the rainbow: Rural gay life and its relevance for family providers. *Family Relations, 52*(1), 72–81.

Vontress, C. E., Woodland, C. E., & Epp, L. (2007). Cultural dysthymia: An unrecognized disorder among African Americans? *Journal of Multicultural Counseling and Development, 35,* 130–141.

Weston, K. (1995). Get thee to a big city: Sexual imaginary and the great gay migration. *GLQ: A Journal of Lesbian and Gay Studies, 2*(3), 253–277.

White, M. (2007). *Maps of narrative practice.* New York, NY: Norton.

World Health Organization. (1992). *International statistical classification of disease and related health problems* (10th rev., Vol. 1). Geneva, Switzerland: Author.

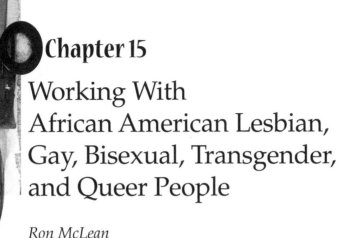

Chapter 15

Working With African American Lesbian, Gay, Bisexual, Transgender, and Queer People

Ron McLean

Throughout this chapter, I attempt to help readers better understand how cultural oppression promotes depression in same-gender-loving (SGL) Black men. First, I share with readers a brief synopsis of theoretical concepts that have influenced my development as a practicing counselor. Second, after presenting a case history, I offer some ideas or methods for how to help Black SGLs work through a process of overcoming cultural dysthymia, primarily through the use of narrative counseling and other therapeutic concepts. Lastly, I articulate and describe implications for counselors to improve practice in this area.

Theoretical Orientations (Guides for Practice)

Over the years my development as a counselor has evolved and been informed by many theoretical orientations. I'll speak briefly about three elements of these theoretical orientations that have been influential in my practice of counseling. I began my career with a strong identification with Rogerian counseling, embracing the idea that the therapeutic relationship is the single most important element for healing psychological wounds. To that orientation was added cognitive–behavioral concepts that purport that individuals frequently upset themselves because of their irrational thoughts, and later narrative concepts were integrated into my brand of helping out of the recognition that we live our lives according to a social script. Sometimes the script needs to be rewritten in order for us to live a life of meaning and purpose. Finally, two larger philosophies, multiculturalism and spirituality, are overarching frameworks that guide my decision making when helping others because of their emphasis on fairness, self-definition, love, and transcendence. In this chapter, I elaborate further on the therapeutic relationship, cognitive–behavioral concepts, and narrative counseling.

Therapeutic Relationships

Over the years I have come to see just how critical relationship building is to the counseling process. Clients come to counselors in need of help and typically have exhausted other resources for solving the problem (e.g., friends, relatives' advice). In the initial session, the client can often be characterized as anxious, uncomfortable, distrusting; they may be feeling weak or hopeless to solve the concern and may be judging the counselor. It is into this clinical arena the counselor steps to accomplish his or her first goal of successfully connecting with the client. For example, in North America, many clients accept direct eye contact, a pleasant tone of voice, and positive body language (e.g., a firm handshake) as indicators that the counselor cares about them. For me, making contact is subtle and intentional or deliberate. I become very aware of how I am using my choice of words, tone, and nonverbal signals to communicate a basic message: *You are a valuable person. I am willing to be nonjudgmental, to understand, and to help you, in an environment of care and support, discover your best decision about your concerns.*

For example, in the case of JC, I became aware early on that he appreciated eye contact and immediate responses. (See JC's case study in the next section.) Sometime he would look at me with a sustained gaze and would ask, "Are you hearing me?" I responded to his gaze by mirroring it back to him, and I would often reflect the feelings I was sensing by responding in the moment, something like, "I can sense the intense hurt you must have felt fearing rejection by your mother." I observed that my warm gaze and attempt at capturing and expressing his emotions caused him to lower his defenses and motivated him to deepen the bond with me. When I am able to consistently and genuinely convey this type of message, the process of trust and therapeutic attachment begins. This early connecting was crucial and help set the foundation for the work that was to come.

Cognitive–Behavioral Concepts

It is interesting to observe the explanations that clients provide when positing reasons for their emotional or mental distress. I feel a sense of intrigue and expertise in understanding the linkages between the quality of one's thoughts and their impact on the client's emotions and behavior. One concept that is of particular interest is the psychoeducational theory rational emotive behavior therapy (REBT). Specifically, the ABC (Activating event, Behavior, Consequences) theory offers strong explanatory power that enhances clients' understanding of how their perceptions of everyday events affect their resultant feelings and behavior. I find that REBT concepts align well with clients who have a proclivity toward cognitive pursuits because such clients prefer rational explanations for phenomena.

Although JC was quite expressive emotionally speaking, he also seemed to have an appreciation for compelling explanations (that is, ones that were irrefutable or rational). The use of REBT aided me in helping JC confront some of his errors in thinking as they related to being gay. Throughout our work together I aimed to teach JC about the ABC theory and how his thinking about being gay (not his being gay itself) contributed to his chronic depression. For example, consider the following client–therapist therapeutic interaction:

JC: I am flawed . . . just wrong.
Counselor: I am confused . . . why do you say that?
JC: I feel depressed . . .
Counselor: There is a part of me that wants to ask you where is the evidence that just by being gay one is flawed or wrong?
JC: My mother says it's wrong . . . it even says it in the Bible.
Counselor: So far I'm hearing you tell me about things you have learned from your upbringing (the way you were socialized) about being gay, but I've not heard any evidence that in fact being gay means being flawed (or less than anyone else).
JC: You know what I mean . . .
Counselor: JC, the fact is that being gay does not mean you are flawed. What is factual is that being gay just means that you are sexually attracted to some males. It is not something to be understood in terms of right or wrong or flawed or unflawed. You have learned from your family and others that being gay is wrong, and that kind of thinking contributes to your feelings of depression. When you house strong negative and irrational thoughts in your mind it influences your feelings, which, because of their complimentary nature, are negative as well.

Here I am attempting to use the REBT concepts to help JC see that his thinking may be irrational and that this contributes to feelings of depression.

Narrative Counseling

To a degree, narrative counseling is quite similar to cognitive–behavioral concepts because it examines how one perceives his or her environment and resultant emotional/behavioral reactions. However, it differs in that its core premise is to view how social or societal forces impinge on one's life, primarily through cultural institutions. For example, one narrative counseling assumption is that we are all living a sociocultural script that is typically imposed by major social institutions such as the government, religion, school, and family. If one complies with the imposed script then he or she is rewarded (e.g., the preferred gender in America is male—males enjoy more of the available privileges). If one does not comply with the social script, then he or she enjoys fewer of the available privileges (e.g., the preferred sexual orientation in America is heterosexual—people who are not heterosexual are subject to all kinds of cultural rejection in important areas of life such as the workplace, schools, family, and legal arenas). *My role as the counselor is to help the client see how hegemony and subjugation has developed in his or her life because of a social script that benefits the powerful and often decimates the client. Next I work with the client to develop the courage to write his or her own script, one that is aligned with who he or she is as an authentic self.* Following the case study of JC, I show how I integrated these concepts in my work with JC.

The Story of Jackster (JC)

JC was an African American gay man on the down low. He was 34 years old and was quite nervous and highly secretive when he came to counseling (e.g., he gave me his home address and then emphasized that I should never send mail to that address). He had graduated from high school and completed 2 years of college. He was employed as a blue-collar worker and lived alone.

JC described his family background as unpleasant. He was the oldest of four children born to his parents and the only boy. His father was physically abusive and eventually left the family when JC was 12. His divorced mother worked long hours to care for him and his three sisters. As the oldest sibling, he was expected to take care of his sisters and managed the home while his mother worked. He was called "the rock" in his family because he was the one everyone in the family depended on.

Though his mother worked long hours, it was hard for her to make ends meet. JC reported many occasions when he was hungry and recalled moving from place to place because the rent had not been paid. Moreover, he remembered that his mother had several live-in boyfriends, some of whom he was secretly fond of.

JC described himself as a feminine boy and had known from an early age that he was attracted to boys. His mother was the central figure in his world, and he adopted many of her values about men. For example, he learned that men can't be trusted. He also learned that it was wrong for a man to be sexually attracted to another man, and this caused him substantial angst, as he was becoming aware of his same-sex attractions.

This angst caused him to develop a false personality in an attempt to deny his true gay self. He consciously worked to develop this false personality or "The Rock" identity. He became his mother's quasispouse and helped her rear the younger children, listened to her speak about her soured relationships, and offered emotional support when the next eviction notice came. He helped his siblings with their homework, got them ready for school, and stood up for them when they were bullied at school. He was the foundation, a solid rock for everyone!

JC learned how to be The Rock so well that he fooled himself into believing that this persona was who he really was. He felt happier and worth something when everyone depended on him. He stated, "I felt in control." However, he was paying an emotional price for denying his emerging gay awareness. He said that as a teenager "I developed another life . . . it's like I am living two lives . . . ." JC began having sexual encounters with other men on the down low. He described many of these experiences as negative, leaving him feeling guilty, ashamed, and worthless. Yet these feelings did not stop him from having sexual encounters. The soul-killing thoughts and feelings became more intense as time passed. Soon he added alcohol and drugs to help him escape his undesirable emotions. He admitted that he was on a downward spiral that, by the time he reached his 20s, had left him chronically depressed and occasionally suicidal.

JC's Problem-Saturated Narrative (How it Might Be Told in His Voice)

"Hi, my name is JC. I am 34 years old and feel very depressed. You might ask why? Well, I have been trying to answer that question for some time. All I know is that I am extremely unhappy, lonely, sad, and angry. I feel like I can't be myself. It's like I live two lives, and I feel like a fake.

"On the one hand, I am considered the "rock" in my family. I am the oldest child in my family and always helped my mother raise my younger siblings. Growing up I cooked, cleaned, and did my sisters' hair. Since my dad abandoned us, I knew I had to be the man of the house. In the role of the rock I had power and I was in control because everyone depended on me. I felt good about that part of me.

"On the other hand, I am an SGL Black man. This is the part of me that I have kept secret for so many years. I can remember back when I was a teenager and becoming aware that I might be gay. For example, I developed an attraction to my mother's boyfriend and tried to get him to pay attention to me. I had mixed emotions of shame and guilt because I knew it was wrong for me to feel this way toward another male. On the rare occasions he gave me attention (e.g., giving me a compliment) it made me feel good and I would just smile because I could not share my true self, not even to him. I recall crying a lot at night and even thinking about suicide.

"I had to cover up my feelings. I lived in a family and a region that is homophobic. I would not be accepted for being gay because it is wrong for two males to have sex together. What is wrong with me? I am a freak! I prayed, *Lord please take this thing off my back and make me straight.*

"Now that I am in my 30s, I am breaking apart. Though I still am the rock and now I help a new generation (i.e., my siblings' children) deal with their problems, it is becoming harder to hide who I am. I have come to the unbearable awareness that either my family is in deep denial of who I am or my true self is genuinely unknown to them. Either way, I remain invisible, alone, and more empty than ever. I want companionship with a man but I fear I will be found out and rejected. Life is too hard . . . I do not want to live like this."

Assessment/Diagnoses

From a narrative counseling perspective, JC was embedded in a culture that devalued who he was as a sexual minority. Social scripts from the general society and the Black community had been imposed on him and included strong negative messages about nonheterosexual identities. As a result of these socially imposed cultural scripts, JC had been unable to reconcile his authentic self (i.e., an SGL Black man) with the cultural mores and social roles expected of men. As a result, there was a large and looming gorilla on

JC's back that caused significant distress and that was manifested as major depression or cultural dysthymia. JC felt out of control and was uncertain how to get the gorilla off his back.

Although narrative counselors do not necessarily subscribe to the use of the *Diagnostic and Statistical Manual of Mental Disorders* because of its focus on the intradynamics of an individual, I take clinical latitude here to outline the following assessment of JC that is more aligned with the *Diagnostic and Statistical Manual of Mental Disorders* (American Psychiatric Association, 1994):

Axis I	Major depression
Axis II	None
Axis III	None
Axis IV	Cultural oppression against sexual minorities
Axis V	Global Assessment of Functioning = 48

JC admitted feelings of chronic sadness, hopelessness, and suicidal ideation. He found it difficult to concentrate or take action on daily activities and often got agitated easily. He reported no known or observed personality disorders or general medical conditions. There was evidence to suggest that he was having major challenges adjusting to life as an SGL Black man in a society that was racist, homophobic, and discriminatory toward him. I estimate that JC's global functioning was at 48, which indicates moderate emotional impairment.

Goals and Treatment

Working from a narrative perspective, in a real sense, involves educating the client about how dominant social scripts are used to subjugate Black SGL men and identifying appropriate tools (e.g., externalization, deconstruction, reauthoring) for eradicating this kind of trauma. It was important to help JC understand that his personal identity as an SGL Black man was not the problem. Rather, the problem was the social forces imposed on him to comply with expected social roles. Dominant groups in society (e.g., Whites, heterosexuals, Black community leaders) use their power to their advantage to subjugate and/or force weaker groups (e.g., SGL persons) to comply with their expectations (e.g., become heterosexual or keep their nonheterosexual orientation invisible). I used an interrelated process called *externalization* and *deconstruction* to help JC become aware of how cultural oppression subjugates him.

Externalization or externalizing helped JC see the problem of social oppression against Black SGL people as something being pushed into his life and see that his personhood and value were separate from the prejudice and discriminations that may be levied at him. Moreover, a concomitant process called deconstruction or deconstructing provided JC a way of evaluating the merits of hegemonic cultural scripts and literally breaking down those social expectations or assumptions that promoted further subjugation of JC's personhood.

For example, requesting that JC give the distressing problem a name, such as the "gorilla on my back" or the "black cloud that hovers over me," helped him to begin the externalizing process. Externalizing helped JC change the location of the distressing problem from inside himself (e.g., "I am defective" or "I must be an awful person") to outside himself (e.g., "It is unfair that others place social expectations on me that do not fit who I am as a person"—the gorilla). Externalizing decreases debilitating self-blame and motivates the client to take action to solve the problem. It is a first step to deconstructing proscribed misaligned social scripts and later opens up avenues for alternative social scripts, or what I call "reauthored stories."

Dominant narratives had shaped JC's views of himself. For example, the larger society told him that he was sinful, flawed, and unworthy of respect or social privileges because he was a Black SGL man. *Thin descriptors,* superficial definitions of a subjugated group or community typically used by outside observers, had been used to further oppress JC and people like him (e.g., by calling them child molesters, a threat to the family, and other derogatory names). JC's current problem-saturated narrative was characterized by shame and guilt, and he saw himself as defective. So in effect, his internalized messages were telling him that he was twice flawed in being Black and gay.

Similar to externalizing, narrative counseling helped JC to deconstruct the oppressive thin descriptions and assumptions that had been pushed into his life by the dominant society. Deconstruction is a strategy for breaking down the repressive assumptions made about his identity and evaluating them. The assumption that Black SGL men do not deserve respect was a serious challenge for JC, and this became the centerpiece of his own self-narrative. This perception was so deeply planted in his consciousness that he struggled exhaustively to keep his SGL personality hidden and invisible.

I used deconstruction to help JC examine his self-narrative by asking certain key questions to break down assumptions and increase JC's awareness of the oppression in his self-narrative. For example, I asked, "How is this problem getting in the way of you living your life?" "What does your mind tell you about why you should keep living this way?" "When was the last time you were able to stand against homophobia?" "What would it be like if you took a stand against homophobia?" Through the use of these type of questions, then, deconstruction helped JC to see that there were other possible alternatives to living his oppressive self-narrative. As his awareness increased, so did his motivation to make changes and to reauthor his life.

In order to demonstrate how a counselor might use narrative questions, let's consider the following interaction:

Counselor: JC, it seems that you have this monkey riding your back with a very tight grip. The monkey tells you that you must never let anyone know that you are a gay man because being gay is evil and you will be rejected. I am wondering if you would tell me more about how internalized homophobia is getting in the way of you living your life?

159

JC: I am always hiding and feeling ashamed. I feel like if anyone knew who I was they would not want to associate with me. I feel like such a fake, but it is the only way that I can keep from being rejected by my family and friends. I feel so lonely because my true self is invisible to people.

Counselor: I'm wondering if you can give an example of that kind of invisibility?

JC: Yes, I can give you an example. I went to my mother's house a few weeks ago for our annual holiday dinner. My Aunt Mabel was there, and she asked me when I am going to get married. I responded, "When I meet the right girl." I felt my mood drop immediately because I chose to hide. I was angry with myself for being such a fake and weak. I was depressed the rest of the day.

Counselor: So when the monkey is riding you with a tight grip it causes you to think and do things that are hurtful to you and it leaves you feeling very bad. What would it be like if you took a stand against the monkey or internalized homophobia?

JC: Wow! That is hard for me to imagine. I think I would feel pride. What I should have told Aunt Mabel was that I will marry when I find the right man!

First, I used wording to externalize the problem and evoke imagery as to how difficult the problem is (this helps the client to see the counselor's empathic understanding, it paraphrases a core theme that is problematic for the client, and it places the problem outside of the client). Second, "I am wondering if you would tell me more about how internalized homophobia is getting in the way of you living your life?" is a question I used to help increase JC's awareness of how his homophobic narrative was a barrier to his growth and movement toward self-affirmation. Third, the question "What would it be like if you took a stand against the monkey or internalized homophobia?" was used to help JC begin to explore new possibilities for responding in authentic ways. Implementing the use of narrative questions assists the client in moving from being stagnant in the problem to exploring new or better ways of responding to the problem.

Put another way, when the client realizes that his or her previously held assumptions about being gay are part of a dominant-culture script that does not value his or her personhood and that has been forced on him or her as the right way to think, the deconstruction process begins. That is, the client begins breaking apart previously held assumptions and reexamining those assumptions and whether they have merit for who the client is as a person. Typically the sexual minority client discovers other ways of thinking about sexual orientation that are meritorious. As these new understandings become more dominant in the client's awareness, this paves the way to the client taking charge of his or her self-definition and initiates the reauthoring process.

Reauthoring is a term used by narrative counselors to indicate when a client reaches a level of awareness at which he or she begins to coconstruct a new story or social script that is better aligned with who he or she is as a person.

JC's Alternative Narrative (Reauthored in His Voice)

After some time JC began to recognize that his self-narrative was saturated with problems, and he began to make a shift in his thinking. The following is a brief synopsis of his reauthored narrative:

"I have come to see that I am a valuable person worthy of love and respect and that I have the right to create positive meaning and purpose in my life. I now recognize how people who have cultural power have the ability to negatively dominate the lived experiences of those who do not have that power. Frequently, Black SGL men like me have been subjugated in this society, and our 'truth' has been marginalized because it has been misrepresented through thin descriptors of who we are. It is up to me now to find my own voice, continue to reauthor the social script that promotes Black SGL authenticity, and work for social justice to improve my quality of life and the Black SGL community."

JC's reauthored storyline helped him respond to cultural dysthymia in a more effective way. One indication of this is that he no longer assumed that his sexual orientation caused him to be inherently flawed. In fact, the more JC embraced and lived his new social script, the more his feelings of depression and hopelessness dissipated because his new storyline was in alignment with who he was as a person.

Conclusion

Goldenberg and Goldenberg (2004) noted that narrative counselors assist clients in gaining access to a preferred story about their identity instead of the self-defeating and restrictive narrative often imposed by the larger culture. Here I have shown how JC was able to work through a process of externalizing the problem and deconstructing assumptions that distorted his authentic self. JC began to develop his own story about who he was, to live his truth, and to oppose both the restrictive self-narrative and institutionalized cultural narratives that had previously oppressed him as a Black SGL man. I assert that the narrative counseling process is one method for helping this population move beyond cultural dysthymia.

A note of caution seems appropriate at this juncture: Counselors should stay alert to transference and countertransference issues, particularly when they and the client share the same sexual minority status or ethnicity. The power of cultural oppression in this population should not be underestimated. The counselor should "know thyself," be aware of unresolved issues regarding race and sexual orientation, and make sure to avoid projecting onto the client. In addition, once trust has been established, the client may experience the counselor as a beloved authority figure. The client may appear very vulnerable or childlike, and boundaries may become blurred. It is imperative the counselor, while conveying genuine kindness and hope, maintain clear boundaries when assisting the client in reauthoring a new narrative.

My recommendation for JC was that he continue to "thicken" or strengthen his new narrative so that it had sustainability. One idea was to develop a network of individuals who would support him as he further established his authentic story and, by extension, his authentic self (in narrative language we sometimes refer to this as *creating supportive leagues*—groups of people who band together to support the healthy changes that are being made). Finally, JC was encouraged to increase capacity in his authentic self by moving beyond his own personal situation and getting involved in activities for the greater good of humankind that promote respect for human dignity and reaching one's full potential (e.g., participating in an affirming spiritual group or in political activism).

References

American Psychiatric Association. (1994). *Diagnostic and statistical manual of mental disorders* (4th ed.). Washington, DC: Author.

Goldenberg, I., & Goldenberg, H. (2004). *Family therapy: An overview* (6th ed.). Pacific Grove, CA: Brookes/Cole.

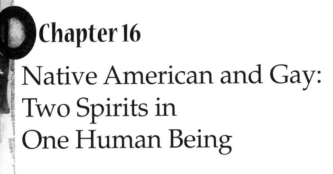

Chapter 16

Native American and Gay: Two Spirits in One Human Being

Mark Pope

The terms *gender roles* and *sexual orientation* give mental health professionals an easy way to talk about these issues, but to traditional Native Americans these are false conceptualizations. Traditional Native Americans never analyzed human sexuality in such dichotomous and categorical ways—ways that are more allied with a European individualist approach. In traditional Native American tribes, there was a continuum of human sexuality and gender behavior that was appropriate for different people. People did what they did best. If one woman was particularly adept at making and shooting arrows instead of beadwork, that is what she did, and maybe she went on war parties and became a chief someday.

Wilma Mankiller was Principal Chief of the Cherokee Nation of Oklahoma from 1985 to 1995. She spoke eloquently in her family biography about the role of the Christian missionaries and federal government in trying to destroy the traditional culture of the Cherokee people:

> Back in the bad old days, the [Bureau of Indian Affairs] representatives who maintained boarding schools such as [the] Sequoyah [School] would go hundreds of miles and return with native children. The philosophy, reflecting an errant missionary zeal, was to get native children away from their families, their elders, their tribes, their language, their heritage. They isolated native children so they would forget their culture. The boarding-school concept was simply another way for the federal government to deal with what its officials always called "the Indian problem." After first trying to wipe all of us off the face of the earth with violence, they attempted to isolate us on reservations or, in the case of many people [such] as the Cherokees, place us in an area that the government called Indian Territory. All the while, they systematically conjured up policies to kill our culture. So the federal government rounded up Indian youngsters and forced them to attend boarding schools whether they wanted to or not. This was true for most tribes, not just the Cherokees. (Mankiller & Wallis, 1993, p. 7)

At Sequoyah School, which was just south of Tahlequah, the capital of the Cherokee Nation of Oklahoma, Mankiller's father and his younger sister were forbidden to speak their native language. Even though they could not speak a word of English when they first entered the school, when they tried to talk to each other in Cherokee they were whipped repeatedly (Mankiller & Wallis, 1993). The whole idea behind these boarding schools, whether they were operated by the government (like Sequoyah School) or by a religious operation, was "to acculturate native people into the mainstream of white society and, at the same time, destroy their sense of self. The boarding-school officials hoped to make the 'little Indians' into 'ladies and gentlemen'" (p. 8). Thus, the teachers cut the Cherokee children's hair short and did not allow them to utter one word of their native language. Often, visits to family and friends back home were denied. The idea was to "civilize the heathen children." There was even a popular expression about "killing the Indian and saving the man."

> Still, the fact remains that the primary mission of Sequoyah and the other boarding-schools was for the children to leave everything behind that related to their native culture, heritage, history, and language. In short, there was a full-scale attempt at deracination—the uprooting or destruction of a race and its culture. (Mankiller & Wallis, 1993, p. 8)

The Native American way of passing on knowledge uses the tradition of storytelling to educate children in cultural values and to reaffirm those values for adults. From those stories, we learn that those who are different have something important to contribute and that we are all related to all things—whether person, animal, plant, or rock.

Various terms have been used to describe "two-spirited" Native American gender roles and sexuality, including *winkte* (Lakota Sioux), *lhamana* (Zuni), *nadleehe* (Navajo), *hwame* (Mohave), *warharmi* (Kamia), *tainna wa'ippe* (Shoshoni), as well as *berdache*. Many different phenomena are defined by the concept of "two spirits" as well as the term *berdache*, including cross-dressing or transvestism, effeminacy in males, the carrying out of female tasks and activities by males, the entering into of homosexual relationships, intersexuality or hermaphroditism, and the carrying out of male social roles by females. The traditional roles of two-spirited people included healing and herbal wisdom, child care, teaching, spiritual leadership, keeping the knowledge of the elders, mediation, interpretation, and all forms of artistic expression.

Native American culture consistently promotes context and would therefore rarely use such dichotomous categories as "gay and straight" or "male and female" to describe such complex phenomena as gender roles and sexual orientation. In fact, in the Native American worldview, even the entire adoption of the feminine gender role by a male does not lead to him being described as female, as there is a difference between gender category and gender status in the Native American way of thinking.

Gender category is more biological, but gender status is more culturally defined. Accordingly, one's gender status may be either man (masculine), woman (feminine), or not-man/not-woman. Not-man is not the same as woman in this model, and not-woman is not the same as man. Women are, by definition, not-men; however, other social groups within a society may consist of males whose gender status is that of not-men but who are also defined as not-women. Such multiple genders are part of gender role construction in Native American societies, and those who serve such cultures must be cognizant of this contextual ambiguity.

Christian missionaries had a much more dichotomous view of the world, and their role was to impose their beliefs onto their new aboriginal converts—the Native Americans. Issues of sin, therefore, became prominent and traditional beliefs were questioned. The demonization of two-spirited people was part of that process and has led to increasing rejection and harassment of two-spirited people on modern-day reservations. This is not surprising, however, considering the efforts of Indian agents, missionaries, and boarding schools to suppress all forms of traditional Indian culture. Many Indian people have been taught by these outsiders to be ashamed of such roles as the *berdache*, and Indian leaders, even traditionalists, have adopted the attitudes of White society toward gay people. Only the elders remember, but even they have been reluctant to speak up.

The cultural characteristics that promoted the acceptance of two-spirited people are extremely important in understanding and fully appreciating traditional Native American cultures. In turn, such appreciation is critical to being able to provide appropriate mental health services to these communities.

The Case of Erik, the "Fancy Dancer"

Erik was a 32-year-old gay Cherokee male. He presented himself at my office with a number of questions that began with one focused on a career decision but soon expanded over the next three sessions to relationships with his partner, aging parents, and tribe as well as his own health.

Erik was originally from a small rural town in northwest Arkansas. His parents had been raised there after his grandparents had escaped from the Trail of Tears death march, which was intended to resettle peaceful Cherokee tribes people from the Carolinas to Oklahoma after the U.S. government had stolen their lands. Erik was the youngest child of parents who were now in their late 70s. He was well educated, had attended a large state university in Kansas on an Indian scholarship, and had completed his undergraduate degree in social work.

Erik had spent the past 10 years living in St. Louis, Missouri, where he moved when he found out that he was HIV seropositive. He had a fairly extensive network of friends and lived with his partner of 10 years. Erik had worked in a number of jobs in social welfare agencies but was currently unemployed because 6 months ago he had become symptomatic with recurring pneumocystis. He was now taking a combination of medications that seemed to have the pneumonia under control and was ready to go back to work.

He had come to see me for career counseling to explore his career options because he was not sure that he could work a full 40-hour week and as a social worker he was burned out by having to listen to other people's problems as well as deal with his own. He was at a loss as to what to do.

Erik loved nature and being outdoors. He talked about how he used to sleep out in the backyard at his grandparents' house all by himself and stay awake all night listening to the insects and feeling the morning dew settle on the sleeping bag. It was truly his happiest childhood memory. He would have loved to return to Arkansas to be with his parents and grandparents, but his AIDS and the required medical care kept him in the city. Erik also loved his Cherokee heritage and had been a prize-winning Native American dancer at powwows all over the country. He competed in the "Fancy Dancer" category, which is a highly costumed dance characterized by intricate footwork and rapid spins. Also, his partner was an attorney and had a thriving legal practice. Erik was aware of how difficult it would be to move such a practice to another state.

Erik had previously been seen by a career counselor at his university when he had made a decision to go into social work. That counselor mailed me Erik's results on some inventories, including the Strong Interest Inventory and the Myers–Briggs Type Indicator. These inventories had been taken 8 years earlier, and they indicated a preference for Social, Artistic, and Investigative (on the Strong Interest Inventory) and Extraversion, Intuition, Feeling, and Perception (on the Myers–Briggs Type Indicator).

At the initial interview Erik presented as a medium-height, slender, well-groomed, and, even at age 32, "young" man with medium-brown hair and hazel eyes. He was intelligent, soft-spoken, but quite verbal as he discussed what had brought him to my office that day. It was obvious to me that he had been thinking about all of this a lot. He first discussed his presenting problem: He was not sure what direction he wanted to go with his career.

He then began to lay out in detail all of the many contextual issues that made this decision so complicated for him. With little prompting from me, he presented a coherent narrative that described his life from birth to the present day. He seemed to have great insight into many facets of the issues but could not put it all together, make a plan, and move forward. He said "I'm stuck" as he ended his lengthy narrative and looked at me, seeming to say, "Now what do we do?"

I responded to his narrative by keeping the focus on the career issues but knew that he had even more to discuss. Those other issues would emerge naturally as we progressed with the career counseling, I was sure.

At the next session Erik appeared excited and yet sad as he entered the office and sat down on the couch. I did not have to prompt much before he began to talk about the anniversary celebration that he and his partner had just had. It was their 10th anniversary and his partner had taken him to San Francisco for the weekend. They had eaten at restaurant in the Castro (the primary gay neighborhood in San Francisco) that focused on French–Japanese fusion cuisine. They had sat at a romantic table for two in a candlelit dining room with soft modern Japanese music by Agatsuma playing in the background.

It was very special for Erik, but he was also aware of his sadness immediately after the evening ended and even during the meal. He said, "It's not fair to my partner." When I responded, "Not fair?" he went on to say that it was his own sadness that was not fair to his partner. Here they were in this very special restaurant, in this very special city, celebrating this very special and most important event in their lives, and suddenly he was aware of being sad, very sad. At a time when he was "supposed" to be happy for having 10 years together with this very special man, he was sad. And he was confused because he did not understand why.

What remained of the weekend went very well and they returned home to St. Louis late Sunday night, both very happy with their anniversary celebration in San Francisco. But Erik wanted, needed to understand why this had happened.

I worked with him to brainstorm all of the possible causes of the sadness—problems with his relationship, problems with his HIV status, problems with his career—but nothing was emerging. He was way up in his head and staying there.

I decided to use a Native American story to help him access his feelings. In counseling, we might use this as a type of guided visualization, but in Indian country we call this a "story" because that is how many of our intergenerational lessons are imparted and how our history is kept. So I told him that I had a story for him.

I then proceeded to use a guided visualization intervention to see whether that might help uncover the reason for Erik's sadness. And as I led him through the visualization, during a section in which I had presented his parents as part of the process, he started to gently cry. I brought him out of the intervention process to explore what had happened. He said, "I was sorry that we did not spend our anniversary with my family in our tribal home in Arkansas."

He said, "I miss my parents, my family, our tribe. Our tribe has always been truly one big happy family, and we always have celebrated our special events together."

I asked about the tribe's and his family's feelings about his sexual orientation and his HIV status.

He replied, "Cherokees have a long history of accepting two-spirited people."

I told him that I knew that two-spirited people—the phrase that has come to be used in Native communities for anyone who is lesbian, gay, bisexual, intersex, or transgender—were generally accepted in our Cherokee community, especially the more traditional ones that practiced the old Cherokee spiritual ways, but I also knew that some fundamentalist Christian denominations had also found their way into our *Tsalagi* (the Cherokee word for "Cherokee" or "human being") communities and had turned some against the people of two spirits. I was just trying to find out whether his community was more traditional or more fundamentalist Christian in its ways. Erik said, "No, we have maintained our traditional ways, but there are some who now also go to the Baptist church and other churches near where we live."

He told me the story of how his family, including his parents, aunts, uncles, nephews, nieces, brothers, sisters and their partners, all their children, and his parents' neighbors along with the principal chief and elders of the tribe had welcomed him back when he returned from college. They knew that he was two spirited, and they all turned out at his parents' home to honor his family for their son's achieving a college degree and returning to his tribal home.

Furthermore, in his tribe his two-spirited status actually gave him special recognition. He was, in fact, accepted and loved and honored for this. The tribe also believed that this gave him special powers that flowed through him when he danced at tribal celebrations. His great uncle, who was two spirited as well, was the medicine person for the tribe, so his family had a long history of accepting and loving their two-spirited family members, as did his tribe.

As his narrative deepened, Erik became aware that his sadness was about more than not just spending the anniversary celebrating with his family and tribe. It was intertwined with his HIV status, which always hung over his remaining life. It wasn't that his HIV status was always in the foreground of his consciousness, but it did pop into his mind at what seemed to be inopportune times, like when he had been celebrating with his partner, as he became aware that this might be the last anniversary that he and his partner might celebrate together and the last celebration that he might have with his entire family and tribe. And so with the awareness that each celebration might be his last, he was sad. Not always sad, not every day, but this sadness was part of his life. Together we conceptualized this issue as one of feelings of sadness impinging on daily life events. Together we worked to develop a coping approach.

I again used a story. This time it was to remind him of the story of the Cherokee Trail of Tears death march, when the U.S. government forcibly removed the Cherokees from the Carolinas and marched thousands them across Tennessee, Kentucky, and Missouri in the dead of winter to new lands in Oklahoma. It is a story that every Cherokee and almost all Native Americans know, but this time I helped Erik focus on the feelings of those who were in the march—their great feelings of sadness about losing their homes, watching their families die along the way, being mistreated by the soldiers, and finally arriving in a new land they neither wanted nor understood the way that they had understood the lands they had left behind. I spoke about the personal internal process of how they survived along the trail and how they began to first cope and then thrive in these new lands as the Cherokee Nation of Oklahoma and the United Keetoowah Band of Cherokees. I also spoke about how our people had learned to both feel the feelings and then let them go—for to harbor such hatred and resentment and allow it to fester would only do harm to themselves and our people. (But also we must cognitively never forget.)

With this issue, I wanted to help him accept this—to learn to stay in the moment, accept the feelings of sadness when they arose, and let them go. I also wanted to help him reframe this a bit so that he could also begin to feel that it was then also a time to enjoy and celebrate the moment by staying in the moment, by maintaining full awareness, and, as the feelings of sadness came, by letting them pass through him.

We did not directly address any of Erik's career issues at this session. Erik decided that he wanted to stay focused on the issues of sadness first, to see where this might lead. He even said that it might resolve some of the career issues if we addressed these other powerful feelings first.

In the third session, Erik wanted to talk about his partner and his family, especially his parents. He and his partner had been talking about returning to northwest Arkansas and his family's community. Erik was pining for nature. He had recurring dreams of being wedged tightly into the bottom of a big concrete hole in the street, feet up, head down, hundreds of feet deep and three feet wide, arms caught tightly at his side, unable to move. He could not get out. He was smothering to death, ever so slowly but surely.

Erik knew that he wanted to go home to be near nature with his parents on their farm in the Ozark Mountains, but he also knew that he would have to leave his partner to do that, because his partner's legal practice was located in St. Louis and was not readily transferable to another location. There were many reasons not to go—his partner was not admitted to the bar in Arkansas, he was not known there, he was of Irish–German ancestry and had always lived in an urban environment, he owned a house in the city, and he and Erik both currently lived off of the money his law practice provided because Erik had not been working for quite awhile. Although Erik loved his partner deeply and had accepted the fact that he would not be able to return to nature, it did not remove the yearning.

Erik did not seem to be able to resolve this dilemma.

I asked Erik whether we might "smudge" at this point. *Smudging* is the Native American practice of using an herb, such as sage, sweet grass, or cedar chips, for purification. The herb is burned, creating smoke, and the smoke is directed over the person or into the space that is being purified. For example, it is common for all new events in a person's life (a new home, a new baby, a new coupling) and all difficult events (a problem negotiation, a difficult meeting, and many others) to begin with smudging.

My feeling was that the smudging might serve to symbolically carry off the blockage to creatively resolving this dilemma. It is powerful spiritual and social imagery among Native Americans and can serve to center the person and calm inner conflictual voices. For those who are Native, it seems to trigger a meditative response. We smudged at the start of a recent meeting of the Native American Concerns group of the Association for Multicultural Counseling and Development, and that process helped facilitate the smooth functioning of a potentially difficult meeting.

Erik eagerly agreed to the smudging and afterward was able to access his dilemma more clearly. His brainstorming of options flowed easily then. Part of all this were his feelings of great responsibility to his mother and father and family back home. Sure, he missed nature, but he could go to nature whenever he wanted to—he had his garden in the city as well as Forest Park, the largest metropolitan park in St. Louis proper. There were even parts of Forest Park that reminded him of back home, and he could and did go there often on an as-needed basis. And most of all, he was with his partner who loved him deeply and wholly. That love replenished his soul, and the thought of living apart from this dear person was too much for him to bear.

I knew that he would still pine for the Ozarks, but he had more resolution of this important issue. It would not go away, but it became manageable when he clarified his values and options and accepted the dilemma. As at the previous session, as the feelings of sadness came, he was resolved to allow himself to acknowledge them, feel them, and let them pass through him. He did not have to hold on to them and let them fester.

With some resolution of these issues, Erik was ready to go on and so he began the next session with the issue that he had presented when he first came to me—career. He said that he was ready to address this now.

I took him at his word and pulled out his results on the Myers–Briggs Type Indicator (Extraversion, Intuition, Feeling, and Perception) and the Strong Interest Inventory (Social, Artistic, and Investigative). I first wanted to verify that he felt that these were accurate. He said that they were.

Then I asked him what he felt was wrong for him about being a social worker. He replied that he had so many of his own medical and emotional problems that he felt he had "burned out about hearing others' problems right now."

I reflected back to him that "felt" was a past tense verb, and he responded that the past few sessions with me had moved him to a different place emotionally. He just felt differently now than he had previously about career issues. He said, "Maybe social work and helping others is not the problem," that he really did like helping others but his issues had overwhelmed him and the bout of pneumocystis especially had scared him. Now that the crisis part of all this had passed and he felt more resolution with his family, partner, and place issues, he was questioning his previous questioning of his career choice.

He also informed me that he had even danced recently at an intertribal gathering at the Cahokia Mounds just east of St. Louis. It was the first time that he had danced at such a gathering in over a year.

The rest of that session and a few more were spent discussing his career and tweaking his relationships with his partner, friends, and family, but he had new tools now—awareness and letting go. Those tools were life affirming and life changing. And he had a new approach to life and an appreciation of both "the moment" and what he already had.

This was manifested in many ways but was reported to me by his partner, who noticed that Erik began saying "I love you" more to his partner each time he left for work or went on a business trip. If something happened to his partner when they were apart, Erik wanted the last words that he had spoken to his partner to be "I love you." And his partner gladly reciprocated this new behavior.

The other issues did not evaporate into thin air, but they were all much more manageable, as Erik had resolution and new tools.

Issues

The issues Erik faced included the following:

- The right vocation for him
- His HIV status and its role in his life
- The salience of his various cultures
- The growing fundamentalist religious influence in his tribe that could potentially affect his relationships with other tribal members
- His relationship with his partner

- His relationship with his parents, family, and tribe and the role of nature in his life
- His sadness at not being at home with his parents and his big extended family

Diagnosis

Axis I	309.9	Adjustment Disorder (unspecified)
Axis II	V71.09	No Diagnosis
Axis III	042.0	AIDS, with pneumocystis (in remission) (*International Classification of Diseases*, Ninth Revision, Clinical Modification)
Axis IV		Occupational problems
Axis V		Global Assessment of Functioning = 75 (highest level in the past year)

It is important to note here that what Erik was experiencing was sadness and unawareness of feelings, not depression. Certainly there were some aspects of depression, but as the symptoms never grew into a full-blown mood disorder diagnosis or even 309.0 Adjustment Disorder with depressed mood, diagnoses were ruled out. Furthermore, the diagnosis of psychological factors affecting medical condition was ruled out because it was actually medical factors affecting the psychological condition.

There were no manifestations of a personality disorder or pervasive cognitive impairment that might lead to an Axis II diagnosis.

The Axis III (General Medical Condition) diagnosis was based on Erik's HIV status and manifestation of symptomatology (pneumocystis, but in remission).

The Axis IV (Psychosocial and Environmental Problems) diagnosis was based on Erik's initial statement of his problem.

The Axis V (Global Assessment of Functioning) was based on his medical status (in remission) and his response to treatment.

Implications for Counseling

My theoretical orientation is cognitive–behavioral with a dash of humanistic–existentialist thrown in. I was trained by a radical behaviorist (Dr. Steven Zlutnick) at the University of San Francisco, who had been trained at the University of Utah and who had grown up in University City, Missouri, a major suburb of St. Louis.

When a mental health professional sees a two-spirited person or someone who is trying to cope with a loved one who is two-spirited, here are some things to keep in mind. First, it is important to assess the degree of acculturation of the individual and his or her family into the dominant U.S. culture. The more the person has been acculturated into the dominant U.S. culture, the fewer of these recommendations will apply. The more the person has maintained his or her traditions and beliefs as a Native American, the more likely these recommendations will apply.

Second, it is important to assess the degree of religiosity (Christian religion) of the individual and his or her family. The more the person has been acculturated into a Christian sect (especially a fundamentalist one), the less likely he or she will be able to accept his or her sexual orientation.

Third, it is important to keep in mind what kind of gender role and sexual orientation the individual identifies with—for example, cross-dressing, transvestism, effeminacy in males, the carrying out of opposite-gender tasks and activities, the entering into of homosexual relationships (sexual orientation), and intersexuality or hermaphroditism. Any or all of these may be included in that person's definition of two spirited or gay/lesbian. It is important to clarify specifically the individual's operational definition so that any proposed interventions can proceed in an accurate context. Remember that the issue of gender role or sexual orientation may not be the problem; however, it is always the context for the individual.

Fourth, use readings such as this chapter to assist the client in understanding the issues of sexual orientation and gender role from a Native American perspective.

Fifth, consider protracted cultural immersions in traditional Cherokee situations to reverse dominant-culture programming.

Sixth, assess your own prejudices as a professional counselor toward gay and lesbian culture or toward Native American culture to be sure they are not getting in the way of your client's healing.

Seventh, consider consultation or cocounseling with a Native American medicine elder. This other person may provide the necessary objectivity to allow you to be an effective counselor, and you may learn something about traditional ways of healing.

Eighth, consider involving the entire family in the counseling process. Rarely are decisions in a traditional Native American family made by a single individual. Rather, the entire extended family is involved in this process. Bring the entire extended family and make this system an ally instead of an antagonist.

Ninth, acknowledge that joking or humor is a traditional Native American way of imparting important information to another person. Mental health professionals may use humor to present important information to a client.

Tenth, use symbols and stories in your counseling process. These are well understood and have much power in Native American culture.

The bottom line is that the concept of two spirits in Native American culture broadly encompasses all gender status behaviors, including but not limited to sexual orientation, and that understanding this is important to providing effective services to this important American population.

References

Mankiller, W., & Wallis, M. (1993). *Mankiller: A chief and her people.* New York, NY: St. Martin's Press.

Chapter 17

"Why Did God Make Me This Way?" The Case of a Chinese American Gay Christian Man

Terry S. Gock

Identifying Data

Sam was a 34-year-old Chinese American. He had a tall and slim build. He dressed fashionably but conservatively in business attire for our sessions.

Background Information

Sam had been sent by his parents from Taiwan to the United States when he was about 14 years old to live with his adult sister and her family. They lived in a medium-size suburb with a relatively small Asian population. His parents had sent him to the United States in hope that he could get a better education and future.

Sam had grown up in a middle-class family in his home country and reported a relatively uneventful childhood. He was the younger of two children born to his intact parents. He was a better than average student in terms of his academic performance and was relatively popular and outgoing with his peers. He was unprepared for the culture shock when he was suddenly moved to the United States. He became socially withdrawn in his predominantly Caucasian American school and neighborhood because he felt "they were unwelcoming at best." He felt out of place because the few Asian American students at his school were U.S. born and he was considered an "FOB" (fresh off the boat). He kept to himself at school and spent his free time in high school concentrating on his academic work. His primary social outlet was his sister's family and the members of a small Chinese fundamentalist Christian church he attended with them in a nearby city.

Because of his good academic performance in the United States, Sam was admitted to a well-known university in a metropolitan city with a large Asian American population. He became more socially outgoing and began to become conscious of his attraction to other men. He felt confused and conflicted about these feelings during his first year in college but did not act on them. Rick, his assigned dormitory roommate during his junior year, turned out to be an openly gay Caucasian American man. Sam found the courage to open up to Rick about his emotional conflicts surrounding his attraction to other men after the two of them became friends that year. Rick introduced him to the lesbian, gay, bisexual, and transgender (LGBT) organization on campus, some of his own gay friends, and the various resources available on the Internet.

Sam gradually began to meet some other gay men through the Internet and the LGBT organization on campus and had his first sexual experience near the end of his senior year. However, he remained quite secretive about such encounters. In fact, except for with a few close friends, he remained quite closeted throughout his college years and beyond. As time went on, he became more accepting of himself as a gay man. However, he kept telling himself that he should not have to disclose his same-sex attraction to others, as his sexual orientation was "nobody else's business." He also came to recognize that his attraction to other males had begun when he was quite young, although he had not had any understanding of or label for such feelings. He thus had tried hard to ignore it.

After receiving a master's degree in business administration, Sam began to work as a financial analyst in a large investment firm in the same city where he had attended college. Because of his good technical skills he was rewarded with promotions despite being perceived as quiet and socially aloof around his office. He stayed closeted at work for fear of jeopardizing his career. He also kept his gay sexual orientation from his parents and sister (all of whom, by this time, had moved to the city where he was living). He was concerned that they would disapprove of, and be disappointed with, him. In particular, he was afraid that his sister would not allow him to see her children, whom he adored, because of her conservative Christian beliefs.

With respect to his current religious practice, Sam indicated in our sessions that he still shared most of the religious beliefs of the fundamentalist Christian faith he had subscribed to since his teenage years and considered himself to be a "devout Christian at heart." However, he related that he had seldom attended worship services in the past few years and had avoided participating in other church activities, to the disappointment of his sister. He explained that this was because he had difficulty resolving the conflict between his sexual orientation and the antigay rhetoric espoused by his church. Moreover, although he had learned of gay-affirmative Christian churches in the metropolitan area where he was living and had gone to some with Jim (the man he was dating), he found it difficult to relate to their generally more progressive religious tenants despite being "somewhat drawn to their belief in God's unconditional love." He thus had not felt comfortable returning to these religious institutions, although he was aware they existed.

About 3 years ago, Sam met Jim, a Caucasian American man about his age, through a gay dating website. Their ensuing romance led to their considering themselves as "steady boyfriends" although they did not live together primarily because of Sam's concern that his family would become suspicious about his sexual orientation. In fact, Sam's closeted lifestyle became a source of constant conflict in their relationship, as Jim was much more open with others about his sexual orientation. Although Sam became quite well integrated into Jim's social, work, and family circles, Jim was virtually shut out of Sam's. A few weeks ago, Jim broke up with Sam because he reportedly could not stand repeatedly having been excluded from Sam's "other life" of his family, work, and straight friends when they were a couple.

Presenting Issues

Although Sam was seldom demonstrative about his feelings, it was not difficult for his friends and coworkers to notice that he was sad about something. However, they didn't know why. When he asked his primary care physician for medication to help him sleep after his breakup with Jim, the physician suggested that he might also consider psychotherapy. Although he was initially resistant to this idea, he agreed after Rick (his gay college roommate with whom he had remained friends throughout the years) also urged him to do so. His first treatment session occurred about 6 weeks after his relationship breakup.

In our initial session, Sam reported that he would often cry when he thought about his breakup with Jim (and did so during our initial session when this topic was discussed). In addition, he noted that he had difficulty falling asleep and would reminisce about his relationship with Jim whenever he would close his eyes. He also related that he had not felt like eating after they had broken up. In fact, his parents and sister had commented recently that he appeared to be thinner and expressed their concern about him. Despite his desire to just stay home, Sam had made himself go to the office everyday. However, his work productivity and quality had suffered, as he would often find himself ruminating about his breakup instead of attending to his work. Sam blamed himself for the breakup because of his reluctance to open up to others about his sexual orientation and his relationship with Jim. He also felt hurt that Jim could not be more accepting and understanding of his fear about coming out to his family, including his having to go on dates with women arranged by his family occasionally in order to maintain his facade as a straight man.

As our sessions progressed, Sam related that he had often felt that he was not as good as others, although he had never told anyone about that. He could not say for sure when such feelings began but related that they had been getting more intense in the past few years. Although his difficulty accepting his sexual orientation and his relationship breakup contributed to his low self-concept and feeling of inadequacy, it appeared that such feelings had been pervasive for a while despite his outward appearance of being successful at school and at work. Along this line, Sam related that for periods of time from "a few days to more than a week practically every month" in the past few years he would feel depressed and disinterested "about everything." During such periods, he would prefer to be left alone after work and on weekends. Although he would spend time with Jim when invited to do so, he would not initiate any contact. He would also begrudgingly perform such social obligations as visiting with his parents and sister's family, but whenever he could he would try to make excuses to cut short their time together. As we explored these presenting issues, Sam acknowledged that his depressed mood, sense of insecurity about himself, and periods of social withdrawal had likely been problematic throughout his relationship with Jim, although he did not recognize it at that time.

Diagnostic Impressions

Based on the presenting issues and background information described previously, the following are the diagnostic impressions using the *Diagnostic and Statistical Manual of Mental Disorders* (4th ed., text rev.; American Psychiatric Association, 2000) criteria:

Axis I	309.0	Adjustment Disorder With Depressed Mood
	300.4	Dysthymic Disorder, Late Onset
Axis II	V71.09	No Diagnosis
Axis III	None reported or apparent	
Axis IV	Problem with primary support group (relationship dissolution with same-sex partner)	
Axis V	Global Assessment of Functioning = 52	

An adjustment disorder with depressed mood was considered to be the principal diagnosis for Sam at this time because it was the primary reason for his seeking psychological intervention. Because further exploration in our sessions revealed a pattern of chronic depressive symptoms with an insidious onset for at least a few years before his relationship dissolution, an additional diagnosis of dysthymic disorder was included. Although it was unclear when these depressive symptoms first began, Sam reported that they had become more prominent and frequent in the past few years. A "late onset" qualifier was thus used here.

No personality disorder was included in his diagnostic formulation at this time. In terms of personality pattern, Sam exhibited a sense of inadequacy and periods of social withdrawal. Although these may be suggestive of avoidant personality disorder, the available data did not warrant such a diagnosis, as these personality traits did not appear to be overwhelmingly inflexible and maladaptive. They also did not seem to be so pervasive that Sam appeared odd or eccentric in a manner that is often typical of those with Cluster A personality disorder diagnoses. In addition, his life experience as a person of color and as a sexual minority who had been living in communities that did not seem to be supportive of his minority status may also have contributed to his negative self-perception.

Sam's multiple behavioral symptoms (such as crying spells, sleeping difficulty, appetite loss) were considered to be in the moderate-to-severe range in terms of severity. Given this and his work and social difficulties as a result of the emotional distress he was experiencing during our initial sessions, a numerical value of 52 was assigned to reflect the moderate-to-severe level of functional impairment he was exhibiting according to the Global Assessment of Functioning Scale.

Theoretical Framework

Although a number of different conceptual frameworks can be used to understand Sam's presenting issues, a strength-based integrative approach that includes cognitive–behavioral, psychodynamic, and social–ecological elements is offered here. I use this framework for this particular case study because I believe this holistic approach can provide a fuller appreciation of those intrapersonal, interpersonal, developmental, and sociocultural factors that contribute to Sam's current psychosocial stressors, behavioral symptoms, and dysfunctional beliefs. It also recognizes those personal strengths and environmental support that are available to assist him in dealing effectively with his presenting concerns.

To appreciate the context of these dynamics, it is necessary to understand the intersectionality of the social identity dimensions that were salient to Sam. Based on his presentation in our sessions, these relevant dimensions include his self-identification as Asian, gay, and Christian. Along this line, despite his developmental experience with social oppression arising from his being both Asian and gay, he appeared to be relatively comfortable and integrated in terms of his Asian and gay identities when he first came in for treatment. His emotional conflicts tended to be more pronounced in the area of his integrating his Christian faith with his being a gay man.

Before highlighting the specific intervention approaches used to help Sam address his presenting issues, I offer a brief description of the key psychological constructs that seem to be pertinent in this case based on this theoretical framework. They form the conceptual guide to inform the selection of interventions described in the "Interventions Used" section.

From the background information mentioned previously, Sam's psychological distress as a result of his relationship breakup was considered to be the proximal impetus for his seeking psychological intervention. His past experience surrounding rejection and abandonment may also have contributed to his current depressive symptoms. In particular, it is likely that the relationship breakup initiated by Jim may have evoked his unresolved emotional experience of perceived abandonment by his parents when he was sent ill prepared to live in this country as a teenager.

In our initial sessions, Sam's negative self-attribution was apparent in his repeatedly making statements such as seeing himself as a failure because he "messed up [his] relationship with Jim." He also made comments like "I will never find another partner like Jim." Although how these negative self-statements and catastrophic generalizations had led to his current presenting symptoms was quite apparent from his presentation in our sessions, he was not aware of the connection initially. Such disapproving and damaging self-beliefs about his relationship breakup seemed, however, to be just one aspect of the pervasive sense of negative self-concept that had fueled his depressive mood and related behavioral symptoms prior to this emotional crisis. In addition to exacerbating his negative self-beliefs and clinical symptoms after his relationship dissolution, it is likely that his poor self-esteem may have significantly and adversely hindered his relationship intimacy with others (including with Jim).

Although Sam's tendency to be socially withdrawn and isolated at work and in his personal life can be attributed to his low self-concept and other depressive symptoms, the impact of the social milieu in which he had grown up in this country needs to be taken into account. In particular, one cannot ignore how the recurrent microaggression he had experienced (e.g., his unwelcoming and rejecting experiences by both his mainstream and his Asian American peers at school) may have contributed to his low self-esteem. In addition, the lack of supportive resources at home and in the community to help him deal effectively with his culture shock and his rejecting experiences after arriving in this country probably further exacerbated his emotional turmoil during that period. Given this and the social conformity expected by his Asian cultural upbringing and reinforced by the fundamentalist Christian church that was his primary social outlet aside from his family in his developmental years, it is understandable that Sam would experience difficulty developing a positive and integrated identity as an Asian gay Christian.

In addition to the conceptual understanding described previously, the emotional assets Sam possessed and the supportive resources he had in his life would need to be recognized in order to complete this theoretical formulation. Along this line, his history of being able to attain both academic and professional success despite his negative self-perception and self-doubt can be considered a strength. In addition, his interpersonal strengths seem evident from his being able to maintain relatively long-term social relationships (such as with Rick, his college roommate) and to seek support from these relationships when needed. Moreover, his willingness to follow through with the recommendation to seek psychological help despite his initial trepidation about doing so was indicative of his positive internal drive and motivation for change.

Treatment Goals

The proximal reason for Sam to seek treatment was the emotional crisis precipitated by his breakup with his boyfriend. In our first session, Sam was quick to acknowledge that reducing such physical and cognitive symptoms as crying spells, sleep problems, concentration difficulty, and appetite loss was foremost on his mind (and that of his primary care physician who had referred him for psychological treatment). We thus agreed on weekly sessions to help him address this treatment goal. With further exploration in subsequent sessions it became clearer for Sam that the emotional turmoil arising from the grief process and his self-blame for his relationship loss was associated with the physical and cognitive symptoms he was experiencing. He thus agreed to include working on these areas as part of his treatment goals.

As the initial presenting symptoms associated with his emotional crisis subsided between 2 and 3 months into our treatment process, Sam's focus in our weekly sessions shifted from his breakup with Jim to both his social discomfort at work and his relationship issues with his family. Along this line, it became more apparent that he had been experiencing depressive feelings and disinterest in "about everything" for at least a few years prior to his relationship dissolution with Jim. Although it was likely that these symptoms had negatively affected his relationship with Jim, Sam felt that "it was just part of [his] personality" at that time. He thus "did not think [he] could do anything about it." Through our sessions, however, he became more aware of how his feeling of inadequacy and his low self-concept were holding him back in his family, professional, and social relationships. He acknowledged that he wanted to work on improving these areas of his life. They thus were included as part of our treatment goals despite his initial belief he could not change them.

Interventions Used

The psychotherapeutic treatment process with Sam spanned a period of 2 years. Although the intervention approaches used varied and were tailored in response to different concerns he presented at different times during the treatment process, they included, in general, crisis stabilization, medication monitoring, supportive exploration, cognitive reframing and belief challenge, resource linkage, and corrective experience. Examples of how these intervention approaches were used with Sam are briefly described here. It should be noted, however, that they were not sequential approaches that followed one another during our treatment process.

As part of the therapeutic engagement process (see "Process Issues" for further discussion), Sam was helped in the initial session to normalize the emotional crisis and functional problems he was experiencing by helping him understand that his grief reactions in response to his relationship loss were uncomfortable but expected. Because he complained that his sleep difficulty and appetite loss had been negatively affecting his daily functioning, we spent time in the first few sessions exploring his past experiences with such symptoms and what had been effective for him in those situations. Along this line, he was able to recall having sleep and appetite problems when he had felt isolated and overwhelmed by culture shock after arriving in this country as a teenager. He also remembered that it had helped for him to "take it easy" with relaxation rituals (such as visualizing favorite places and friends in Taiwan) so that he could "clear [his] mind before bedtime." How these approaches could be updated to assist him in his present predicament became a primary focus during these initial sessions. Besides instilling hope by reminding him of his past success in dealing with similar problems, he was helped to implement practical and realistic ways to experience symptom relief and restore his sense of self-efficacy instead of feeling that he was "out of control in [his] life."

Another area that was explored during the initial sessions was Sam's need for referral for a psychotropic medication assessment to address the moderately severe depressive symptoms that were significantly impacting on his daily functioning. Sam reported that he had been prescribed some sleep medication and an antidepressant by his primary care physician. However, he had felt drowsy and groggy the next morning after taking them. He thus had not continued taking these prescribed medications and expressed his desire to hold off on considering other medications if he could. Moreover, he mentioned that his parents had been cooking him Chinese herbal concoctions to help him restore balance to his *chi* (energy or life force). He remarked that he felt more comfortable with these herbal medications because he was more accustomed to taking them and, unlike the psychotropic medications he was previously prescribed, he experienced no adverse side effects when he took them. Given his trepidation about using psychotropic medication, we agreed to monitor his depressive symptoms and revisit his medication needs if his presenting symptoms did not subside. Because his depressive symptoms reduced over time, the psychotropic medication referral issue was resolved without the need for further follow-up.

A significant amount of time during our treatment process was devoted to helping Sam explore those developmental experiences that had contributed to his pervasive sense of low self-concept. They included but were not limited to his being sent to this country as a teenager with inadequate emotional preparation by his parents, his recurrent experiences with microaggression by his peers in this country, and his constant fear of being ostracized by his family and his faith community if they found out that he was gay. The emphasis was on helping him better understand how these experiences had led to and sustained his low self-concept as well as contributed to his depressive feelings and social isolation even prior to his breakup with Jim. Moreover, how his negative self-attributions had hindered his embracing his gay Asian identity more fully and his emotional availability in deeper interpersonal connections (such as romantic relationships) was a theme we often came back to during our psychotherapeutic treatment sessions.

Increasing Sam's understanding of the negative impact some of his life experiences (e.g., his encounters with unwelcoming peers who put down his ethnic and cultural background when he had first arrived in this country) had on his self-concept was instrumental in enabling him to become more open to tackling his negative self-statements and attributing less self-blame for his predicament. In addition, such understanding was used to help him reframe his self-perception from that of being inherently unworthy to needing to remind himself to counteract these negative self-statements whenever they occurred. Along this line, he was encouraged to increase his pride in his background by recognizing how his cultural values (e.g., harmony and self-improvement to support family goals) had actually been a source of strength for him in attaining his academic and career success.

During our sessions, Sam's explicit and implicit beliefs that gay relationships could not last and that he would "never find another partner like

Jim" were gently but repeatedly challenged by helping him acknowledge the relationships he had been able to develop with other gay people (such as Rick). In addition, he was helped to look at the "source" from which he had come to develop these beliefs (such as his internalized homophobia and the antigay beliefs espoused by the fundamentalist Christian church he attended) in an effort to assist him in counteracting the validity of these beliefs. He was also encouraged to challenge his negative self-attributions surrounding his racial/ethnic identity and sexual orientation and deepen his self-acceptance as a gay Asian man.

Although this gentle challenge was effective in helping Sam develop a healthier gay Asian identity, it was less successful in assisting him to integrate his religious beliefs and his sexual orientation. For example, when an alternative understanding of the biblical passages that had been used by his fundamentalist Christian church to condemn homosexuality was pointed out, he had a problem accepting it. On one occasion he explained his dilemma by saying "I want to, but I can't" when he was asked why it was so difficult for him to consider these other interpretations. Through further exploration, it became clearer that he was afraid to contradict the teachings of his faith tradition because he would not want to "jeopardize [his] salvation" by questioning the scriptural understanding he had been taught.

Although focusing on the conflict between his faith and his sexual orientation through a cognitive approach was less successful, Sam seemed responsive to the empathic exploration offered to him as he struggled to come to terms with his religious beliefs and his sexual orientation. Along this line, he was helped to minimize his negative self-judgment surrounding his emotional conflicts in this area. For example, besides empathizing with his emotional dilemma about being gay and feeling he was condemned by God for it, I gently reminded him of his self-acknowledgment that he had "always tried to be a good Christian" in his daily life. In addition, any question to me about how he should resolve these conflicts was used as an opportunity to encourage him to stay with the exploration process.

About a year into our treatment process, Sam posed the following question rhetorically in one of our sessions when he talked about his continued conflict surrounding his sexual orientation and his faith: "Why did God make me this way?" With his budding shift away from believing in a retributive God, the focus in our sessions changed from dealing with his concern about condemnation to helping him discern the meaning from the Divine of his being gay. This process was bolstered by his previous experience with other Christian churches that had proclaimed God's unconditional love for him. As our treatment progressed, Sam was able to better integrate his sexual orientation within the context of his Christian faith and diminish his initial perspective that these two dimensions of his life were mutually exclusive.

The psychotherapeutic treatment process provided Sam with a supportive and safe space to work on reducing his depressive symptoms by diminishing his emotional dilemma and negative self-attributions surrounding his racial/ethnic identity, sexual orientation, and Christian faith. His efforts in developing an integrated identity were further helped by the community resources that were available in the area where he was living. As our treatment progressed, Sam began to ask whether there were "other people like [him]" and where he could connect with them. In response to his query, he was helped to explore the available supportive resources via the Internet before contacting them. Through this process, he became interested and active in a gay Asian support and social organization. He also began to attend a gay Christian peer support group and together with these new friends started to attend a church that was both gay affirming and theologically familiar to him. By being involved in these community groups, Sam gradually became both more socially active and further integrated in terms of his identity as a gay Asian Christian.

About 16 months into our intervention process there was a change in the health insurance plans offered by Sam's workplace. He reported that our sessions would no longer be covered by the new plans. He expressed his desire to continue his treatment with me, and he appeared sad when he asked whether I could refer him to someone else on the new insurance plan. He was surprised and on the verge of tears when I indicated that I was willing to work out some arrangement with him if he wanted to continue with our treatment process. Not only did he have the treatment option he desired, but his emotional reactions to my offer were used to help him counteract the expectations of rejection and abandonment that he had come to expect from others as a result of his development experience. Through this and other corrective experiences during our treatment process, Sam was helped to deepen and further nurture his sense of self-worth.

Outcomes

About 2 months prior to the termination of treatment, Sam indicated that he wanted to start thinking about "going at it on [his] own for a while." Through our exploration of his desire in this regard, he acknowledged his therapeutic progress as including "getting over the breakup with Jim," significantly decreasing those symptoms associated with the dysthymic disorder from which he was suffering to the point that he "had not been feeling depressed for a while now," having a positive experience with coming out to some coworkers, becoming more socially active with friends, and feeling "generally more positive about [himself]." We thus agreed on using our last few sessions to further bolster his treatment gains and help him prepare for treatment closure.

Process Issues

A few process issues that were relevant to working with Sam and not necessarily apparent from the case study so far are briefly discussed here. They include the use of self-disclosure for trust building and the challenge of negative transference and countertransference as a result of client–therapist similarity.

At the beginning of our treatment process, Sam politely asked me a number of questions about my personal background, including but not limited to my racial/ethnic background, age, sexual orientation, and religious affiliation. Based on his cultural background and expectation, it would likely have been counterproductive to the development of the therapeutic relationship and the trust-building process had I not answered his questions with some self-disclosure. I therefore responded with sufficient (but not excessive) personal information and was always mindful to ensure that my self-disclosure would work toward enhancing our therapeutic alliance. Many of my answers to his questions included two parts to support the therapeutic engagement process. For example, when asked whether I came from Taiwan, I responded, "I am Chinese but not from Taiwan, and I wonder if you are concerned that I may not be able to truly understand you if I am not from there."

Although our similar backgrounds (such as being Chinese and gay) were helpful in enhancing our therapeutic engagement, they also presented some relational challenges. A few months into our treatment process I noticed that Sam would keep some distance with me in our interactions. For example, although he was polite and verbally interactive, he tended to be formal and seemed to have some difficulty delving deeper into his feelings and issues when encouraged during our sessions to do so. When this observation was brought to his attention, he stated that he was not aware that he appeared to keep his distance in both our relationship and from his own feelings. Although I invited him to let me know whether I could do anything to help him feel more comfortable in our sessions, he repeatedly stated that he could not think of anything. Through our exploration over a number of sessions he remarked that he was concerned that he was not meeting my expectation and that I would give up on him. In addition to helping him recognize his projection from his developmental learning of conditional acceptance onto our therapeutic relationship, I learned that he was feeling uncomfortable with me because my background was so close to his own. Along this line, he remarked, "It's like looking into a mirror and not liking what you see." Through much verbal and behavioral reassurance of my nonrejection of him he was helped to reduce his emotional guard between us as he addressed his negative self-attributions and other presenting issues.

In addition to his negative transference, our similar backgrounds created some negative countertransference on my part surrounding his difficulty integrating his sexual orientation and his religious faith. I found myself feeling frustrated and increasingly impatient when it was difficult for him to accept the alternative scriptural interpretations about his sexual orientation that were less condemning of him as gay. My reactions became a reminder for me to stand back and monitor my own feelings surrounding the negative impact and painful conflicts caused by condemnatory religious beliefs for sexual minorities, especially gay men and lesbians. This reminder helped me to have a deeper appreciation of Sam's emotional struggles in this area and to redirect our therapeutic efforts from using cognitive challenges to utilizing patient self-exploration as we addressed his concerns in this area.

Other Recommendations

Sam made positive strides during our treatment in terms of integrating the different identity dimensions that were significant to him (i.e., race/ethnicity, sexual orientation, and religious faith). When treatment terminated, he acknowledged that he "still had some way to go" before he felt comfortable coming out to his parents and his sister. However, he felt "it would probably just be a matter of time" before he would do so. In addition, although he had been dating a few men during the last year of our treatment, he still had some reservations about opening himself up to the possibility of "settling down with someone" despite his desire to do so. We acknowledged that these would continue to be "growth areas" for him to work on. He was also reassured of my availability to support him with further psychotherapeutic intervention in the future if needed.

References

American Psychiatric Association. (2000). *Diagnostic and statistical manual of mental disorders* (4th ed., text rev.). Washington, DC: Author.

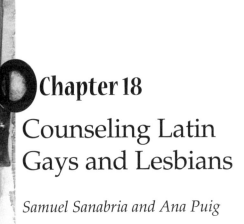

Chapter 18

Counseling Latin Gays and Lesbians

Samuel Sanabria and Ana Puig

Any study of gays and lesbians in the context of Latino culture can be complex because Latinos are not a homogenous population. Yet within the diversity of national backgrounds, social ideals, and distinct cultural histories that make up the vibrant Latino community there are some general themes. It is important to keep this in mind when counseling gay and lesbian Latinos. In general, the ideals of familial duty, gender roles, and religious observance are strongly emphasized, although individual clients may or may not present these factors. These principles can lead to less tolerance of lesbian and gay individuals within the Latino population. Thus, it is also important to note the challenge that gay and lesbian Latinos face in integrating their ethnic identity with their sexual orientation. For example, Latino societal pressures may come with many homophobic messages from family and community, and the gay and lesbian culture may not reflect the fundamental ideals of the Latino culture. Gay and lesbian Latinos may be afraid, therefore, to disappoint their families. They hide their true selves to avoid this but may also separate themselves from other gays and lesbians and the support that they could provide. These stressors can lead to depression, anxiety, substance abuse, and in some cases suicidal ideations. The goal of therapy should be to recognize and respect the individual's ethnicity and within that context, reduce the effects of homophobia, integrate cultural identities, encourage positive social relationships, and promote self-acceptance.

Case Study 1

Hector grew up in the Dominican Republic, the youngest of four siblings. His parents raised him with traditional Catholic beliefs and values, and as a child Hector was an altar boy at Iglesia de Cristo in Santo Domingo. Being involved in his church was very important to him, and at one time he aspired to be a priest. Hector was very close to his family, especially his oldest brother Freddie. He looked up to his older brother, who was *guapo* (handsome) and popular in their *pueblo* (community).

From an early age Hector knew that he was different from other boys his age, but he was not sure why. In high school he began to develop romantic thoughts for his best friend, Juan Carlos. Hector had his first sexual experience at a graduation party with Juan Carlos. Juan Carlos rejected Hector shortly thereafter and refused to speak to him. This was particularly upsetting for Hector. At one point Hector attempted to contact Juan Carlos but was told to stay away or he would tell his parents that he was a *pato* (homosexual male). Hector realized that he was gay but was afraid of coming out to his family for fear that he would disappoint them. He was afraid of being stigmatized and losing the love and support of his *familia*.

After high school Hector moved to St. Louis on a scholarship to attend Washington repressive environment. In his new surroundings he was able to explore his sexuality more freely. He started going to the local gay bars and expressed his newly found sexual freedom with a variety of men. He enjoyed his autonomy but soon grew tired of the bar scene and became more interested in developing a meaningful and long-lasting relationship. He stopped going out to gay bars because he believed that the men he would meet there would only be interested in sex. He decided to join the campus lesbian, gay, bisexual, and transgender (LGBT) student organization hoping to find a different connection with the gay community.

After his freshman year, Hector started dating one of his classmates, Benjamin. They had originally met during an LGBT meeting at the student recreation center on campus. They talked a lot after their weekly LGBT meeting and expressed interest in each other. Hector quickly developed strong feelings for Benjamin and asked him out on a date. They dated for 3 months but the relationship ended when Hector discovered that Benjamin was seeing other men. Hector was upset and felt betrayed not just by Benjamin but by the whole gay community. In his disillusionment he was convinced that he was not going to find a loving and committed relationship with another man. He stopped attending the LGBT meetings and spent more time alone in his dorm.

Hector became increasingly homesick, phoning his family more often. He still had not revealed his sexual orientation and was not comfortable talking about his relationship problems. When he expressed his loneliness to his father he was told to "man up" and stay focused on his studies. Hector's isolation increased and he decided that he needed to reconnect with his Hispanic and religious roots, so he joined the local Catholic church, which held a Spanish Mass every Saturday evening. Despite his attendance in church, Hector still felt disconnected as guilt for his past relationships with men grew. Hector, who had always been a good student, started missing classes. When Hector failed one of his classes he was placed on academic probation. He had a meeting with his academic advisor, who encouraged him to seek help at the university counseling center for his depression.

Hector started seeing Jill, a counselor at the center. During his first session Hector inquired about a form of therapy he had read about in a church pamphlet called reparative therapy. Hector was conflicted about his sexual identity and was interested in being "normal." He explained to the counselor that his attraction to other men was wrong and that it was not natural to be gay. He expressed his belief that there could not be any real or significant relationship in the gay culture and his desire to one day be married and have children.

Presenting Issues

Gay individuals grow up receiving homoprejudicial messages mainly through socializing agents such as parents, teachers, peers, religious organizations, and popular media. As a result of these negative messages, some individuals who struggle with their gay identities seek a controversial form of treatment called reparative therapy in hopes that they can change their sexuality and become nongay. They believe that their lives would be improved and they would gain more acceptance in a predominantly heterosexist society. Although it is likely that a perceived change in sexual orientation would help individuals gain more acceptance in society, there is a question about whether their lives would be improved. Reparative therapy overlooks a fundamental tenet of counseling—the client's unconditional acceptance of self. As counselors, it is important to be aware of clients' motivations for seeking to change their sexual orientation and to explore them during therapy. Counselors experience a unique challenge in working with clients who seek reparative therapy for religious convictions. Counselors need to be respectful of clients' rights to seek the best therapeutic path for themselves while promoting self-acceptance through discovery. In this case, it appears that Hector's Catholic upbringing had an integral part in his sense of self as a gay male. Hector was raised with Catholic values, and the Catholic Church has a long history of denouncing sexual minorities. Most likely Hector received many messages that reinforced homoprejudicial values. As a result, Hector sought out reparative therapy in order to fit in to what he saw as religiously acceptable.

An important part of developing a positive gay identity for ethnic minorities is coming out to family and community. The Latino culture places great value on family unity, harmony, and conformity. Many traditional Latino families have negative attitudes toward gay individuals. Being openly gay is often viewed as contributing to conflict in the family. In order to avoid conflict many gay Latinos choose to live a double life and not reveal their sexual orientation. The experience of many gay Latinos includes rejection by their families. Hector was afraid to come out to his family for fear of causing discord and being rejected. By not revealing his sexual orientation Hector had isolated himself from his family and his main source of support. In addition, Latino cultures generally have strong traditional expectations regarding appropriate male and female behaviors. Men are encouraged to flaunt their masculinity. Hector's brother, Freddie, was well liked in his community. Freddie exhibited a high level of *machismo* and won admiration from his parents and community. Hector admired Freddie and wished to have this same level of acceptance for himself.

Some racial or ethnic sexual minorities believe that they need to choose between their gay and racial or ethnic identities. They may feel split between their dual identities. It is not uncommon for gay Latinos to experience oppression both from the Latin community and from the dominant culture. Hector was not comfortable revealing his gay identity in the Latin community for fear of ostracism. Hector also detached himself from the gay community because he believed it did not share his cultural ideal of love and commitment in relationships. It did not help that Hector was thousands of miles away from home and living in a community significantly different from the one he was used to in the Dominican Republic.

Diagnosis

Hector reported symptoms of depression soon after his breakup with Benjamin; these intensified after he attempted to reconnect with his Latin culture and faith. On further exploration, Jill discovered that Hector experienced sad moods most days, anhedonia, difficulty sleeping at night, fatigue, and feelings of worthlessness. He denied past or current suicidal ideations. Jill also determined that Hector's depression had begun in the past year and that he had not previously experienced symptoms comparable with his current ones. He admitted to missing classes as a result of his depression. After seeing Hector, Jill did not believe that a personality test was necessary. Hector had no history of physical or sexual abuse and reported being physically healthy. As a result of the information provided, Jill reported the following diagnosis:

Axis I	296.2	Major Depressive Disorder, Single Episode, Mild, Without Psychotic Features
Axis II	799.9	Diagnoses Deferred
Axis III		None reported by client
Axis IV		Homesickness, educational problems, identity conflict
Axis V		Global Assessment of Functioning = 68

Goals of Treatment

Hector's initial treatment goal was to change his sexual orientation. Not accepting her client's goals at face value, Jill explored Hector's motivation for wanting to change while making sure to respect his religious and cultural beliefs. Through therapy, Jill exposed Hector's internalized homoprejudicial attitudes and beliefs and their cultural and religious origins. She also discussed the limitations and potential harm that reparative therapy presents. Realizing these things, Hector accepted his fundament need for self-acceptance and agreed on the final goal of integrating his cultural, sexual, and religious identities.

Interventions Used

Jill's first concern in therapy was to develop a high level of trust with Hector. She knew that in order for counseling to be effective a strong therapeutic relationship needed to be established. She empathized affectively with his conflicting emotions and took special care to reinforce that Hector was in control and was responsible for making choices about all aspects of his life. Jill's genuine concern for Hector's well-being prompted her to take a very deliberate approach to therapy, being careful to respect his cultural and religious beliefs.

One of the goals of therapy that Jill identified was to help Hector move toward developing a healthy sense of self by increasing his acceptance and integration of his sexual, religious, and ethnic identities. Jill decided to use Cass's (1979) gay and lesbian identity model and the racial/cultural identity development model (Atkinson, Morten, & Sue, 1989) to help Hector develop a positive and integrated personal identity. Jill recognized that exploring Hector's desire to be nongay was a critical part of his therapy. Jill inquired about how he had come to the decision to seek to change his sexual orientation. In this case Hector had found literature regarding reparative therapy. He was convinced that he would not be able to find a meaningful long-term relationship with another man and was interested in eventually having a family. Jill worked with Hector by gradually introducing him to various aspects of the gay community. She presented several examples of same-sex couples in meaningful and long-lasting relationships, some of whom, through adoption and assisted reproductive therapies, were able to have families of their own. By exploring these aspects of gay culture she hoped that Hector would realize that he could find happiness in a same-sex relationship. Jill also introduced Hector to a local gay Latino group and gay-affirming churches like the Metropolitan Community Church.

Jill also encouraged Hector to address his relationship with his family, specifically to consider coming out as gay. The decision to come out is an important part in the development of a strong and positive gay identity, but Jill knew that Hector might also experience painful rejection. The fear of losing family support is not exclusive to gay Latinos but may be intensified by Latinos' strong acculturation of appropriate behavior. Jill led Hector to develop an understanding of the possible outcomes, positive and negative, of both deciding to come out and deciding not to come out. For both options they developed a plan to deal with the potential consequences of his decision. Jill and Hector repeated the same exercise when considering the specific cases of coming out to Hector's brother and coming out to the Latin community at large.

Outcomes

Hector continued to work toward integrating his gay, Latino, and religious identities. He reconnected with the gay and lesbian student group and started a subgroup for Latino individuals. He started coming out to select friends and, after receiving affirming responses, developed enough confidence to come out to his family. His brother was supportive and, after some initial anger, so was his father. His mother had a hard time believing that she was not to blame and still struggled with her sense of guilt. Hector gave up the idea of reparative therapy and instead started to attend the gay-affirming

Metropolitan Community Church in St. Louis, where he has been able to connect with other gay minority individuals. He hasn't started dating yet but feels that it won't be long until he's comfortable enough with his own self to begin doing so.

Case Study 2

Sofia was a 41-year-old divorced Venezuelan American female who had been living in southern Florida for the past 15 years. Sofia's two younger sisters and their elderly parents had been living in Venezuela until recently. A year ago, because of the increasingly tense political situation in Venezuela, Sofia's parents and siblings had asked her to help them immigrate to the United States. Sofia had attended graduate school in Miami, where she had met her ex-husband. She was in her mid-20s and her parents were already pressuring her to marry and start a family. After a brief courtship, Sofia married Carlos, a second-generation Cuban American. Soon after they married, Carlos became domineering, verbally abusive, and controlling. Sofia was independent and smart and reacted defensively to his behavior. They had intense verbal altercations. Sofia felt that she had made a mistake and filed for divorce after 3 years. She was grateful that they had no children. Her family, although disappointed, supported her decision to divorce.

Soon after, Sofia began to explore her sexual identity and realized that she had married not only because of her parents' pressure but to escape her attraction to women. In retrospect, Sofia saw that her intense friendships with girlfriends in high school were filled with deep emotional bonding and unspoken sexual tension. She began to socialize with other professional lesbians through a small and discreet circle of friends. Sofia had had a couple of short-lived relationships that had ended when the women asked for more serious commitment. Sofia refused to live openly as a lesbian, and this created strain in her relationships. She had not agreed to cohabitation until she had met Marisa, a Puerto Rican, 5 years ago. Although both women identified as lesbians, they had never come out to family or coworkers. Marisa's family of origin was chaotic and dysfunctional, and she had been estranged from them for many years. Although both women maintained a covert lifestyle, were only physically intimate at home, and lived as roommates to the outside world, they were emotionally committed to each other. As closeted lesbians, their relationship had never been a topic of discussion, particularly within Sofia's family.

Since her family had immigrated to the United States 4 months ago, Sofia had been wrestling with their being nearby and finding out about Sofia and Marisa's relationship. Although they lived together as a couple, Sofia and Marisa maintained separate bedrooms to cover up their relationship. Sofia's family made frequent requests for support as they negotiated the new city and culture, and Sofia was increasingly unavailable to Marisa. These demands and Sofia's fear of being found out were beginning to take a toll. Although Marisa understood Sofia's fear, she was very concerned about the impact the situation was having. Sofia had become sullen, withdrawn, edgy, and unapproachable.

On a recent Sunday morning Sofia's parents showed up unannounced while Sofia and Marisa were still in bed. Sofia scrambled to get to the door while Marisa hid in her bedroom, pretending to be asleep. After Sofia's parents left, the women had a heated argument. Sofia was angry, screaming, and crying. Marisa was scared and confused. She had never seen Sofia this upset and emotionally out of control. The incident scared Sofia as well, and she realized she had to do something. Sofia looked through the phone book and decided to call a mental health counselor who specialized in LGBT issues.

During the first session Sofia emphasized to Dr. March how important complete confidentiality was to her. Sofia was leery of anyone finding out she was there and wanted to make sure everything they discussed would be confidential. Dr. March reassured her that their sessions would be confidential to the extent provided by law and reviewed the limits to confidentiality before they began talking about the stressors that had brought her to therapy.

Presenting Issues

Sofia was struggling with internalized homophobia and a triple-minority status. In addition, Sofia was a lesbian in middle adulthood trying to maintain a closeted lifestyle with her *pareja* (partner) of 5 years. With her family's relocation, she had been forced to come face to face with her sexual orientation and the probability of their uncovering the truth about her. As the oldest daughter of elderly parents, there were tacit expectations about Sofia's role in supporting the family's needs. Because she did not have a family (husband and children) of her own, she was held to a different standard than her younger sisters, who had husbands and children to take care of. Furthermore, the Latino/a family structure can interfere with privacy, and interpersonal boundaries are quite fluid; it is common for family members to ask multiple questions and offer opinions, even when unsolicited. Sofia became the point person for helping them acclimate to a new environment. She was now facing an extremely stressful adjustment.

Sofia did not doubt or resist her sexual identity; however, she was grappling with deeply ingrained homophobia; her family's expectations of her as the oldest, unmarried daughter; and her partner's frustration with the impact of this situation on their relationship. After her arrival in the United States, Sofia had integrated the American values of independence, self-reliance, and freedom into her lifestyle. Since her family's immigration to the United States, these individualistic values were now in conflict with her collectivistic sense of duty as the eldest daughter and sister and her relationship to Marisa. A central therapeutic issue for Sofia was her lack of self-acceptance and the fact that she had not resolved her homophobic feelings. In addition, Sofia needed to reconcile her new responsibilities to her family of origin and her loyalty to Marisa as her life partner.

Coming out to family and community is a crucial part of developing a positive gay identity for ethnic minorities. This process would allow Sofia to become aware of, accept, and ultimately affirm her sexual identity. Sofia had chosen to live a closeted lifestyle to avoid upsetting her family and creating conflict. She had always been a source of pride to her parents, who valued her professional accomplishments and responsible attitude. She had already disappointed them by divorcing Carlos after only 3 years of marriage. Sofia was afraid that her sexual orientation and her relationship to Marisa would bring shame to the family and alienate her parents and siblings. Latin cultural expectations for appropriate female behaviors were incongruent with Sofia's lifestyle. Sofia was already exhibiting culturally nonnormative behaviors by choosing, in her family's eyes, to be a single, childless, career woman.

Sofia felt a deep split between her dual identities. She had been negotiating dominant and nondominant cultures (Venezuelan, Cuban, and American) most of her adult life. All had homoprejudicial elements and gender-based expectations. Sofia was not comfortable revealing her sexual identity to the Latin community because she feared rejection. She also had a successful professional life that she believed might be jeopardized by her lifestyle.

Counseling Considerations and Diagnoses

Sofia reported that since her family's arrival, she had been experiencing depressed and anxious moods, irritability, tearfulness, hopelessness, excessive worrying and jitteriness, loss of appetite, headaches, stomachaches, trouble sleeping, and difficulty focusing at work. She had also pulled away from Marisa and was unable to express affection or be sexually intimate. Sofia acknowledged emotional abuse by her ex-husband but denied a history of physical or sexual abuse. She denied suicidal ideations. She was in good physical health; however, she had recently begun taking prescription medication for gastroesophageal reflux disease. Sofia was especially conflicted about her relationship with Marisa. Although they were not without problems, they had a fairly good relationship. Sofia acknowledged that her relationship to Marisa was making it exhausting to conceal her sexual orientation. After completing her initial assessment, Dr. March documented the following diagnoses:

> Axis I 309.28   Adjustment Disorder, Acute, With Mixed Anxiety
>   and Depressed Mood
> Axis II 799.9   Diagnoses Deferred
> Axis III Gastroesophageal reflux disease
> Axis IV Identity conflict, relational conflict
> Axis V Global Assessment of Functioning = 65

Goals of Treatment

At the beginning, Sofia was unable to articulate a goal for therapy. She simply stated that she felt "overwhelmed, torn, stuck, confused, and powerless." She wanted relief from the intense pressure she had been feeling. She also wanted to avoid hurting her family and Marisa. She became tearful when acknowledging that Marisa had the worst of it. Sofia had so far concealed her stress from her family, although her youngest sister Raquel had asked her what was wrong with her, commenting that she seemed on edge and grumpy. Sofia eventually said that she wanted to work through her impasse. She acknowledged that something had to change and that she had to begin by exploring her own fear of coming out. She told Dr. March that she knew this had been a problem for a long time and that it had now reached its peak. Dr. March helped Sofia to see how her relationships to her family members and to Marisa also needed to be explored. The idea of bringing Marisa into therapy was raised, but Sofia said she wanted to work on herself first. Sofia and Dr. March agreed to initially explore the fear of coming out and healthier ways of coping with current stressors.

Interventions Used

Dr. March was aware of Sofia's guardedness and her need for reassurance about the confidential nature of their sessions. Dr. March emphasized her understanding of and respect for this need and worked to establish trust with Sofia. She helped Sofia by using McCarn and Fassinger's (1996) model of lesbian identity formation. The model attends to the unique influences of race, ethnicity, and gender as well as the dual nature of lesbian identity "as an *individual sexual identity* that results in *membership in an oppressed minority group*" (p. 509, emphasis in the original).

Dr. March helped Sofia explore her movement toward an internalized, synthesized individual and group identity. When she had married Carlos, Sofia was not yet consciously aware of her sexual orientation. It was not until her divorce that she became aware of her attraction to other women and began exploring these feelings. Her choice to begin dating women moved her toward a deepening commitment to her sexuality in her individual identity; however, personal involvement with a larger group of lesbians never took place. Sofia was selective and guarded about her social relationships and aware of the potential consequences of her choices as seen by her ethnic group membership. She was also aware of the conservative occupational culture she inhabited. These multiple oppressions silenced her and created a sense of paranoia that kept her closeted and afraid. Meeting Marisa and entering into a partnership with her made this choice easier to manage. Neither one had fully embraced their identity as members of the broader LGBT minority group.

According to the model used by Dr. March, lesbians may remain professionally closeted while individually integrated in terms of their sexual identity. However, the final phase of full internalization and synthesis in both individual and group membership identity requires an exploration of oppressions associated with minority group memberships (gender, ethnicity/race, LGBT). Sofia realized the impact that being caught between worlds had had over the years and began to identify ways to negotiate and come to terms with her multiple identities. Sofia was able to make connections that helped her unravel the complexities of her situation. A crucial part of this process was the identification and unlearning of the heterosexist and homophobic notions she held. Understanding these processes alleviated some of the tension, anxiety, and depression Sofia had been experiencing and normalized the intensity of her emotional states.

193

Eventually Sofia agreed to bring Marisa in for couples counseling. Dr. March helped them understand their unique developmental trajectories regarding individual and group membership identities. Dr. March also helped them clarify their positions and explore ways to negotiate, compromise, respect, and support each other. Both women began to see similarities and differences between their identities and the role these played in the current situation.

Outcomes

Sofia began to recognize the central role that her sexual identity and group membership issues had on her well-being and the quality of her relationships. She recognized the roles that heterosexism and homophobia had on her choice to remain closeted. She saw how concealing her sexual identity had taken a toll on her peace of mind and kept her from developing a circle of supportive friends and connections to the lesbian community. She began to consider coming out in small steps, beginning with her youngest sister Raquel, to whom she felt closest. She also invited Marisa to join her in therapy sessions so they could discuss the issue and "come to an agreement about what to do and how to be."

Although she made strides toward coming out to her sisters, Sofia would not consider coming out to her parents. She felt the harm would outweigh the benefits. Coming out to Raquel and eventually Miriam was as far as she could go at the time. Sofia and Marisa had begun to spend more time together as a result of Sofia's ability to set some boundaries with her parents. Although Miriam, Sofia's middle sister, had taken the news harder than Raquel, both sisters were supportive of Sofia and understood her dilemma. They helped by looking after their parents more often, lessening their demand for Sofia's time.

Recommendations for Further Counseling or Training

The cases of Hector and Sofia illustrate some of the common issues that affect gay and lesbian Latinos. Although the broader Latino community is highly diverse, homophobia and homoprejudicial messages are common. These negative values, along with the basic ideals of family, collectivism, harmony, and respect for elders, among others, may be internalized by gay and lesbian individuals. Thus, gay and lesbian Latinos may present to counseling with complaints about the impact of these messages and related stressors. In Hector's case, religion played a critical role, whereas Sofia's status as an older daughter who did not adhere to normative behaviors for Latina women placed her in a highly stressful situation with her partner and her family. Also evident were the distinct developmental issues faced by each—Hector as a young man in emergent adulthood and Sofia as a middle-aged career woman.

Counselors must be properly trained and prepared to help clients such as these address their unique presenting issues. Therapists need to be able to recognize and explore the impact of a client's race, ethnicity, gender roles, sexual identity, nationality, spirituality and/or religiosity, degree of acculturation, and family background on the client's ability to accept his or her sexual orientation. For example, Sofia's and Hector's experiences are markedly different yet similar, as both felt pressure to behave in a manner that fulfilled the cultural expectations for people of their genders.

The goals of therapy may include an exploration of the client's internalized homophobia, the integration of cultural and sexual identities, the creation and maintenance of positive social relationships, and the promotion of self-acceptance. Counselors have a responsibility to learn about and understand the impact that multiple identities have on individual development. To this end, counselors must become acquainted with the various theories about gay and lesbian identity development and learn to apply them in a competent manner. It is also vital that counselors learn multicultural competencies (Arredondo et al., 1996) and spiritual/religious competencies (Association for Spiritual, Ethical, and Religious Values in Counseling, 2009) to support the fundamental counseling goal of self-acceptance and to recognize how their own values affect their ability to provide effective therapeutic help.

Ultimately, counseling Latino gay and lesbian individuals involves counselor self-awareness and competency in working with individuals of multiple minority backgrounds, creating a foundation of trust, and carefully assessing presenting issues. Special attention should be given to the cultural, racial/ethnic, and religious values clients may hold and to the influences their national origin and degree of acculturation may have on their acceptance of their sexual identity. Carefully guiding the process toward self-acceptance and integration is essential for a successful therapeutic experience to take place.

References

Arredondo, P., Toporek, M. S., Brown, S., Jones, J., Locke, D. C., Sanchez, J., & Stadler, H. (1996). Operationalization of the Multicultural Counseling Competencies. *Journal of Multicultural Counseling & Development, 24,* 42–78.

Association for Spiritual, Ethical, and Religious Values in Counseling. (2009). Spiritual competencies: Competencies for addressing spiritual and religious issues in counseling. Retrieved from http://www.aservic.org/resources/spiritual-competencies/

Atkinson, D. R., Morten, G., & Sue, D. W. (1989). A minority identity development model. In D. R. Atkinson, G. Morten, & D. W. Sue (Eds.), *Counseling American minorities* (pp. 35–52). Dubuque, IA: Brown.

Cass, V. C. (1979). Homosexual identity formation: A theoretical model. *Journal of Homosexuality, 4,* 219–236.

McCarn, S. R., & Fassinger, R. E. (1996). Revisioning sexual minority identity formation: A new model of lesbian identity and its implications for counseling and research. *The Counseling Psychologist, 24,* 508–534.

Chapter 19

Multiracial/Multiethnic Queer and Transgender Clients: Intersections of Identity and Resilience

Annelise A. Singh and Kirstyn Yuk Sim Chun

I remember how being young and black and gay and lonely felt.
A lot of it was fine, feeling I had the truth and the light and
the key, but a lot of it was purely hell.

—Audre Lorde

Multiracial/multiethnic queer and transgender clients present with unique opportunities for counselors and psychologists to explore the intersection of not only their multiple identity development processes but also how these intersections are sites of resilience and liberation. Multiracial/multiethnic queer and transgender clients may face numerous challenges because of their multiple identities. Clients may often feel caught between two (or more) worlds such that they feel acceptance of their queer or transgender identity in one area of their life but feel they need to hide or refrain from sharing other salient identities. Queer and transgender multiracial/multiethnic clients may also endure and/or have internalized a tremendous number of societal stereotypes based on race/ethnicity, sexual orientation, gender identity, and gender expression.

However, in addition to exploring these many barriers to well-being, counselors may work with queer and transgender multiracial/multiethnic clients to collaboratively identify the unique resilience and coping strategies these clients have developed despite these barriers. This chapter presents two case studies (one queer case study from a cognitive behavior therapy theoretical lens and one transgender case study from a narrative theoretical lens) in order to further explore how counselors may work with common issues that arise in counseling these clients. Throughout both case studies we use a feminist and social justice framework in order to identify issues of power, privilege, and oppression within both the counseling relationship and the experiences the clients have had in society that influence their well-being. We also integrate the Competencies for Counseling Gay, Lesbian, Bisexual and Transgendered (LGBT) Clients (ALGBTIC, 1997) and the Competencies for Counseling With Transgender Clients of the Association for Lesbian, Gay, Bisexual, and Transgender Issues in Counseling (ALGBTIC, 2010) in our discussion of the case studies (see Appendixes A and B, respectively).

Queer Multiracial/Multiethnic Case Study

Background Information

Rosa Nakano-Gonzalez is a 28-year-old Catholic, female, partnered lesbian graduate student who identifies as Mexican American and Japanese American. Her father immigrated from Michoacán, Mexico, in his 20s and married her mother, who is a second-generation, *Nisei*, Japanese American. (*Nisei* describes an individual whose parents emigrated from Japan.) Rosa has been living with her girlfriend Thanh, a 33-year-old female, first-generation Vietnamese American Buddhist engineer, for the past 2 years. This is Thanh's first similar-gender relationship, and she prefers not to label her sexual orientation.

Aware of her similar-gender attractions in high school, Rosa began secretly dating other women in college and even attended a few LGBTQQI events on campus. When Rosa tried to come out as *lesbiana* to her parents in her early 20s, however, her mother fidgeted uncomfortably while her father called his daughter "sick," put his head in his hands, and softly started crying.

Despite her parents' lack of support for her sexual identity, Rosa has tried to live as openly as she can in her relationships with other women. Now in her late 20s, Rosa prefers to hold hands or put her arm around Thanh when they are out in public. Thanh tolerates this in certain areas of town but quickly pushes Rosa away in parts of the city with high concentrations of other Asians and Asian Americans. Thanh's family thinks of Rosa only as a roommate. Recently Thanh started to bring Rosa with her to family gatherings, but she quietly scolds Rosa whenever Rosa sits too close to her. Thanh's siblings make awkward attempts at polite conversation, but her parents stare past Rosa, pretending not to see her.

Reasonably certain of her sexual identity as lesbian, Rosa continues to struggle with her multiracial identity. When asked about her racial background, she shrugs, describing herself as "just American" or "a mutt, I guess." She adds, "I've always been too Mexican for the Asians and too Asian for the Mexicans." Rosa is drawn to Thanh and her family for their strong sense of Vietnamese heritage, their use of the Vietnamese language, and their adherence to cultural traditions. "I just wish I could fit in somewhere like that," she adds softly. However, the women's differences in sexual identity development, degree of candor regarding sexual orientation, and experience with same-sex relationships have contributed to increased tension in the relationship. Rosa explains, "I've worked so hard to be proud of who I am, how I live, who I love. I don't understand why Thanh is so ashamed of me, of us, of our love for each other."

Presenting Issues

Referred to counseling by her dissertation chair, Rosa presented with mild symptoms of depression that had persisted for the past 18 months. She reported a lack of motivation and increased feelings of "emptiness" for part of the day, most days of the week. Changes in appetite, sleep patterns, concentration, energy levels, and libido were reported. Rosa acknowledged significant academic impairment and some social impairment. She discussed ongoing struggles with depression since high school, with symptoms worsening in her early 20s. However, Rosa reported managing to distract herself with academic demands until about 18 months ago, when she began to feel overwhelmed by her dissertation project, her first domestic partnership, and ongoing disapproval from her parents. "I just wish I could feel like someone really *got* me, was on my side," she whispered. Rosa denied being an immediate risk to herself and others but expressed concern about her ability to be happy in the future. "Sometimes I just feel so lost, so alone. I wonder if anyone will ever love me for *all* of me."

Diagnosis

Axis I	311	Depressive Disorder, Not Otherwise Specified
	313.82	Identity Problem
	V62.4	Acculturation Problem
Axis II	V71.09	None
Axis III	None reported	
Axis IV	Family problems, romantic relationship problems, problems related to the social environment, educational problems	
Axis V	Global Assessment of Functioning (GAF) = 61 (at intake) GAF = 70 (at termination)	

The intensity and frequency of Rosa's depressive symptoms do not meet criteria for a major depressive episode, ruling out major depressive disorder. Though ongoing, the intensity and duration of her depressive symptoms also do not meet criteria for dysthymic disorder. However, the symptoms have persisted too long to warrant a diagnosis of adjustment disorder. Without a report of manic episodes and other psychotic symptoms, her presenting depressive symptoms do meet criteria for depressive disorder not otherwise specified because she reported significant academic and occupational impairment. Rosa denied substance use or medical problems that might contribute to her depressive symptoms. Her report of ongoing sexual and racial identity issues indicates that diagnoses of identity problem and acculturation problem are appropriate. Rosa denied symptoms of anxiety, psychosis, and other Axis I disorders.

Theoretical Frameworks and Goals of Treatment

As mentioned previously, both cases here are approached from feminist, multicultural, and LGBTQQI-affirmative perspectives. In this clinical vignette, a cognitive–behavioral approach is also applied. A common thread among these four theories is the importance of understanding the individual's difficulties in the context of the environment.

From a cognitive–behavioral perspective, Rosa's symptoms of depression can be understood as the result of automatic thoughts stemming from faulty assumptions and negative core beliefs about herself, others, and the world in which she lives. Cognitive behavior therapy begins by understanding the environmental context in which one's automatic thoughts, mood, behavior, and physical reactions interact but ultimately emphasizes change at the *individual* level. However, the feminist, multicultural, and LGBTQQI-affirmative approaches mentioned earlier often highlight the need for change at *systemic* as well as individual levels. If Rosa's case is examined from the perspective of these theories, then it becomes clear that an environment intolerant of female; multiracial; and lesbian, gay, bisexual, transgender, queer, questioning, and intersex (LGBTQQI) identities is likely to serve as both a cause of and ongoing contribution to the negative core beliefs and assumptions that fuel Rosa's automatic thoughts and depressive symptoms.

Consistent with cognitive–behavioral, feminist, multicultural, and LGBTQQI-affirmative approaches to therapy, the following treatment goals were developed in collaboration with Rosa:

1. Improve mood.
   a. Identify automatic thoughts, examine available evidence, and develop more balanced thought patterns.
   b. Increase social support for multiracial identity development.
   c. Increase social support for LGBTQQI identity development.
2. Improve functioning in the romantic relationship.
   a. Identify automatic thoughts as well as assumptions and core beliefs that interfere with functioning in the romantic relationship.
   b. Develop skills to dialogue with Thanh about Rosa's multiracial identity development, especially in the context of her LGBTQQI identity development.
   c. Develop skills to dialogue with Thanh about similarities and differences in LGBTQQI identity development, especially in the context of her and Rosa's respective cultures.
3. Cope more effectively with family relationships.
   a. Understand the development of automatic thoughts, assumptions, and core beliefs in the context of family relationships.
   b. Identify realistic goals regarding family relationships.
   c. Continue to identify automatic thoughts, examine available evidence, and develop balanced thought patterns in response to any distress regarding family relationships.
   d. Explore ways of continuing the process of multiracial identity development through possible contact with family.

Interventions

The treatment plan developed in collaboration with Rosa required cognitive–behavioral interventions delivered from feminist, multicultural, and

LGBTQQI-affirmative perspectives. As is typical with most cognitive–behavioral interventions, treatment commenced with psychoeducation about the impact of automatic thoughts on mood, behavior, and physical reactions in the context of the environment. Rosa was given an opportunity to identify her own automatic thoughts about her self-worth as a lesbian of Mexican and Japanese American descent, her romantic relationship, and her family relationships. When asked about her automatic thoughts, she stated with certainty, "I don't belong anywhere. People will never accept *all* of me, and I will end up alone."

Given her background and the nature of her presenting issues, it seemed especially important to also utilize a systemic approach to treatment that explored the sociopolitical context in which Rosa's automatic thoughts had developed. To address these environmental issues, the therapist recommended increased contact with potential sources of social support (e.g., a multiracial support group at the counseling center, a weekend diversity conference at school, attendance at the school's LGBTQQI Diversity Week event). Rosa's involvement in LGBTQQI and people of color community groups was monitored throughout treatment, and opportunities for greater involvement and empowerment were discussed as appropriate. At first she reported feeling nervous about meeting new people and possibly facing rejection by them as well. Over time, however, Rosa reported meeting more people who could relate to her experiences of feeling marginalized on multiple fronts. "The other students," she added, "some of them are more out than I am . . . and they're 'brown' too. It's just nice not to feel like I have to be the brave one all the time."

As Rosa continued to increase her social support regarding her multiracial and LGBTQQI identities, the individual treatment continued to use cognitive–behavioral strategies regarding her automatic thoughts. "Thought records" were introduced, and she learned to identity automatic thoughts, examine available evidence, and develop more balanced thought patterns first in session then eventually between sessions. Over time, for example, Rosa learned to use words like *never* and *always* less frequently. Instead she stated, "It's hard to be 'mixed' sometimes, because lots of people don't 'get' it . . . but some people do understand what it's like to be gay and brown and mixed and how it feels to love a girl who makes you ache when she pulls her hand away from you just 'cause you're in the Vietnamese part of town. I guess it's just meant to be hard . . . but at least I don't have to do it alone."

This cognitive–behavioral approach to therapy also included "behavioral experiments" in which Rosa learned to test her newly developed balanced thoughts in her daily life. For example, she practiced talking to students she met at the LGBTQQI Resource Center who seemed friendly in spite of her fears that they would reject her. Rosa set goals for communicating more openly with Thanh about her feelings, learning over time to express her emotions and needs without interpreting Thanh's inner conflict as commentary on her own self-worth.

The introduction of "action plans" to therapy involved blending both cognitive–behavioral and systemic approaches. In this phase of treatment,

Rosa developed the following action plan with strategies for improving her mood and functioning:

1. Talk to new people in multiracial and LGBTQQI groups on campus.
   a. Practice using thought records to challenge automatic thoughts about self-worth and interpersonal relationships.
   b. Go to the multiracial support group at the counseling center.
   c. Sign up for the weekend diversity retreat at school.
   d. Volunteer to help with the LGBTQQI Resource Center's upcoming LGBTQQI Diversity Week.
2. Talk to Thanh more about feelings and needs in the relationship.
   a. Practice using thought records to challenge automatic thoughts about self-worth and romantic relationships.
   b. Express appreciation for positive aspects of the relationship.
   c. Discuss each person's coming out process, especially regarding family.
   d. Express feelings and needs regarding different coming out processes.
3. Dialogue about multiracial and *lesbiana* identities with parents.
   a. Practice using thought records to challenge automatic thoughts about self-worth and family relationships.
   b. Ask parents about their cultural backgrounds and traditions.
   c. Read anthologies of multiracial and LGBTQQI narratives with parents and discuss.
   d. Attend Parents, Families, and Friends of Lesbians and Gays meetings and eventually invite parents to attend as well.

Outcomes

After 15 weeks of individual therapy, Rosa terminated treatment because the semester was ending and she anticipated being busy with her upcoming summer internship. At termination she described mixed feelings about having to end therapy before she felt fully "done" with treatment. During the final three sessions, she reported feeling much more hopeful about her ability to manage her mood, especially in regard to her multiracial and LGBTQQI identity development. Identifying automatic thoughts had become much easier, and she was growing more proficient at examining available evidence through her regular use of written thought records. However, she still struggled to develop balanced thought patterns that she truly believed. As termination approached, she challenged herself to engage in a behavioral experiment at the local LGBTQQI community center in which she approached multiracial individuals in her support group to discuss current events about multiracial issues. The duration of therapy did not permit a full exploration of Rosa's negative core beliefs, but at termination she expressed satisfaction at having at least identified assumptions and core beliefs contributing to her automatic thoughts.

During the course of treatment, Rosa made progress in her efforts to discuss her multiracial identity development as a lesbian with her partner

Thanh. In regard to her goal of dialoguing about similarities and differences in LGBTQQI identity development with Thanh, Rosa practiced communicating these thoughts and feelings through role plays in session. However, she remained somewhat ambivalent about taking the risk of confronting her partner in person. Given Rosa's own experiences with rejection by her parents, it was difficult for her to overcome the assumptions and negative core beliefs she then carried into her romantic relationship. In addition, Rosa's ongoing struggle to appreciate her own multiracial identity contributed to fears about not being able to connect on a cultural level with Thanh, who was of a different ethnic identity and acculturation level.

At termination Rosa reported feeling most disappointed with her efforts to address her family conflicts. Despite Rosa's efforts to dialogue with her parents about her multiracial identity, the ongoing tension regarding her lesbian identity and current girlfriend made it difficult for them to establish an environment in which such conversations would be possible. Although she had become more skilled at identifying automatic thoughts, examining available evidence, and developing balanced thought patterns in other settings, Rosa reported feeling much more overwhelmed in dealing with her distress regarding her family. This disclosure presented an important opportunity for additional exploration of the ways in which sociopolitical factors such as heterosexism and other forms of marginalization may cause and continue to contribute to the development of negative core beliefs, assumptions, and automatic thoughts.

As treatment concluded client and therapist discussed ways in which Rosa could continue working toward her goals of improving her mood, friendships, romantic relationship, and family relationships through cognitive–behavioral, feminist, multicultural, and LGBTQQI -affirmative approaches. Rosa reported feeling pleased with some of the progress she had made thus far regarding the action plan developed in therapy. At termination she expressed a desire to continue working on the remaining goals on her own, with the support of her new campus and community connections.

Transference and Countertransference Issues

Because both client and clinician in this case were LGBTQQI women of color, the possibility of overidentifying with each other existed. Toward the beginning of therapy, Rosa did seem to make assumptions that this therapist could understand her identity struggles on a more personal level. This was addressed through discussions about what it was like for Rosa to work with a nonmultiracial, Asian Pacific Islander, queer woman of color in the context of therapy. Demographic similarities and differences were processed, and the clinical pros and cons of this particular client–therapist match were reviewed.

Countertransference on the therapist's part was also quite likely in this situation. There is the possibility of overidentifying with the client and not recognizing ways in which the client's experiences were unique. There is also a risk of under- or overpathologizing the client when there is shared understanding of the sociopolitical context of mental health issues related to sexism, racism, heterosexism, and other forms of marginalization. Finally, there is the possibility of becoming overly protective of the client. This may lead to ambivalence about challenging clients and encouraging the development of their independence. In this case, awareness of these risks promoted increased vigilance on the part of the clinician. Consultations with colleagues about this case became particularly useful for the maintenance of an ethical and effective approach to clinical work with Rosa.

Transgender Multiracial/Multiethnic Case Study

Background Information

Jeremy Nichols was a 22-year-old client who identified as a transgender man despite having been assigned female at birth. His father was African American and his mother was Euro-American. Jeremy reported that when he is "forced" to check a box of race/ethnicity, he checks African American. However, when there is an "other" choice, Jeremy prefers to check that box. Jeremy was in his senior year of college and applying to graduate school in economics when he reported at the university counseling center. He described himself as polyamorous, meaning that he did not subscribe to a monogamous model of relationships. Rather, Jeremy believed he had the capacity to have many types of relationships in his life. Jeremy identified as queer and reported that his affectional attractions went "beyond gender." He had not been in a relationship since he had made his social transition from female to male 1 year ago.

Jeremy reported that he experienced a mixture of support, misunderstanding, and conflict with his family as he made his social transition as a first-year student in college. Jeremy had lived with anxiety for most of his life, and he reported that much of this anxiety was alleviated after his social transition to male. College provided supportive places for Jeremy to feel comfortable sharing his gender identity as transgender with other peers. He attended a support group at the college counseling center for queer and transgender students, and he also became involved with transgender education and advocacy on campus.

Jeremy did not want hormonal or surgical body modifications, reporting he "felt comfortable in the body [he] had." He had experienced some stress related to this both within and outside of the transgender campus community. Within this community, Jeremy had sometimes felt like an outsider because his "friends who were trans men always talked about how many chin hairs they are growing." In addition, Jeremy shared that he felt lonely as the only transgender man of color on campus. Outside of the transgender community Jeremy was "tired of getting questions about hormones and surgery." He wished more people respected his gender identity without "feeling the need to know what was in [his] pants all the time." Jeremy's parents initially were not supportive when he had disclosed his gender identity to them, but they had begun to read books and watch movies on transgender issues.

Presenting Issues

Jeremy reported to the counseling center with complaints of increasing anxiety. He shared that he had been "stressing" about what he would do after graduation and what types of jobs he could apply for where he "wouldn't get interrogated about his gender." Jeremy also reported that he was nervous about his family coming to campus for his graduation next month. His father had recently told Jeremy that he would "never be a true man" and was worried that Jeremy's gender presentation would impact the types of jobs he could get after college. Jeremy reported "feeling distant" from his transgender peers at school "because their conversations don't go deeper than hormones." He shared that he had been spending more time alone than usual. He reported that he was afraid his "anxiety would come back" and interfere with him passing his final exams. He reported having difficulty sleeping, feeling a general sense of fear throughout the day, and having difficulty concentrating on his work—all over the past 4 weeks. Jeremy reported no suicidal ideation and no history of depression.

Diagnosis

Axis I	300.00	Anxiety Disorder, Not Otherwise Specified
	302.85	Gender Identity Disorder
Axis II	None	
Axis III	None reported	
Axis IV	Problems related to the social and career environment, family problems	
Axis V	GAF = 65 (at intake)	
	GAF = 80 (at termination)	

The counselor engaged Jeremy in a collaborative exploration of diagnosis. Jeremy's symptoms did not meet the criteria of generalized anxiety disorder because of the length of time (4 weeks) he had experienced symptoms. Jeremy was having difficulty sleeping, yet he did not report symptoms of hopelessness, worthlessness, sadness, suicidal ideation, or other symptoms that would have indicated clinical depression. The counselor and Jeremy discussed the advantages and disadvantages of including a diagnosis of gender identity disorder on Axis I. The disadvantages included both the counselor's and Jeremy's shared beliefs that this diagnosis was not appropriate for inclusion in the *Diagnostic and Statistical Manual of Mental Disorders, Fourth Edition, Text Revision* (American Psychiatric Association, 2000). However, Jeremy also discussed that he wanted to "keep the door open" for any future decisions he made about hormonal and surgical treatments and to acknowledge the societal stressors that transgender people encounter. Jeremy identified recent family, social support, and career-related stressors that were appropriate for inclusion on Axis IV.

Theoretical Framework and Goals of Treatment

We discuss Jeremy's case vignette through a narrative therapy lens. In order to bring a feminist and social justice emphasis to the use of narra-

205

tive therapy with Jeremy, we pay specific attention to issues of the power differential in the counselor–client relationship and the issues of societal privilege and oppression that were influencing Jeremy's well-being as a multiracial/multiethnic transgender person. In collaboration with Jeremy, the following goals of therapy were identified based on a narrative therapy approach used within a feminist and social justice framework:

1. Collaboratively understand the dominant narrative.
   a. Identify the current dominant narrative about being a transgender man of color.
   b. Identify the individual and societal aspects of the dominant narrative.
   c. Externalize the "problem" experiences of anxiety, career, and social support issues.
   d. Identify exceptions to the "problem" experiences of anxiety, career, and social support issues.
2. Collaboratively reauthor the dominant narrative to a more fulfilling and satisfying one.
   a. Identify client strengths and resilience to reauthor the dominant narrative.
   b. Identify and develop "witness" supports (people who can support the reauthored narrative).
   c. Identify the necessary context for the reauthored narrative.
   d. Explore future opportunities and barriers for the more fulfilling, satisfying narrative.

Interventions

The initial session with Jeremy focused on collaboratively identifying his goals for treatment. The counselor was clear in sharing that she viewed her role as the helping professional as one of serving as a consultant (rather than an expert) who would reflect back to Jeremy his story and his goals for counseling (White, 2007). The question guiding the collaborative goal setting was "Imagine we are at the end of counseling and you are looking back on the main story of what worked. What would have happened?" Jeremy answered this question, sharing that he would like to have (a) established a good relationship with his parents and (b) decreased his anxiety.

After identifying counseling goals, the counselor began to explore Jeremy's dominant narrative—or the main storyline of his life related to his presenting issues. Jeremy shared that he had felt more isolated recently, missed the support of family and peers, and felt uncertain about how he as a transgender man would be respected in the workplace. The counselor used the "miracle" question to collaboratively identify how Jeremy might reauthor his current dominant narrative. She asked, "If you woke up tomorrow morning and everything in your life was just as you wanted it to be, what would be the story of your life?" Jeremy's response was that he would have increased his connection with transgender men of African heritage, established a closer relationship with his family, decreased his anxiety, begun to feel happy in his job and career, and begun to feel that his anxiety would "go away."

The counselor used an externalizing technique to encourage Jeremy to think of his anxiety as an experience separate from who he was as a person. In this externalization, the counselor explored what images came to mind when Jeremy thought of his anxiety. Jeremy shared that his anxiety felt like "a huge weight on [his] shoulders." The counselor and Jeremy collaboratively identified the metaphor of a backpack loaded with stones representing Jeremy's fears in order to symbolize and externalize his anxiety. The counselor also engaged Jeremy in redefining the "problems" he was experiencing so that they could identify the thoughts, feelings, and behaviors that Jeremy had when the problems were not occurring in his life. The counselor also explored how societal expectations of how he should live his life were influencing his definition of "problems." Jeremy shared that he had felt he "always does [his] best in everything, especially in being a Black man." The counselor explored stereotyping about Black men that Jeremy had experienced (e.g., being labeled the "angry Black man") and/ or had internalized and validated these aspects of his narrative. Jeremy also shared that he often felt like he was "caught between being Black and White" because he felt like he had to "choose one side or the other." The counselor explored Jeremy's dominant narrative about his racial/ethnic background and the reauthored narrative he would like to have. Jeremy shared that he thought he would be less anxious if he could "claim 100% of both of his parents' heritage." The counselor validated this reauthored narrative. The counselor also explored how Jeremy wanted to be seen in terms of his multiple identities. In addition, the counselor sought to understand and affirm how Jeremy experienced his multiracial/multiethnic and gender identities intersecting with a focus on his resilience in order to identify positive images, thoughts, and feelings about himself (Singh & McKleroy, 2011). Jeremy shared that he saw himself as a "phoenix that had risen from the ashes and wanted to fly." The counselor explored how Jeremy might want to use the metaphor of the phoenix in relating to his parents, identifying new ways of relating and expressing his authentic thoughts and feelings about his parents. Jeremy shared that he wanted his father to know that he viewed his father as a role model of what being a strong African American man "looked like."

Outcomes

After 6 weeks of individual counseling, Jeremy terminated treatment because of his graduation from college. As termination approached, the counselor worked to find a referral to a transgender-affirmative counselor in Jeremy's home town, where he would be living with his parents until he began graduate school. Jeremy reported feeling less anxiety about interacting with his parents at his upcoming graduation. He decided to use the metaphor of the phoenix rising from the ashes as a way to "start to see things in a new light" with his parents. Jeremy was able to connect with other African American transgender men by signing up for an electronic mailing list geared toward this group. He reported being surprised at the support and care he received from simple e-mail interactions, which gave him hope to connect with more people in his community offline. Jeremy had decided to write a letter to his father telling him how much he needed his help as his son and as a Black man in society. He also wrote a letter to his mom sharing that he wanted to learn more about his European heritage. Such letter writing represented common narrative therapy techniques.

Jeremy reported still feeling "caught" between two distinct racial/ethnic identities, and he also shared that he wanted to keep learning about his heritage. Jeremy said that he had found the metaphor of a backpack very helpful to identifying his anxiety levels. He shared that he still had anxiety about his next career steps. He and the counselor discussed various online career and transgender resources he could access while transitioning to his next counselor. They also discussed the realities of job discrimination and prejudice in the workplace before identifying a brief list of requirements he would want in a job. This list included transgender awareness, gender-neutral bathrooms, supportive coworkers, a relaxed work environment, and the ability to use his leadership and creativity. During the last session the counselor explored which aspects of counseling had worked for Jeremy and which aspects he might have reauthored. Jeremy shared that the focus on his multiple identities, especially how they influenced his interactions with his family and peers, was helpful and that he would have reauthored the counseling experience to give more time to his career concerns.

Transference and Countertransference Issues

Jeremy assumed that his counselor was Latina, and he asked about her racial/ethnic background. After exploring why this was important for Jeremy to understand, the counselor shared her multiracial/multiethnic identity as White and South Asian. Jeremy expressed surprise at the counselor's background and had several questions. The counselor welcomed the questions and used them as ways to explore how Jeremy's dominant narrative might be reauthored around his multiple identities.

Both Jeremy and his counselor had multiracial/multiethnic identities. Therefore, the counselor was careful to ensure that in her countertransference she did not assume that she was aware of Jeremy's definition of his racial/ethnic identity. In order to avoid these assumptions, the counselor considered her own racial/ethnic identity development. She felt comfortable with both her White and South Asian heritage and had integrated these identities. There were times during the counseling relationship when the counselor could readily relate to Jeremy's struggles in feeling he had to choose one identity or another. Because the counselor and Jeremy had discussed her multiracial/multiethnic identity, at times she affirmed Jeremy's struggles with appropriate self-disclosure and validation.

Conclusion

The two case vignettes presented here share three themes that often arise when counselors work with multiracial/multiethnic queer and transgender people. First, counselors should be mindful of the different diagnosis issues regarding either under- or overpathologizing around cultural factors. In other words, multiple cultural and identity factors are at play when working with this group. Counselors should avoid underpathologizing presenting issues because of an overattribution to cultural factors. At the same time, they should avoid overestimating psychopathology because cultural factors have not been fully integrated into the case conceptualization.

Second, few counselors use one particular theory or set of interventions based on a particular theory. Therefore, as counselors integrate theoretical approaches to working with this group, they should select approaches and techniques guided by the client's counseling goals, the client's presenting issues, and the relevance of the approaches to multiple marginalization experiences. Theory integration should be conducted in a thoughtful manner that fully attends to experiences of oppression and resilience.

Third, individuals from historically marginalized groups—especially those who are multiply marginalized—face potential barriers to accessing mental health services. Therefore, reflecting on the case vignettes of Rosa and Jeremy, counselors and the counseling settings in which they work should engage in outreach and advocacy with these groups to ensure that services are accessible. These outreach and advocacy efforts should reflect the overall movement of counselors (and the settings in which they work) toward the provision of multiculturally competent clinical services to multiracial/multiethnic queer and transgender clients.

References

American Counseling Association. (2010). Competencies for counseling with transgender clients. *Journal of LGBT Issues in Counseling, 4,* 135–159. doi:10.1080/15538605.2010.524839.

American Psychiatric Association. (2000). *Diagnostic and statistical manual of mental disorders* (4th ed., text rev.). Washington, DC: Author.

Association for Lesbian, Gay, Bisexual and Transgender Issues in Counseling. (1997). *Competencies for counseling gay, lesbian, bisexual, and transgendered (LGBT) clients.* Alexandria, VA: Author.

Singh, A. A., & McKleroy, V. S. (2011). "Just getting out of bed is a revolutionary act": The resilience of transgender people of color who have survived traumatic life events. *Traumatology, 17,* 34–44.

White, M. (2007). *Maps of narrative practice.* New York, NY: Norton.

Chapter 20

Transsexual Case Studies: Transition Is Not the End of the Road

Randall D. Ehrbar

Terminology

Writing a chapter about clinical work with transgender people was difficult because *transgender* is often used as a superordinate term covering a wide range of gender identities and expression that all differ from the gender one is assigned at birth (see, e.g., American Psychological Association, 2009; Stryker & Whittle, 2006, p. xi). As I realized there was no way for me to pick one or two cases that would meaningfully exemplify the experience of transgender people, I decided to narrow my focus to people who *transition* from one social gender to another. I had two main reasons for this. First, although the term *transgender* covers a wide variety of people who do not permanently transition socially or medically, people who transition are often the ones who come to mind when the word *transgender* is used. Second, people who transition have a unique set of experiences and needs that impact clinical work. Sometimes people who are seeking medical transition will enter psychotherapy simply as a step along the path toward accessing desired medical care. This impacts the therapeutic relationship and at times can lead people to tell their providers what they believe the providers need to hear in order to approve desired medical interventions rather than exploring their experiences openly.

Often the term *transsexual* is used to describe people who transition socially and medically from one gender to another. On the one hand, not all people who identify as transsexual define this term in the same way; for example, some use it to refer to people who permanently transition socially regardless of which (if any) physical interventions are part of the process. On the other hand, not all people who permanently transition socially and medically identify as transsexual. Furthermore, both *transgender* and *transsexual* are terms with political weight: For example, some transsexual people reject the term *transgender* because they do not align themselves politically with the broad range of gender-variant people included in that term but see themselves as having unique needs that are lost in this broader assemblage (see, e.g., O'Keefe, 2010).

One of the people I describe in this chapter has a physical intersex condition. The term *intersex* is used to describe people who have one of a wide range of variations in sexual development (see, e.g., Dreger, 1999). Just as with other identity terms, the language in this area is shifting, with some preferring *intersex,* others *disorders of sexual development,* and others still other terms. I use *intersex* in this chapter because this is the term my client used. Although most people with intersex conditions develop gender identities consistent with those assigned at birth, some later transition to a different gender.

Some people conceptualize intersex conditions as falling within the category of transgender. This conceptualization highlights the wide range of ways in which people can differ from societal expectations for sex and gender. Other people conceptualize transgender, and especially transsexual, people as having a type of intersex condition related to brain structure. This conceptualization highlights biological aspects of transgender etiology. Another conceptualization is to see neither transgender nor intersex as subsuming the other but to see them as separate categories that refer to different experiences. This is the conceptualization I find most useful, as the experiences and needs of these two groups of people are sufficiently distinct that they should not be obscured. Although intersex and transgender are different categories, they can overlap. One of the people described in this chapter has both the experience of a physical intersex condition and a gender identity different from that assigned at birth and self-identifies as both intersex and transgender.

A Note on Context

Both NG and RF were people with whom I worked at a lesbian, gay, bisexual, and transgender (LGBT) community mental health center. At a community mental health center, many clients have multiple needs. Many are poor. Many face multiple sources of oppression. The complexities of these cases reflect this context rather than being inherent to work with transgender clients.

I practice from a transaffirmative therapy perspective informed by feminist and client-centered therapies. For further discussion of transaffirmative therapy, please see the Association for Lesbian, Gay, Bisexual and Transgender Issues in Counseling's (2009) Competencies for Counseling With Transgender Clients; Bockting (2008); Lev (2004); Vanderburgh (2007); or World Professional Association for Transgender Health (WPATH; 2011). For further discussion of how I see feminist and client-centered therapies as interrelating, please see Ehrbar (2004).

NG

NG, who was 40 when we first started working together, had immigrated to the United States from Europe as an adult. NG has a physical intersex condition and when we began working together identified as a woman. She tended to dress very stylishly, with many beautiful accessories such as bright scarves and dangling earrings. We began our work together when NG enrolled in the substance abuse program at the LGBT community mental health clinic where I worked. NG's drug of choice was methamphetamine, and she had been involved in dealing methamphetamine as well as in sex work.

We worked together to explore why NG used, why NG wanted to stop using, what needs methamphetamine use met, and how to satisfy those needs in other ways. One of the major needs methamphetamine served for NG was that it allowed NG to avoid dealing with a variety of difficult issues in her life (discussed in more detail below). The approach to substance treatment in this program was very individualized, with clients free to explore a wide variety of goals from complete abstinence from all drugs and alcohol, to abstinence from particular drugs that are causing problems for them, to harm reduction or substance use management. We also explored other issues in NG's life, and addressing substance abuse issues was one aspect of helping NG to engage in personal growth and develop a better life.

One of the issues that we explored was how having a physical intersex condition affected her sense of identity, in that it left her with a sense of uneasiness around her identity as a woman. Other issues we addressed included NG's choices about whether to continue engaging in sex work and NG's extensive trauma history and associated complex posttraumatic stress disorder. In each of these areas I did not assume any particular right answer but helped NG explore what her personal answers were. For example, I explained that I did not view sex work as inherently problematic in all cases but that by the same token I did not assume that it was *not* an issue or problem either, and I invited NG to tell me about her experience of sex work and what it meant for her. One of the things that emerged was that although NG enjoyed some aspects of sex work, other aspects were problematic, and she could not imagine engaging in sex work without using methamphetamine. Because of NG's goals, transitioning out of sex work became her choice rather than something imposed from the outside.

In the past, conversations about having an intersex condition had often been simplified either to "It doesn't really matter—you're a woman in spite of this" or "So does that mean you are really a man?" By separating the impact of having experienced unusual physical development related to NG's reproductive system and medical interventions aimed at correcting this from NG's gender identity, NG was able to both integrate experiences related to the experience of being intersex as well as be free to explore gender identity without assumptions of what gender NG should identify as. NG recalls that as a teen medical interventions were done but was not told exactly why (as was common practice in treating intersex conditions at the time). The specifics of the treatment left NG confident that an intersex condition was involved, but not which one. During the exploration process, NG tried to discover what the intersex condition was through family or old medical records. Unfortunately, these efforts were unsuccessful, as the old records had been destroyed and NG's mother was also unsure about what the condition was. This in some ways paralleled NG's trauma history, as NG had only fragmentary memory of some past traumas. Together we worked toward accepting that although there was enough information to be pretty sure of some things, other aspects of NG's history remained unknown.

During this exploration of identity, NG became more and more clear that rather than identifying as a woman, he identified as a gay man. Although I would not have predicted this shift in identity when I initially met NG, because we shared the exploration of his identity it was not a surprise when his identity crystallized as male. In the process of identity exploration, I worked carefully to deepen my understanding of NG's experience (which helped NG to deepen his own understanding) and not to lead or presume either NG's experience or the meaning NG made of it. This coming out process included revisiting memories from previous parts of his life through this lens. For example, NG's previous relationships with men were reconceptualized from being those of a straight or bisexual woman to being those of a gay man. NG had repeatedly had relationships with gay men who had told NG that they could not imagine being with women in general but found something different about NG, an experience that was affirming of his emerging gay male identity. NG also became clearer that he wanted to transition socially and physically to male. In addition to working with me individually, NG engaged in group therapy with other trans people dealing with substance issues. This group included people of a wide variety of gender identities and histories who had a wide variety of drugs of choice and treatment goals. Many group members also had serious trauma histories. Fortuitously, the group also included another member involved in sex work.

NG began the process of transitioning while living in a women's supportive living environment. NG's gender presentation gradually shifted from clearly feminine to more androgynous to clearly masculine. NG began to come out to some of the housemates both about being intersex and about the decision to transition to male. Whereas some of the housemates were supportive, others were actively hostile. In one incident, someone wiped themselves with NG's towel after a bowel movement. The staff at the house generally discouraged NG from talking about these emerging identity issues, describing them as a barrier to addressing sobriety. This, of course, was contrary to my own conceptualization that one of the purposes methamphetamine served was to help NG avoid these issues. I directly acknowledged that NG was faced with a situation in which different treatment providers had fundamentally different approaches and empowered NG to choose which approach was most helpful. I supported NG in continuing to explore his identity at his own pace, always being careful not to overwhelm him. Initially a supportive environment, the house became an obstacle and NG moved out.

Ultimately NG decided that it was time to engage in physical transition and set up an appointment at a local health clinic to begin hormone therapy. Surgical interventions were not in reach financially at that time, and NG did not know when he might be able to afford desired surgeries (including breast removal). NG learned to live in the male gender role and was increasingly recognized and accepted as male. NG also learned to navigate sexual and romantic situations with a nonstandard male body that retained various female aspects. NG used therapy to process these issues as they emerged in his life, and I supported him in understanding his experience and formulating strategies to respond to these challenges on an ongoing basis.

During treatment NG transitioned out of sex work and got a job as a peer counselor at an agency focused on working with sex workers. NG also resolved several trauma-related issues and became much more relationally competent with appropriate interpersonal boundaries. By the time NG and I ended our work together, he had been sober for a year. NG integrated developmental processes related to understanding his self-identity and his relationship with others in all of these areas simultaneously. NG developed a sense of himself as male and as sober at the same time.

Because of the structure of the substance abuse treatment program, NG and I had to end our work after 18 months together. NG had clearly succeeded in his initial treatment goal of addressing methamphetamine use. NG had also made a successful transition socially from female to male (although some aspects of his medical transition were still out of reach). Although NG had made great strides in addressing his trauma history, this work was not yet complete. Therefore, I worked with NG to transfer him to another therapist with whom he could continue this work. I discussed NG's case with the manager who reassigned him, describing the progress he had made in therapy and his current needs. Although NG had largely resolved his gender-related concerns at that point, I felt it was important for him to be assigned to a therapist familiar with trans and intersex issues.

Since Then

NG has now been sober for 2.5 years. His transition was successful and is not a current issue in his life. He works at a gay sex club whose policies are inclusive of trans men regardless of the extent of their physical transition. This club has also hosted several community forums for trans men who have sex with men to support community inclusion and HIV prevention. NG is out and open about being trans at work and is encouraged and supported there. He finds this work meaningful, which is important to him in maintaining his sobriety: "If I'm not doing something that matters, I might as well go back to using." Unfortunately, NG has also been dealing with a variety of physical problems, including chronic pain from a knee injury and depression partly associated with his pain medication. He uses his ongoing involvement in therapy to address these concerns. Although NG has continued to try to gain information about his intersex condition, he has been unable to do so. He has had to accept that the more time that goes by, the less likely he will be to get more information.

NG and Me

When NG's exploration of gender identity had made it clear that he identified as a man and was considering gender transition, I encouraged him to join the transgender substance abuse support group I facilitated often along with a practicum student coleader. I felt that the opportunity to meet people with a wide range of transgender identities (some pretransition, some posttransition, and some nontransitioning) as well as a wide range of substance abuse treatment goals would be helpful to NG.

This was also the time for me to disclose my own gender history as a man who was assigned female at birth and who has transitioned medically and socially. When working with *cisgender* (nontransgender) clients, I do not usually disclose my gender history unless I am directly asked by my clients, as I feel it would be distracting and would not facilitate our clinical work. When working with transgender clients I usually disclose my own history at some point. This can be useful in terms of providing relief from fears that I will be judgmental or won't "get it." Because I am transgender, I can also serve as a successful role model. I am also careful to clarify that I don't assume that others should have experiences or make choices similar to my own in order to help keep a wide range of options open for exploration. Because of the assumptions NG had faced about how his intersex conditions should (or should not) impact his gender identity, I felt it was important not to disclose my own history prematurely so as to give NG as much room as possible to explore what it means to have an intersex condition and what gender identity feels most accurate.

NG was the first client with whom I had worked after moving to the San Francisco Bay Area who initiated the process of medical transition while in therapy with me. I had had a great deal of experience working with transitioning clients previously and was used to the process of documenting and justifying their eligibility for and readiness to begin the process of medical transition required by their providers based on the WPATH Standards of Care (Meyer et al., 2001; WPATH, 2011). These standards are flexible guidelines regarding the transition process that establish eligibility and readiness criteria for client access to medical aspects of transition. This often takes the form of a letter documenting a client's gender identity, gender history, and mental health. Having a reality-based understanding of the transition process on both a medical and social level is an important part of being ready. Unlike the providers I was used to working with before, the providers NG accessed in San Francisco used an informed consent model for hormone prescription. In this model, hormones are prescribed by experienced medical providers confident in their own ability to assess clients presenting for care who do not request additional documentation from mental health professionals. The most current version of the standards of care (produced after my work with NG; WPATH, 2011) make it clear that this informed consent model is consistent with the standards. It was thus a first for me when NG came in and told me that he had an appointment to begin hormone therapy the following week. I told him how different this was for me, especially as he had not put together an explicit transition plan, something I had found useful in helping to assess and document one's readiness to transition. NG took this in, and the following week not only did he have his first shot of testosterone but he presented me with a transition plan. NG's transition plan addressed issues of coming out to members of his support system and planning for dealing with foreseeable challenges in the transition process. For my part, this experience helped solidify my understanding of how context influences providers' interpretation and implementation of the WPATH Standards of Care (Ehrbar & Gorton, 2011; WPATH, 2011).

RF

RF was a participant in a group for transgender people with mental health concerns (not the same group NG participated in). This group was structured to include six members, three on the transmasculine spectrum of transgender identities (transgender people assigned female at birth) and three on the transfeminine spectrum of transgender identities (transgender people assigned male at birth). Because this group included people with a wide variety of mental health conditions, I asked that all group members also be in individual therapy. When a group member left, I filled the opening with a new group member. All group members were prescreened by me (and sometimes the group coleader) before joining. I led this group with practicum student coleaders, each of whom was with the group for an academic year. Because of group consensus to maintain the gender balance, I recruited coleaders who identify as female because I identify as male. During the time RF was in the group the coleaders were first a woman with a feminine gender expression, then a woman with a masculine gender expression, and finally a genderqueer person assigned female at birth who had not transitioned physically or socially. I also asked that coleaders be willing to disclose their gender identity and history. When someone new joined the group, introductions include gender identity and history, and I disclosed my transgender status to group members at that time. I believe that this helped to establish the group as a safe and accepting place.

RF is a straight Caucasian woman who had transitioned from male to female both physically and socially while in her 40s. She was in her early 50s when she joined the group as one of its founding members, and she stayed in the group for about 3 years. RF suffered many losses due to her transition. She lost the middle-management job she had in environmental compliance. She lost social status: From being someone who was socially a middle-class heterosexual man she became a poor woman who was visibly transsexual (because of physical characteristics, such as height, that are impossible to change). Even before her transition, RF had ended her marriage to her former wife, and this made contact with her son more difficult. In addition, RF has a physical disability—a hearing impairment on her right side. She had never been able to find another responsible job and recounted that in job interviews, interviewers would often back away from her. She found the stigma and discrimination she faced traumatic and depressing.

Although I describe RF as visibly transsexual, the phenomenon of how we are perceived is social. Thus, in some contexts RF might be perceived and interacted with as a woman, whereas at other times she might be treated differently or even subjected to discrimination because the person she was interacting with perceived her as transsexual. Cultural context also affects whether observers are predisposed to seeing RF as transgender. The unpredictability of how she would be perceived and when she might face discrimination was in itself an additional stressor.

When RF initially joined the group she was frequently suicidal. Other group members, suffering from their own trauma histories, sometimes found it hard to sit with her intense depression and suicidality. She was frequently hopeless and overwhelmed by the oppression she faced, including the practical difficulties of living in poverty.

At that time she did not present a conventionally feminine physical appearance. For example, she did not wear makeup and often wore sweat clothes. This stirred up intense emotions from other transsexual women in the group, who found presenting an attractive and conventionally feminine appearance crucial to both ensuring their own safety and achieving recognition of their gender identity in social interactions. One group member repeatedly offered to help RF change her style, but RF insisted that she had done all of these things for years and they did not help. Although non-transgender women would probably not be assumed unfeminine or have their gender identity doubted because they chose not to wear makeup or wore sweat clothes, the pressure RF faced on this front reflects a combination of sexism and transphobia that can be internalized by transgender women. Paradoxically, transgender women can also face criticism for being overly feminine in their gender expression, and the authenticity of their gender identity may also be questioned on this basis, suggesting that no "real" woman would dress in such a way. Thus, sexism and transphobia can present a catch-22. In addition, the chilly weather in San Francisco can make skirts impractical, and RF's options for clothing she found attractive were limited by her finances. As the group grappled with these interlocking oppressions, I tried to maintain room for multiple possible responses such that neither RF nor other group members were scapegoated. In order to do so, I directly pointed out the inherent unfairness, sexism, and transnegativity involved in the situation being addressed and how different strategies for navigating oppression might work best for different people at different times.

When she first joined the group, RF's hearing impairment interfered with her connection to the group. Because she found it difficult to hear and engage with what other group members were sharing, she rarely gave them feedback. Instead, she mainly talked when sharing her own distress. Later she was able to secure an assistive listening device that she placed on a table in the center of the room and that allowed her to understand group members and interact more.

Early on in her group participation, RF had a tendency to talk repeatedly about specific difficulties she was facing related to her overall oppression. Because she related these difficulties so concretely, she tended to receive equally concrete feedback, often consisting of suggestions she did not find either helpful or supportive. For example, when she expressed frustration with navigating systems aimed at serving the poor, such as Social Security or medical care, she was looking for empathy rather than strategies of how best to do this. With some guidance, she was eventually able to share the emotional aspect of her concerns more clearly and in turn receive feedback that was more emotionally supportive.

RF talked about how she had transitioned physically and socially as quickly as she was able with little regard for possible pitfalls, only to be devastated not to be received as a woman afterward but to face discrimination as a visibly transgender woman. Although she was able to access some support through LGBT community spaces, at times she also faced discrimination there. Also, in LGBT spaces she was unable to connect with men who were romantically interested in her as a woman. The group became one of the few places where RF could experience acceptance. She also expressed unhappiness with San Francisco, contrasting her experience there with the Midwest where she had grown up and spent much of her life. Eventually she decided to return to the Midwest and ultimately did so. She left the group when she moved, expressing that the group was one of the few things she would miss about her time in San Francisco.

During her time in the group RF decided to convert to Judaism, which she enthusiastically and energetically pursued. She shared that she had studied theology in the past and had been drawn to Judaism, and as she joined an LGBT-affirmative synagogue and explored the teaching of Judaism she felt more and more drawn to it. Over time she felt more in alignment with conservative rather than liberal interpretations of Judaism. She was also drawn to the supportive community she found and became sensitized to (and began to speak against) anti-Semitism. Her decision to convert to Judaism was reached prior to, and independently of, her decision to return to the Midwest. When she did move back to the Midwest, connecting with a local welcoming synagogue was an important part of building a support system in a new place. Several members of the group repeatedly cautioned RF not to pin all of her hopes for acceptance on becoming Jewish. Her shift in identity was incorporated into many aspects of her life. For example, as RF became less depressed and more self-confident she began to present herself in a more conventionally feminine way. She still did not wear makeup but often wore long skirts and a few pieces of jewelry. This did not seem to reflect a strategy of navigating social oppression but rather an increased sense of worth and an enjoyment of dressing in a more feminine manner. This style of feminine expression also reflected RF's sense of belonging to a community of conservative and orthodox Jewish women who dressed similarly.

Unfortunately, shortly before she was to engage in the ceremony to become Jewish (and shortly before leaving San Francisco), RF was involved in a situation in which she was accused of writing obscene graffiti (an action completely out of character for her). She was unable to complete the ceremony at that time and was devastated that people she trusted believed she could do something so heinous based on so little (entirely circumstantial) evidence. The group joined RF in her bafflement about how this could have happened and was supportive of her innocence and her emotions.

Since Then

RF is still in touch with a woman she met through the transgender group. She still misses the group as well as a group for LGBT seniors in which she'd been involved. The city RF moved back to had changed in the decades she was away in ways she did not expect, but she is adjusting. The lower cost of living is helpful, but some hidden costs have cut into the disposable income she was hoping to have. She has been able to connect with a welcoming synagogue where she is continuing the process of converting to Judaism. There is also an active local transgender community through which she has made a new friend who identifies as intersex. Although she has not had much contact with the local transgender community thus far, it is a potential resource. Since moving back to the Midwest, RF has been able to find a supportive feminist women's therapy group. Most of the other women in the group are also heterosexual (and cisgender) and fully accept her. RF says that this has been a wonderful experience. She has also been working to establish a closer relationship with her son, which has been facilitated by her being geographically nearer to him (although still 2,000 miles away—the Midwest is large!). Age-related health concerns continue to be an issue.

RF and Me

The intensity of RF's emotions as well as the implacable nature of her challenges (multiple social inequalities and structural aspects of society) sometimes made it hard for me to maintain my empathy. At times I was equally outraged with the social inequalities and just as frustrated and hopeless about how to change such massive problems as she was. I had to start by accepting my own feelings about the world and acknowledge that the world really does present inequalities that are impossible to overcome as an individual. Only once I had come to terms with these facets of the situation was I able to empathically connect with RF, a woman who had been traumatized, who was despairing, and who was angry, outraged, and outspoken—a woman for whom transition had not been easy and for whom transition had in fact consisted of trading one set of difficulties for another. And yet transition has also provided RF much greater freedom to become more authentically herself. Despite the very real external obstacles she faces, transition has been worthwhile for RF.

The group provided RF with a safe haven in which she was able to begin addressing the trauma she had experienced because of societal oppression. She was better able to access her emotions and to connect with others at the end of the group than at the beginning. As important as it was for RF to have a space in which her gender history was accepted and understood, it was also important for her to be accepted by a peer group of other heterosexual women. RF agreed to share her story because it is important to know that transition is not the end of the road, that living as a transgender person can be incredibly hard. Sharing her story publicly is part of RF's ongoing passion for social justice and indicative of her tendency to speak up in the face of oppression. She hopes that ultimately everyone will be able to fully express their authentic selves free from fear and danger.

Conclusion

Work with clients who transition from one gender role to another is influenced by many factors, including where clients are in their identity development process, gender identity, intersections of other aspects of identity, trauma history and discrimination, and any other co-occurring concerns. Because mental health providers often serve as gatekeepers to needed medical interventions, it is especially important for us to empower trans people to articulate their own goals rather than imposing goals on them. It is also important for counselors to be prepared to directly address their role in treatment. Counselors should be aware of issues of sexism, cissexism, transphobia, and other forms of oppression. Just as with other clients, I see trans clients growing, integrating different facets of themselves, and reaching their goals as key indicators that the therapy process is in fact helpful.

References

American Psychological Association, Task Force on Gender Identity and Gender Variance. (2009). *Report of the Task Force on Gender Identity and Gender Variance.* Washington, DC: Author.

Association for Lesbian, Gay, Bisexual and Transgender Issues in Counseling. (2009). *Competencies for counseling with transgender clients.* Alexandria, VA: Author.

Bockting, W. (2008). From gender dichotomy to gender diversity: Implications for psychotherapy and the Real Life Experience. *Sexologies, 17,* 211–224

Dreger, A. D. (1999). *Intersex in the age of ethics.* Hagerstown, MD: University Publishing Group.

Ehrbar, R. D. (2004). Taking context and culture into account in the core conditions: A feminist person-centered approach. In G. Proctor & M. B. Napier (Eds.), *Encountering feminism: Intersections between feminism and the person-centered approach* (pp. 154–165). Ross-on-Wye, Herefordshire, England: PCCS Books.

Ehrbar, R. D., & Gorton, R. N. (2011). Exploring provider treatment models in interpreting the standards of care. *International Journal of Transgenderism, 12*(4), 198–210.

Lev, A. I. (2004). *Transgender emergence: Therapeutic guidelines for working with gender-variant people and their families.* New York, NY: Haworth Clinical Press.

Meyer, W., III, Bockting, W., Cohen-Kettenis, P., Coleman, E., DiCeglie, D., Devor, H., . . . Wheeler, C. (2001). *The Harry Benjamin International Gender Dysphoria Association's standards of care for gender identity disorders, sixth version.* Retrieved from http://www.wpath.org/documents2/socv6.pdf

O'Keefe, T. (2010). *Don't call me transgender.* Retrieved from http://www.thescavenger.net/glbsgdq/dont-call-me-transgender.html

Stryker, S., & Whittle, S. (2006). *The transgender studies reader.* New York, NY: Routledge.

Vanderburgh, R. (2007). *Transition and beyond: Observations on gender identity.* Portland, OR: Q Press.

World Professional Association for Transgender Health. (2011). *Standards of care for the health of transgender, transsexual, and gender nonconforming people. Seventh version.* Retrieved from http://www.wpath.org/documents/Standards%20of%20Care%20V7%20-%202011%20WPATH.pdf

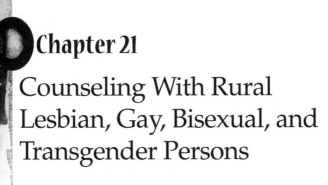

Chapter 21

Counseling With Rural Lesbian, Gay, Bisexual, and Transgender Persons

Paul A. Datti

In urban areas, there are often many signs that a lesbian, gay, bisexual, and transgender (LGBT) community exists. LGBT bookstores, community centers, bars, and LGBT-owned and -operated businesses proudly display their affiliations and rainbow flags. All of this evokes an air of common and normalized culture in which LGBT persons may easily exist among a larger population. This perceived ease of city living is part of what Weston (1995) portrayed in her essay on the rural-to-urban migration of lesbians and gay persons. She contrasted the benefits of communities and acceptance in cities with the absence of communities and the abundant persecution in rural areas and suggested these as reasons why many rural LGBT persons relocate to big cities. However, many LGBT persons from rural areas stay in rural areas. And whether or not they choose to migrate, their experiences and worldviews may be very different from those of LGBT persons from urban or suburban areas. This chapter outlines the case of a rural LGBT client (fictional but based on clinical and personal experiences), addresses common internal and external issues encountered by these individuals, and presents a counseling approach and recommendations for better serving this population.

The Case of Joe

Joe was a friendly 30-year-old Italian American gay man from a rural Ohio town (population 2,400). Born into a tight-knit middle-class family, he grew up with his mother, father, and older sister. Joe was family and commu-nity oriented and had an affinity for where he had grown up. He liked his apartment and his job at the country store where he quickly moved up to manager. Until he was a young adult, Joe knew of no other gay people, with the possible exception of Mr. Jones and his 'friend' who lived across town. As a teen Joe had begun fantasizing about boys and could not understand why. His friends talked about and dated girls, in which he had no interest. Joe was sometimes taunted by others for his effeminate non-gender-conforming qualities and because he did not initially date girls. He had a high voice, swayed as he walked, and, unlike most other boys in the neighborhood, did not like to get dirty when playing outside. He experienced occasional bullying and sometimes feared going to school. As a teenager he attempted to fit in by doing "manly" things such as fixing up motorcycles, but this never really captured his interest. Because he was not like everyone else he believed something was wrong with him and did not talk about it to anyone. He felt a need to remain anonymous and hide his sexual and romantic desires, and he did this in his late teens and early 20s by dating women and escaping to the city (an hour away) on occasion to have intimate relationships with men.

A few years out of a heterosexual relationship and in his first real same-sex relationship (found through an online chat room), Joe presented in counseling with symptoms of anxiety that had begun in high school in social situations, particularly when subjects of sex or dating arose with peers or girls. The anxiety continued across similar social situations but had recently heightened and spilled over to others, such as work, relationships, and finances. Joe related much of his anxiety to issues associated with sexual orientation, such as fear of being found out, worry about lying, and guilt for not feeling and acting heterosexual. Early on he stated that although being straight would be better, he was okay with being gay but wanted to feel better about his situation and stop always having to think about being gay. For example, at family dinners his parents would inquire when he was going to go back to his ex-girlfriend, get married, and have kids. Joe was particularly fearful of his father learning his sexual orientation, as he described his father as a typical Italian macho man for whom he believed it would be difficult to have a gay son, mainly because of expressed hopes for Joe to carry on family traditions and the family name. He also worried whether customers at work would assume he was gay and dreaded personal questions such as, Do you have a girlfriend? or Why aren't you married yet? There were also issues with his relationship. Joe's partner, who lived in the city, was out to many and had aspirations of living with Joe; however, Joe's fears had thus far prevented this, and Joe preferred to keep the relationship secret. Joe had no history of counseling and pursued it at the urging of his partner, with whom he was often at odds. Although he had friends, he was not out to them or comfortable talking to them about these concerns.

Joe also experienced restlessness, irritability, and difficulty concentrating. His symptoms had been significant for about a year, at which time his physician prescribed Xanax, which Joe reported was somewhat helpful. His mother had a history of bipolar disorder, but no known mental health issues existed on his father's side. Joe's strengths included intelligence, a willingness to collaborate, and a sense of responsibility for change. A detailed assessment was conducted that included the frequency, duration, and antecedents of Joe's anxiety. The following diagnoses were assigned:

Axis I	300.23	Social Anxiety Disorder
	300.02	Generalized Anxiety Disorder
Axis II	None	
Axis III	None	
Axis IV	Problems in primary relationships, lack of an adequate support system	
Axis V	Global Assessment of Functioning = 63	

Not comfortable seeking counseling in his town, Joe traveled 45 minutes to my office, which is advertised as LGBT friendly. Initial stated goals for counseling included controlling anxiety, becoming less nervous in social situations, and feeling better about himself. Negotiated goals included feeling increased comfort with his relationships and eventually coming out to loved ones (something he had been considering for years). Joe stayed in weekly or biweekly counseling for 6 months.

Approach to Counseling

At the outset of such cases, it is helpful to consider that, especially in rural environments, LGBT persons may be considered nonexistent, go unaddressed, or, when discussed, be presented in a negative light. Indeed, Joe experienced significant negative attitudes and victimization at an early age, and in his rural area there was no known LGBT community or related resources to provide support. When we consider the Association for Lesbian, Gay, Bisexual and Transgender Issues in Counseling (ALGBTIC; 1997) human growth and development competency and understand that psychosocial factors influence the course of LGB orientation and transgender identity development, we can surmise that the negative experiences of many rural LGBT youth and limited exposure to LGBT persons and communities likely do not set the stage for comfort in the self-acceptance or coming out process. Joe's rural environment allowed for only limited information about his sexual orientation, and that which he absorbed and comprehended represented shame, negativity, and even pathology; therefore, he had significant difficulty integrating it into his life. Furthermore, when we consider the ALGBTIC social and cultural foundations competency we understand a need to be aware that heterosexist worldviews can be internalized and can affect healthy functioning. Indeed, from a young age Joe experienced auras of heterosexism in the worldviews of his rural peers and adults, and these became instilled in him. As a result, his gay identity was less understood and subsequently complicated by a perceived need for isolation and invisibility.

Although many counseling approaches are conducive to working with LGBT persons, here I present a combination of three known to be helpful with this population: person-centered counseling, feminist theory, and cognitive behavior therapy. Person-centered counseling's focus on honest relationships and nonjudgment can be greatly applicable to rural LGBT persons, a group who may not have experienced many relationships with regard to sexual orientation or gender identity. At the outset, and consistent with the signage in my office, it was communicated to Joe that he was in a safe, nonjudgmental space in which all persons were regarded as valuable. Indeed, after an initial hesitation Joe expressed relief in being able to communicate honestly on the subject and relate to someone he felt would be trustworthy and objective. Joe commented on several occasions that he had never been so honest with someone, particularly with regard to his sexual orientation. For the first time Joe felt he had a voice and thus was subsequently able to release many thoughts and feelings that until then had gone unexpressed. Joe also learned that if he was able to have such communications in counseling, he was indeed capable of doing so on many levels in his daily life. In addition, like many LGBT persons from rural areas, Joe experienced consistent (perceived or actual) judgment by others. It was helpful for Joe to have his orientation affirmed, as he had not experienced this in the past and never from a professional in a position of authority. These experiences helped set the stage for us to strengthen our relationship and to begin and maintain meaningful work to address Joe's presenting and underlying issues.

When we consider the ALGBTIC competency of helping relationships, a feminist perspective helps us to acknowledge and address the societal prejudice and discrimination experienced by these individuals and provides the framework for addressing internalized negative attitudes toward sexual orientations and gender identities. Many rural LGBT persons like Joe may be unaware of the ramifications of heterosexism, internalized homophobia, and oppression. Psychoeducationally speaking, this information was helpful for Joe, as he began to increasingly appreciate his life and develop a more positive identity when he was able to better understand LGBT history and culture. He benefited significantly from information about numbers of LGBT people, the etiology of their minority status, oppression fostered by heterosexism, and strict binary gender roles. When I communicated these perspectives to Joe, new knowledge was gained and a sense of collaboration heightened. These discussions helped him realize that there are many others like him and that because they are not a majority does not mean they are inferior. Joe was able to synthesize how external forces—including treatment by others when he was young, his father as a role model, and religion—contributed to his issues. Joe began to realize that perceptions of past issues were related to current feelings of inadequacy and fears of being judged as not worthy, particularly by those about whom he cared. He was able to put into perspective that he felt less than as a result of experiences and messages he received; therefore, the pathology began to shift from within himself to the attitudes, beliefs, and behaviors of others.

Although Joe was becoming more comfortable with himself, he continued to have some negative thoughts and feelings related to being gay. Cognitive behavior therapy and cognitive–behavioral techniques were explained to him, met with enthusiasm, and used in conjunction with feminist and person-centered approaches to address these issues. Specifically, Joe's common and problematic thought processes were examined and more adaptive responses were developed. The following is an example of dialogue that resulted from Joe being asked what it was like to be gay:

Joe: It's hard. It's like you're not as good as straight people.
Counselor: What makes straight people better people than gay people?
Joe: Well, you know, you're always hearing lousy things about gays . . . never about straights.
Counselor: What do you hear about being straight?
Joe: [pause] Hmm. Nothing really, now that I think about it.
Counselor: So, people don't generally talk about being straight.
Joe: No reason to talk about it I suppose. Most people are straight.
Counselor: Since there are less gay people in the world, it makes them not as good?
Joe: Well, maybe "different" is a better word.
Counselor: And thus perhaps less understood?
Joe: Absolutely.
Counselor: Okay, being straight is more common and more understood. How does this translate to better?
Joe: (pause) It really doesn't, I guess.

When revisiting the question, Joe was able to respond more productively: "Being gay means that I'm not straight and that I may have more difficulties because of how society may treat gay people." Continuing with this approach, Joe was asked to keep a log of thoughts with regard to being gay that occurred within him in between sessions. During subsequent sessions the log was reviewed, and if the thoughts were deemed problematic, more productive responses were developed.

Although there was much progress with self-acceptance and worth, Joe's anxiety and fears about being found out, judged, and rejected, particularly in social situations, continued on some level. The focus of counseling then shifted to anxiety reduction in specific situations and the development of more effective coping strategies for these and other instances. Specific situations that caused anxiety for Joe included discussing LGBT issues with non-LGBT persons, being seen by friends alone with his partner in public, and coming out to loved ones. We addressed many of these throughout counseling via role play and homework. For example, we performed role plays encompassing mock conversations with coworkers about recent gay marriage news to help him work through the anxiety and fear surrounding such situations in a relaxed environment. Joe was also able to learn and practice responses and behaviors with which he gained comfort. He also agreed to homework (e.g., going to the movies or dinner alone with his partner, first in the city and then closer to his town) in order to gradually sensitize him to situations and to process it in counseling. These activities served the two-fold purpose of directly addressing specific situations that caused anxiety and allowing for knowledge acquisition and increased coping skills to transfer to the broader spread of anxiety.

Counseling results for Joe included anxiety reduction, particularly in social situations, and the belief that if he were out or outed it would not be nearly as disastrous as he had initially imagined. With the approval of his physician Joe was able to decrease his use of Xanax to an as-needed basis. His Global Assessment of Functioning improved to 75. He had made strides with improving his self-esteem and self-worth, understanding his place in the world, and looking at himself more positively in a heterosexually biased community. He gained helpful tools to maintain and improve these perspectives as well as address thoughts, behaviors, and situations more productively. Although Joe needed to hold off on further sessions because of time and monetary constraints, he agreed to return for follow-up services (including support in coming out) as needed. He was provided with a packet describing LGBT-friendly resources and services in his surrounding area, including a free LGBT-friendly counseling center in the city. He was also referred to an LGBT-friendly couples counselor so that he and his partner would have an appropriate avenue for working on relationship issues as needed, particularly in light of their sometimes differing perspectives on being out and how this may impact the future of their relationship.

Further Recommendations

Counselors in rural settings, as in all areas, will inevitably work with LGBT clients and would do well to understand and be comfortable with their own sexuality, biases, and prejudices about LGB orientations and transgender identities. Counselors who are not in touch with themselves with regard to these issues risk having a limited understanding of clients' issues or potentially conveying a heterosexist or sexist bias. Either of these not only can hinder or negatively affect the counseling relationship or direction but indeed may cause harm. Although there are several potential strengths, problems, and differences to matching clients and counselors in terms of sexual orientation (e.g., gay counselor with gay client), if they are understanding and comfortable with these issues counselors of all sexual orientations and gender identities will be better able to work effectively with this population.

In addition to being self-aware, it is imperative that counselors be knowledgeable of issues that affect LGBT persons and be familiar with their communities, cultures, and worldviews. Given the dearth of LGBT communities in rural areas, all counselors in these areas risk having limited training opportunities and experience working with LGBT persons; therefore, actively seeking out such training opportunities and experiences is essential to better serve LGBT clients. Because LGBT persons from rural areas have different experiences from those of LGBT individuals from urban or suburban areas, it is helpful for counselors to become familiar with rural culture and the LGBT persons who have been a part of it. This is important for counselors in all areas, not just rural ones. Although migration to cities may foster changes toward urban worldviews, counselors must consider that client behaviors and attitudes may still reflect rural culture and world-views. Furthermore, although it may be no easy task, making deliberate and thoughtful efforts to reach out to LGBT persons in rural areas may set the stage for needed advocacy and social action.

On the practice or agency level, counselors who are competent working with LGBT clientele should consider advertising this in mainstream arenas as well as in LGBT publications or websites. It may also be helpful to have LGBT publications and materials (e.g., Human Rights Campaign materials, *The Advocate, Transgender Tapestry*) visible in offices to promote a more inclusive atmosphere. In addition, Oswald and Culton (2003) provided excellent suggestions for assessing and promoting welcoming climates for LGBT clients in rural areas. These include having sexual orientation and gender identity–sensitive wording on intake forms, providing training on LGBT issues to staff, and including LGBT persons on lists of clientele served in brochures.

Finally, it is important to know about and help develop LGBT resources and services for rural clients. A helpful phone or Internet resource is the GLBT National Help Center (www.glbtnationalhelpcenter.org), which assists individuals of all ages with peer counseling, information, and local LGBT resources. In addition, through client recruitment or advertising, counselors can create support or process groups for LGBT individuals in rural areas and develop quality programming or activities in an attempt to increase socialization, target specific issues, or foster the beginnings or expansion of LGBT communities. For clients who have and prefer to use the Internet, counselors may create online resources or suggest existing ones such as Daily Strength (www.dailystrength.org), which offers LGBT support groups. In addition to keeping abreast of any helpful resources that may be available in their area, counselors working with rural LGBT persons need to be aware of clinical considerations relevant to this population as well as understand the sociocultural contexts of being LGBT in rural areas in order to foster appropriate service provision to this client base.

References

Association for Lesbian, Gay, Bisexual and Transgender Issues in Counseling. (1997). *Competencies for counseling gay, lesbian, bisexual and transgendered (LGBT) clients.* Alexandria, VA: Author.

Oswald, R. F., & Culton, L. S. (2003). Under the rainbow: Rural gay life and its relevance for family providers. *Family Relations, 52*(1), 72–81.

Weston, K. (1995). Get thee to a big city: Sexual imaginary and the great gay migration. *GLQ: A Journal of Lesbian and Gay Studies, 2*(3), 253–277.

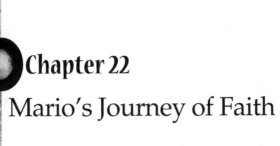

Chapter 22

Mario's Journey of Faith

Kathleen Y. Ritter and Anthony I. Terndrup

Identifying Data

Mario is a 23-year-old Caucasian male. He is the fifth of seven children of parents who have been married for more than 30 years. He has two older sisters, two older brothers, one younger brother, and one younger sister. His father is a partner in a family farming business with his mother's father and brother, and his mother is an instructional assistant for a special education teacher at a public high school. Mario lives with his parents and oldest brother in their family home in southern Oregon. His brother is disabled with a mental illness, a bipolar depression with psychotic features. While his youngest sister is completing her college education at a Catholic university in eastern Washington, the rest of his siblings have begun developing their professional careers and raising families of their own.

Mario's ethno-religious identity is rooted in his northern Italian cultural heritage and Roman Catholic faith tradition. His maternal grandfather and grandmother emigrated from their respective villages in Veneto and Toscana to the rural valleys of southern Oregon, met there, and were married in the late 1950s. His mother's parents have been a strong influence in his young life. His paternal grandfather died before Mario was born. He seldom sees his father's mother, who now lives with her daughter and granddaughter in Arizona.

Background Information

Mario was raised within the sociocultural matrix of the local Italian Catholic community. He was born in their hospital, baptized in their church, and educated in their schools. The folk beliefs and customs of his maternal grandparents and their *paisanos* (fellow countrymen) from the "old country" have deeply influenced Mario's faith development and religious instruction. Although he idealized the priests and sisters assigned to his hometown parish, Mario formed a rather anxious attachment to religious authority and became very conscientious in his religious practice. In the 12th grade he studied Christian morality at his Catholic school, led retreats for Catholic students at the public school, and received the annual award for religious loyalty and service to his alma mater at his commencement ceremony.

After graduating from high school, Mario earned his associate's degree at the local community college before transferring to a small Catholic liberal arts college in northern California where he studied philosophy, psychology, and religion. As he was completing his bachelor's degree, he considered entering the priesthood but instead decided to postpone his admission to the seminary in order to join the Jesuit Volunteer Corps (a 1-year Catholic program of volunteer service). Following his college graduation, he spent 12 months in Texas teaching English as a second language to immigrant families from Mexico. Meanwhile, he developed an intimate emotional attachment to Carlos, one of his male peers on the missionary team with whom he was living and working. When Mario began to fall in love for the first time with this other young man, he felt anxious and confused. During his religious education, Mario had learned that "homosexual acts are intrinsically disordered" and therefore morally wrong. Thus, he felt ashamed of admitting his attraction and afraid of expressing his affection for his companion. He tried to convince himself that he was not gay but was just falling in love with Carlos.

At the end of their year of service, Mario and Carlos distanced themselves from each other emotionally as well as geographically, as each returned to his hometown to resume life as he had known it before their forbidden and forsaken romance. Within weeks of returning to live with his parents and oldest brother in southern Oregon, Mario began to feel depressed. His determination to deny his emotional attachment to his beloved friend further complicated his grief. Against these odds, however, Mario found a job with the help of his maternal grandmother as an admitting clerk on the graveyard shift in the emergency room at the local Catholic hospital. At the end of each night of work, he attended morning Mass in the chapel where he would pray for God's grace to live a chaste and celibate life in obedience to church teaching. In the meantime, his work schedule was contributing to his sleep disturbance and social isolation.

Presenting Issues

Mario eventually succeeded in suppressing his affection for Carlos. However, he began to notice his attraction to other young men in his local community with whom he was unacquainted. His feelings for these relative strangers deeply troubled him. No longer able to attribute his erotic desire for men to his romantic love for Carlos, Mario confided his confusion and anxiety to his parish priest. Rather than reinforce his religious defenses, as Mario had hoped and expected, his progressive pastor affirmed the validity of his feelings and referred him to a professional counselor for affirmative psychotherapy.

At the onset of his treatment, Mario presented with a broad range of clinical issues. He alternated between depressed moods and anxious states. He was feeling empty over the loss of his attachment to Carlos and discouraged and hopeless about his lack of vision for the future. At present, he could foresee for himself neither a religious vocation nor any other professional career. He was feeling guilty for his fantasies about other young men and worthless for his failures to deny or repress them. He ascribed his poor concentration and fatigue to his insomnia and his sleeplessness to his graveyard shift in the emergency room. However, he further admitted to feeling distracted and exhausted by his obsessive fear of surrendering to sexual temptation and immorality. Mario was afraid of inadvertently flirting with other young men and inevitably yielding to their advances and was continually worried about losing self-control.

Diagnoses

After interviewing Mario and evaluating his presenting issues, his counselor completed the following multiaxial assessment:

Axis I	296.22	Major Depressive Disorder, Single Episode, Moderate
	300.00	Anxiety Disorder Not Otherwise Specified
	V62.89	Religious or Spiritual Problem, Phase of Life Problem
Axis II	V71.09	No Diagnosis
Axis III	None	
Axis IV	Brother's mental illness, loss of friend, stressful work schedule	
Axis V	Global Assessment of Functioning = 55 (at intake)	

The forthcoming discussion reflects the clinical decision making the counselor used to formulate her appraisal.

On Axis I, Mario's counselor based her primary diagnosis of her client's distress on his clinically significant symptoms of major depression. Requisite symptoms of depressed mood and loss of interest were both present, as well were six other criteria (five are required): feeling sad or empty, diminished pleasure in all activities, insomnia, fatigue or loss of energy, feelings of worthlessness or guilt, and diminished concentration.

The counselor also considered diagnosing Adjustment Disorder With Mixed Anxiety and Depressed Mood (309.28) given that Mario appeared to have developed these symptoms in response to separating from Carlos. However, her consideration of his premorbid anxious attachment to religious authority prior to the onset of this stressor, along with his family history of mental illness, led to her suspicion that his symptoms might persist for more than an additional 6 months. Therefore, she settled on a secondary diagnosis of Anxiety Disorder Not Otherwise Specified (300.00) in order to account for his continual worry, obsessive tendencies, and numerous anxiety-related symptoms, none of which appeared to meet full criteria for any specific anxiety disorder.

In addition to Mario's primary and secondary diagnoses on Axis I, his counselor itemized two other conditions on which to focus her clinical attention. Both of these focuses shared the same diagnostic code (V62.89). Accordingly, she identified a Religious or Spiritual Problem with Mario's struggles to reconcile his sexual orientation with his Catholic faith and to differentiate between the moral authority of his individual conscience and that of the institutional church. In addition, she associated a Phase of Life Problem with his developmental challenges to leave parental control and to start a new career.

The counselor further considered diagnosing an Identity Problem (313.82) but reconsidered coding an "uncertainty about . . . sexual orientation and behavior" in his clinical profile (American Psychiatric Association [APA], 1994, p. 685). She recognized the ease with which authorized third parties could confuse this rather benign condition with a "persistent and marked distress about sexual orientation" (APA, 1994, p. 538), one of three clinical examples of a Sexual Disorder Not Otherwise Specified (302.9) enumerated in the *Diagnostic and Statistical Manual of Mental Disorders* (4th ed.). This category of sexual disturbance appears to be the reformulated remnant of an archaic and obsolete classification (i.e., ego-dystonic homosexuality) removed from the diagnostic nomenclature after the revision of the *Diagnostic and Statistical Manual of Mental Disorders* (3rd ed.; APA, 1980). Mario's counselor was careful to avoid any suggestion of psychosexual pathology in her multiaxial assessment and thus chose not to include either of these two categories.

In general, Mario's mental health and physical wellness had been rather stable. On Axis II, therefore, his counselor identified no "enduring pattern" of personality dysfunction that "is inflexible and pervasive across a broad range of personal and social situations" (APA, 1994, p. 633). Likewise, she specified no general medical condition related to his mood and anxiety disorders on Axis III.

On Axis IV, Mario's counselor reported three psychosocial problems that she assessed could affect her client's diagnosis, treatment, and prognosis. First, she considered how his brother's mental illness might suggest a family pattern of vulnerability to stress. She also recognized how Mario may compensate for his sibling's psychiatric disability by not wanting to disappoint and further burden his parents. Second, she considered how Mario's disenfranchised and suppressed grief over his loss of friendship with Carlos might complicate his depressed mood. Third, she recognized how his stressful work schedule on the graveyard shift in a clerical position for which he was overqualified might depress his vocational ambition and exacerbate his social isolation.

On Axis V, Mario's counselor used the Global Assessment of Functioning Scale to report her estimation of his overall level of psychological, social, and occupational performance. Based on the moderate severity of his clinically significant symptoms of depression and anxiety, she assessed his current level of impairment at 55.

Theoretical Framework(s)

Given the severity of Mario's depression, his counselor decided first to treat the case from cognitive and behavioral perspectives. She selected the cognitive approach because she reasoned that if Mario wasn't able to reduce his dichotomous and negative self-referent ideations, the possibility of him feeling better and less fretful in the near future was unlikely. For example, Mario thought that his only choice was to choose between living as either an "obedient" son or a "prodigal" son of his church and family. He also believed that if he could not embrace and embody church teachings about mandatory celibacy for homosexual Catholics, then he was fundamentally opting for a disobedient and dissolute lifestyle. Furthermore, using the cognitive and behavioral approaches allowed the counselor to address Mario's punitive superego, which was causing him to feel extreme guilt for even the slightest discordant thoughts (e.g., "I think he's handsome"), feelings (e.g., "I feel excited when I see attractive men"), and behaviors (e.g., "I could not stop stealing glances at him"). She initially felt it was also important to target Mario's isolation and hopelessness, so she helped him initiate some behaviors that had the possibility of increasing his interaction with others, his exploration of alternative careers, and his sense of pleasure in the activities of living. Accordingly, Mario's counselor encouraged and challenged him to introduce himself to one new coworker in the hospital cafeteria or chapel each week between counseling sessions, to check the newspaper for interesting job titles and descriptions, and to join one of the social justice ministries at his church. As some of the initial symptoms began to lessen, she added an existential focus, particularly regarding Mario's conflicts of meaning and valuing regarding his religion and sexual orientation. Psychodynamic and family-of-origin perspectives were also woven into the treatment when it became obvious that there were many parallels between Mario's feelings about his religion and his family of origin. For instance, Mario likened his church to a maternal parent who demanded his obedience. Although his own mother was not quite so demanding, he did expect himself to please her and his Italian grandmother as well as to become and to be a source of pride for the entire family. Finally, psychoeducation and support were provided throughout the course of therapy (see "Interventions Used" for examples).

Goals of Treatment

Given Mario's significant level of distress, the following goals were formulated:

1. Reduce Mario's depression and elevate his mood.
2. Decrease anxiety and obsessive features.

3. Initiate career planning.
4. Lessen cognitive dissonance.
5. Facilitate grief recovery.

Interventions Used

Because of the seriousness of Mario's depression, the first intervention was to rule out suicide. When answering the counselor's question to assess risk of danger to self, Mario said that although he felt as if a part of him was dying, he would never take his life because of the principles of his Catholic faith and his strong attachment to his family. Attempts were made to join with Mario in reflecting the depth of his sadness, hopelessness, and fears. He described a profound moral dilemma regarding his strong same-sex attractions, the fear of hurting his parents, and the intense desire to be faithful to his religious beliefs. During this time, his counselor empathized, supported, and then gently challenged when his dichotomizations became obsessive and led to an increase in anxiety. Mario explained to his counselor how much he wanted to be attracted to women and how he desired to marry and have a family and that he needed "evidence" that this would not be possible. In order to gather that evidence, he and his counselor developed a plan in which he was to meet women, initiate conversation with them, and then ask for a date. Mario attempted this strategy with two women and even had a slight attraction to one, which gave him a glimmer of hope. This hope lasted barely a week before he lost the interest and motivation to continue the experiment. During this time his counselor provided psychoeducation (such as information about the continuum of sexual responsiveness and attractions) when an explanation or an illumination might help Mario increase his perspective and reduce his cognitive dissonance.

Along the way, Mario's counselor encouraged him to take a career exploration class at the local state college. He agreed to do so as well as to take two additional classes to investigate other areas of interest. When the results of the vocational interest inventories he had taken were available, Mario discovered that all of the scores were in the midrange. These findings, along with the "failure" of the dating experiment, seemed to convince Mario that his situation was "completely" hopeless. At this point, his counselor actively began to challenge his dichotomies and conclusions about himself (e.g., "I am a failure," "I should be able to control myself," "I shouldn't feel so awful," "I should be able to be happy").

Four months into treatment it appeared as if Mario's meaning system had collapsed and an existential perspective was added to the therapy. He told his counselor that he was "sad" about the awful reality of his situation. At the same time, he denied any anger, although his verbalizations (e.g., "I played by the rules," "It is not fair") led his counselor to believe that underneath his somewhat flat demeanor there was unexpressed ire. Nonetheless, she challenged his dichotomous thinking and offered psychoeducation regarding grieving and loss. She further explained the process of faith development and the distress that James Fowler (1995) contended occurs when conventional systems of belief fail and tumultuous individuative-reflective processes occur. Mario possibly internalized some of these concepts, because a few sessions later he told his counselor that he was ready to acknowledge his homosexuality. He said he felt relieved and that things were "settled" for now. Furthermore, he realized how much he needed to belong to his church and, although he may be lonely and celibate, at least he would be a "faithful son." With renewed commitment, he applied for and was offered a job teaching religion at the local Catholic high school. Shortly afterward he told his counselor that he was discontinuing therapy and was going to "try it alone for awhile."

Mario returned to therapy 3 months later in much pain. Knowing he was gay and yet teaching Catholic doctrine had reactivated his cognitive dissonance and feelings of alienation from both his church and his family. Seeing that the feelings of attachment to, and estrangement from, his religion and his strong Italian Catholic family and community were quite similar, Mario's counselor began to approach his dilemma from family systems and psychodynamic perspectives. Emotions of precarious attachment existed in both situations, and the fear of separation from either was intense. This state of affairs continued for 2 months, and Mario finally quit his job in order to reduce the pain and decrease the emotional conflict. This choice was somewhat successful because it freed Mario from having to face church doctrine on a daily basis, but it still did not reduce his feelings of marginalization from religion and family. However, the decision to terminate his employment in spite of family pressures to continue somewhat empowered Mario to make other courageous choices, such as to fall in love with a man. Unfortunately, the man moved away and he and Mario were forced to continue their relationship through correspondence. The departure led to an activation of separation anxiety for Mario, and his counselor again resumed psychoeducation regarding loss and grieving as well as challenged his dichotomous and defeating cognitions (e.g., "I'll never fall in love again" and "No one will ever love me in the same way"). These processes, however, seemed to trigger something in Mario, and his loneliness forced him to reach out to other gay men. As he began exploring the local gay community, Mario described feeling more "free." He became less bland in affect, had fewer dichotomous cognitions, and was more interpersonally relational. At the last meeting, he reached out to shake the hand of his counselor for the first time in the 10 months of therapy.

Outcomes

Mario's counselor has seen him several times since the termination of therapy. Shortly after they discontinued meeting, Mario came out to his large Italian family, who, incidentally, has welcomed each of his two long-term partners (the first of whom died of HIV infection) into the *famiglia*. He transferred his need to serve others into a helping profession and has continued his relationship with his faith but has redefined it on his own terms. From time to time he continues to struggle with institutional authority and often is taken aback by yet another pronouncement from the Vatican related to sexual minorities. Still, he continues to be a "faithful son" but in accordance with his own conscience.

Transference and Countertransference Issues

From early adolescence, Mario idealized his parish priest. When his progressive pastor referred him for affirmative psychotherapy, Mario likewise developed an idealizing transference with his professional counselor. In the initial phase of his therapy, he experienced her as all knowing, all loving, and all powerful in much of the same way as he envisioned God and religious authority. She became for him his childhood image of the perfect parent. His idealization of his counselor reflected his developmental need to participate in her psychological strength and stability and to merge with her for emotional safety and security. In other words, Mario's imagination of his counselor's perfection bolstered and empowered him to feel sturdier and steadier, as well as more sound and confident, within the relational context of their psychotherapeutic alliance.

As his therapy progressed, however, Mario noticed that his counselor's empathy was not always accurate. Occasionally he felt misunderstood and disagreed with her interpretations and recommendations. Once, for example, she prematurely reflected the anger she felt that he suppressed beneath his flat affect. Mario was not ready for her explanation and thus resisted her intervention. He thought she must be mistaken because he tried so hard to be gentle and kind to everyone. These inevitable empathic breaches, along with her utmost respect for his autonomy and regard for his integrity, gradually allowed and enabled Mario to differentiate between his and her understandings without fearing the loss of their attachment and to internalize her unconditional esteem for his human dignity. Eventually these developmental processes and outcomes were replicated in Mario's relations with his family and his church.

Mario's counselor had several of her own countertransference issues to confront throughout the course of this case. The first was her sense that Mario was primarily same-sex attracted although he was not ready to acknowledge this reality at the beginning of therapy. Being more extroverted and fast moving than Mario, she had to make a conscious effort to slow herself down and become synchronized with Mario's cautious and reflective pace. Watching him struggle so tediously was painful for her, and she sometimes had to restrain herself from offering comfort or reassurance before he had concluded something intellectually for himself. Furthermore, also being from a Catholic tradition, his counselor had to guard herself from projecting her own beliefs onto Mario. For example, when he expressed strong views about the sinfulness of same-sex feelings and behaviors and subsequently of himself, she had to remind herself that he had to struggle through this conflict in his own way and at his own speed. Being aware of her own pulls, however, helped her to keep her differences with the institutional church separate from Mario's.

Recommendations for Further Counseling or Training

It is recommended that counselors who assist sexual minority clients in resolving religious issues familiarize themselves with the thinking of James Fowler (e.g., Fowler, 1987, 1995, 1999). His descriptions of the various phases through which individuals typically proceed during the often painful processes of developing an authentic and personal faith can be helpful guides for therapists. Mario's counselor often used Fowler's ideas as a framework for conceptualizing his struggles and for assisting him in reframing his relationship to his religion and to his faith. Similarly, therapists might become familiar with the processes of loss and transformation described in many models of grieving (e.g., Schneider, 1994). This framework was essential for helping Mario's counselor see that all is not lost with loss and that renewed vision often occurs after the death of someone or something that an individual holds sacred.

References

American Psychiatric Association. (1980). *Diagnostic and statistical manual of mental disorders* (3rd ed.). Washington, DC: Author.

American Psychiatric Association. (1994). *Diagnostic and statistical manual of mental disorders* (4th ed.). Washington, DC: Author.

Fowler, J. W. (1987). *Faith development and pastoral care.* Minneapolis, MN: Fortress Press.

Fowler, J. W. (1995). *Stages of faith: The psychology of human development and the quest for meaning.* New York, NY: HarperOne.

Fowler, J. W. (1999). *Becoming adult, becoming Christian: Adult development and Christian faith.* San Francisco, CA: Jossey-Bass.

Schneider, J. M. (1994). *Finding my way: Healing and transformation through loss and grief.* Colfax, WI: Seasons Press.

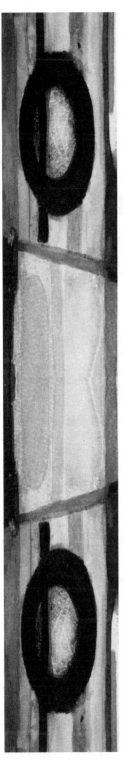

Section 4
Wellness Issues

Competent counselors will:

- recognize that their own sexual orientations and gender identities are relevant to the helping relationship and influence the counseling process.
- seek consultation or supervision to ensure that their own biases or knowledge deficits about LGBT persons do not negatively influence the helping relationship.
- understand that attempts to alter or change the sexual orientations or gender identities of LGBT clients may be detrimental or even life-threatening, and, further, are not supported by the research and therefore should not be undertaken.
- identify the heterosexist assumptions inherent in current life span development theories and account for this bias in assessment procedures and counseling practices.
- affirm that sexual minority persons have the potential to integrate their GLB orientations and transgendered identities into fully functioning and emotionally healthy lives.

In the chapters that compose this section, authors look at the various wellness issues that face lesbian, gay, bisexual, and transgender (LGBT) clients—sex in lesbian relationships, sexual addiction, HIV and

AIDS, substance abuse and dependency, lesbian health issues, so-called conversion therapies, domestic violence, the use of psychological tests, and the fact that their sexual minority status can be used as a political target. Overarching all of these chapters is the question of how LGBT persons, couples, and families maintain their psychological and physical health in a world filled with stressors.

The first chapter in this section is "Sex and Lesbian Women" by Joy S. Whitman. According to Brown (2000), the heteropatriarchal view of sex is often that of genital contact and orgasm wherein women are passive in the initiation and active in the reception. The frequency of that contact becomes the measure of sexual health, and other types of sexual play are seen as less significant to that health. Framed in this context, lesbians have been characterized as losing a desire for sex and decreasing the initiation and frequency of sex more quickly than women in heterosexual couples (a phenomenon referred to popularly as "lesbian bed death"; Nichols, 2004). Dr. Whitman exposes this phenomenon as being grounded in a heteronormative framework and asserts that lesbian sex needs to be explored and framed within the context of what is normal and regular for sex between women.

Nichols (2004) cited studies comparing lesbian and heterosexual relationships and findings of sexual satisfaction between lesbian women that does not include genital contact or orgasm. These studies also indicate that the length of time lesbians spend in a sexual encounter is greater than for heterosexuals and that lesbians are more sexually assertive and more arousable than heterosexual women. These alternative perspectives offer counselors broader ways to intervene clinically when lesbians present with issues around sexuality. Dr. Whitman discusses these issues, which are of considerable clinical importance to lesbians and their sexuality, using a case study of a female couple that presented with sexual concerns. In this case, she discusses the clinical interventions and the process used to tease apart the various components of sex between women.

For some gay men, sex can turn into sexual addiction. This is the focus of Brian J. Dew and Misti A. Storie's chapter "Sexual Addiction and the Gay Male Client." The study of addictive behaviors among LGBT persons has most often focused on substance-related disorders. Only recently have there been investigations into process-oriented addictions such as food, gambling, and, in particular, sex (Adams & Robinson, 2001; Kuzma & Black, 2008). However, sexual addiction is not considered a unique mental disorder in the *Diagnostic and Statistical Manual of Mental Disorders* (4th ed., text rev.; American Psychiatric Association, 2000). Dr. Dew and Ms. Storie present a case study of a 37-year-old gay male who has been assigned to his employee assistance program counselor as a result of decreased work performance, depressed mood, and having been caught by his employer viewing sexually explicit images on his office computer.

According to the preponderance of research, issues of sexual compulsivity are best addressed using cognitive behavior therapy (Walch & Prejean, 2001). Prochaska and DiClemente's (1983) model of change is essential to providing effective counseling services to an addicted client, especially one who is sexually addicted. Matching the client's identified stage of change with appropriate interventions is necessary for increasing the potential for successful client outcomes. Recognition of the Triple A engine (accessibility, affordability, and anonymity) as a primary appeal of online sexual behavior is a fundamental component of counseling sexually addicted clients (Cooper & Griffin-Shelley, 2002). Counselors must help their clients recognize the flawed cognitions associated with these various perceptions of online sexual activity.

In the recent past the gay male community was devastated by the AIDS epidemic. AIDS is no longer a death sentence, but many clients live with HIV. David W. Hart examines this issue in "Counseling HIV-Positive Gay Men." HIV and AIDS have been a part of the gay male community for more than 40 years now. This spectrum of diseases has changed the culture of gay men and requires addressing in any counseling work with gay men. In the case presented here, Mr. Hart uses queer-affirmative psychotherapy, which was born out of the feminist movement and which draws the analogy between misogyny and homophobia in a society in which gay men may be hated or feared because they are perceived as being or behaving like women (Lebolt, 1999). In the practice of queer-affirmative psychotherapy, the first goal is to openly acknowledge that gay men live in a heterocentrist culture that actively legitimizes and perpetuates stigmas related to sexual orientation and diagnosis. Within the dominant cultural lexicon, HIV/AIDS is deemed to be a "gay" disease, and the diagnosis is analogous to a scarlet letter—marking the diagnosed individual as "one of them."

The second goal of queer-affirmative therapy is to unconditionally affirm queer lives and experiences. Ultimately it is the job of the counselor to normalize the rage, fear, and hurt that a client is feeling as a result of the stigma and marginalization he or she is experiencing. This is accomplished by practicing traditional humanistic principles, including demonstrating unconditional positive regard, demonstrating neutrality through body language, and reflecting content and underlying feelings. Therefore, the first interventions always involve simply listening, responding with empathy, and avoiding making any assumptions about the client's experiences. In the case study described here, Mr. Hart addresses such issues as depression, religion/spirituality, transference/countertransference, and race sensitively and with great compassion.

Drug and alcohol use and abuse have historically played a significant role in the LGBT community (Kominars & Kominars, 1996). Often the abuse of drugs and alcohol has been attributed to a struggle with sexual identity. A. Michael Hutchins's chapter "Moving Through the Void: Counseling Gay Men With Histories of Chemical Abuse and Dependency" discusses this struggle. The relationship between the complex dynamics of sexual identity development and drug and alcohol abuse is not necessarily a causal one. In a complex and rapidly changing world, counselors are called on to be agents of change and supporters of growth and development; addressing cultural issues is a critical part of treatment (Wright, 2001). In the case described here, Dr. Hutchins works with his client Carlos in an integrated and holistic manner that focuses on growth and development rather than on pathology.

Health and wellness issues also impact lesbians as well as their sex lives, something addressed by Jane E. Rheineck and Catherine B. Roland in "The Case of Eve: A Picture of a Lesbian Health Journey." A broad and expanding area of research focuses on health care for diverse LGBT persons. These individuals not only struggle with the same health issues as their heterosexual counterparts but also experience health issues that are often passed over or ignored entirely by health care providers. Heterosexism and discrimination are often present within the health care system, and as a result there is disparity (Johnson, Mimiaga, & Bradford, 2008; Weisz, 2009).

Discrimination and social stigma can impede both access to and utilization of programs and services. LGBT persons are significantly more likely than heterosexual persons to be uninsured, with lesbians, LGBT youth, and transgender individuals representing the highest percentage of the underinsured (Johnson et al., 2008). Without health insurance, access to programs is limited, and as a result a health disparity exists.

The American Public Health Association (1999) has acknowledged the special concerns of the LGBT community in a policy statement on the need for health care research. In addition, the U.S. Department of Health and Human Services (2000) has produced a manual addressing the public health needs of LGBT persons. All of these policies will hopefully influence research and funding and will impact the lives and well-being of LGBT people and their families.

Drs. Rheineck and Roland's case provides an example of some of the health care issues faced by many members of the LGBT community. Understanding health concerns is always important, but it is imperative for counselors to also understand secondary tangential issues such as physical and emotional support received from health care institutions and medical professionals, the psychological well-being of patients and their families, and overall standards of care.

For many LGBT persons wellness includes recognition by religious and spiritual organizations. Some LGBT persons who embrace certain denominations of Christianity find that homosexuality is condemned and that they are expected to change their sexual orientation. Douglas C. Haldeman uses two case studies to examine this in "Sexual Orientation Conversion Therapy: Fact, Fiction, and Fraud." Today mental health organizations consider same-sex attractions a normal variant of human behavior (American Psychological Association, 2009). However, not all segments of the population agree with this (American Psychological Association, 2009; Tozer & Hayes, 2004). Notably, Christian fundamentalists do not agree and attempt to change homosexuals into heterosexuals through the use of reparative therapy. The term beginning to be used now in the professional literature to describe this process is *sexual orientation change efforts* (SOCE) because the process is not therapy. Therapists often see clients who have gone through SOCE and must help them with the impact of this experience. Post-SOCE trauma often includes depression, guilt, suicidality, demasculinization, and/or intimacy avoidance (Haldeman, 2002). Because SOCE are aimed primarily at men, the individuals in Dr. Haldeman's two case studies are male.

Domestic violence occurs in LGBT relationships at about the same rate as it does in heterosexual relationships (see Burke & Follingstad, 1999). Yet most domestic violence services are geared toward heterosexuals and don't consider the needs of LGBT victims, as Connie R. Matthews and Peggy Lorah discuss in "Domestic Violence in Same-Sex Relationships." Few shelters for victims of domestic violence make the necessary accommodations for those in same-sex relationships, and LGBT individuals who have used such shelters have not found them to be very helpful (McClennen, Summers, & Vaughan, 2002; Merrill & Wolfe, 2000; Renzetti, 1992). This may be one reason why most LGBT persons who experience domestic violence are likely to rely on friends and family rather than shelters for support and sometimes for protection (Merrill & Wolfe, 2000; Renzetti, 1992). Most domestic violence is perpetrated by men against women, and when theories and services are geared toward male/female violence, same-sex violence becomes difficult to identify and to treat (Letellier, 1994; Pitt & Dolan-Soto, 2001; Seelau & Seelau, 2005). Drs. Matthews and Lorah describe two domestic violence cases that therapists might come across in their daily practice.

Therapists who use psychological assessment often forget that these tools have not been normed on LGBT populations. Therefore, they must be used carefully, as Jeffrey P. Prince and Michael J. Potoczniak argue in "Using Psychological Assessment Tools With Lesbian, Gay, Bisexual, and Transgender Clients." When interpreting assessment results from an LGBT client, the therapist must minimize homophobia and heterosexism as much as possible. Drs. Prince and Dr. Potoczniak describe how the use of assessment tools can help guide explorations of diagnosis, past experiences, and the future all within the context of multiple intersecting identities. In the case of Leo, many intersecting identities (ethnicity, religion, sexual orientation, health, economic status) impact the interpretation of his assessment results and the direction of treatment. Leo is being seen at a short-term counseling facility for academic problems, and the therapist knows that using assessment tools can speed up the therapy process. The counselor provides interpretations tentatively as he operates from a social cognitive career theory (Lent, Brown, & Hackett, 1996) approach.

Finally, this section ends with Glenda M. Russell discussing how anti-gay political referendums seen in almost every state impact the wellness of LGBT people in "When the Political and the Personal Collide: Lesbian, Gay, Bisexual, and Transgender People as Political Targets." Therapists rarely examine with clients the psychological impacts that negative campaigns against same-sex marriage can have on them. Dr. Russell's chapter explores the adverse effects such political campaigns can have on clients and how to use a cognitive framework to combat this. As with many of the other authors of this book, cognitive reframing is a major piece of Dr. Russell's therapy process. Dr. Russell also uses mirroring and explains how to apply this approach. A primary aspect of working with the adverse psychological impacts of antigay political referendums is helping clients develop active coping skills. Some of this active coping is specific to the distressing event, and some includes exploring internalized homophobia. Here Dr. Russell describes James, a gay man who is referred for counseling with depression. James includes the passage of Proposition 8 (which banned gay marriage in California) as affecting his sense of feeling "doomed." The chapter ends with a discussion of how James uses new active coping skills developed in therapy.

References

Adams, K. M., & Robinson, D. W. (2001). Shame reduction, affect regulation, and sexual boundary development: Essential building blocks of sexual addiction treatment. *Sexual Addiction and Compulsivity, 8,* 23–44.

American Psychiatric Association. (2000). *Diagnostic and statistical manual of mental disorders* (4th ed., text rev.). Washington, DC: Author.

American Psychological Association. (2009). *Report of the Task Force on Appropriate Therapeutic Responses to Sexual Orientation.* Washington, DC: Author.

American Public Health Association. (1999). Policy statement 9819: The need for public health research on gender identity and sexual orientation. *American Journal of Public Health, 89,* 444–445.

Brown, L. (2000). Dangerousness, impotence, silence, and invisibility: Heterosexism in the construction of women's sexuality. In C. B. Travis & J. W. White (Eds.), *Sexuality, society and feminism* (pp. 273–298). Washington, DC: American Psychological Association.

Burke, L. K., & Follingstad, D. R. (1999). Violence in lesbian and gay relationships: Theory, prevalence and correlational factors. *Clinical Psychology Review, 19,* 487–512.

Cooper, A., & Griffin-Shelley, E. (2002). The Internet: The next sexual revolution. In A. Cooper (Ed.), *Sex and the Internet: A guidebook for clinicians* (pp. 1–15). New York, NY: Brunner & Routledge.

Haldeman, D.C. (2002). Therapeutic antidotes: Helping gay and bisexual men recover from conversion therapies. *Journal of Lesbian and Gay Psychotherapy, 5*(3–4), 117–130.

Johnson, C. V., Mimiaga, M. J., & Bradford, J. (2008). Health care issues among lesbian, gay, bisexual, transgendered and intersex (LGBTI) populations in the United States: Introduction. *Journal of Homosexuality, 54*(3), 213–224.

Kominars, S., & Kominars, K. (1996). *Accepting ourselves and others: A journey into recovery from addiction and compulsive behaviors for gays, lesbians, and bisexuals.* Center City, MN: Hazelden.

Kuzma, J. M., & Black, D. W. (2008). Epidemiology, prevalence, and natural history of compulsive sexual behavior. *Psychiatric Clinics of North America, 31,* 603–611.

Lebolt, J. (1999). Gay affirmative psychotherapy: A phenomenological study. *Clinical Social Work Journal, 27,* 355–370.

Lent, R. W., Brown, S. D., & Hackett, G. (1996). Career development from a social cognitive perspective. In D. Brown & L. Brooks (Eds.), *Career choice and development* (pp. 373–421). San Francisco, CA: Jossey-Bass.

Letellier, P. (1994). Gay and bisexual male domestic violence victimization: Challenges to feminist theory and responses to violence. *Violence and Victims, 9*, 95–106.

McClennen, J. C., Summers, A. B., & Vaughan, C. (2002). Gay men's domestic violence dynamics, help-seeking behaviors, and correlates. *Journal of Gay and Lesbian Social Services, 14*, 23–49.

Merrill, G. S., & Wolfe, V. A. (2000). Battered gay men: An exploration of abuse, help seeking, and why they stay. *Journal of Homosexuality, 39*(2), 1–30.

Nichols, M. (2004). Lesbian sexuality/female sexuality: Rethinking "lesbian bed death." *Sexual and Relationship Therapy, 19*(4), 363–371.

Pitt, E., & Dolan-Soto, D. (2001). Clinical considerations in working with victims of same-sex domestic violence. *Journal of the Gay and Lesbian Medical Association, 5*(4), 163–169. doi:10.1023/A:1014266212280

Prochaska, J. O., & DiClemente, C. C. (1983). Stages and processes of self-change of smoking: Toward an integrative model of change. *Journal of Consulting and Clinical Psychology, 51*, 390–395.

Renzetti, C. M. (1992). *Violent betrayal: Partner abuse in lesbian relationships.* Newbury Park, CA: Sage.

Seelau, S. M., & Seelau, E. P. (2005). Gender-role stereotypes and perceptions of heterosexual, gay, and lesbian domestic violence. *Journal of Family Violence, 20*, 363–371. doi:10.1007/s10896-005-7798-4

Tozer, E. E., & Hayes, J. A. (2004). The role of religiosity, internalized homonegativity, and identity development: Why do individuals seek conversion therapy? *The Counseling Psychologist, 27*, 722–742.

U.S. Department of Health and Human Services. (2000). *Healthy People 2010: Understanding and improving health* (2nd ed.). Washington, DC: U.S. Government Printing Office.

Walch, S. E., & Prejean, J. (2001). Reducing HIV risk from compulsive sexual behavior using cognitive behavioral therapy within a harm reduction framework: A case example. *Sexual Addiction & Compulsivity, 8*(2), 113–128.

Weisz, V. K. (2009). Social justice considerations for lesbian and bisexual women's health. *Journal of Obstetric, Gynecologic, & Neonatal Nursing, 38*, 81–87.

Wright, E. (2001). *Cultural issues in working with lesbian, gay, bisexual, and transgender individuals: A provider's introduction to substance abuse treatment for lesbian, gay, bisexual, and transgender individuals.* Rockville, MD: U.S. Department of Health and Human Services, Substance Abuse and Mental Health Services Administration.

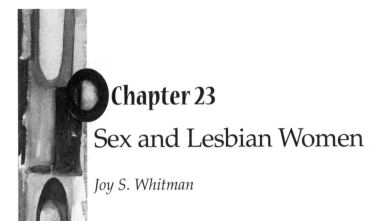

Chapter 23
Sex and Lesbian Women

Joy S. Whitman

The expression of a lesbian's sexuality can and does take a variety of forms, through romantic touches or glances, holding and cuddling, and sexual play. How it is defined and understood, however, has often been by using heterosexist definitions of normal sexual expression. Brown (2000) noted how the heteropatriarchal view of sex is often that of genital contact and orgasm wherein women are passive in the initiation and active in the reception. The frequency of that contact is often the measure of sexual health, and other types of sexual play are seen as less significant to that health. This view leaves little room for the spectrum of lesbian sexual expression.

This definition can cause problems between lesbian women when they attempt to understand their sexual relationships through a heteronormative lens. These perspectives lead to one of the greatest myths of lesbian sex in a coupled relationship: lesbian bed death. This myth has been bantered about in the lesbian communities for decades, and its mention in this chapter is important for clinical reasons. Lesbians have historically been characterized as losing a desire for sex and decreasing the initiation and frequency of sex more quickly than women in heterosexual couples. Unfortunately, this characterization has been understood using a heteronormative framework, leaving lesbians afraid of this phenomenon.

The research, however, indicates that this is not the case and that sex between women needs to be explored and framed within the context of what is normal and regular for sex between women. Nichols (2004) offered an alternative perspective, citing studies comparing lesbian and heterosexual relationships and findings of sexual satisfaction between lesbian women that does not include genital contact or orgasm. These studies also indicate that the length of time lesbians spend in a sexual encounter is greater than for heterosexuals and that lesbians are more sexually assertive and more arousable than heterosexual women. These alternative perspectives offer counselors broader ways to intervene clinically when lesbians present with issues around sexuality.

Because the issues of desire, initiation, and frequency are of considerable clinical importance to lesbians and their sexuality, in this chapter I discuss these issues using the case of a couple who presented with these concerns. I also discuss clinical interventions and the process used to tease apart the various components of sex between lesbian women.

Liz and Maria

The Presenting Issue: Where Did the Sex Go?

Liz and Maria sought counseling because of a change in their sexual relationship. Liz was a 37-year-old lesbian of Italian descent, and Maria was a 35-year-old lesbian of Mexican descent. They each had been in a variety of short- and long-term relationships with women. They had been together for more than 2 years and noticed early on that Liz enjoyed sex play more frequently than Maria. When asked, Liz stated that she preferred having sex at least twice a week, whereas Maria preferred it twice a month. At the beginning of their relationship, they found themselves highly sexually aroused by each other and engaged in sexual contact at least twice a week. Liz found this satisfying, and though the frequency was more than usual for Maria, she started enjoying it. As the newness of each other's bodies began to wane and the relationship became more routine, the frequency of sex decreased, resulting in sex play once a week. Most recently they had realized that they had fallen into a pattern of having sex perhaps once a month, something neither was content with. In particular, Liz found herself often feeling sexually frustrated and wanting more sexual contact with Maria.

Assessment: Gathering Background and Sexual Histories

It was important to first rule out any medical condition, health issues, or prior or presenting mental illness that might have been impacting their relationship. They both denied any physical illness, mental illness, or abuse of drugs or alcohol that may have been interfering with their desire. In addition, it was important to take a history of any childhood sexual abuse given the frequency with which it presents in relationships between women (Barret & Logan, 2002). Neither reported a history of having been sexually abused as children, and their trauma histories revealed no other kinds of abuse. This helped to clear the way for a less complicated exploration of their sexual histories.

We explored what sex meant for each. Of primary clinical interest was how each woman defined sexual contact and what being sexual meant for them. I wanted to understand through what lens each perceived sexual play and whether they subscribed to the heteronormative definition. As it turned out, Liz had a more narrowly defined and heteronormative definition, seeing sex as an act that involved the sexual touching of breasts and genital contact leading to orgasm. Maria agreed that these acts were sexually satisfying for her, but she had a broader view of sex that also included cuddling, holding, and massages that did not necessarily lead to orgasm. Maria said she liked holding Liz, cuddling while watching a movie, and being held by Liz when falling asleep at night. Maria said she found immense satisfaction in these nonsexual contacts; Liz found these contacts comforting but also sexually frustrating at times because she became sexually aroused through this physical contact.

In addition, each discussed the role of initiating physical contact, whether it led to orgasm or not. Liz stated that she was typically the partner to initiate sexual contact, enjoying the control and play that went with it. She said she liked to think about ways to entice her partner to be sexual and gave examples of this behavior, including both subtle cues and straightforward advances. Maria offered that she usually waited for her partner to initiate sexual contact, unsure of her own sexual interest at times but usually receptive when approached. She said that this pattern had been typical for her in past relationships, that she often derived satisfaction from a mix of sexual and nonsexual touching, and that she often initiated nonsexual touching with Liz.

Over time, Liz had begun to decrease acts of initiation in response to Maria's decreasing interest in contact leading primarily to orgasm. A pattern had developed of Liz feeling rejected by Maria and Maria feeling pressured to be more "sexy." Liz said that she was very attracted to Maria, and though she enjoyed all of the nonsexual touch, she also wanted to have more sex play between them. She offered that she was typically the partner to seek more sexual contact in past relationships.

We also explored time spent in sexual play and the expectation each had in regard to time allotted for sex. Liz enjoyed both spending a long time in love making and also having "quickies" when time is limited. She and Maria agreed that when they had time for sex, they enjoyed kissing and fondling each other without moving quickly to orgasm. In fact, Maria said that this was her favorite form of having sex with Liz and wanted more of it. Liz agreed that this was her preference as well, but given their lack of time during the week, simply having a quick orgasm before going to work or drifting off to sleep was also satisfying to her. Maria did not find the need to have this kind of sex play between them but would sometimes engage in it for Liz.

We explored these patterns between them and their roles in the patterns. What was helpful to each was to notice how their present relationship mirrored past ones in regard to sexuality and how neither was to blame for what was occurring between them. They had been blaming each other for the changes in their sexual relationship, seeing the other as asking too much and asking for the other to change. Noticing how they each had a history of different sexual desires and energy allowed them to normalize their desires and to reframe their difference as just that—a difference—and not as deficient.

It was also therapeutic for them to explore their understanding of sex and how they each came to the expression of it differently. Liz started to become more aware of how goal directed she was in her desire for orgasm and how that the pursuit of that goal often disregarded an intimacy Maria desired. Maria began to see how her desire to be pursued sexually left her with less power in the relationship. All of these issues were also connected to remnants of sexism and homoprejudice.

Exploring Homoprejudice and Sexism

It was crucial that Liz and Maria explore any underlying homoprejudice (Logan, 1996) and sexism they had carried unconsciously into the relationship. When I brought up the possibility that this may exist and might be affecting their sex play, they both agreed that this was present but had been unaware of it until we discussed it. Maria believed that women should not be overtly sexual but should be demure in their desire, something she had learned from the women in her family and culture. She had also struggled in the past around her sexual identity as lesbian, coming out in her mid 20s after having had relationships with men. For her, sex was something that was enacted out of love and only in a relationship. She did not feel comfortable having sex for the release of sexual tension or desire but instead saw it exclusively as an act of love for another person. We explored how this connected to her understanding of what it meant to be a woman and a lesbian and how, because of lingering unresolved internalized homoprejudice, she held back from allowing herself the pleasure of her sexual desire. She voiced being uncomfortable at times with her sexual identity and ashamed of her desire for women. The effect of these feelings on her relationship with Liz resulted in her holding back and waiting to be overcome with desire before giving in to the pleasure of it.

Liz had come out in late adolescence, having had one boyfriend in high school but thereafter exclusively relationships with women. She identified as a feminist lesbian and took pride in being a lesbian woman. For her being lesbian was powerful, yet when discussing frequency of sex and goal direction of orgasm she was aware of how she had bought into the heteronormative means of expressing her sexuality. In addition, she was aware of holding back at times sexually with Maria, wanting to include penetration or the use of dildos but not doing so because of Maria's past experience with men. She felt embarrassed by her desire for power at times and did not want to mimic heterosexual sex play, not only because of Maria's relationships with men but because she believed being a feminist lesbian meant she should not want to have power over women. Sexism and homoprejudice had caused her to frame her desires as imitating heterosexual intercourse or recreating a power differential with her partner, precluding her from framing her desire as normative within a lesbian relationship.

Our work in this area continued to more deeply explore how each saw themselves as women and the messages they had received about sex from their families and communities. As we did this, they understood more complexly how the mixed messages received about their desire, their expression of it, and the power in it connected to sexism and interfered with their freedom to initiate sex in their relationship. Exploring homoprejudice and internalized messages of what it meant to be lesbian allowed Maria to move toward healing painful beliefs of herself as bad for wanting to be with women and for having desires and gave Liz room to express her sexuality more fully and to integrate the strength of her desire as a powerful lesbian.

Communication: Looking at Patterns In and Out of the Bedroom

As we worked together, I watched how the two women communicated with each other and focused on this in treatment. It was important that they understand how they talked with each other in general and around sex specifically. It was apparent that Liz spoke more frequently and more directly than Maria, yet when Maria was passionate about an issue, she spoke frankly. I again directed our work to explore how these patterns were a product of how they had been socialized as women and within their cultural backgrounds. Liz spoke of the strong women of her Italian heritage who spoke their minds. Yet she noticed how at times this assertive quality became aggressive. She also noticed how this carried into her assertion for sex, sometimes pushing Maria away with her direct approach.

As a Mexican woman, Maria had been taught to be less assertive in communicating, waiting for others to speak first. She feared being perceived as pushy, a message embedded in her culture about how women should act more passively. However, when something was important to her, she noticed that she found her voice to speak out. Nevertheless, the message for her around sex and communication was still that women did not ask for what they wanted, often because they did not know and because they did not want to appear aggressive. She was able to articulate in our work that in each of her relationships she learned more about her desires and spoke up more. She was able to tell Liz in session how she had grown and how she wanted to have more room to speak up within this relationship. This was true not just for sex but also for other aspects of their relationship.

This exploration proved to be powerful for them individually and as a couple. Liz learned how her assertiveness was both a strength and liability to her communication with Maria about a variety of issues that had become challenges for them. We worked on the skill of being assertive without being bossy and worked on how Liz could learn to be receptive when Maria spoke up without losing her power as a woman. This work was important to create the safety Maria needed to voice her wants and needs more freely with Liz. Maria was slowly able to claim her power as a woman without becoming "pushy," as she feared. It was important that she not abandon her cultural connections to what it meant to be a woman but that she broaden her understanding to encompass greater flexibility and choice. These conversations helped them create more trust and partnership in and out of the bedroom.

We then focused specifically on how they communicated their sexual interests. I asked them, as homework, to write down how they asked for their desires to be met. When they brought in their homework, we had fun with the language around sex, making it playful and light for them. Liz wanted to use language that was direct, clear, and goal directed. Maria wanted to ask for sex more indirectly so as to avoid feeling embarrassed about her needs. I asked them to reverse roles and play the other to experience what it was like to hear themselves ask for what they wanted and to gain empathy in the role of the other.

Again, this was a pivotal moment in our work together, as they heard their desires spoken out loud and embodied their partner's experience when they were spoken. Liz realized how forceful she was and how it felt uncomfortable to be told to "perform" sexually. She voiced greater empathy for Maria and understood why Maria found ways to avoid Liz's demands. Maria, in being the powerful Liz, experienced the freedom of asking for what she wanted and enjoyed this power as sexual. She said it made her feel "kind of sexy" and was excited to try this on more frequently with Liz. She also had greater insight into the frustration Liz experienced when she asked for sex and was turned away.

In exploring her communication, Maria gained insight into how confusing and powerless her sexual messages were. She learned how Liz often missed her sexual overtures because they were too subtle to be perceived. Liz's experience was also significant because she gained empathy for the discomfort Maria experienced asking for what she wanted and the discomfort she felt because of her desires. The insight each gained allowed them to play with language that was clearer, using words that felt comfortable for them both.

Moving Toward Each Other Sexually

Having laid the groundwork for clearer communication, Maria and Liz were ready to explore their patterns of initiation, frequency, and desire more directly. At this point in our work, talking about sex had become easy and less filled with the tension originally experienced by them both. We began with the initiation of sexual overtures, as that dynamic had become most problematic between them. Liz wanted to get out of the role of always being the initiator of sex, a pattern that had caused her to build resentment toward Maria as a result of being rejected. Because of the role plays they had engaged in, it was a relatively easy transition to encourage them to exchange the roles of initiator outside of the therapy office. As Maria gained confidence in being more assertive about her needs and wants, she enjoyed the freedom and power that accompanied this behavior. Liz also began to learn how to receive, which brought up childhood feelings of wanting to be cared for. I suggested at this point that they discuss their unmet needs for power (Maria) and caring (Liz), and this work allowed for deeper connection. Though bumpy at times, the therapeutic work at this juncture created a temporary reversal of roles between them, and even today they continue to work on how to balance the dynamic of initiator and receiver.

Integrated into the change in initiation patterns was an exploration of erotic interests to create more desire and fun between them. Because homework worked well for them, I again asked them to write a list of the ways they wanted to be sexual with each other, being as creative as possible about real and fantasy options. They were not to share the list with each other outside of session to ensure that they each felt free to be as expansive as comfortable. In sharing the list in session, they were able to see how similar they were in their desires, fantasies, and erotic interests. This exercise also communicated to them that erotic feelings and fantasies for women are healthy and normative. Though they agreed that they did not want to act on all of the ideas generated, they enjoyed the freedom and playfulness with which they were now approaching sexual contact between them. I encouraged them to explore sex toy stores that served lesbians, erotic videos for women, and change of venue for sex. We discussed changing the time of day for sex and allowing each of them to say "no, not now" when appropriate. Significant for each was the freedom to initiate sex play as she wanted without violating the other's boundaries. They agreed to try each other's ideas at least once and to discuss afterward whether it was something they wanted to integrate into their sex life. If not, they agreed to try something new.

Liz was particularly concerned that the frequency of sex still would not be satisfying to her. Her desire for orgasm was greater than Maria's, and she sometimes just wanted the physical release of tension. Maria said that she was willing to increase the frequency as she was feeling more comfortable sexually but that she would not agree to having sex twice a week as Liz wanted. We discussed the possibility of Liz masturbating with Maria present as a compromise when needed, and Maria felt that this helped take the pressure off of her to "perform" on demand. Liz also found this an agreeable solution because sometimes she was not interested in long love-making sessions but only quick orgasms with Maria present. They wondered whether this was "normal" and again we revisited messages around sex between lesbian women. Once I normalized this for them, they relaxed and began to integrate this sexual behavior into their relationship.

Finally, I encouraged them to read Newman's (2004) book on lesbian sex to normalize many of their experiences and to explore new ways to enjoy each other. This resource enhanced our work throughout, and from time to time they would discuss in session what they had read to better understand a healthy approach to sex play and incorporate it into their relationship. And though we are still working together in counseling to manage any glitches that arise, Liz and Maria have found a way to better communicate inside and outside of their sex life, to be more playful in their relationship sexually and otherwise, and to expand their own sexuality and power for themselves individually and as a couple.

Transference and Countertransference

Liz and Maria sought me ought as a therapist because they knew I was lesbian. In treatment we discussed their hopes in working with a lesbian therapist and what they expected from me. Neither wanted to have to teach their therapist about lesbians, coming out, and lesbian sex. It turned out during various moments in our work together that each hoped that I would take her side in the treatment, though she did not explicitly state this. When that arose, I brought it forward and explored her fantasies of having the "perfect lover," someone who would know what she wanted without her having to communicate this. Though frustrated that I would not take sides, they were able to manage the disappointment and gained insight into the work that is required to make a relationship flourish.

In addition, at various times each flirted with me in session, especially when we spoke explicitly about sex. I found those moments particularly uncomfortable for me and the other partner, and redirecting that energy back to the couple was a challenge at times. I did not want to embarrass them by making the behavior explicit, but I did find ways to redirect the sexual energy back to her partner. I would notice with them the sexual tension in the room and process with them how to manage this within their relationship.

My own comfort talking about sex and sexuality and my own experience with issues of variant sexual desires challenged me at times. I found myself relating to each woman, reviewing my own relationship histories and issues around communication and sex. There were times when I found myself wanting to side with and relating to each. It was also difficult at times not to impose my own values about how sexism and homopreju-dice impact lesbian relationships and sex in particular, and I explored this gingerly so as to respect their histories and cultures. As a Jewish feminist lesbian, keeping tabs on my own cultural scripts was at the forefront of my work with them.

I could not help but reflect on my own sexual relationships as I worked with them. They taught me so much about respect, flexibility, and openness in a relationship as they earnestly worked together through these issues. I also revisited my own internalized homoprejudice and sexism and how it has impacted my relationships. Because of their ability to tolerate the often painful process of self- and other exploration, I again was reminded of the resilience of being lesbian and the joys that come with the expression of lesbian sexuality.

Conclusion

This chapter focused on sex between lesbian women and a broader view of how women can express their sexuality in a lesbian relationship. There are multiple means by which counselors can assist lesbian women in exploring their sexuality as women and as lesbians. Counselors who create a safe therapeutic relationship by examining their own biases and worldviews around sexuality for women and lesbian women and who can guide their clients in doing the same will have greater success exploring sensitive is-sues of sexuality. As was illustrated in this case example, teasing apart the various worldviews each partner brings to the sexual relationship; ensuring attention to gendered, cultural, and heterosexist lenses; and assisting both women in redefining sex are significant therapeutic processes in which counselors must engage. Counselors also must be knowledgeable of the unique issues lesbians face as women and as lesbians to avoid overlaying a heterosexist and sexist frame and thereby offering interventions that do not allow for the broad spectrum of lesbian sexual expression.

References

Barret, B., & Logan, C. (2002). *Counseling gay men and lesbians: A practice primer.* Pacific Grove, CA: Brooks/Cole.

Brown, L. (2000). Dangerousness, impotence, silence, and invisibility: Heterosexism in the construction of women's sexuality. In C. B. Travis & J. W. White (Eds.), *Sexuality, society and feminism* (pp. 273–298). Washington, DC: American Psychological Association.

Logan, C. (1996). Homophobia? No! Homoprejudice? Yes! *Journal of Homosexuality, 31*(3), 31–53.

Newman, F. (2004). *The whole lesbian sex book: A passionate guide for all of us* (2nd ed.). San Francisco, CA: Cleiss Press.

Nichols, M. (2004). Lesbian sexuality/female sexuality: Rethinking "lesbian bed death." *Sexual and Relationship Therapy, 19*(4), 363–371.

Chapter 24

Sexual Addiction and the Gay Male Client

Brian J. Dew and Misti A. Storie

Eric was a 37-year-old Caucasian single gay male who for the past 3 years had worked at a major corporation as a financial advisor. Eric was referred to his company's employee assistance program (EAP) counselor because of reports of excessive tardiness, long lunch breaks, and decreased productivity. His supervisor noted that Eric no longer displayed enthusiasm for his work and often appeared "checked out" during meetings. One year ago, Eric had been a top employee in his division and had earned many awards for his performance. The supervisor suspected Eric was having personal problems and opted for supportive services instead of further reprimands.

Eric reported to the EAP counselor that he had difficulty concentrating, was easily fatigued, felt depressed, and had lost pleasure in activities he previously enjoyed doing, including spending time with friends and family. He had recently lost weight, had difficulty sleeping most nights, and often felt restless and worthless. Eric reported having felt this way during the past 8 months but noted that his symptoms had become increasingly worse in the past several months. He identified the reason for the affective change as the frequency and nature of his sexual activities. He remarked that although these brief sexual relationships provided "short-term relief" from his depressed state, they produced a cycle of guilt and shame that was perpetuated by further sexual encounters. Eric acknowledged feeling no sense of "connection" to these sexual partners and stated that "these guys are just a release for me."

Eric admitted to spending the majority of his workday accessing gay social networking and pornography sites online. He had been confronted about this activity once it was discovered by the company's information technology (IT) department, and a notation had been made in his file. Most of his recreational time was spent visiting these online sites at home by himself in an effort to arrange more sexual encounters, which were carried out both in person and online. Eric also reported that he used an application on his cell phone to identify the locations and profiles of potential sex partners within a few miles of his work. He used this application to arrange brief anonymous sexual encounters at work and at home. Eric reported a gradual increase in his sexual acting out behavior over the past 3 years, with the severity of his symptoms peaking during the past 6 months. He occasionally engaged in sex while under the influence of drugs and/or alcohol and frequently practiced unsafe sex. Eric experienced distress and guilt over the escalation of his sex-related behavior and the impact it had on his work and personal relationships.

Eric reported the occasional binge use of alcohol (two to three times per year), a pattern that had remained consistent since his first use at age 17, and occasional marijuana use since the age of 19. Eight months ago he inhaled methamphetamine for the first time with a "trick" he had met on a men-who-have-sex-with-men social networking site. Eric reported to using the drug one weekend per month and adamantly declared that he was not "one of those meth addicts." Eric said that he liked using methamphetamine while having sex because it made him feel "sexier, better in bed, and more relaxed." He also reported that he experienced increased energy and confidence when using the drug, although he identified several instances of work-related impairment due to his recreational methamphetamine drug use. He denied any suicidal or homicidal ideation.

Eric had been born in Macon, Georgia, and had moved to Atlanta after finishing college. He lived alone and had one cat. Eric stated that he assumed that he was HIV negative but acknowledged being unsure of his current HIV status given that he had had more than 60 sexual partners since his most recent test 2 years ago. He had never had a major romantic relationship and last dated someone 18 months ago. He had come out in his early 20s and reported ongoing parental conflict resulting from his sexual orientation. Eric had a small social network of friends but was not openly gay in his workplace. He reported his upbringing as having been "normal overall" and cited church as being an important influence in his life because his father was a deacon at their church. Eric had never received any previous mental health services and had no immediate family history of mental illness or addiction.

Diagnosis

Following Eric's second individual session, the EAP counselor constructed the following diagnosis:

Axis I	302.60	Sexual Disorder Not Otherwise Specified
	296.22	Major Depressive Disorder, Single Episode, Moderate Without Psychotic Features
	305.70	Amphetamine Abuse
Axis II	799.90	Deferred
Axis III	None	
Axis IV	Threat of job loss, conflict with parents due to sexual orientation	
Axis V	Global Assessment of Functioning = 57 (current)	

Given the EAP counselor's previous clinical experience with sexually compulsive clients, she recognized that sexual addiction is not considered a unique mental disorder in the *Diagnostic and Statistical Manual of Mental Disorders* (4th ed., text rev.; *DSM-IV-TR;* American Psychiatric Association, 2000). However, she realized that over the past 12 months Eric had exhibited a pattern of recurring sexual activity with numerous anonymous sexual partners that he objectified and described as "frequent tools for my release." Eric also indicated no interest in maintaining contact with these partners following the sexual episode. It was the counselor's belief that the sexual acting out behavior was the principal diagnosis and therefore she listed it first on Axis I. Eric also presented with symptoms that met the criteria for a major depressive episode. These indicators were not related to a general medical condition, nor were they accompanied by mood-incongruent delusions or hallucinations. Although Eric acknowledged feeling "sometimes down and moody" following his weekend use of methamphetamine, his depressed mood, diminished interest in activities, fatigue, and feelings of worthlessness were present even when he was not using the drug. The counselor determined that Eric had experienced work-related impairment (e.g., poor work performance, tardiness, inability to concentrate) as a result of his methamphetamine use during the past 12-month period, and thus he was given a diagnosis of amphetamine abuse. No diagnosis for methamphetamine abuse exists in the *DSM-IV-TR*. An Axis II diagnosis was deferred pending the collection of additional information. Eric reported no current general medical condition relevant to his Axis I diagnoses. He acknowledged two primary psychosocial and environmental problems that affected his treatment and prognosis: (a) the potential that he may lose his job resulting from online sexual activity at work and (b) continued strife with his parents related to his sexual orientation. His current Global Assessment of Functioning rating of 57 indicated moderate difficulty in his social and occupational functioning.

Treatment and Interventions

The preferred theoretical framework for assisting this type of client would be cognitive behavior therapy. The primary tenet of this theoretical framework is the belief that cognitions mediate (lead to) behavior modification. Outcomes of treatment are based on cognitive, behavioral, and emotional changes. Given that cognitive–behavioral interventions are often directive, structured, goal directed, and time limited, it is imperative that the relationship between the client and the counselor be collaborative and that the client be a major contributor to therapeutic objectives.

The primary aims of treatment include three interrelated goals. The first treatment goal is to identify factors that facilitate the client's sexual compulsivity. This initial step includes identifying irrational beliefs, emotions, and behaviors that contribute to the cyclical nature of the client's sexual behavior. Information obtained from this step becomes the basis for the second therapeutic goal, behavioral modification. With regard to this goal, the client and counselor work collaboratively to change irrational beliefs and to modify the relationship between the client's affective state and his or her sexual acting out behavior. The third therapeutic goal is for the client to create and maintain a self-management plan that allows for self-regulation of his or her cognitions, emotions, and behaviors. These goals allow for the utilization of specific interventions to be implemented at various stages of the therapeutic process.

In an effort to uncover the contributions to Eric's compulsive sexual behavior, the counselor implemented a series of cognitive-based interventions. It was essential that Eric provide a detailed, written sexual history. This narrative included his earliest memories of hearing sex-related topics being discussed; his memories of how the topic of sex was dealt with in the home and church; his first sexual experiences, including masturbation; and his thoughts on these behaviors. It also included dating patterns, any incident of sexual abuse, and sexual patterns throughout college and in early adulthood. Specific attention was paid to Eric's patterns of sexual behavior in the past 12 months, especially the types of sexual activity he engaged in, his patterns for obtaining sexual partners, and his thoughts related to the acting out behavior. This assignment was given at the second counseling session, and its completion was mandatory. In fact, Eric called his counselor 24 hours before the next session asking her whether it would be acceptable to attend the next session without having fully completed the assignment. The counselor acknowledged that this assignment was difficult yet remained steadfast in reminding Eric of their mutual agreement to complete it. Eric appeared at his third session having completed a 12-page, single-spaced sexual history. This allowed him and the counselor to discern the content and sources of Eric's early cognitive messages about sex in general and, more specifically, his earliest recollections of what others shared about being nonheterosexual. This assignment also heightened Eric's cognitive awareness of the progression of his risky sexual activity. Eric acknowledged in the third session that he was now engaging in sexual behavior that just 12 months ago he would have considered "too risky" or "too far out there." While admitting that his sexual activity had increased in frequency prior to his initial experimentation with methamphetamine, he for the first time recognized the link between his unsafe sexual activity and his drug use. This realization specifically contradicted his earlier belief that his methamphetamine use was safe, controlled, and unproblematic.

During the fourth session, an additional cognitive-based intervention was utilized in order to identify irrational beliefs about Eric's sexual self-concept. Following an initial check-in, Eric completed an exercise in which he identified messages he had heard from others about being nonheterosexual. The counselor had a 6-foot laminated outline of a male body hanging on her wall, and Eric was asked to write on the figure as many messages about his sexuality that he could remember. Eric identified more than 20 negative messages he had heard since his childhood from his father, mother, oldest brother, and minister at his childhood church and a few positive messages he had heard from a close female college friend. The counselor recorded each message and then proceeded to have Eric process to what degree he still believed, even remotely, in the message he had heard. The counselor identified six cognitive schemas that still resonated with Eric's view of his sexual orientation: (a) Being gay is not normal and is therefore bad, (b) gay men are unlovable, (c) gay men are all promiscuous, (d) gay men cannot be in committed monogamous relationships, (e) others will not accept me if they know I am gay, and (f) and no one will want to date a man in his late 30s.

Additional cognitive-based interventions allowed the counselor to address the appeal of online sexual activity as described by Cooper's Triple A engine (accessibility, affordability, and anonymity; Cooper & Griffen-Shelley, 2002). Eric was quick to minimize his online sexual activity early in his counseling sessions by stating "the Internet is everywhere, so it must not be a bad thing" and "it's a cheap form of entertainment." For Eric, it was important to acknowledge that accessibility did not mean that online sexual activity was productive or appropriate. The counselor and Eric worked together to enhance his recognition of the costs of his behavior with regard to work (potential loss of employment), friends (increased reliance on the computer at the expense of his social support networks), recreational activities (weight gain of 25 pounds during the past year as a result of ceasing gym activities), and health (potential risk for HIV and other sexually transmitted infections), thereby directly challenging his perception of online sexual activity as being affordable and anonymous.

During the first session, Eric had acknowledged being unfamiliar with sexual addiction. He claimed not to have known anyone who self-identified as a sex addict, nor had he heard of anyone else describe their sexual pursuits as problematic ("especially among other gay men"). As a result, Eric's counselor provided him with reading material in order to challenge his own cognitive schemas as well as to minimize isolation. For example, the counselor provided a list of books on coming out and dealing with the shame of being nonheterosexual, as well as Patrick Carnes's 2001 book *Out of the Shadows* and several articles from the *Journal of Sexual Addiction and Compulsivity* that addressed online behaviors among gay men. Bibliotherapy is an essential intervention in helping to identify and modify existing cognitions.

In addition to cognitive interventions, the counselor utilized several strategies targeting modification of the cyclical link between Eric's affect and his compulsive sexual activities. The counselor asked Eric to keep a 1-week log of the affective states in which he was most triggered to engage in sexual activity, including the desire to masturbate, seek out sexual partners, and/or look at pornography online. This intervention, assigned between the third and fourth weeks of counseling, was instrumental in identifying anxiety as Eric's primary emotional trigger, followed by loneliness, anger, and boredom. The counselor helped Eric to recognize that his online sexual activities had largely replaced his traditional means of meeting other gay men, especially potential dating and/or sexual partners. Eric acknowledged that approaching potential dating partners at parties and clubs produced a high level of anxiety stemming from a fear of rejection that had increased because of his age and increased body weight. Consequently, he had decreased his attendance at parties and gay social venues, relied on the Internet to meet other gay men, and perpetuated his feelings of loneliness and boredom. Eric identified anger as a trigger most profoundly following interactions with his parents and/or older siblings and said this was often because of family members "not caring enough to ask me about my life outside of work, asking me if I am going to church, and being unwilling to visit."

Even more important as an effective intervention, the counselor was able to incorporate Eric's affective state (e.g., unworthy, unattractive, and unwanted) as a facilitator of his using methamphetamine as an affective coping mechanism and as a way of his being sexually active without experiencing the potential of rejection. Eric acknowledged that when he used methamphetamine he relaxed, was more confident, and was sexually appealing to potential partners. He also identified that his negative affect seemed to evaporate while he was under the influence of the psychoactive substance. Furthermore, Eric said, "The men I was with while high on meth never pushed me aside for the younger guys. They never viewed me as overweight. They were just happy to be with me."

A series of behavioral interventions were also used throughout the counseling relationship. It was essential for Eric and the counselor to work together to create a list of behavioral modifications that would assist in interrupting the cycle of online sexual activity. By the third session, a behavioral contract was developed and signed by both parties. This contract contained several interventions. First, Eric removed his sole computer (laptop) from his home and turned it in to the counselor, who stored it in a locked and fireproof filing cabinet. Second, Eric turned in to his IT department his cellular phone containing the application that allowed him to locate other gay men within a particular geographic distance. Third, he negotiated with his supervisor a new cellular device that contained no Internet capabilities or geographic identification software. Fourth, he rearranged his office so that anyone entering could see what he was viewing on his computer. Fifth, while in his office he agreed to leave his door open at all times. In cases when he needed to meet with other coworkers, he used one of the various group meeting rooms located on his floor. Sixth, Eric acknowledged the importance of notifying his direct supervisor of his issues with sexual compulsivity in order to enhance accountability at his work and agreed to a face-to-face meeting with his boss within the first 2 months of counseling.

Next, Eric and his counselor worked together to create a sexual behavior modification plan that identified baseline behaviors in which Eric should not engage. For example, it was mutually determined that Eric would abstain from using methamphetamine; looking at pornography of any kind either in print form or online; and engaging in anonymous sexual activity, including masturbation, oral sex, and/or anal sex. Furthermore, Eric was encouraged to attend two sex-related 12-step meetings per week (e.g., Sexaholics Anonymous, Sex Addicts Anonymous, Sexual Compulsives Anonymous, and Sex and Love Addicts Anonymous) and obtain a temporary sponsor within the first 6 weeks of counseling. Furthermore, he was encouraged to attend a 4-week series of relationship seminars for gay men at the local lesbian, gay, bisexual, and transgender center as well as increase time spent at the gym. A final behavioral intervention was introduced after the third month of counseling, by which time Eric had increased his understanding of sexual compulsivity, reported lower levels of depressive symptoms, and had constructed a larger social support network. Given his history of risky sexual activity, his fear related to his physical health—especially his exposure to HIV—became an increasing focus of concern. It was determined by the counselor that Eric had built up enough social support to handle the results of an HIV test. In addition, the counselor encouraged Eric to obtain a complete sexually transmitted disease (STD) screening, which would test not only for HIV but for other sexually transmitted infections, as well. The counselor, having knowledge of various local confidential HIV/STD testing facilities, provided a list of such sites to Eric.

Despite his initial reluctance to complete the written sexual history exercise, Eric identified his behavior as problematic and was willing to implement changes within the first month of counseling. In the counselor's previous work with clients who struggled with sexual compulsive behaviors, she had found that it was less common for clients to enter into counseling at this developmental stage of change. Given his readiness for personal growth, Eric successfully implemented many of the aforementioned interventions, which allowed for significant modification of his behavior. His completion of the sexual history account; his realization of various contributors to his elevated internalized homophobia via the "body exercise"; and his reassessment of the Internet's accessibility, affordability, and anonymity proved especially helpful. The use of bibliotherapy as an intervention was essential, but the counselor's initial attempts to encourage Eric to purchase books she thought would be appropriate were unsuccessful. Instead, when the counselor provided him with the exact names of books or even allowed him to read her journal articles following a session, the outcome was more positive. The shame associated with purchasing (either in a bookstore or online) books on sexual compulsivity was too great for Eric to complete this task during the first 4 weeks of counseling.

Eric's identification of the influence of his affective states on the cyclical nature of his compulsive sexual activity was a significant outcome of the various counseling interventions. The identification of anxiety as a leading trigger helped the counselor to introduce stress-reducing interventions in the latter stages of counseling, thereby reducing Eric's desire to act out sexually. Also, Eric successfully gained an understanding of how the acting out behavior actually enhanced the loneliness and disconnection he felt from others in the long term. It is important to note that personal growth did not take on a linear formation; rather, two "relapses" were the direct result of Eric feeling angry and rejected following a telephone conversation with his mother. Eric acknowledged these encounters with regret, and the counselor used these opportunities to clarify the affective triggers that contributed to the acting out behavior.

Both Eric and the counselor agreed that therapeutic success would not have been achieved without the multiple behavioral interventions. In fact, Eric admitted to being surprised that the counselor "knew exactly what to do in minimizing my exposure to my old behaviors." Although he realized that he could access the Internet in other venues (e.g., a friend's house, a borrowed laptop, the public library) or simply buy a new cellular device with an array of social networking applications and accessibility to the Internet, Eric noted that not having immediate access was critical to his early success. A stumbling block appeared later on in counseling when Eric took a 2-week business trip. Although both Eric and the counselor knew that this travel was pending, neither took the initiative to modify the behavioral contract or create a new one applicable to Eric's travels. Following the termination of this counseling relationship, the counselor acknowledged that not having Eric locate 12-step meetings in cities he was visiting, as well as not processing how Eric was going to handle having a laptop computer, which was essential for him to complete his job responsibilities while traveling, was an important learning opportunity.

Implications for Counselors

In order to provide clinical services to gay men who struggle with issues of sexual compulsivity, it is essential for counselors to understand the sensitive nature of placing a judgment on same-sex sexual behaviors. Many gay men who are taught that their sexuality is sinful and nonnormative are especially susceptible to critiques of their sexual activity. Counselors working with these issues must concentrate on the consequences of the acting out behavior, including the time spent engaging in the activity, the denial, the potential risks to self and others, and the impact on interpersonal relationships. Counselors must also be aware of their own heterosexism and the belief that there is one true way of being in a relationship or engaging in sexual activity. For example, it would have been detrimental to Eric to assume that all gay men aspire to be in a long-term monogamous relationship.

Counselors must also continue to assist their clients with stigma management, especially around self-disclosure of one's nonheterosexual sexual orientation. Choosing not to come out to others should not be perceived as a lack of sexual identity development. Instead, counselors need to discuss the benefits and costs associated with a client's decision to come out, especially in employment situations. Eric's decision to self-disclose his sexual orientation to his supervisor was circumvented by the IT department's detection of his viewing of pornography online while at work. However, the counselor was able to provide assistance in determining with whom it was and was not safe for Eric to share details of his personal life outside of work.

Similar to other persons who seek treatment for sexual compulsivity, Eric was facing multiple stressors that impacted his therapeutic growth. Potential loss of job, depressed mood, markedly diminished interest in social and other recreational activities, excessive fatigue, and diminished ability to think or focus at work and in his relationships were significant barriers to his overall wellness. Once Eric entered counseling, the primary crisis facing him was his unknown HIV status and his fear surrounding the decision to get tested. Although he acknowledged engaging in risky behavior, it was not until he began modifying his sexual *and* nonsexual behaviors that he began addressing the impending doom he felt surrounding a potentially positive HIV test result. It was important that the counselor wait until Eric have sufficient social support to cope with a positive result before encouraging him to take the test.

Eric was fortunate that he was assigned an EAP counselor who had knowledge of how to work with a gay male client with issues of sexual compulsivity. In reviewing this case study, certain recommendations for counseling and training with this population become evident. First, it is essential that counselors become familiar with the gay male community, including its broad range of interests, attitudes, and unique developmental experiences. It is also imperative that counselors understand the concept of internalized homonegativity, its sources, and the detrimental impact it has on gay male development. Next, counselors must enhance their understanding of sexual compulsivity, its warning signs, and the impact it has on the addict and his or her loved ones. Furthermore, counselors need to be able to assess for sexual compulsivity, especially when clients are reticent about discussing such activities. Counselors need to be aware of particular interventions that can be used to address cognitive, affective, and behavioral changes at varying stages of the counseling relationship. Finally, if they are going to be successful with their sexually compulsive clients, mental health professionals must keep abreast of the latest technological advances and their implications for sexual activities.

References

American Psychiatric Association. (2000). *Diagnostic and statistical manual of mental disorders* (4th ed., text rev.). Washington, DC: Author.

Carnes, P. (2001). *Out of the shadows: Understanding sexual addiction* (3rd ed.). Fenter City, MN: Hazelden Press.

Cooper, A., & Griffin-Shelley, E. (2002). The Internet: The next sexual revolution. In A. Cooper (Ed.), *Sex and the Internet: A guidebook for clinicians* (pp. 1–15). New York, NY: Brunner & Routledge.

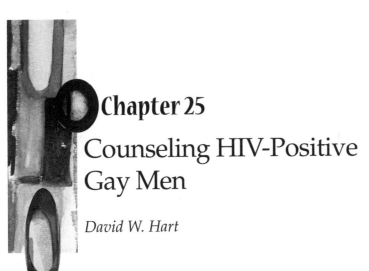

Chapter 25

Counseling HIV-Positive Gay Men

David W. Hart

I will never forget my first client. I was a graduate student in practicum at the local lesbian, gay, bisexual, and transgender center and can vividly remember the excitement I felt when I received the referral. I reviewed the intake form and noted the demographic information: gay male, Filipino, mid-30s, single, never accessed counseling services in the past—and HIV positive. I gasped. What did I know about HIV? I knew gay, I knew culture, I knew single—but HIV? Panic ensued. My palms began to sweat and my mouth felt as if it were packed full of cotton. Not that I lacked a basic understanding of HIV, but I had never *known* an HIV-positive gay man. I had seen the movies *Angels in America* and *Philadelphia* and had even participated in AIDS walks in my community. But what did I really know? In that moment I felt underprepared for the reality of HIV. I worried that I lacked any genuine real-life experience that might serve as a foundation for developing culturally competent therapeutic interventions. Frantically I phoned my supervisor to disclose my fears and persuade her to pass the client on to the next trainee—one who had more experience with HIV-positive gay men than I did. In her infinite wisdom, my supervisor lovingly denied my request and asked if not you, who? In that moment I learned an important lesson about counseling. I knew that as a professional counselor I would be called to work with clients from a variety of backgrounds with a myriad of challenges. I also recognized that it was not required for me to have lived shared experiences with my clients in order to be effective as a counselor. Yet in that moment I bought into the stigma associated with HIV. In my unconscious mind, living with HIV was akin to the proverbial end of the world, and I had not yet experienced such a traumatic prognosis in life. I was projecting all over my client before he even stepped foot in the front door. With the little experience and information I had on HIV at the time I genuinely wondered how I could help this man.

My supervisor suggested that I start by listening to his story, loving him unconditionally, and assessing how I could be of best assistance. Loving him unconditionally, I thought? What a radical concept. I had to push through personal perceptions of HIV that were unconsciously rooted in stigma and fear to see a new reality—one in which I said yes to walking with a client who was on a journey much like that of any other client but who happened to be HIV positive.

Over the 10 years since that first encounter, I have worked with hundreds of gay men representing a number of cultural traditions and personal experiences. The thread that ties their stories together is HIV—whether it be the fear of contracting the virus or the reality of living with it. This chapter focuses on how I have counseled HIV-positive gay men and the powerful professional and personal lessons I have learned through my clinical practice. I next present a case study—a qualitative analysis—of counseling methods and interventions that have been efficacious in the lives of clients with whom I have worked. The chapter is divided into three sections—intake and assessment, treatment goals and outcomes, and potential transference issues and professional implications. I hope to convince the reader of the benefit of using a queer-affirmative narrative approach to working with this population.

The Case of Drake—Intake and Assessment

Drake became my client nearly 3 months after his diagnosis as HIV positive. He was referred to the gay and lesbian center by his physician to access free counseling services funded by the Ryan White Act. During our preliminary phone conversation, Drake indicated that he was suffering from a severe case of "depression" and could not seem to find the motivation to get out of bed in the mornings. Drake reported that he had intense feelings of guilt related to his diagnosis, particularly the "irresponsible" sexual behavior that had led to him contracting the disease. Drake described his goal for counseling as "finding a way to keep on living." It is important to note some specific demographic and mental status data that were gathered on Drake's initial intake form. Drake was an African American male in his mid-30s living in an urban area close to the coast. He was a middle school teacher and reported liking his job "very much." Drake was the oldest of two children and revealed that he was "pretty close" to his mom and sister but remained estranged from his father, who had left the family when Drake was 4 years old. Drake self-identified as a gay man and specified his relationship status as single. Drake disclosed that he had been to see a counselor in the past to get help for a reoccurring depression. At the time of the intake he was taking Paxil to manage his "constant feelings of worthlessness." Drake also reported that he had been attending Sexual Compulsives Anonymous for the previous 2 years and had found a sponsor to begin working the 12-step program. In addition, Drake noted that despite his love for God he had felt "detached" from his church since coming out 5 years ago. As a result, Drake had stopped attending the church he had been going to since he was 7 years old.

At our first meeting I noticed that Drake was meticulously dressed—in a freshly pressed collared shirt accessorized by a brilliantly colored tie and recently polished shoes. His dress was in stark contrast to his mood, described over the phone as depressed, and I wondered what the discrepancy might tell me about Drake's coping style. After reviewing the informed consent and going over general office policies, I asked Drake to describe how his life had changed since his diagnosis. Drake questioned out loud why he had to be the one to contract HIV. He speculated as to God's reasons for inflicting him with HIV. He demanded to know what he had done to deserve the diagnosis. Drake was clearly angry, and at moments his rage would overtake him. I calmly reflected the pain and hurt he was experiencing and validated his feelings at every opportunity. I wanted Drake to know that the range of emotions he was experiencing were all entirely normal and that he had every right to feel each feeling wholly and completely. As he circled through the anger and touched his pain, I asked Drake what he thought he had done to deserve his diagnosis. Drake considered the question for a moment and replied that he was destined to become HIV positive because he was gay and had fallen out of God's grace. I immediately made a note to myself to explore Drake's internalized understanding of himself as a gay man and what negative social experiences and cultural messages had coalesced to shape a somewhat negative self-identity. Drake's disenfranchisement from his religion of origin and his lack of an ongoing spiritual practice would become a major focus of therapy in the months ahead.

Drake also expressed his need for additional information on the topic of HIV. Specifically, he had questions related to the course of the disease and what to expect as time progressed, experimental treatments, the effectiveness of current medications and their potential side effects, and community resources that could potentially help him manage the disease over time. Drake's desire for information vital to maintaining his health and the courage required to address his personal challenges in therapy were framed as unique strengths of his. Hearing this from me appeared to give Drake a small sense of empowerment, evidenced by a slight smile and an affirmative nod at the end of our first session. Drake's attention to the future also helped to assure me that despite his depressed mood and increased risk for suicide due to his diagnosis, he was focused on living rather than dying.

In our second session together, Drake and I continued to address how to best meet his needs in therapy. Drake revealed the sadness he felt as his dreams and vision for the future had begun to slip away. Because of the stigma attached to HIV, Drake believed he would never have a monogamous gay relationship in which he could share his body fully and completely. Drake felt as if he were "contaminated" and "out of order" and feared that he lacked the confidence or the strength to disclose his HIV status to potential partners. Conversely, Drake worried about divulging his diagnosis to his mom and sister and felt a need to shield them from the pain and suffering that knowing his status might bring. Throughout the coming weeks the two of us discovered where and how Drake had learned it was his duty to protect others from his feelings and his reality. This line of exploration would prove to be highly beneficial in terms of Drake's overall awareness of how he coped—and was coping—with negative feelings and experiences.

Drake had imagined that he would someday have children but had given up on that hope. He doubted any man would have children with a partner who had the potential to "die young" and leave him to be a single parent. Drake explained the he felt as if he had three strikes against him in society: he was gay, HIV positive, and Black. He was struggling with an intense fear of rejection from his peers in each of the groups to which he belonged. Drake aptly observed that the gay community looks on HIV-positive gay men as "bad" because they failed to protect themselves in the face of deadly disease. Drake was concerned that he would be unable to maintain his status within the gay community—signaled by his peer group, occupation, and place of residence—because of the stigma associated with the disease. A therapeutic intervention was designed to explore how internalized homonegativity influences the dichotomization of "good" gay behavior (e.g., safe sex, monogamous relationships, "passing" affect, HIV negative status) and "bad" gay behavior (e.g., unsafe sex, open relationships, "flamboyant" affect, HIV positive status) and how this binary understanding of gay identity can negatively influence self-esteem and overall well-being. Furthermore, it was crucial that Drake begin to meet other HIV-positive men who were living meaningful, purpose-driven lives. This component of the therapeutic process became a primary focus of our work together and is discussed in detail in the following section.

Treatment Goals and Outcomes

I met with Drake once a week for 6 months until therapy was terminated after we mutually decided that weekly therapy was no longer warranted. From our initial meeting, I began to assess Drake's self-reported depression and immediately requested a signed release to confer with his prescribing physician. After two sessions of assessment and consultation with his doctor, I determined that Drake met the criteria for a diagnosis of depression. Drake's five-axis diagnosis and rationale was as follows:

Axis I	296.33	Major Depressive Disorder, Single Episode, Recurrent, Severe Without Psychotic Features
	Rule out 302.71	Hypoactive Sexual Desire Disorder
Axis II	V71.09	No Diagnosis
Axis III	HIV positive	
Axis IV	Problems with primary support group, problems with social environment, religious/spiritual challenges	
Axis V	Global Assessment of Functioning = 61	

In my work with HIV-positive gay clients I conceptualize therapeutic interventions within the queer-affirmative and narrative frameworks. Queer-affirmative psychotherapy—born out of the feminist movement—draws the analogy between misogyny and homophobia in a society in which gay men may be hated or feared because they are perceived as being or behaving like women (Lebolt, 1999). In practicing queer-affirmative psychotherapy, my first goal was to openly acknowledge that Drake was living in a heterocentrist culture that actively legitimizes and perpetuates stigmas related to Drake's sexual orientation and diagnosis. Within the dominant cultural lexicon, HIV is deemed a "gay" disease, and the diagnosis is analogous to a scarlet letter—marking the diagnosed individual as "one of them." I could not affirm Drake's diagnosis without also affirming his sexual identity.

The second goal of queer-affirmative therapy is to unconditionally affirm queer lives and experiences. Ultimately it was my job to normalize the rage, fear, and hurt he was feeling as a result of the stigma and marginalization he was experiencing. This was accomplished by practicing traditional humanistic principles, including demonstrating unconditional positive regard, demonstrating neutrality through body language, and reflecting content and underlying feelings. Understanding the therapeutic power of building a solid, authentic rapport with Drake, my first interventions were to listen, respond with empathy, and avoid making any assumptions about his experience.

Within the first two sessions, Drake appeared to trust that I was walking with him on a path we were constructing together rather than pushing him down a road paved on what he should or ought to do. The narrative therapy approach, rooted in postmodern ideology, is focused not on experts solving problems but rather on understanding how stories, or narratives, shape a clients' perspectives on their lives, histories, and futures. My intent was to provide a safe space for Drake to freely share his story without fear of contempt or judgment on my behalf. In partnership, we explored and deciphered the meanings attached to challenging stories (i.e., Drake's story as an HIV-positive man was eclipsing and even subverting more positive narratives that had described his reality prior to his diagnosis) and worked to discover untold stories that included an account of Drake's hopes, life vision, dreams, purpose, and overall meaning in life. Combined, queer-affirmative and narrative approaches to counseling appear to have been most beneficial in my work with gay men generally and HIV-positive gay men specifically.

Initially Drake was immersed in a chapter of his narrative that was saturated in self-blame and internalized homophobia. One of Drake's first questions was "What did I do to deserve this?" To find the answer, Drake and I explored his backstory. I was curious as to how and when he had learned that he could do something to deserve HIV. Over time Drake began to recall his first encounters with gay men—mostly on television talk shows being ridiculed by the studio audience for their apparent aberrant behavior. He recollected a story from his childhood about a family friend who had contracted HIV, had no health insurance, and died alone in the county hospital within weeks of his initial diagnosis. Drake recalled his mother's disdain for the man and sourly noted that his fate was directly tied to his sexual orientation. With tears Drake recanted his mom's pronouncement that "God kills fags dead." We sat together in silence and I witnessed an "aha" moment. Drake realized that his choices were not his alone. As a result of the negative messages he had received related to his sexual identity, Drake was socially groomed to believe that he would become HIV positive and had gone on to construct a reality that matched his belief. Over time Drake was able to replace this outdated narrative with one that accentuated childhood stories that were rooted in his personal strengths and unique characteristics that guided his professional and personal success as an adult.

As Drake retold his story, religion emerged as a persistent theme. Raised as a Southern Baptist, Drake was acutely aware of the church's stance on homosexuality. Some Protestant doctrines regard the expression of same-sex attraction as sinful or immoral. Drake described his relationship with God as "extremely important" but felt disconnected from his spiritual self because he had stopped attending the neighborhood church he had attended for more than half his life. I wondered how the lack of spiritual practice in his life affected his ability or inability to cope with his diagnosis, as his relationship with God appeared to have been such a big part of his life prior to coming out. Drake talked openly about his anger toward God and how he felt "forsaken." He wondered whether there was a place for him in God's house, and we talked about what His house might look like. Drake described an affirmative place of worship that cared more about a person's heart than a person's sexual identity or HIV status. Drake envisioned a church in which he could be totally and completely himself—without fear of retribution or scorn. He described it as a place where being gay would be seen as a gift rather than a stain. Together we explored Drake's understanding of religion and spirituality, and I asked whether one could be spiritual without being religious. Drake reflected on this question for many weeks and finally decided that yes, he could be spiritual without subscribing to a particular religion. I provided Drake with a number of referrals to gay-affirmative Christian churches, some of which had specific HIV ministries. Drake went through a grieving process as he released his religion of origin and eventually found a new spiritual home at the Metropolitan Community Church. He later reported that reengaging his faith and spiritual practice was the most significant outcome of the therapeutic experience.

At the outset of our time together, Drake indicated that his primary goal for therapy was to "find a way to keep on living." I asked Drake to describe what he envisioned living with HIV to look and feel like. Drake's impression of living with HIV was embedded in popular misconceptions about HIV—predominantly that his life would not be worth living. Drake imagined that he would physically waste away over time, become debilitated by pharmacological side effects, and be ostracized within the gay community. Drake feared that his diagnosis would prohibit him from finding true love and dismissed any potential for a committed, monogamous partnership. Although he dreamed of having children one day, Drake had given up hope that any man would agree to have children with a partner who would certainly "die young." I asked Drake whether he had ever known a gay man who was HIV positive—although I was pretty sure I knew the answer to my question before I asked it.

A critical component of Drake's therapeutic plan was to connect him to a social support system that met his individual needs and reframed his understanding of what it meant to live with HIV. There were a number of different programs in the community to choose from, but it was important to extrapolate appropriate referrals from Drake's narrative. For instance, two of Drake's presenting challenges—the consolidation of his religious and sexual identities and the need for social support—could be simultaneously addressed via the HIV ministry at the local gay-affirmative church. In addition, I knew of a social group for HIV-positive gay men that Drake and I believed would be a better fit for his immediate needs—meeting other HIV-positive gay men in a relaxed environment—than a traditional psychotherapeutic support group, which often attracts individuals with severe mental health and sociopolitical challenges. Drake was open to exploring multiple options, became an integral member of the social group for HIV-positive men, and later reported what a "life saver" the group had become.

Part of my job was to be familiar enough with medical issues related to HIV that I could at minimum answer Drake's questions related to the course of the disease and its effect on the immune system, general terminology such as *T-cell count* and *viral load,* and U.S. Food and Drug Administration–approved pharmacological treatments and their potential side effects. For more technical questions, I referred Drake to any number of community partners that were able to provide more precise answers. In this vein, Drake and I agreed that his therapeutic experience would be enhanced by my direct communication with his physicians. In general I recommend integrating a multidisciplinary approach to care when working with an HIV-positive client. Drake's physician and I consulted with one another on a somewhat regular basis and coordinated psychosocial and medical interventions, specifically around Drake's depression. Drake reported having peace of mind knowing that his care providers were committed to his total health and overall well-being.

A core component of Drake's education related to HIV was on the subject of safe sex and the disclosure of his status to potential sexual partners. In addressing this issue, I asked Drake how he felt about disclosing his diagnosis to potential sexual partners, and he quickly replied that he planned to remain celibate for the remainder of his life. When encouraged to explore the cognitive and emotional rationale for his decision, Drake imagined the trauma he would experience if he were rejected by a potential mate for being HIV positive. Now that he was connected to other HIV-positive gay men, Drake was beginning to hear horror stories that substantiated his worst fear—that he would be an undesirable partner because of his HIV status. I asked Drake to describe himself to me as if I had never met him. After a moment of contemplation he rattled off four to five positive personal characteristics. He failed to mention being HIV positive. I wondered whether Drake believed that his HIV status was greater than the sum of his parts. We talked about Drake's former relationship vision and identified what he was looking for in a partner—someone intelligent, loving, compassionate, and secure, among other attributes. Drake came to the realization that his vision had not changed, he had. Many of our sessions focused on the impact HIV would have on dating and developing romantic relationships. We role-played disclosure scenarios and explored how he might cope with any potential rejection. Despite Drake's depressive symptoms, he was naturally optimistic and believed that rejection was another opportunity to find the right guy for him. Drake's experience as an African American living in a society dominated by White male privilege had thickened his skin in a psychological sense. Over time, Drake had developed coping strategies to manage the constant racial microaggressions he faced as a Black man, and these strategies appeared to influence a fighting spirit in Drake.

As Drake began to meet men through his social group and church ministry, we talked about his early declaration that he was to remain celibate for the remainder of his life. Drake smiled and suggested that he may have been overzealous. Drake reported feeling a sense of loss related to his inability to freely have sex without constantly imagining the possibility of infecting a partner. Sex had primarily become a matter of life and death rather than a means of expressing and receiving love and affection. Drake and I talked about the importance of safe sexual practices not only to protect his partners from contracting HIV but also to shield him from additional sexually transmitted infections. I encouraged Drake to speak openly with me about his sexual fantasies and suggested that just as it had not been easy for him to use a condom in the past for all the reasons we had previously discussed, it would not be easy to use a condom in every sexual encounter now. Drake eventually was able to talk openly about the personal meaning and fulfillment he found in having sex without a condom. Having another man inside of him, without barrier, was the ultimate sense of intimacy. Drake felt as if an emotional void had literally been filled when a man would cum inside him.

Despite the guilt he would feel afterward for engaging in "bad" homosexual behavior, he nonetheless continued in unsafe sexual practices as he unconsciously sought to heal familial and social wounds. I decided to try a guided imagery technique to help Drake find the part of his voice that had the strength to describe the emotional void he was feeling at the core of his *self*. The emotional void Drake felt embedded the sense of abandonment and resulting pain he had suffered after his father had left the family when he was 4 years old. I wondered out loud whether Drake was searching for his father's love in sexual encounters with random men. Without hesitation, Drake began to cry. Through his tears, he said, "All I've ever wanted is to be loved. I have never felt fully loved by anyone. My dad left me to care for my mom and sister. I've always been second. I want to be the most important person in a man's life. Believe it or not, I feel like I'm number one when I'm having sex." Drake's insight provided him with a sense of awareness that he later commented had changed his life. For the first time Drake recognized the impetus for his behavior, and that allowed him to have empathy for himself. He was able, as an adult, to care for the 4-year-old child who desperately wanted to be number one. Drake cognitively understood that meeting his 4-year-old needs by engaging in unprotected sex was not in his overall best interest, and together we developed a plan to integrate his 4-year-old self with his mid-30s self. This took a tremendous amount of mindfulness on Drake's part while we facilitated self-integration in the therapy session via role plays, journaling, and guided imagery.

Counseling Implications and Transference Issues

In my work with HIV-positive gay men, I have found it absolutely imperative to first and foremost establish a strong therapeutic rapport with my clients, and I do this through actively affirming their lives and experiences. In my work with Drake I spent the first 2–3 sessions actively listening to his story before making any formal assessments—although I was careful to look for any red flags that might appear in his narrative. Drake had questioned his ability to live as an HIV-positive gay man yet he reported his desire to learn more about HIV and how to better manage it over time. When working with HIV-positive men—or any man with a chronic and potentially terminal illness—it is critical to assess suicidal ideation and any history with suicide (e.g., prior attempts or family history). Assessing a client's history of mental health challenges is also critical. Drake immediately disclosed his diagnosis of depression, and I quickly took action to follow up with Drake's primary care physician. A biopsychosocial model of care is well suited to working with HIV-positive clients because it affords a multidisciplinary, coordinated approach to treating a client's physical and mental health. Drake's physician and I worked in conjunction to treat Drake's depression, manage his medication side effects, and educate him on living as an HIV-positive gay man. The social component of the model was facilitated by the community organizations to which Drake was referred—including the social organization for HIV-positive gay men, the gay-affirmative church and its HIV ministry, and other health care providers within the HIV service community who helped to educate and support Drake along the way. These organizations were essentially community partnerships with which I had developed strong reciprocal relationships. I highly encourage all counselors working with this population to build solid, mutually beneficial relationships with other HIV service providers in the community.

Drake's principal concern—how to live with HIV—was addressed primarily through connecting him to other gay men who were thriving despite their diagnosis. This intervention was designed to give Drake a sense of hope that his life indeed could and would go on—albeit somewhat different than what he had imagined—if he allowed himself the emotional space required to dream about a successful, meaningful life. In order to create this psychic space, Drake and I needed to address the internalized homophobia that was in a sense holding him hostage. Drake believed his sexual identity rendered him broken and out of order. He frequently described himself as contaminated and operated from a place of self-hate. Drake's diagnosis as HIV positive powerfully reinforced his negative self-perception and offered credibility to his mother's admonition that God kills fags dead.

Reaffirming his belief in God was a turning point in Drake's therapy. Multiple studies have demonstrated the influence of religion on decision-making processes, coping strategies, psychological well-being, and sexuality, and the absence of a spiritual practice in Drake's life had negatively impacted his mental health. A key intervention was exploring Drake's understanding of the role his religion of origin had played in the development of his identity as a gay man while also assisting him in differentiating between religious dogma that sought to stigmatize his sexual orientation and a spiritual practice that actively affirmed his greatness in the mind of God. A number of studies in the social sciences have demonstrated a direct link between social support and positive psychological outcomes, so connecting Drake to queer-affirmative places of worship was an imperative therapeutic task. Being able to see his reflection in affirmative places of worship without the obstruction of discriminatory dogma was described by Drake as a critical factor in the construction of a more positive understanding of himself as an HIV-positive gay man.

A number of transference issues were addressed as Drake and I strengthened our therapeutic relationship. It is imperative for counselors working with HIV-positive gay men to remain aware of their motives for working with this population, to refrain from imposing their goals and/or values on clients, and to seek out professional consultation and supervision to maintain appropriate therapeutic boundaries with their clients and their own emotional well-being. Initially my natural optimism had a tendency of getting in the way of my joining Drake in the extreme despair he was experiencing as a result of his diagnosis. I relied too heavily on cultural axioms—something about pulling oneself up by one's bootstraps and about good things coming to good people—but of course these were less axioms than they were my own defense mechanisms. In an effort to defend my own psyche, I preached a litany of false optimism that failed to genuinely validate Drake's suffering. I quickly learned my lesson, with the help of my supervisor and a personal practice of self-reflection and meditation. It came to me that Drake needed less of my opinions about life and more validation, positive regard, and unconditional support of his choices and his story. I also found that my exhortations to follow through on agreed-on interventions (e.g., taking medication, attending support groups) were ineffective in strengthening the therapeutic bond, nor did they have any value in terms of the intervention's overall efficacy. Part of the therapeutic process was exploring Drake's occasional resistance to proactively caring for himself, a behavior that was partially rooted in his depression but was also a symptom of internalized homonegative messages that were constantly repeating in his head: you're not good enough, you don't deserve love and/or happiness, and you're going to die. Releasing these negative messages and rewriting the script of Drake's story-to-be was much more therapeutically fruitful than my attempts to persuade Drake to care for himself without any insight as to why he had stopped taking a medication or had skipped out on a doctor's appointment in the first place.

Ten years have passed since my first encounter with an HIV-positive client, and I have learned many clinical lessons along the way. But more important, my soul has expanded as a result of the relationships I have been privileged to nurture over the years. Working with HIV-positive gay men is truly about respecting the client's story—all of it. Counseling this population is about validating and affirming the despair, the rage, and the uncertainty that often accompanies the HIV diagnosis. In my experience I have found that focusing on more than just the singular dimension of HIV in a client's life is of utmost value. There are numerous chapters to a client's story, and each layer deserves therapeutic inquiry. Drake indicated that his initial goal for therapy was to learn how to live with HIV. I have incorporated Drake's personal objective into a general principle in my work with HIV-positive gay men, one that is best stated in a question: How can I help my clients to live more fully? Within this framework, I have sought to help my clients make connections in their communities and explore the role of religion in their narratives—from a perspective that honors the client's perspective while exploring the potential for a restructured understanding of the benefit of queer-affirmative spiritual practices. I conceptualize my work with this population as intimately engaged encounters that transcend modern approaches to therapy that advocate distant, hierarchal approaches to treating clients. I respect my clients and their choices and have developed a care regimen and supervision schedule for myself that has kept me well when clients make choices I disagree with (unless the choice legally or ethically mandates a professional response). I am only along for the ride—and my proper position is in the passenger seat. With this group of men, it is a position I cherish.

References

Lebolt, J. (1999). Gay affirmative psychotherapy: A phenomenological study. *Clinical Social Work Journal, 27*, 355–370.

Chapter 26

Moving Through the Void: Counseling Gay Men With Histories of Chemical Abuse and Dependency

A. Michael Hutchins

Drug and alcohol use and abuse have historically played a significant role in the gay, lesbian, bisexual, and transgender (LGBT) community. Often the abuse of drugs and alcohol has been attributed to a struggle with sexual identity. The relationship between the complex dynamics of sexual identity development and drug and alcohol abuse is not necessarily a causal one. In a complex and rapidly changing world, counselors are called on to be agents of change and supporters of growth and development. In the case described here, a counselor works with a client in an integrated and holistic process that focuses on growth and development rather than on pathology. The client identified here is a young man who seeks assistance from the counselor. The "greater" client is the community in which he lives.

Case Study: Carlos

Presenting Issues

Carlos is a 26-year-old Mexican American man who is self-referred for counseling. He reports that he had an "anxiety attack" that led him to seek a counselor. He found this counselor through Wingspan, the LGBT community center.

He reports that as a "birthday gift" to his best friend David he paid for a trip for both of them to visit San Francisco for the weekend. While in San Francisco they used alcohol, marijuana, and cocaine. While using, Carlos reports, he realized that he was "in love" with David and wanted them to have a sexual relationship. According to Carlos, David is a straight-identified, Anglo man. In San Francisco, David met a woman and invited Carlos to join them in a sexual liaison. Carlos reports that he "freaked out" and began throwing furniture and breaking things. He left the hotel and spent the night in the airport crying. Upon his return to Tucson, he called his employer and arranged a medical leave of absence.

Background

Carlos reports that he is not certain of his sexual orientation. He was introduced to being sexual by a male cousin when they were both 13 years old. His cousin is now in a gay marriage in Massachusetts. Carlos reports that he has been sexual with men and with women but fantasizes primarily about men. He also reports that his contact with men has been more "exciting" than his contact with women. He was engaged to a woman when he was in his early 20s. He says that she ended the relationship because of his alcohol use and his difficulty being sexual with her. He reports that David is the first man that he has ever wanted to do more than "have sex with," and he is afraid that he has destroyed that relationship because of his drinking and drug use.

Carlos reports using marijuana daily, using alcohol several times per week (although he reports that he does not usually drink to the point of intoxication), and using cocaine several times per month ("almost always with friends on weekends"). He reports that he began using marijuana occasionally at age 15 and began using alcohol "around 17." His use of cocaine is "relatively recent," within 3 months of his first counseling appointment. He reports that his daily use of marijuana helps to calm his anxiety and that alcohol helps him to be "more social." He reports that "cocaine makes me crazy." He also reports that he is more likely to make sexual advances toward other men when he has been using cocaine and that the quality of his sexual connections is enhanced.

Carlos says that his sleep pattern is inconsistent. Sometimes he sleeps as long as 12 hours a night. At other times he sleeps for only 3 or 4 hours per night. He rarely gets to sleep before 1 a.m. He reports that when he goes to bed his mind keeps "going over things that [he] would like to say to David." He reports that he uses marijuana to help him get to sleep.

Carlos also reports an erratic eating pattern. He says that he "craves lots of carbs" when he is using. He identifies that he is overweight and that he has some concern about his weight because he has a family history of diabetes. He reports that he is much more effective at balancing his diet when he is consistently involved in a fitness program in which he combines weightlifting and cardiovascular activity. His primary care physician has recommended that he lose 20–25 pounds in order to be healthier. Carlos indicates that he recognizes that he is anxious and would like to decrease his anxiety without taking prescribed medication.

Carlos reports a family history of diabetes, primarily on his mother's side. He also reports that hypertension "runs in [his] father's family" and that strokes and heart attacks are common among his father's relatives. In addition, he reports that alcohol dependence/addiction and other chemical abuse is common on both sides of his family. He indicates that he was 13 when his mother divorced his father partly because of his father's drug and alcohol use.

Neither of Carlos's parents graduated from high school, and both are encouraging him to continue his education. Carlos shares that he has a maternal uncle who has been living with his male "friend" for as long as Carlos can remember. He says that these men are included in family events but are "talked about behind their backs."

Carlos is a student at the University of Phoenix. His classes are almost completely online and he has no face-to-face contact with any other students. He reports that he feels very isolated and, although he is "doing okay" academically, he would like a greater social connection. He has thought about taking courses at the local community college in a field that is different from his field of study at the University of Phoenix and that, he says, is much more interesting to him. He uses Facebook and has "about 500" Facebook friends, most of whom abuse substances and are gay-identified. His screen name indicates that he is "chemically friendly." He occasionally uses Internet chat rooms, although he denies using any gay dating sites. He is familiar with these sites and reports that he "almost hooked up" once on Craigslist but got "too scared" to show up for the date.

Carlos's pattern of isolation and introversion dates back to early adolescence when his biological father left the family. Carlos reports that he has never been "really close" to his father but that they continue to maintain a cordial relationship. He reports great tension in the family before his father left, but he denies any form of abuse. His mother has had a series of boyfriends; Carlos has liked some of them and not others. Carlos believes that he is responsible for his mother and lives with her and his younger siblings. His mother is currently not in a relationship. He reports that she knows that he and David are friends, but she doesn't know how much he cares about David. She also continues to encourage him to date "Spanish-speaking girls" and has arranged some dates for him with daughters of her friends. He reports that her involvement in his life contributes to his use of marijuana.

Cultural Issues

Having grown up in a Mexican American family in a largely Hispanic community, Carlos has integrated many of the values of the Mexican American Catholic community. His family has a strong expectation of heterosexuality and the importance of family connectedness. It is not uncommon for men in Carlos's peer group to live in the family home until they marry. Carlos has been able to avoid becoming involved in the street gang culture that was a part of his parents' experience and that is common for many of his friends. He graduated from high school and continued on at the University of Phoenix. He identifies that this may not be the most appropriate academic course for him, but his mother encouraged him to matriculate there in order to get a business degree. He is more interested in the arts, particularly those rooted in his cultural heritage. He is beginning to recognize that his educational interests may isolate him from his family, whose interests and experiences are different from his.

Tucson has a history of awareness and action in integrating the LGBT members of its community. In 1976 the city council passed an antidiscrimination ordinance outlawing discrimination on the basis of sexual orientation. Gender identity was added to the antidiscrimination ordinance in 1998. This ordinance prohibits discrimination in housing and employment. The City of Tucson also passed a Domestic Partnership Ordinance in 2003 recognizing same-sex relationships. The Gay, Lesbian, Bisexual and Transgender Advisory Commission to the mayor and city council celebrated its 10th anniversary in 2010 and continues to actively address issues within the community at large. Wingspan, the LGBT community center, was established in the mid-1980s and serves as a resource center for the general Tucson community. Strong ethnic LGBT organizations exist within the community, and a variety of social, spiritual, religious, political, intellectual, educational, academic, artistic, athletic/sports, medical, social justice, philanthropic, and business/financial organizations are available as resources for counselors and clients alike. Yet discrimination continues to be problematic.

Theoretical Framework

The counselor in this case develops a plan of action based on the integration of several growth and development models. Initially Carlos and the counselor collaborate using a cognitive–behavioral approach to understanding Carlos's presenting concerns. The counselor integrates existential and gestalt approaches in working with Carlos in both individual and group sessions. Experiential group work is integrated into the insight-oriented verbal group counseling. Carlos is strongly encouraged to participate in nontherapy experiential group activities as well. The counselor draws heavily from developmental and advocacy models in order to not pathologize Carlos's responses to the world in which he lives. The counselor uses sexual identity and racial/cultural developmental models to structure both individual and group sessions with Carlos. The counselor also frames the community in which Carlos lives in terms of its cultural development. The ACA (American Counseling Association) Advocacy Competencies (Lewis, Arnold, House, & Toporek, 2002); the Association for Lesbian, Gay, Bisexual and Transgender Issues in Counseling (1997) Competencies for Counseling Gay, Lesbian, Bisexual and Transgendered (LGBT) Clients; and the Association of Multicultural Counseling and Development Multicultural Counseling Competencies (Arredondo et al., 1996) provide a framework for both Carlos and the counselor. In addition, the counselor integrates the Association for Specialists in Group Work (1999) Principles for Diversity-Competent Group Workers and the ACA Code of Ethics (ACA, 2005) into his work with Carlos. Remaining vigilant to ethical standards, the counselor and Carlos collaborate with physicians, nutritionists, personal trainers, and other resources from Wingspan, the LGBT recovery and educational communities, and the Mexican American community.

Vision

Carlos has indicated that he wishes to "get his life together" and be clean of substances so that he can be independent, live on his own, have a career that he likes, be clear about his sexual orientation, and move toward having a healthy relationship.

The vision that Carlos and his counselor create includes the following:

- Ending his alcohol and cocaine use. He is unsure about ending his marijuana use.
- Staying at his job without experiencing anxiety and without feeling overwhelmed.
- Being physically and emotionally healthy, integrating a healthy eating and sleeping pattern into his life, having a regular fitness routine, and decreasing his anxiety-/fear-based lifestyle.
- Becoming clearer about his sexual orientation and his place in the Mexican American community and developing a healthy LGBT social system, if appropriate.
- Completing school; transferring to the community college for the social opportunities it presents and changing his major to the arts rather than business with the plan of continuing in a more traditional academic program.
- Being in a loving, healthy relationship in which he is monogamous.
- Establishing and maintaining a healthy and loving relationship with his family of origin.

Plan of Action

The counselor and Carlos agree to pursue an integrated, holistic approach to exploring Carlos's growth and development. The first step in this approach is to assist Carlos in reducing and eliminating his substance abuse, which both see as symptomatic of a lack of integration in Carlos's life. Carlos sees his primary care physician to gather medical information that may be critical to changing his life path. Carlos has determined that he does not wish to take medication as part of his plan. He agrees to work for 3 months with alternative approaches and to revisit his situation at the end of the 3 months. In addition, he agrees to participate in individual and group counseling focusing on cognitive, affective, and behavioral integration. He agrees to participate in support group meetings and to work with a peer who will encourage him in his efforts to reduce and eliminate his use and abuse of alcohol, marijuana, cocaine, and other substances.

With the assistance of Carlos's physician, Carlos and his counselor explore the biochemical components and implications of Carlos's chemical use and abuse. Carlos agrees to work with a nutritionist and fitness trainer to develop a plan that will help to bring his physical health back into balance. He also commits to participating in a martial arts or yoga program associated with his fitness center.

Carlos acknowledges that beneath his abuse of substances much of his life is based on fear. He explores his fear-based lifestyle with his counselor in both individual and group counseling settings. He also acknowledges that anxiety inhibits him from making the social contacts that would enhance his life. Such anxiety contributes to his isolation and alienation. He expresses an interest in participating in hiking and bicycling activities but historically has been too anxious to join any group. The LGBT community offers many opportunities to participate in a wide range of activities. Prior to being able to participate fully, Carlos explores issues related to sexual identity development in individual and group counseling sessions. He reads stories and accounts of the coming out process and discusses them tentatively in group counseling sessions, becoming more certain of himself as the group progresses and as he receives supportive feedback from group members. In addition, he explores attending an LGBT social group within the Mexican American community.

Carlos changes his online screen name to reflect his changing sense of self as a recovering, sexually healthy person. He begins to make tentative contacts on local websites through Wingspan. His Facebook profile changes, and he becomes more honest in the information he provides.

At the end of the first month of counseling, Carlos returns to work. His medical leave of absence has ended and he needs the income in order to move forward with his life. Carlos acknowledges that he is fortunate that his employer provides limited medical insurance and commits to continuing his changes, acknowledging that his change in lifestyle is less expensive and less anxiety producing than his alcohol and drug use has been. Much of what he is able to accomplish is greatly enhanced by his access to health care coverage.

Carlos also acknowledges that he still has "cravings" for alcohol, cocaine, and marijuana and that these will continue. As he becomes more attuned to the changes he is making, he is more capable of identifying dynamics that "trigger" his cravings, and with support he develops alternatives to "using." After 3 months of his "New Carlos Program" he reports a decrease in anxiety and a clearer sense of direction. However, he acknowledges that the changes are tentative. He recognizes that one of the dynamics that he continues to explore is the relationship between "shame" and his alcohol and drug use and abuse. He recognizes that he carries conflicting information about his sexual orientation and continues to integrate cognitive, affective, and behavioral dynamics that lead to greater centeredness. Carlos has terminated his friendship with David, which was painful for him. He acknowledges that this friendship was heavily reliant on alcohol and drug use and that his "payoff" for being involved in the friendship was that he continued to experience anxiety, pain, shame, and anger. He further recognizes that he had lost respect for himself when he was involved in this friendship.

Throughout his process, Carlos continues to take business-related courses at the University of Phoenix. As he becomes more centered, he explores courses at the community college and is preparing to register for his first class. His anxiety in social situations is decreasing and he participates more in group sessions. He has greater difficulty maintaining a weight and fitness program. He acknowledges that he has the tendency to "take on more than [he] can handle" and continues to reframe ways to redirect his life.

After 6 months Carlos has decreased his participation in individual counseling sessions, seeing the counselor every 2 weeks with the intent to decrease sessions to once a month. He continues to participate in group sessions and does not plan to eliminate his group participation at the 6-month review date. He has not relapsed and continues to participate more in the community. He continues to live in the family home and does not yet have the financial resources to move into his own apartment. He is exploring the possibility of sharing an apartment with someone from the hiking group he has helped to organize. He continues to increase his involvement in the community at large and anticipates a time when his anxiety will not interfere with his decision-making process and activity.

Interventions

The counselor in this case directly encouraged Carlos to make contact with his primary care physician at the beginning of their work together. In addition, Carlos signed releases for the counselor to work with his physician, nutritionist, and personal trainer to collaboratively develop an integrated plan of action. Carlos was directly encouraged to make contacts within the community. The counselor had a network of resources within the community, in which he himself was also actively involved. The counselor encouraged Carlos to be an advocate for himself and others in the community and helped him plan ways to do this.

Counselor Issues

Counselors walk a fine line as advocates and supporters of growth and change. The dynamics of addiction are such that dependency can manifest itself in a variety of ways, including in the counselor/client relationship. At times, individuals who have histories of substance abuse are adept at inviting counselors to step into a chaotic world. It becomes essential for counselors to be vigilant about maintaining healthy boundaries and allowing the client to move through his or her process in a manner that is congruent with life-enhancing growth. Particular vigilance must be maintained when moving beyond more traditional forms of intervention and when using experientially oriented methods. In addition, counselors must be counted on to establish and maintain ethically sound and congruent boundaries when working across disciplines to create an action plan with the client. Too often counselors can move into a parental role with clients when serving in a more adult role would be more helpful to both parties.

Counselors are encouraged to continue to take care of their own mental, physical, spiritual, cognitive, affective, social, and emotional lives. As participants in intimate relationships on a daily basis, counselors serve themselves well to have a social, physical, and spiritual balancing point. As persons committed to growth and change, counselors need to participate in ongoing clinical supervision as part of their own self-maintenance process.

Recommendations

The following recommendations are made to Carlos:

- Continue in counseling to explore identity development concerns by expanding his definition of what it means to be a sexual man who is attracted to other men. Also, continue in counseling to reframe experiences to operate from self-respect rather than from anxiety or fear.
- Continue to be involved in social activities that increase his opportunity for meeting like-minded and like-spirited individuals and groups.
- Continue to build on his health, diet, and fitness program for the purpose of decreasing the physical manifestations of anxiety and increasing the likelihood of maintaining sobriety.
- Continue the appropriate use of the Internet as a resource for social contact.
- Maintain connections with his family of origin as he creates a family of choice, explore ways to integrate his interest in Mexican American art, and continue balanced the family's community involvement.
- Continue academic and career exploration with the assistance of resources at the community college and the university.

Conclusion

Carlos is encouraged to pursue a path of integration into the complex community while learning to speak his voice in a clear manner. He is encouraged to operate in the world from a position of self-respect and strength. He is an intelligent and creative individual who has the potential to take on leadership roles in his workplace and in the community at large. He has begun a transformational process.

References

American Counseling Association. (2005). *ACA code of ethics.* Alexandria, VA: Author.

Arredondo, P., Toporek, M. S., Brown, S., Jones, J., Locke, D. C., Sanchez, J., & Stadler, H. (1996). Operationalization of the Multicultural Counseling Competencies. *Journal of Multicultural Counseling & Development, 24,* 42–78.

Association for Lesbian, Gay, Bisexual and Transgender Issues in Counseling. (1997). *Competencies for counseling gay, lesbian, bisexual and transgendered (LGBT) clients.* Alexandria, VA: Author.

Association for Specialists in Group Work. (1999). ASGW principles for diversity-competent group workers. *Journal of Specialists in Group Work, 24,* 7–14.

Lewis, J. A., Arnold, M. S., House, R., & Toporek, R. L. (2002). *ACA advocacy competencies.* Retrieved from http://www.counseling.org/Resources/Competencies/Advocacy_Competencies.pdf

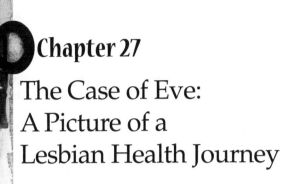

Chapter 27

The Case of Eve: A Picture of a Lesbian Health Journey

Jane E. Rheineck and Catherine B. Roland

A broad and expanding area of research focuses on health care for lesbian, gay, bisexual, and transgender (LGBT) persons. These individuals not only struggle with the same health issues as their heterosexual counterparts but also experience health issues that are often passed over or ignored entirely by health care professionals. Heterosexism and discrimination are often present within the health care system, and as a result there is disparity (Johnson, Mimiaga, & Bradford, 2008; Weisz, 2009).

Discrimination and social stigma can impede both access to and utilization of programs and services. LGBT persons are significantly more likely than heterosexual persons to be uninsured, with lesbians, LGBT youth, and transgender individuals representing the highest percentage of the underinsured (Johnson et al., 2008). Without health insurance, access to programs is limited, and as a result a health disparity exists.

In addition, social stigma is a stressor with significant mental health consequences, such as shame, anxiety, depression, and even suicide. A sense of hopelessness and low self-esteem coupled with the resulting despair can lead to the use of unhealthy coping devices. Lesbians and bisexual women have higher incidences of alcohol consumption, greater cigarette and marijuana use and greater risk for breast and gynecological cancers than heterosexual women (Steele, Tinmouth, & Lu, 2006). Gay men have disproportionately higher rates of HIV/AIDS (Centers for Disease Control and Prevention, 2006), experience higher rates of major depression, and also report more frequent panic attacks than heterosexual men (Johnson et al., 2008).

The American Public Health Association (1999) has acknowledged the special concerns of the LGBT community in a policy statement on the need for health care research. In addition, the U.S. Department of Health and Human Services (2000) has produced a manual addressing the public health needs of LGBT persons. All of these policies will hopefully influence research and funding and will impact the lives and well-being of LGBT people and their families.

The following case example highlights some of the health care issues faced by many members of the LGBT community. Understanding health concerns is always important, but it is imperative for counselors to also understand secondary tangential issues such as physical and emotional support received from health care institutions and medical professionals, the psychological well-being of patients and their families, and overall standards of care.

The Case of Eve

Eve was a 48-year-old woman of Irish descent who had worked as a career hotel management executive for more than 20 years. She had much responsibility at a well-known hotel in an urban area and traveled widely for her job. Eve, a lesbian with a life partner of 9 years, was completely out at work and with her strictly Irish Catholic family. She had one brother, Alan, 43 years old, who was gay. Eve was not particularly close with her mother, however she spent a good deal of time touching base every day or so and visited often.

Eve made an appointment with me (Catherine B. Roland) at my private practice, having found my information on an LGBT website in the area. Her main concern, as stated in an initial call, was that she was in a "dying mode" and that she wanted help with end-of-life issues. I immediately sought information from her to determine whether this was a medical issue, and she said it was and didn't want to go into it on the phone. Having never been in counseling before, she shared that she was nervous but knew it was what she needed to do. We made the appointment for the end of that week.

Eve presented as somewhat depressed and hesitant, however her eye contact, demeanor, and ability to converse were impressive. She began to talk right away—she clearly was ready to share some of the pain and have someone else carry it with her. One year ago, while Eve had been experiencing general tiredness and irritability, she had been persuaded by her life partner Grace to take the BRCA (BReast CAncer) test—a test that is said to be able to predict one's likelihood of being diagnosed with cancer, especially for women who have previously had breast cancer (Manne et al., 2004). Eve tested positive for some genetic influence and from that point forward began to live her life differently. One of the important changes she made was to stop drinking and begin to attend Alcoholics Anonymous, and she had been sober for 8 months. Eve noticed that communication issues were emerging in her relationship with Grace, but because she felt fine physically she expected the interpersonal issues "to take care of themselves and be better."

Her life seemed, as reported, "just fine," and then a medical issue emerged. Five weeks before she had called me, Eve had experienced acute abdominal pain that had caused her to miss two trips for work and to cancel a birthday party for Grace. She went to a doctor, who referred her to a specialist. Eve's physician advised a very quick surgery, and she had a full hysterectomy the following week. Immediately following this, Eve was diagnosed with Stage

III ovarian cancer with multiple complications. She was immediately scheduled for a full regimen of chemotherapy that would begin in the hospital—the
physician felt she would be too weak to stay at home. Her first hospital visit
would occur 2 weeks after our initial therapy appointment, and Eve was ter-
rified. Part of the terror was that this was not her first experience with cancer.
What she shared next helped me to conceptualize the situation.

Twelve years ago, when Eve was 36, she had been diagnosed with breast
cancer. At that time she went through radiation and a light chemotherapy
regimen and was said be to "cancer free" after 1 year. During that period
Eve was with a younger women named Janet, who cared for her and offered
support. When they decided to end their relationship it was mutual, and
Janet and Eve remain good friends. Eve had experienced another significant loss after her first cancer diagnosis—her father had suddenly passed
away from a heart attack 5 years ago. The profound realization of mortality
impacted Eve, as she had never lost anyone before, and in fact she hadn't
known anyone intimately who had yet lost a parent. She began drinking
and developed a dependence on alcohol about 4 years ago.

The work we began to do together that day centered on her current
feelings of desperation coupled with her fear of a lack of support from
the medical community. Although during her first round of cancer she
had had a willing helper in her partner, they were both treated poorly
in Eve's estimation—no one talked with them about any possible social
services, and it was constantly difficult for Janet to visit with Eve during
nonvisiting hours at the hospital, even though "family" members were
always permitted to do so. Hospital staff who were informed that Eve was
partnered seemed to dismiss that and treated Janet with disrespect and,
at times, rudely. Eve shared that once Janet and her mother had come to
visit—the nurse on duty had asked Janet to leave because "the mother is
the most important if you don't have a husband." Eve was understandably apprehensive that this experience would be repeated with her partner
Grace, and given some of the issues with which they had been struggling
recently, Eve was anticipating that Grace would gravitate away from her
and ultimately leave her to die alone.

The experience after her recent surgery was better, although Grace did
not participate as much as Janet had years before—in fact, it was her friend
and ex, Janet, who stayed with Eve most often in the hospital, and as "just
a friend" Janet was treated fairly well, as any friend might be. When Grace
did appear she was not allowed in the room once because it was right after the surgery and "only family" was allowed. This was rectified shortly
afterward; however, the pain of it caused Grace to feel embarrassed and
angry. Eve's anxiety level was very high, and I felt that this was one of
the first issues to consider in therapy. Eve would need all her strength—
emotional and physical—to engage in both our therapy process and her
medical treatment. This was quite a bit of information for a first session; I
felt that because Eve would begin her chemotherapy in a few weeks, we
should set twice-weekly appointments until that time. Eve agreed, and we
set the next appointment for 3 days later.

During those 3 days I did some research on my own concerning ovarian cancer and the stages, prognosis, and medical and social structures in place for women in general and lesbians specifically. Although I found information on the disease, I found very little information or referral sources specific to lesbians. We just didn't seem to exist in the literature—scholarly or otherwise. I knew my support for Eve would be vital for her process, and I wanted to be as up to date as possible. We would begin to construct a support system and a mode of operation around the medical professionals if necessary, which was a topic in her therapy.

Over the next few appointments Eve and I were able to develop a list of goals that were time sensitive. We agreed that her anxiety in general was primary, and this was followed by her being able to remain hopeful and trusting of her doctors during chemo and to cope with the social and physical issues that might occur, such as hair loss, loss of self-esteem, an inability to work, and feelings of helplessness at conducting herself as she once had as a professional and a partner. We accomplished the second goal to some degree, so that she did grow to trust the doctors, through developing lists of questions for her doctors and her medical team as well as further research on the disease. When she shared that her first appointment had yielded virtually no answers to her questions, and that the response from her doctor was "That's a question I don't have time to answer now," we practiced her being more insistent on getting her answers. We role-played the situation several times, each time with Eve being more and more assertive. She learned that she had the right to know information and that if a primary doctor wasn't forthcoming, he or she had to point her in the direction of another professional who could help. In this way, she found her "person," as she referred to her—a medical assistant in the surgeon's office who happened to be a lesbian. Given what Eve had done professionally, dealing very successfully with all types of people for many years, we were able to have her put into practice her skills, and she was able to confide in her doctor, directly asking for help. He referred her to his assistant. It became clear that the doctor didn't know about lesbians but that he also didn't care that Eve was lesbian—he just seemed in general not to like talking with his patients. The assistant was, in Eve's estimation, "a godsend" to her in that she offered personal support, sometimes ran interference with medical staff, especially during treatment, and all around seemed to understand her personal and health-related situation.

The first goal, lessening anxiety, was more difficult to address. After a deep exploration about her feelings of loss and of being left alone as a result of the disease, Eve admitted that she felt that she and Grace had been drifting apart before the diagnosis and surgery. She had dismissed it as her fault because she had just recently started Alcoholics Anonymous and was certain if she made changes, all would be well. I asked her to tell me what she was most afraid of—and I admit I was ready to hear that the greatest fear would be her own death. That is not at all what she reported. Eve said that when her father had died so suddenly, she had become aware that she really only had her mother left, and that she would be left alone after her mother passed away. I mentioned her relationship with her brother Alan, and Eve shared that although she was close to him, he had separated from the rest of the family and was "just never there for me when I needed him to be—all my life." Eve said she felt that Grace was going to abandon her "just like my father did" and that she would live alone with this diagnosis. We discussed the loss of her father, and I asked her tell me about him, to describe their closeness and her sadness. She cried a bit but was able to talk about what he meant to her and how much she had missed him for the past 5 years. At one point she said, "He would know what I should do." When I asked her to clarify, she said, "You know, if I should even do chemo or not—is it worth it?" No one trains counselors to field a question like that; I softly reminded her that all issues of her life and how she lived it were hers and that she had supportive people around who loved and needed her in their lives. She nodded and smiled a little and said that she knew she needed to try all possibilities because she wanted to "get better and live my life with Grace." At the mention of her partner, she broke down and sobbed. Loss permeated the room—the loss of her father, the anticipated loss of her partner, and the feared loss of her life were palpable. I moved to the couch and held her hand, and after a few minutes Eve straightened and shook her head, saying she felt a little better.

It seemed to me that we needed to assess just where Grace was at this point, so I asked Eve how she would feel if Grace came with her for a session. She immediately agreed and seemed to relax a bit—she said if Grace agreed she thought she would be able to tell Grace how she felt. We planned it for the next session at the end of that week. Eve asked whether it would be okay for her to call Grace right then on her cell and ask about the time, and I agreed. Normally I would not do that in session, however we were on a time constraint of which I was acutely aware. The date and time were set, and Eve breathed deeply for perhaps the first time in almost an hour.

Grace and Eve came to see me, and immediately there was a calm about Eve I had not seen. We began with a general overview of why the session had been requested, and then I invited Eve to begin. Eve quickly was able to synopsize her feelings and fear that Grace would leave her given the medical situation she was in, the past disrespect that Grace had suffered already, and the problematic issues that had been happening between them before the diagnosis. Eve sat back on the couch, exhausted. She was clear and relaxed, however, and I got the impression that she had been holding this, and more, for a very long time.

Grace looked at Eve, then looked at me, and said nothing. She covered her face with unsteady hands and began to cry softly. I allowed that to play out a little and then asked whether she would like to share with us. Grace reached over, took Eve's hand, and nearly whispered, "It's nothing like that—I just don't want to lose you. I thought if I avoided you and the hospital, it would all go away. I don't want to live without you." Eve was totally quiet, but I could see her eyes and sensed she was holding back tears. I asked Eve what she was feeling, and the strong resolve crumbled before us. Eve cried in Grace's arms, and Grace clung to her. We teach our master's students that it is okay for the therapist to emote—well, that's a good thing, because my eyes were clouding with tears, and the lump in my throat caused me to stay more quiet than I might have. After a few minutes, Grace sat back and breathed and looked very relieved. She offered that as long as Eve knew she was afraid, too, they would be able to stay close and loving. She would be comfortable with her fear and would be able to help Eve through this very difficult physical and emotional juncture.

Eve responded by looking at me and smiling, perhaps the first genuine smile I had seen since meeting her several weeks earlier. I felt from that smile that some hope had been restored; her will to live seemed to magically begin to emerge, perhaps not strong at first but growing. Eve asked whether we could share the goals we had discussed for her, and of course it was up to her to share whatever she wanted with Grace. We continued to discuss the goals of lowering Eve's anxiety and gaining trust in her doctors, therefore assisting her to reestablish her positive outlook. At each statement Grace had suggestions, such as that she would go with Eve to the assistant next time and be a "second set of ears" as I had mentioned to Eve several times. Grace also pledged to help with researching support groups in the community for lesbians and committed to attending those with Eve if necessary—or not, depending on the situation. Grace volunteered to give Eve a backrub and massage if she was up to it, and Eve seemed especially pleased with that. The session concluded with a good deal having been accomplished, most important the melding of Eve's and Grace's feelings of loss and a consideration of how that had impacted their relationship and attitudes. Eve now had trust in the most vital advocate possible, her loving partner.

We arranged that Eve and I would meet once more alone before her first chemotherapy treatment and that Eve and Grace and I would meet once as well. Eve asked me before we parted whether I would be able to come to her home if she was not able to come to me through her chemotherapy appointments. I replied that I could and that we would arrange that if necessary. I felt that Eve needed to know that I would be there for her, regardless of where that was.

In the next sessions before the chemo I separated issues of the couple and the individual. As a rule I do not see a couple as well as one person of that dyad individually; this was a situation that was very short term and intense, and I viewed it as completely about Eve, her support systems, and how we would work to raise her feelings of hope. My view is that Yalom (2005) was correct, that the installation of hope is arguably one of the most important aspects of therapy, especially in situations that are life threatening in some way. Eve's life was indeed threatened, medically and emotionally.

Future Counseling Sessions

Eve endured five treatments of advanced chemotherapy before she decided to discontinue that treatment. She was not able to come to the office, and I met her at her home once and the hospital once. Her diagnosis did not change after the chemo; Eve felt ill most of each day. She was unable to leave the house for the first few weeks, then began to physically become a bit stronger and could go to the grocery with Grace, go out for a very short walk, and sit out in the backyard. She lost her hair and was given the opportunity to choose many wigs, which she did not do. She made the decision to purchase one wig for when she was in public with people she did not know; she choose to go natural all other times. She had her left ear pierced with two extra holes so she could wear multiple earrings in that ear. It seemed as though Eve was determined to make the best of this very difficult time.

Our two sessions consisted of support and open discussion of her father, her relationship with her brother Alan, and how those two were entwined. She was able to begin to separate the fact that Alan and her father were both men but different and that Alan's being gay and then being estranged from the family had been something that had kept her from trusting him throughout the past few years. She felt that Alan had been wrong about staying away from the family and that he should have been more communicative with their father and not shut him out. Eve felt strongly that her father had died a very sad man because he had in effect banished his son, and he finally felt that loss through the years. Eve shared that she had tried several times to ask Alan to come home for holidays, but he had refused. She felt that now she was sick, and he wouldn't be there for her either. We discussed the possibility of her telling Alan the truth about her medical status after I found out that he thought her surgery had been elective and prophylactic in nature. Eve promised to think about that and discuss it with Grace.

The second to last time I saw Eve in session we discussed the possibility of writing her will. She took me by surprise that day—she had been looking a bit better and had researched several alternative cancer treatment centers outside the United States, one in Mexico and one in Sweden. Neither had received great reviews from her research, but she was feeling like she had to "just do something at this point." She brought in a list of attorneys who she had found online who were gay or gay friendly and wanted to know whether I had knowledge of one or two. She reported that she and Grace had tried to consult Eve's mother's attorney about setting up a will, a living will, and a trust, but the attorney had not seemed interested in assisting. He had met with them but then asked Grace to leave because it was "Eve's issue and it was a private legal matter." Eve and Grace immediately left the meeting together. When Eve reported that incident to me, I could feel the anger in my heart and the sadness as well. We discussed attorneys and I did give her two names, one of whom was on her list and the other of whom I knew did work with gay and lesbian individuals and couples in the area. We confirmed that we would see each other later that week.

The morning of our next planned meeting Grace called me. She told me that Eve had been taken to the emergency room for pains in her chest and trouble breathing and that she had been admitted. After apologizing that Eve would miss her time with me (imagine!), she asked whether I would come to the hospital if Eve wanted me to sometime soon. I agreed. Grace called me every day for a week to report on Eve's progress and to let me know that one of the attorneys that I knew was indeed working with them and that he had already done what Eve had asked. Eve slipped into a coma and was unable to approve or deny any treatment. The living will specified that no unnatural means were to be used if it came to that and that Grace would make all those decisions. Eve was not able to come back from the coma; her cancer had spread and the chemo had not been effective. Grace later shared that there seemed to be respect and acknowledgment for her feelings and decisions at the hospital and during all of the service arrangements. Sadly death brought about a final resolution.

Conclusion

My work with Eve and Grace was finished, I assumed. We addressed many issues: health education, anxiety, depression, relationship issues, and legal and discrimination issues, to name a few. Yet 3 months later Grace made an appointment and we worked on her grief for a few sessions before she took a different position in her company and moved to another city. She shared that she could no longer live where Eve had lived, that the sadness was too much. Grace said she needed "a new place and a new start." I hear from her occasionally at holiday times; she is doing well. Eve's case has stayed with me, humbled me, for several years. I imagine it always will.

References

American Public Health Association. (1999). Policy statement 9819: The need for public health research on gender identity and sexual orientation. *American Journal of Public Health, 89,* 444–445.

Centers for Disease Control and Prevention. (2006). *HIV/AIDS surveillance report, 2005* (Vol. 17). Atlanta, GA: Author.

Johnson, C. V., Mimiaga, M. J., & Bradford, J. (2008). Health care issues among lesbian, gay, bisexual, transgendered and intersex (LGBTI) populations in the United States: Introduction. *Journal of Homosexuality, 54*(3), 213–224.

Manne, S., Audrain, J., Schwartz, M., Main, D., Finch, C., & Lerman, C. (2004). Association between relationship support and psychological reactions of participants and partners to BRCA1 and BRCA2 testing in a clinical-based sample. *Annals of Behavioral Medicine, 28,* 211–225.

Steele, L. S., Tinmouth, J. M., & Lu, A. (2006). Regular health care use by lesbians: A path analysis of predictive factors. *Family Practice, 23,* 631–636.

U.S. Department of Health and Human Services. (2000). *Healthy People 2010: Understanding and improving health* (2nd ed.). Washington, DC: U.S. Government Printing Office.

Weisz, V. K. (2009). Social justice considerations for lesbian and bisexual women's health. *Journal of Obstetric, Gynecologic, & Neonatal Nursing, 38,* 81–87.

Yalom, I. (2005). *The theory and practice of group psychotherapy* (5th ed.). New York, NY: Basic Books.

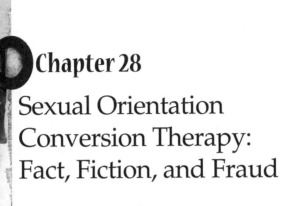

Chapter 28

Sexual Orientation Conversion Therapy: Fact, Fiction, and Fraud

Douglas C. Haldeman

The practice of attempting to change the unwanted same-sex attractions of homosexual and bisexual individuals predates any other form of treatment for lesbian, gay, bisexual, and transgender (LGBT) clients. Clinical assumptions about the pathology of same-sex attraction were derived largely from prevailing cultural norms (Haldeman, 1994). However, the "mental illness" model of homosexuality was discarded by the major mental health organizations in the 1970s, and same-sex attractions are now considered a normative variant of the human experience (American Psychological Association [APA], 2009).

Not all segments of contemporary American culture have fallen in line with the social scientists, however. The overwhelming motivation of those seeking to change their sexual orientation through therapy or other means derives from incompatibility with religious beliefs (APA, 2009; Tozer & Hayes, 2004). It has been estimated that up to one quarter of the American public believes in traditional conservative Christian concepts such as an active interfering deity, an afterlife featuring a day of judgment, and "the rapture" (Herman, 1997). Therefore, conversion therapies, or sexual orientation change efforts (SOCE) as these practices are now called (owing to the fact that most of such efforts surely do not qualify as therapy), still have a considerable following.

Because of the fact that such interventions are unsuccessful (APA, 2009), clinicians who work with LGBT clients can expect to see, at least on occasion, individuals who have undergone such efforts and failed. The residual effects of such "treatment" failures vary from person to person. For some, the interventions themselves simply serve to underscore the constant and unchangeable nature of sexual orientation. The failure to change comes as something of a relief. The individual who has prayed, resisted, and done any other number of "antigay" activities prescribed by the ex-gays is finally able to let go of what is often experienced as an impossible quest.

For others, however, the interventions result in posttraumatic effects, and for some it is the treatment failure itself that is at issue. The discomfort with being gay, compounded with the shame of having been unable to change it, is difficult enough. When these factors are paired with rejection by family and the community of faith, the results can be devastating. In this chapter, a sampling of case material, contextualized by cultural factors, is used to reflect some of the complicated reactions of those conflicted individuals who have sought unsuccessfully to change their sexual orientation.

First, however, we must acknowledge that SOCE are firmly rooted in a sociocultural context that pathologizes same-sex attraction and homosexual/ bisexual orientation. There can be no discussion of SOCE without mentioning the fact that the notion that sexual orientation can be changed is the cornerstone of arguments presented by religious conservatives in the service of abrogating civil rights for LGBT individuals. According to them, everything that protects vulnerable LGBT individuals—from hate crimes legislation to antidiscrimination laws to same-sex marriage—is unnecessary because sexual orientation can be changed. This renders LGBT people a "pseudominority" irrespective of the fact that civil rights are granted to all manner of individuals whose lives are based on variables of choice (e.g., freedom of religious expression). If indeed sexual orientation is in fact a normal variant of the human experience (APA, 2009), all of the arguments against LGBT rights fall like a house of cards.

At the same time, it is essential to note that the identification with and expression of any kind of religious practice or dogma is a personal right and beyond the scope of any criticism or disrespect from mental health organizations (APA, 2008). As social scientists, we acknowledge the importance of religious affiliation for many people and do not attempt to evaluate or interfere with the construction of religious tenets. They lie outside the scope of science. Conversely, we do not view religious dogma as an appropriate basis for social policy or mental health interventions. Furthermore, our respect for religious tradition does not prevent us from evaluating the psychological effects of religious identification when it conflicts with an individual's experience of sexual orientation—in fact, it calls us to do so. For the individual embedded in certain conservative religious traditions, the notion of living as a gay person is unthinkable because of the ostracism that would result from family and community as well as the confusion that is associated with integrating into the gay community. Heterosexual marriage or celibacy thus becomes a personal imperative.

This is not to imply that all communities of faith, or even all conservative communities of faith, include heterosexual identity as a requirement for membership. However, it is clear that nearly all individuals who have undergone SOCE in some form have done so in the service of their religious beliefs (APA, 2009; Tozer & Hayes, 2004) and their understanding that heterosexual identity is a requirement for good standing in their families and communities of faith. Therefore, the clinician working with this population must be sensitive to the role and import of religion in the client's life while attempting to orient the client to the reality of the self and to assist him or her in navigating the LGBT community as a means of recreating an experience of family and community.

This makes it necessary to tread in a delicate way with some clients whose coming out process has resulted in significant losses of family and social network with no replacement immediately available owing to an unfamiliarity with the LGBT community. The literature has documented clinical interventions for those who have been harmed in SOCE (Haldeman, 2002).

Following are two cases that demonstrate the complexities of working with SOCE survivors. It should be noted from the outset that both cases are of gay males. The SOCE literature, such as it is, has focused nearly all of its efforts on men. It has been speculated that this is because conservative religious groups, and U.S. culture in general, are more tolerant of women's same-sex attraction.

A Case of Familial Religious Extremism

Justin was raised in a conservative Christian family. His parents belonged to a nondenominational Bible church in which behaviors such as "talking in tongues" and a concept of hellfire and damnation were assumed truths. He expected, correctly as it turned out, that if he were to come out as gay his family would reject him. Nevertheless, Justin's self-awareness as gay was so strong that he knew no amount of praying or therapy would change it. He came out to his family at age 23, after a long period of soul searching, and brought to session an e-mail he had subsequently received from his mother. It should be noted that Justin had engaged in ineffective religious-based SOCE for several years prior to his coming out.

In the message, Justin's mother told him that she knew Satan had inhabited his soul and that she would pray for him. She requested that he not contact any family members until he had disavowed his "evil lifestyle" and accepted Jesus as his personal savior. Justin is diagnosed with an acute adjustment disorder with depressed mood as well as self-defeating and masochistic personality features.

Justin's attempt to adopt a rational perspective about his family's cruel behavior is quickly eroded because on a profound, almost cellular, level he is devastated. He has been brought up to believe in a harsh, judgmental deity and everlasting punishment for those who do not follow the rules. It would be impossible to overstate the role of mindfulness-based ACT work to help Justin accept his grief and anger about having been so badly treated by his family. The clinician working with people such as Justin needs to be patient as the warehouse of negative affect is unpacked. In Justin's case, anger over being betrayed by those who claimed to have loved him alternates with grief associated with abandonment. This arouses no small amount of countertransferential desire to comfort and soothe him; therefore, frequent reminders that he has done nothing wrong serve to help him neutralize his shame about being gay. For the first few months in treatment Justin is in an acute phase of grief and needs support and reassurance.

At the same time, it is reasonable to reinforce Justin's sense that his sexual orientation is not amenable to change; this he understands after years spent trying to "pray away the gay." Just as the ACT work aids in the acceptance of emotional experience, it is also useful in the integration of same-sex attraction into the identity. SOCE, after all, are ineffective in large measure because they demand a disintegration of the self and a compartmentalization of sexual desire. This is as unhealthy as it is unrealistic.

As the mourning period of losing his family gives way to a more pragmatic perspective (that sounds something like "So now what do I do?"), it is appropriate to orient Justin to the reality before him. This involves the strategy of constructing the replacement family. The families of LGBT individuals often include people who are not legally or biologically related. As Justin's grief over the loss of his family of origin gives way to loneliness, it becomes appropriate to raise this issue with him.

"Have you thought about who your friends will be?" the therapist asks.

"No. I mean, yes, I miss my family and my old friends but I know I can't be around them anymore."

"Who would you like to be around?"

"People who accept me for who I am."

Most models of sexual orientation identity development include some aspect of relationship with other LGB people, as well as some concept of how to live in the gay community (Fassinger & Arseneau, 2006). There are several reasons for this: it solidifies the individual's identity and also provides the very necessary human comforts of companionship and social interaction.

It is useful for the therapist to have some idea about local LGBT resources. All major cities and most urban areas have an array of LGBT social and interest groups; these are easily accessed through online searches. In Justin's case, however, connecting with the gay social world would prove challenging. He finds the social environment of gay bars to be foreign and intimidating; in addition, he is not a drinker. Joining social interest groups within the gay community likewise proves difficult for Justin. Unlike some who are in recovery from SOCE, he is not interested in an alternative gay-positive religious group. Justin seems intent on deleting all references to religion from his consciousness. In addition, he is not keen on any particular sort of athletic, political, or cultural activities for which there are gay groups. He feels uncomfortable around groups of his "own kind," so to speak, and experiences a particular aversion to men he perceives as "effeminate."

Justin's entry into the world of romantic relationships with other men is further complicated by the fact that although his same-sex fantasy life is well developed, he has never actually had sex with another man. Justin's sexual fantasies have a sadomasochistic orientation. Whether his fantasies about being punished in sexual situations are the result of his internalized shame about being gay is speculative. What is apparent, however, is that as his sexual behavior developed, it appeared likely to lead him into potentially dangerous situations.

"Well, I finally had sex!" Justin reports brightly at the opening of one session.

"Oh? Do you want to tell me about it?"

"Well, I found an S&M club where you can join and get into 'scenes' with different kinds of people. I found a guy who wanted me to be his servant, and we had a great time."

The therapist proceeds very carefully, not wanting to be perceived as passing a negative judgment but also wanting Justin to be thoughtful about his sexual adventures. This is compounded by the countertransferential difficulty the therapist is developing with Justin's sexual exploration, fearing that Justin is missing a more "conventional" step in the evolution of his psychosexual expression.

At one point, Justin finds a "master" online who is said to be well known for his management of sexual domination scenarios. Justin engages in a scene in which he is physically bound to the point of severe discomfort. Despite the master's request that Justin inform him when the line between pleasure and serious pain has been crossed, Justin tolerates the procedure. At the end, he has suffered temporary but serious neurological consequences resulting in the partial loss of the use of his right arm and hand. Fortunately Justin recovers full function, but the recovery takes weeks.

This episode is a wake-up call for the therapist. "Justin, I am very sorry to hear about what happened to you; it must be so painful. I also think we should talk, when you are ready, about the sexual choices you are making."

"I know," he replies, very downcast. Justin is understandably frightened by this experience; it also activates his "shame core" associated with being gay. When he starts regaining his full motor function, he and the therapist revisit the issue.

"What do you think about the future of your sexual life, now that you are recovering from your injury?" asks the therapist. Justin commits to revising his internal "sexual script" and states his intention to focus on developing a circle of friends, exploring the possibility of finding a boyfriend, and being more careful in his sexual behavior. Revising a long-rehearsed internal sexual script is not easy. In this case, the therapist works with Justin to make mental "bridges," using visualization and masturbatory reconditioning, between his erotic fantasies of punishment and humiliation and potentially less dangerous erotic behaviors. Justin moves toward revising his choice of partners from those that reside purely in the domain of sadomasochistic fantasy to those whose characteristics (dominant, strong, assertive) retain some element of his historical fantasy repertoire but are ultimately better suited for life with a real partner.

Justin makes admirable progress toward these goals. The experience of allowing himself to be a participant in a homopositive society starts to erode his internalized shame and negativity. Justin is also able to start confronting his intimacy avoidance and begins to date. He meets a man who is 15 years older than himself, whom Justin describes as "smart, kind, and protective." The couple has been together for 2 years and are doing very well.

In retrospect, it is easy to attribute Justin's internalized (and actual physical) torture to a homophobic cultural upbringing and a vicious rejection by his family of origin. Although this is likely, we cannot say it with certainty. We can, however, say that the sociocultural influences to which Justin was subjected in early life and the subsequent family rejection had a negative effect on his mental well-being. The assessment and treatment of trauma, therefore, become important elements of treatment with men who have been involved in SOCE.

This case evoked a spectrum of countertransferential feelings on the part of the therapist, many of which necessarily were screened out or minimized given Justin's fragility. At first, Justin's recounting of harsh treatment by his family aroused feelings of protectiveness in the therapist. Here it was important for the therapist to remain empathic without veering into being overly soothing; in being empathic, the therapist guides the client to soothe himself or herself with mindfulness and self-statements. As Justin became sexually active, the therapist's feelings of comfort gave way to ones of alarm and concern that his client was out of control. Yet the therapist needed to be measured in response to this as well. Tempting though it may have been to ask, "What were you thinking?" upon Justin's disclosure that he had become injured in a sadomasochistic sex scene gone wrong, it was more productive to address his behavior from a value-neutral, problem-solving perspective. This way, the therapist would enable Justin to come to his own conclusions about how to integrate his sexual interests into his life and feel positive about sex—as opposed to risking exacerbating his client's already significant feelings of shame with a judgment-laden response.

A Case of Post-"Ex-Gay" Social Isolation

Mark, 32, comes to treatment with concerns about intimacy in adult interpersonal relationships. He states that he is a successful businessman in the area of real estate development and that he is very conscientious about his work. As a result, he is financially well off and his opinion is sought after among his peers. Nevertheless, he is socially reclusive, spending most weekends by himself, seeking sex online. He rarely hooks up. When he does, it is with others who are sexually submissive, endorsing their devotion to him as the primary component of their erotic stimulation.

Mark wants to develop a healthy primary relationship but has no idea how to go about it. He reports that as a youngster he was an only child raised by a single mother who left him with his grandparents for long periods of time. Mark states that he missed her greatly and attributed her absences to his misbehavior. When she would return, he states that he would do anything to please her.

At 18 Mark came out to his mother as gay. She was horrified and immediately demanded that he enroll in an "ex-gay" program, a request with which he complied. He reports having tried unsuccessfully for nearly 10 years to redirect his primary erotic attraction to men. When Mark finally announced to his family that he had given up trying to change his sexual orientation, his mother grudgingly accepted that he would be gay.

Despite his professional success, Mark is lonely and feels that his sociosexual life is dysfunctional. He desires companionship in the form of a primary relationship with another man. He is diagnosed with dysthymic disorder and social anxiety.

The primary themes of post-SOCE trauma typically include those felt and enacted elements (depression, guilt, suicidality, demasculinization, intimacy avoidance; Haldeman, 2002) that are evident in Mark's attitudes and behavior. The negative sequelae of failed attempts at SOCE most typically manifest in terms of interpersonal problems. The original community has been relinquished when, finally, the individual recognizes that his same-sex attractions cannot be subverted through engaging in traditional masculine activities, cannot be deleted by developing a "healthy" relationship with a father figure, and will not be eradicated through prayer. When the individual hits the "SOCE bottom," to use a recovery term, he must grieve the loss of the connection and privilege associated with his historical origins and face the challenges of navigating a new social world. This often creates anxiety as well as profound loss. Furthermore, because the individual has been trained to associate male identity and gender role expectations with heterosexuality, he often feels a sense of demasculinization upon coming out.

Mark's story illustrates a secondary theme of life after SOCE: the experience of the self as a failure. This sense may be generalized throughout the person's life, or, as in Mark's case, it may be limited to social and romantic interactions. Mark's work life, for example, is a model of accomplishment: professional advancement, prestige and power, as well as monetary reward. Mark takes his work seriously and handles his responsibilities in ways that exceed expectations. His productivity appears to be exceptional. However, his internal experience of it is meaningless. Mark describes his work as a role that he understands and fulfills to the best of his ability. It provides a structure in which he functions like a machine.

With sense of identity confused with the inappropriate application of traditional gender norms, Mark invests all of his sense of personal efficacy in work. His sexual encounters are episodic and always with strangers whom he has met online, for one time only. These erotoromantic events become episodic, quick ventures into a fantasy world in which he is sexually worshiped and adored in an effort to compensate for an arid lack of emotional connection with other men. "I only feel something when someone is kneeling at my feet," he explains, "and even then, it doesn't last."

Mark's experience of his professional self is undermined by the profound sense of despair associated with his personal life. He knows many people and has a variety of superficial relationships but does not experience close friendship, let alone romance. Mark is lonely and has never overcome the shame associated with failing his many attempts at changing his sexual orientation. He grudgingly accepts his same-sex attractions and is unable to sustain an intimate connection.

Mark's case offers a complex interplay between his history and his present life. It challenges him to resolve long-unfulfilled attachment fantasies but also to cope with a present-day life that is absent any real emotional intimacy. His association with male identity and the expression thereof in an intimate relationship is deeply connected with his unsuccessful attempt to change his sexual orientation. His erotoromantic life remains firmly embedded in a landscape of sexual mastery and servitude in which a submissive partner adores him. In reality, his life is devoid of any intimate relationships. Mark's "shame core" is an obstacle but also a sense of being less than a real man, or demasculinized, because of the toxic effects of the conversion therapy and ex-gay programs he attended, which reinforced the notion that "real" men can't be gay.

To be sure, Mark's interpersonal dysfunction cannot be wholly attributed to the negative effects of SOCE; the social context promoting SOCE shares some of the blame as well. At this juncture, it is reasonable to consider approaches to healing the wounds caused by SOCE. These involve a reclaiming of the masculine self in a (gay) context that is appropriate for the client. Learning that real men can indeed be gay is a primary task for Mark. Comprehending the relevant dimensions of gender identity (Englar-Carlson & Stevens, 2006) and reinforcing this in the therapeutic relationship is of primary importance.

Behavioral plans between sessions are critical. It is essential that Mark develop a support network before attempting to engage in a romantic relationship. And how does one develop that support network? One day, Mark offers his therapist a hint in response to an important question.

"Mark, tell me about one thing that you think real men do," the therapist says.

"They play sports."

"And you don't?" asks the therapist.

"No."

"You don't like them?"

"No, it's not that," Mark explains. "I'm actually a big sports guy. I just don't want to play on a team like it was high school and go through all that again." Here Mark explains that "all that" referred to the humiliation he suffered because of the teasing and bullying of the other boys.

"Maybe it's possible for you to rethink not only what it means to be a gay man but what it means to be an athlete. You say you don't think you can be both. But it sounds as though you are both," observes the therapist.

The therapist then explains that there are a number of gay sports leagues and teams in the area and asks Mark to investigate something athletic he thinks he might like. Mark seeks out a local gay runners group. He is then able to engage in an activity he has always enjoyed and associated with his sense of being male and transform it into a gay social context. After making friends within the group, he begins to explore other gay sports groups (skiing, baseball) and takes his enthusiasm to the Gay Games, where he competes in several track and field events. He comes back with a new sense of pride, a reclaimed identity as a gay man, and continues to integrate his gay sexual orientation into the sense of identity from which it was truncated by SOCE long ago.

As explained with Justin's case, countertransference can be a complex factor in working with survivors of SOCE. Given some of the egregious harms endured by clients at the hands of inept reparative therapists, it is easy for the therapist to fall into an alliance with the client and join in the outrage or whatever emotion is aroused. This should be avoided in favor of an empathic but more neutral stance. It is always easier for the client to heal without the emotional interference of the therapist's personal reactions. This is particularly true of survivors of SOCE, however, because these clients have sought to change their sexual orientation in an attempt to please others. This tendency can easily be replicated in a therapeutic effort to undo the damage of SOCE.

Conclusion

These cases illustrate some of the harmful effects of SOCE as well as provide suggestions for how they may be therapeutically addressed. Why is there no policy opposing SOCE altogether? There are two reasons. First, those on both sides of the argument have only anecdotal claims of harm. Proscribing any form of "treatment," even one as poorly based and described as SOCE, is an unusual step and would require sufficient scientific evidence. Second, it is clear that not all who undergo some form of SOCE experience sustained or even short-term harm. As long as there are cultural and religious groups who harbor sexual prejudice and raise their children in such an atmosphere, there will be a market for SOCE. Time, however, is against them. If trends in public opinion continue, the interest in SOCE will eventually die out along with the homophobia that promotes them.

In the meantime, it is in the interest of clients who have attempted some form of SOCE for clinicians to be aware of their numerous potential negative effects on some people. It is also important for clinicians to be aware of appropriate practice guidelines for work with LGBT clients (APA, 2011; Association for Lesbian, Gay, Bisexual and Transgender Issues in Counseling, 2009). After all, SOCE are not ineffective because it is not possible to instruct some bisexually oriented people in the ways of heteroeroticism. SOCE are ineffective because they demand a fragmentation of the spirit and a suppression of desire—neither of which is sustainable or in the best interest of the client.

References

American Psychological Association. (2008). Resolution on religious, religion-related, and religious-derived prejudice. *American Psychologist, 63*, 431–434.

American Psychological Association. (2009). *Report of the Task Force on Appropriate Therapeutic Responses to Sexual Orientation.* Washington, DC: Author.

American Psychological Association. (2011). *Practice guidelines for LGB clients: Guidelines for psychological practice with lesbian, gay and bisexual clients.* Retrieved from http://www.apa.org/pi/lgbt/resources/guidelines.aspx

Association for Lesbian, Gay, Bisexual and Transgender Issues in Counseling. (2009). *Competencies for counseling with transgender clients.* Alexandria, VA: Author.

Englar-Carlson, M. & Stevens, M. (2006). *In the room with men: A casebook of therapeutic change.* Washington, DC: American Psychological Association.

Fassinger, R., & Arseneau, J. (2006). I'd rather get wet than be under that umbrella: Differentiating the experiences of lesbian, gay, bisexual and transgender people. In K. Bieschke, T. Perez, & K. DeBord (Eds.), *Handbook of counseling and psychotherapy with lesbian, gay, bisexual and transgender clients* (2nd ed., pp. 19–49). Washington, DC: American Psychological Association.

Haldeman, D. C. (1994). The practice and ethics of sexual orientation conversion therapy. *Journal of Consulting and Clinical Psychology, 62,* 221–227.

Haldeman, D. C. (2002). Therapeutic antidotes: Helping gay and bisexual men recover from conversion therapies. *Journal of Lesbian and Gay Psychotherapy, 5*(3–4), 117–130.

Herman, D. (1997). *The anti-gay agenda.* Chicago, IL: University of Chicago Press.

Tozer, E. E., & Hayes, J. A. (2004). The role of religiosity, internalized homonegativity, and identity development: Why do individuals seek conversion therapy? *The Counseling Psychologist, 27,* 722–742.

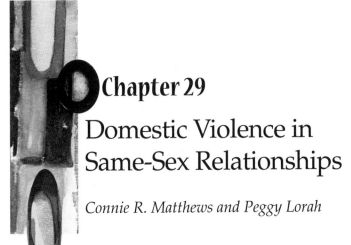

Chapter 29

Domestic Violence in Same-Sex Relationships

Connie R. Matthews and Peggy Lorah

For a variety of reasons, recognizing and intervening with same-sex domestic violence might fall to individual counselors who work with lesbian, gay, bisexual, and transgender (LGBT) clients despite the fact that many counselors receive little or no training in any of these areas. We offer a case to serve as an example of the kinds of situations in which counselors might be called on to address this issue. Because there are two authors, we use the pronoun *we* in discussing work with this client. This is a stylistic choice we have made to best convey the fact that there are multiple authors; we do not intend to suggest that we would both work with this client together.

James

James is reluctantly seeing a counselor following an arrest for driving under the influence of alcohol. He was arrested after he missed a turn and ran off the road into a tree. He was not seriously hurt, but the police were called. Because of the nature of the accident and the fact that officers smelled alcohol on his breath, the police took him to the hospital to be examined. Blood tests showed that he had a blood alcohol content of .20, more than twice the legal limit in his state. During the exam, the doctor found two cracked ribs that had begun to heal and several bruises that were too advanced to have happened in the accident. James told the doctor that he had fallen while hiking about a week ago but did not go in for treatment. The doctor's notes indicated some question as to whether the injuries were consistent with James's explanation.

During the counseling intake James reports that he is a 27-year-old African American male graduate student at the local university. He says that he is single, does not date much, and lives with another graduate student. He is in law school; his roommate, also an African American man, is a doctoral student in English.

307

James has been in for three counseling sessions, during which time he has not been very forthcoming. He has made it clear that he is only coming to counseling to meet the requirements of the treatment alternative program he is in because of his arrest. He must complete the program to stay in law school. Although he admits to having been drinking, he is angry with the police, who treated him roughly and handcuffed him even though he was being cooperative. Rather than send him to the hospital in the ambulance that was at the scene, they transported him in the back of the police car. He has spent much of his counseling time thus far venting his anger at the police.

James arrives at the fourth session with a black eye and bruised and swollen lip and nose. Although he initially mumbles something about falling into the corner of a desk, with gentle challenging he begins to cry and is more forthcoming. He says that the drunk driving incident occurred after he had been drinking following a violent episode with his roommate Robert. James says that he and Robert are a couple. They have known each other since both attended the university as undergraduates. Midway through their junior year they began dating, and they moved in together when they started graduate school 2 years ago. Robert is very charming and really courted James when they were dating. James says that Robert could have any man he wants and that he has always felt flattered that Robert wants to be with him. Although they cannot be married, they privately shared vows of commitment when they decided to live together.

At first things went well. They both were pretty focused on graduate school. After a few months, Robert started complaining that all they ever did was work; he wanted to socialize more. The demands of law school meant that James had to spend a lot of time working. Robert was busy as well but seemed more able, or at least willing, to set aside work to have fun. There were lots of fights about this. Then Robert started to chastise James for being more interested in law school than their relationship, saying that James just wanted to be an uppity lawyer like his dad.

This is another area of contention. Robert is very close to his family and has always been out with them. James admits that they are wonderful and have warmly welcomed him into the family. James then qualifies the statement by saying that Robert's mother and sisters are wonderful. Robert's father had left the family when Robert was a baby. His mother had a series of awful boyfriends whom Robert described as drunken brutes. However, his mother has been on her own as long as James and Robert have been together.

James says that he is not estranged from his own parents; they are just not close. James says that his father grew up in poverty but was able to attend law school and has become a very successful attorney. His mother is a cardiologist. Both work long hours and have instilled in James a strong work ethic. He is cordial with his parents and suspects that they know he is gay; however, they have never talked about it. They are cordial to Robert but rarely see him. This works for James but not for Robert, who tells James that if James really loves him he would tell his parents who Robert really is. They fight a lot about this. Robert insists that James is ashamed of him and their relationship. James acknowledges that there might be some truth to that, so sometimes he just doesn't respond when Robert says these things. That upsets Robert further.

James says that his parents are very religious and that he was raised in a conservative Christian church. Both of his parents are pillars in the church. James says that he was raised to believe that homosexuality is a sin, an abomination against God. He says that he is working to adjust his thinking and to come to peace with his religion and his sexuality but that it is a struggle, especially when it comes to negotiating his relationship with his parents. Robert berates him for even trying, often saying that James is indeed an abomination and an embarrassment to the gay community. Robert frequently calls James names and tells James he disgusts him.

A few empathic responses about how difficult it must be to hear these things from somebody who claims to love him lead James to remark that these comments hurt more than Robert's fists. We attempt to assess the extent of emotional abuse, although it is clearly difficult for James to discuss this. We are able to determine that emotional abuse preceded the physical abuse and has escalated over time, along with the physical abuse. Robert seems very adept at triggering and exacerbating James's shame around being gay as well as isolating him from any support he might get from the gay community.

James explains that Robert is very active in the gay community on campus. He is a leader in the community and highly regarded. In fact, Robert frequently reminds James that "any man in the community would love to fuck me" and that he gets many offers. James reports that over the past year, Robert has begun acting on those offers. James alternates between hurt and anger when discussing this. He is hurt because he and Robert have made a commitment to be faithful to each other. He is angry because Robert seems to have sex with other men to punish James. Furthermore, Robert refuses to practice safer sex either with the other men or with James. When James tells Robert he will not engage in sexual relations unless and until Robert gets tested for HIV and stops this behavior, Robert "forces the issue." When asked, James replies, with eyes and head lowered, that yes, Robert has forcefully had anal intercourse with James when James did not want to. When it is suggested that this is rape, James vehemently argues that it is not rape if the person is your partner. He adds that this has only happened "a few times," that now he mostly goes along if Robert starts getting upset. This makes James uncomfortable, but he strongly denies that he is a victim of sexual assault or domestic violence.

James says that a lot of the physical violence has occurred since Robert started having sex with other men. When James refuses Robert's advances, Robert physically goes after James. James says that he has pushed and shoved and even occasionally hit Robert when he "gets like this," so any violence is two way. James insists that he is not the only victim. Still, he acknowledges that he eventually ends up having sex with Robert when he doesn't want to. When asked, he also acknowledges that he has never cracked ribs or bloodied Robert as Robert has done to him.

The most recent incident occurred when Robert learned that James had changed his ATM account. James explains that it is important to him to support himself. He says that his father makes money available to him through a checking account into which he deposits money. James says that it is his father's way of showing support because he is "not the touchy-feely type." Still, James knows that this support is conditional and that if his father knew he were gay he would withdraw it, at least initially. James says that he does not want to accept such conditional support and does not want to get accustomed to something that could be withdrawn at any time. Robert argues that they should take advantage of it while they have it. He has started taking James's ATM card and withdrawing money from the account. James says that Robert was livid when he discovered that James had changed the account.

James is resistant to suggestions that Robert is abusing him and is completely against filing charges or taking any action against Robert. He says that he knows things have to change in his relationship with Robert but that he is not willing to subject Robert to the police, whom he describes as racist and always looking for an excuse to go after Black men. He also suspects that Robert would tell them about the times James has been physical and that the police would likely go after him too, which would further jeopardize his status in law school. Furthermore, the whole process would expose the fact that he is gay. Robert would get all kinds of support from the gay community and James would be ostracized. Still, he acknowledges that he is at a loss as to how to change things and admits that he is scared.

Working With James

We both operate from a primarily feminist and multicultural framework, with strong person-centered and existential influences, although we are eclectic enough to draw from other theoretical perspectives when they have things to offer a particular client. We tend not to be technique oriented but rather build on the therapeutic relationship. We recognize the expertise that the client brings to the work, as well as our own. We work to create a safe and empowering environment that facilitates the client finding his or her internal and external resources for addressing the problem that precipitated the counseling. This is important with James because he comes into counseling from a very unsafe and disempowered position.

We believe that our theoretical approach would be appropriate for James. Some people hold the mistaken belief that a feminist approach works only with women. We disagree. James is experiencing disempowerment on multiple levels, so an approach that helps him to articulate this and respond to it has the potential to help him move beyond feeling stuck. He is also dealing with a number of contextual factors, including the physical and emotional violence in his primary relationship, his arrest and mistreatment by police, his status in law school, his parents' homophobia, and the role his upbringing has had on his own beliefs and feelings about his sexuality. It is important to approach counseling with James in a manner that recognizes these contextual factors rather than pathologizes him for his response to them. Indeed, given James's expressed anger at the racist treatment he received from the police, an approach that fails to take into account his lived experiences is not likely to engage him in the counseling process.

We recognize that because we are White women, James might be slow to trust us, especially because we represent part of the system that is punishing him for his arrest. We raise that issue and allow James to respond, recognizing that his life experiences might encourage him to be less than forthcoming in the early stages of his work with us. We see this as a reasonable response and not pathology. Likewise, we do not assume that he is lying; rather, we understand his responses to be his reality at the time. Should James be assigned an African American male counselor, it might initially be easier for him to talk openly about his experiences of racism; however, given his current level of discomfort with being gay, in addition to his victim status in an abusive relationship, he might struggle more with discussing those aspects of his situation. A number of cultural factors intersect for James, so it is likely that there will be challenging cross-cultural issues with any counselor.

Our feminist and multicultural framework leads us to be resistant to diagnosis because we believe that there are times when diagnosis pathologizes individuals for contextual and systemic ailments. This can be particularly true for people from marginalized groups. We recognize that many of the issues that bring people to counseling represent efforts at survival in a dysfunctional environment. For example, James faces the social stigma of being Black and gay in a world that is racist and heterosexist. He also faces a situation in which the person he has counted on to be a source of love and comfort has become more threatening than the world outside their relationship. We recognize that because of this, it might take him longer than others to feel comfortable and safe in the counseling relationship. This is likely heightened by the cultural concerns discussed previously. We understand that he might scrutinize us, unsure that he can trust us. We see this as the survival skill it is and not as pathological paranoia or fear of intimacy.

Yet we understand that there are times when diagnosis is necessary for external reasons. Given the manner in which James has entered counseling, it is likely that a diagnosis will be required. We attempt to diagnose James in a manner that accurately reflects his current situation without pathologizing him. Thus, our diagnosis is as follows:

Axis I	995.81 Victim of Physical Abuse
	Rule out 309.81 Posttraumatic Stress Disorder
	305.00 Alcohol Abuse
Axis II	V71.09 None
Axis III	Current and past physical injuries from abuse
Axis IV	Emotional and physical abuse in primary relationship, concerns about parents discovering sexual orientation, stress and anger related to treatment as a man of color during police interventions in the course of driving under the influence
Axis V	Global Assessment of Functioning = 61 (current)

There are some immediate concerns to attend to with James. Although James has not indicated that Robert has used a weapon, the violence is escalating. Furthermore, by having sexual relations with other men and refusing to practice safer sex, Robert is putting James at risk. James should be tested for HIV. Because he is afraid of running into people locally who might tell Robert, we help James locate HIV testing and counseling services out of the area and facilitate a referral. James seems visibly relieved to have access to testing that feels safer. He is alternately appreciative and surprised that we would do this for him. There appears to be some small movement in his level of trust.

A safety plan is also important, and we discuss this before we end the session in which he reveals the violence. At this point James does not see his family or the LGBT community as viable sources of support. We explore this further to see whether there is anybody who might seem safe to approach. Although it is important to help James think of people he might not have considered, we trust his judgment about who he thinks might or might not be safe. We also help James begin to build a support system elsewhere. We ask whether there are students in his program who are oriented toward social justice and who might be open to helping him. James does think of a woman in his study group whom he might be able to contact. He says that she is studying law to do community advocacy, and he believes she would be helpful. She knows Robert as his friend. He is not willing to approach her unless he needs to, but he does promise to reach out to her if Robert becomes violent again. Although we might like to see him be more proactive here, we believe it is important for James to know that we will honor his choices. We do watch him put her number on speed dial in his cell phone.

In addition to our work with individual clients, we make it a practice to maintain knowledge of local resources so that we can feel confident that clients we refer, especially those who are marginalized, will not be further victimized when they reach out for assistance. These resources include local clergy, physicians, attorneys, human services professionals, and others who are affirming with LGBT people and diverse cultural groups and who also understand domestic violence, keeping in mind that all elements are critical. We work with James to try to come up with other resources he could turn to in an emergency. Any decisions about who to reach out to are left to James. He remains reluctant to act right away but does show some interest when we tell him about the pastor of a local church that has made a congregational decision to be open and affirming with LGBT people. He tells us he was unaware that any churches had perspectives on homosexuality that were different from those of the church in which he was raised. We offer to help make a connection should he decide he wants to pursue this.

In addition to the emotional and physical abuse, there is clear evidence of both sexual abuse and financial abuse. Using James's ATM card without his permission and against his wishes constitutes financial abuse, reflecting Robert's attempts at using power and control to get what he wants in the relationship. James has already taken steps to address the financial abuse by changing the ATM account. We use this as an opportunity to help James recognize his strength and ability to act. This seems to be an area in which James was able to recognize the abuse and to do something about it, even though those actions brought about consequences. We work with him to help translate the resolve he showed here into other areas and to build his confidence.

Forcing James to have sex when he doesn't want to, whether or not James eventually acquiesces, constitutes sexual abuse and puts James at risk for HIV and/or sexually transmitted disease. James resists seeing himself as a victim of sexual abuse, so we combine education about what actually constitutes sexual abuse and rape with an analysis of his own situation. We try to be sensitive in doing this, as we understand that James's sense of himself as a man and as a Black man might be fragile. He has already indicated that he struggles with reconciling his sexual orientation with what he has been taught growing up. If he has incorporated a social myth of gay men being less than real men, this could be exacerbated if he also perceives rape, sexual victimization, and domestic violence to be things that happen to women. Thus, we work on debunking both sets of myths. We combine our feminist multicultural approach with a cognitive approach or narrative approach to help James explore the ways in which all of these aspects of himself interact, as well as ways in which he can revision himself as a strong and healthy man. We remain conscious of the fact that race, gender, and sexual orientation intersect for James, so we must incorporate all of these factors; they cannot be addressed one at a time.

James has already addressed his concerns about racism. We pay attention to him, empathize with him, and validate his anger. Given his role in the drunk driving accident, we resist the temptation to move him away from his anger at the police toward taking more responsibility for his own actions. We know that he will eventually have to examine the role that drinking is playing in his life; however, he will be better able to do this after trust has been established. Our feminist multicultural approach informs us that there are serious contextual factors that should not be ignored. If James's description of his interactions with the police are accurate, and we would do best to start with believing they are, his anger is legitimate and should be treated as such. Thus, his reluctance to seek help from them is understandable. We honor this and do not try to persuade James to report Robert's actions to the police. Indeed, doing so could bring about more ramifications than relief. We remain concerned for James's safety and express this, yet we also know that the trust he is slowly building with us is fragile.

Although taking this position might cause doubts or conflicts for many counselors, our feminist orientation to working with victims of abuse informs our belief that we do not have the right to make these choices for our clients. This theoretical stance and our resulting experience with the sense of empowerment many clients report when their choices are honored inform our belief in the effectiveness of this way of working. Our work in the field of domestic and sexual violence has taught us that clients who deal with such matters are the experts about their own lived experiences and that we need to trust their expertise. We are aware that this stance can present a struggle for some clinicians, particularly those who are just beginning to practice and those who practice from more directive theory bases. It is important to address such struggles in supervision in order to offer effective support and advocacy to clients.

As a general practice of advocacy, we understand that it is important to know the local and state police departments, including their level of understanding of domestic violence in general as well as their cultural sensitivity with respect to working with LGBT people and racial and ethnic minorities. Sometimes even the most problematic departments can have one or two people who are victim-sensitive and knowledgeable about the issues. We know one such officer in the local police department with whom we have worked closely in other domestic violence situations. We offer James the opportunity to talk with that person, without the pressure of filing a formal complaint, to help him come to a better understanding of what actually is occurring in his relationship. We offer to accompany James to the meeting and to act as his advocate should the need arise. James immediately dismisses our suggestion, vehemently stating that he wants nothing to do with the police department. We sense a minor setback in his trust just at the suggestion. We address this directly. James reluctantly acknowledges our perceptions and we validate his response. We stress that he is the one who gets to decide if and when to go to the police. We watch him visibly relax a bit. We do, however, leave the door open by letting him know that the offer stands should James want or need to take action.

Several sessions later, James reports that he is afraid that Robert is "getting ready to blow again." He reluctantly agrees to meet with the officer, and we accompany him to the meeting. The officer begins by reaffirming that James was not responsible for any crimes committed against him and that he could share his account of the violence in his relationship with Robert without filing a formal complaint. As James talks, the officer asks questions about the history and pattern of behaviors and reinforces the idea that James's attempts to defend himself from Robert's attacks are not grounds for his being charged with physical abuse. The officer stresses that, given what she has heard, James has the option of filing charges against Robert but that he is not obligated to do so. She says that she can keep his report on file so it could be used at a later date if he chooses. She names what happened as domestic violence; reiterates that domestic violence is a crime that is difficult for any victim to report; and articulates her awareness of the added layers of difficulty for someone in a same-sex relationship, particularly a man of color. Her verbalizing this to James leads to a noticeable lessening of his anxiety. He clearly feels heard and understood, and even though he still does not want to press charges against Robert, he indicates that he wants the officer to keep a record of their meeting. Upon leaving the police department, James states that even though he still feels angry at the officers involved in his arrest, he found this officer to be informed and respectful of his sexual orientation and race.

We want to stress here that it is important to know ahead of time that the person with whom one's client will talk is knowledgeable and sensitive around *all* issues, including domestic abuse, race, and sexual orientation. Had we not personally known such a person in the local police department, then the police would likely not have been an option for James and we would have avoided subjecting him to further victimization. We also recognize that in addition to our individual work with James, there appears to be the need for systemic advocacy in helping the police department to better address all of these concerns.

James remains resistant to seeing his situation as domestic abuse, so we are patient as we offer information and help him to do power analysis before we even discuss referral to a domestic violence program. We address James's belief that because he occasionally defends himself by pushing, shoving, or hitting, he is also an aggressor. The idea of mutual combat is one that victims, perpetrators, police, and helping professionals can all be lulled into believing, particularly when two men are involved. We focus on issues of power and control when assessing the degree to which a situation involves mutual combat or self-defense. In James's case, Robert is using violence to gain power over James, to make James do what he wants. James responds physically to defend himself from being hurt. Through power analysis we help James to reframe the experience, to recognize that his own reactions are defensive responses and that Robert's aggressiveness reflects abusive use of physical and emotional power.

We know that domestic violence programs and shelters are not necessarily any better than police departments when it comes to issues of race and sexual orientation. Framing domestic violence between two men as mutual combat is a way that professionals, especially if they are prone to racism and/or homophobia, can be either dismissive of requests for help or inclined to punish both men. Should the time come when James is open to it, we would only make a referral to a domestic violence program if we had enough knowledge of the program to feel assured that he would not face further victimization through racism or homophobia. In addition, we would only refer to a program that we knew was effective in working with male victims. Race, gender, and sexual orientation intersect for James, so any referrals we make would only be to programs that we know can effectively address that intersectionality. In this instance, we do not refer James because although the local shelter is very good with female victims, we have concerns about how well it will work with male victims. We note that systemic advocacy will likely be necessary if we cannot feel comfortable referring somebody with intersecting concerns.

Given that James is seeing us as a consequence of his arrest for driving under the influence, we do have to address his drinking. When he first enters counseling we assess his drinking to gauge the extent to which it is a problem. We do a clinical interview using the *Diagnostic and Statistical Manual of Mental Disorders* (4th ed.) diagnostic criteria because we believe that it allows for flexibility in considering contextual factors. We determine that James's drinking is indeed causing problems for him and hence give him a diagnosis of alcohol abuse. At the same time, listening to James's description of his drinking, we believe that it might be a symptom of his abusive relationship as much as a primary problem. Thus, we focus first on the abuse while monitoring his drinking to ensure that it does not escalate while we work on other issues. We also note that James does seem to have some conflicts around his religious upbringing and his sexual orientation. We leave open the possibility that internalized homophobia might be contributing to his drinking, although his descriptions thus far seem to link his abusive drinking to violent episodes.

We refer James to specific Alcoholics Anonymous meetings that we are certain will be welcoming and affirming, leaving any decisions about what he chooses to share in those meetings up to him. The meetings can provide an opportunity for James to begin building a support system while also learning ways to cope that don't involve drinking. As with any referrals, we know that it is important to be familiar enough with the local meetings to have confidence that James will not be further victimized. James does not attend the Alcoholics Anonymous meetings. Given his court referral to treatment, we could require him to attend, but we choose not to, focusing on empowering James to make his own decisions. Had we been concerned that his drinking was the more serious problem, we would have addressed that in more direct ways earlier in his treatment.

We understand that working individually with James is only part of our role. We are also attentive to areas in which systemic intervention might be appropriate. James's case has shown us that, even though both the local police department and domestic violence program have strengths, there are areas in which they struggle. We realize that as counselors we have a responsibility to work with both systems to help them to become more culturally competent.

James completes his mandated treatment but chooses not to continue beyond that. His sense of accomplishment at completing mandated treatment leaves us comfortable with his decision. He does reduce his drinking and has no further drinking-related incidents. Although there have been no more explosive incidents with Robert, James expresses understanding that Robert is not likely to change. James is beginning to build a network of friends in law school, although he has not come out to any of them. He has also attended several services at the open and affirming church to which we referred him. He seems less stressed about his sexual orientation. We review his safety plan with him during termination and leave the door open for him to return. We believe that he now views counseling as a viable option in the future.

Conclusion

Clearly, a number of factors are present for James. The concerns that brought James to counseling are not primarily his sexual orientation, although that does factor into his current situation. The counselor who makes sexual orientation the primary issue as well as the counselor who ignores James's sexual orientation altogether will likely struggle in establishing a meaningful therapeutic relationship with James. Furthermore, making sexual orientation the primary issue fails to recognize the pressing and potentially dangerous concerns of domestic violence and problematic drinking. Likewise, failing to acknowledge the role that sexual orientation plays in James's situation runs the risk of further victimizing James and exacerbating his shame. The same is true for failing to acknowledge the role that James's race plays. The counselor working with James must be able to help James integrate multiple identities and address multiple problem areas. This counselor must also have personal familiarity with potential referral sources to ensure that such sources are also capable of treating James as a whole person in an affirmative and empowering way.

It is also worth noting that there appears to be a relationship between substance abuse and same-sex domestic violence for both men and women. In working with LGBT clients experiencing either substance abuse or domestic violence, it is good practice to assess for the presence of the other. Indeed, it is good practice to assess for both substance abuse and domestic violence during intake while remaining open to the possibility that either might be present without being immediately revealed.

Chapter 30

Using Psychological Assessment Tools With Lesbian, Gay, Bisexual, and Transgender Clients

Jeffrey P. Prince and Michael J. Potoczniak

The following case study demonstrates a number of complex factors that are important to consider when using standardized psychological assessment tools in counseling lesbian, gay, bisexual, and transgender (LGBT) clients. The most commonly used empirically based tools have not been normed on LGBT populations, nor have their items and scales been developed to tap the full range of concerns and experiences that form the context of each LGBT client's life (Prince, 1997). Consequently, this case study attempts to highlight ways in which the multiple influences of sexual identity, discrimination, and cultural factors can be integrated into the use of these assessment tools to minimize bias. Specifically, this case study attempts to demonstrate the importance of minimizing homophobia and heterosexism through both the choice of instruments and the integration of those instruments into the counseling process.

Background Information

Leo was a 19-year-old Latino, Columbian American male. Leo had been born in the United States. His family was originally from Columbia and had fled during a civil war during which many close relatives had been kidnapped. He stated that he had always been close to his family and that they have shared a strong bond based on their struggles to survive in the United States. He also reported that his parents were both Evangelical Christian and that they had recently converted from being Catholic to Baptist. Leo revealed that his relationship with his mother had been very close until recently and stated that "secrets have begun to drive us apart lately." Leo attended a small religious school in Southern California, where he had frequent contact with his church youth group until college. His primary language was Spanish, and this was the primary language of many of his friends as well. Leo explained that it was rare for people to move away from his small town and that most of his friends went to a local junior college. He also reported that his family and friends had "mixed emotions" about his decision to leave the town and move hundreds of miles away to attend a large state university. Leo reported that soon after starting college he had begun to have frequent sexual experiences with other men. He expressed intense shame about these experiences and wondered whether he might be gay. Leo had disclosed his sexual attractions to only one or two friends. He also disclosed that he had tested HIV positive about 1 year ago and was receiving services through a city agency. However, he had recently begun to question whether he wanted to continue treatment. Leo also explained that he continued to have sexual relations with the man who had given him HIV and was not sure how to handle the situation.

Presenting Information

Leo presented for counseling at his university's counseling center primarily because he was unable to concentrate on his academic work. He felt "stress and anxiety" related to making a decision about his major—a decision that he needed to make within the next few weeks. His tentative major was mechanical engineering. His family was urging him to choose this field because the only other member of his family to attend college, his uncle, was a successful mechanical engineer in Columbia. Leo stated that he felt pressure to help his family financially and had never considered a different major until now. He stated, "I might not be around for a long time, so I don't know what the point would be to choose a major other than one that would help my family with a little bit of money." Despite these beliefs, he began to consider other options because he feared dismissal from school due to his difficulty focusing and his resulting poor grades. Leo had taken a course in civil engineering that he had enjoyed and was considering changing to that major. However, he reported a general lack of academic motivation. He described his lifestyle as increasingly isolated and socially withdrawn. He admitted to frequent bouts of crying along with feelings of hopelessness and guilt. In addition, he acknowledged occasional suicidal ideation. At the end of the initial assessment session, Leo stated, "I have always felt this way about my life—I have always hoped that someone would understand me and show me the way." In addition, he stated that he felt strongly connected to his family but that "there have always been things I could not tell them; they are all I have." Leo also reported that he wanted to learn more about how to have "healthy relationships with other men" as well as "how to tell my parents that I have HIV."

Introducing Assessment Tools

Because the university counseling center followed a time-limited model for psychotherapy, the counselor introduced the idea that they might consider having Leo initially complete several psychological assessment tools to efficiently gather information about his strengths and concerns. However, because the use of psychological testing has historically been associated with labeling and discriminating against sexual and cultural minorities, the counselor suggested using psychological assessment tools in a tentative manner. He introduced the topic with a collaborative approach to assess Leo's attitudes toward testing and to evaluate whether both could agree that this would be a helpful strategy to pursue. The counselor asked Leo for his opinion about completing some assessment inventories. Leo expressed a wariness of testing. He stated that he did not have much faith in the accuracy of tests. He described an experience in elementary school when he was erroneously tracked into a special needs class because of his scores on an English achievement test. Leo also admitted that he experiences test anxiety and "freezes up" when completing timed tests. The counselor agreed that tests are sometimes misused and clarified how the assessment tools he was considering were not "tests" that Leo could pass or fail. The counselor explained that these were psychological surveys that were different from achievement and other tests; they would not be timed. He also explained that if they decided to use these assessments, and any of the results did not seem accurate to Leo, he would trust Leo's beliefs over the instrument.

The counselor proceeded to describe a few of the assessment tools that might be helpful in Leo's situation and gave examples of specific personality and career inventories along with brief descriptions of the types of information each one could provide (Association for Assessment in Counseling, 2003). Leo expressed curiosity and interest in completing both a psychological inventory and a career interest inventory. They agreed that Leo would complete the Minnesota Multiphasic Personality Inventory–II (MMPI–2) and the Strong Interest Inventory (Strong) before the next session and that they might consider additional assessment tools later in the course of counseling if needed. The counselor was aware that neither of these tools contained items or scales inclusive of specific LGBT content, but the counselor planned to connect the results in a meaningful way to Leo's sexual identity development during their discussion of the results.

Diagnostic Impressions

Based on the outcome of the MMPI–2, the clinical interview, and behavioral observations, the following tentative diagnosis was made:

Axis I	296.33	Major Depressive Disorder, Recurrent, Severe Without Psychotic Features
	316	Psychological Factors Affecting Medical Condition (HIV)
Axis II	Deferred	
Axis III	042	HIV Infection
Axis IV	Problems with primary support group	
	Financial problems	
	Educational problems	
Axis V	Global Assessment of Functioning (GAF) = 53	

Leo reported a sense of isolation, social withdrawal, and hopelessness. He also described periods of excessive crying, intense guilt, and occasional suicidal ideation. He stated that he had felt this way "most of [his] life." If he had not reported that the symptoms had existed for most of his life, then a diagnosis of an adjustment disorder related to his HIV status would have been made instead. The diagnosis was supported by a spike in elevation on Scale 2 (Depression) of the MMPI-2 along with elevations on a number of the clinical subscales of the Depression scale. Similarly, Leo's Strong profile also indicated that his depressed mood was interfering with his enjoyment of life. He endorsed very few "like" responses, resulting in a "depressed" profile with very few elevations on the Basic Interest Scales or General Occupational Themes.

It also appeared that Leo's symptoms were affecting his decision making not only with regard to his choice of an academic major but also with respect to his ambivalence about continuing to take his medications. Therefore, the second part of Axis I diagnosis included Psychological Factors Affecting Medical Condition (HIV). Leo's GAF score was set at 53 because his symptoms were severe enough to moderately affect his ability to function. Although Leo's passive suicidal ideation might otherwise have kept his score below 50, his ability to function well at a large state university convinced his counselor to assess his score at just above a more severe threshold that would connote lower functionality. It is especially noteworthy that Leo had been in a prolonged, conflicted state of sexual identity development and for the past few years had been in the process of questioning his identity as a gay man. Leo's family history of depression also supported a diagnosis of depression. In addition, some of his depressed mood could have been attributed to the normal developmental course of his coming out process.

Goals of Counseling

One goal of counseling was to assist Leo in determining his academic major. A related goal was to identify and address a variety of issues that were impacting that decision, especially his depression. Obstacles that appeared to impede Leo from making a decision were partially developmental, partially diagnostic, and somewhat existential. Leo was struggling with the impact of a diagnosis of HIV at a young age, he was dealing with issues related to coming out, and he was lacking adequate and culturally appropriate social supports and role models related to both his medical diagnosis and his career aspirations. The goals of counseling, therefore, focused on integrating his sexual identity development with relevant environmental factors. Counseling goals included addressing his depression through enhancing social supports related to his HIV diagnosis, addressing his sexual identity development, and broadening his limited exposure to culturally congruent career role models and occupational information.

Theoretical Orientation

Leo's counselor relied primarily on social cognitive career theory (Lent, Brown, & Hackett, 1996) to conceptualize Leo's situation. Social cognitive career theory is composed of three building blocks: (a) self-efficacy, (b) outcome expectations, and (c) personal goals. Leo demonstrated low self-efficacy in his belief that he could not be successful in a number of arenas. He believed that his life was going to be short and unproductive because of his HIV status and that his sexual orientation as a gay man would be a barrier to success. In addition, he did not have a strong role model to demonstrate how a gay Latino man could be highly successful in college or in a career. In addition, Leo's self-efficacy was influenced by the social pressure from his family, his primary support system, to follow a particular path that caused him conflict. Leo's family supported him in attending a university but did not support his decision to attend a university far from where they lived or to study a field other than engineering. Leo experienced guilt about not following their advice. Leo's outcome expectations were based on his belief that he was going to "die an early death." Furthermore, he believed that once his family discovered his sexual orientation they would most likely disown him and he would be alone. At the same time, Leo stated that the only reason for him to attend a university was to provide for his family.

Other key considerations included developing Leo's interests, exploring the impact of his attitudes and values on his self-efficacy, and strengthening his identity as a gay Latino man. Consequently, exploring both Leo's sexual identity development and the context of his environment (e.g., barriers and influences in his academic, social, and family environments) were important aspects to understanding ways in which Leo's career beliefs and decisions may have been shaped through discrimination and cultural stereotypes—and thereby may have lowered his self-efficacy and forestalled his academic and career development. The counselor's approach integrated psychological assessment tools not only to assist with clarifying Leo's diagnosis but also to structure the exploration of Leo's past experiences and to guide Leo in identifying and developing new areas to explore. Because of Leo's narrow focus on financial security he had not been exposed to a wide array of career options and he had taken little time explore his interests. The counselor integrated the Strong in a structured and nonthreatening way to introduce testing and to help Leo identify specific areas of interest he could investigate further. The counselor introduced the MMPI–2 to assess the degree to which Leo's depression might direct the course of counseling and to provide additional information regarding the interplay of Leo's personality, attitudes, and values with his beliefs of self-efficacy. The counselor presented the MMPI–2 within a model that followed the basic guidelines for administering the assessment; however, care was given to provide for a more collaborative experience. For example, he encouraged Leo to formulate some questions that he hoped the inventory might be able to address. The counselor also emphasized that Leo was an equal partner in the test administration and interpretation in order to provide for a testing experience that was disarming and helpful to Leo.

Interventions

In formulating and creating interventions with Leo, the counselor frequently sought consultation to check for biases based on his cultural identity and to assess his comfort in working with a client from a different background. In addition, the counselor sought consultation to address how Leo's intersecting identities (i.e., ethnicity, race, HIV status, sexual orientation) were affecting his development. The counselor examined and discussed with Leo some of the inherent heterosexist and cultural blind spots that existed in the assessments. For example, these individualized assessment tools did not address Leo's cultural context, and the MMPI–2 includes a scale (Scale 5, Mf: Masculinity–Femininity) that can be provocative and challenging to interpret with LGBT clients. The counselor and Leo worked collaboratively to understand Leo's scores and to develop subsequent interventions that were culturally appropriate to his intersecting identities.

Self-Efficacy

To address Leo's self-efficacy as a student who was living with HIV and experiencing depression, the counselor collaborated with the office for students with disabilities at his university to obtain accommodations for Leo based on a medical and psychological disability. Leo and the counselor discussed his need for accommodations, such as extra time on tests as well as a reduced course load. Furthermore, the counselor coached Leo through role-playing exercises and assertiveness training on how to communicate with his professors when he was experiencing more acute symptoms that were preventing him from being more present in class discussions. Leo was mostly agreeable to receiving the accommodations but was concerned that this was considered "cheating." He and the counselor spent a few sessions addressing this concern because it had become an obstacle for him in obtaining the assistance that he needed to feel successful. The counselor also emphasized Leo's various strengths by engaging in a brief cognitive restructuring activity at the beginning of each session. In this activity, Leo would name one of his personal strengths and how it might enable him to achieve some of his goals in the future. In the beginning, Leo was too depressed to participate in this intervention; however, as his depression lifted, he was able to identify and discuss many of his strengths.

Environmental Influences

The counselor and Leo designed a treatment plan that incorporated the medical and social support systems that were impacting Leo's life. Because Leo was isolated from a Latino community and family, they agreed to pursue community-based interventions that would increase his connections. They formulated a plan for Leo to attend support groups at a local HIV community agency with bilingual Latino counselors. Leo was able to adjust his career outcome expectations as he gained more realistic and accurate expectations about his life expectancy through these programs.

Outcome Expectations

Leo took advantage of a mentorship program offered by his university and worked with an engineering alumni mentor who was Latino and identified as gay. In addition, he attended a couple of meetings of a local engineering organization for gay-identified men. By identifying with these men, he was able to develop newer, more affirmative, and more realistic beliefs about the challenges to his career path based on his ethnicity and sexual identity.

Leo's level of depression hampered his active engagement in counseling. He missed some sessions; came late to others; and often did not complete agreed-on goals between sessions, such as connecting with social supports, pursuing informational interviews, and gathering occupational information. However, the counselor rewarded each step that Leo took with praise and encouragement. Throughout the course of counseling, there was careful assessment of and attention to his level of depression.

To address the full range of Leo's treatment goals, the counselor used a variety of interventions that examined Leo's depressive symptoms, career concerns, adjustment to HIV, and coming out issues. The counselor initially used the results of the MMPI–2 and a structured clinical assessment interview as stimuli to discuss and evaluate Leo's depression. Together they examined how his struggles with his coming out process, and his separation from his family, influenced his mood changes. In addition, the counselor was able to arrange for medication evaluation and treatment with Leo's medical providers; this was critical to his progress.

The counselor spent several sessions discussing Leo's Strong profile to assist him in exploring and developing his interests and to help him evaluate his academic options. Leo's interest profile matched that of successfully employed engineers. However, his profile also indicated that he shared interests with men in a number of creative careers, such as florists and interior designers. Leo initially felt that he was being stereotyped by the inventory because he was gay and began to dismiss the relevance of the results altogether. Although Leo had no interest in pursuing those occupational fields, he eventually was able to view his high scores on those scales as representing his broad artistic interests in creativity and self-expression. He agreed that he was motivated by creative thinking and problem solving and realized that he could meet this need through his approach to his engineering work and through avocational activities. These interests could also result in Leo being more expressive and insightful in his career as an engineer. Leo also found the Strong helpful because it indicated that many careers—not just one or two—fit his interests. This prompted him to consider a wider array of options beyond the narrow few to which he had previously been exposed.

The MMPI–2 was interpreted in a way that encouraged a discussion of the interplay of Leo's personality, attitudes, and values with his beliefs of self-efficacy. These discussions helped Leo clarify factors that were influencing his worldview and obstacles that were interfering with his career decision making. Leo was initially skeptical about the value of this personality inventory. When the counselor asked him what it felt like to take such a long inventory, Leo explained that he was somewhat fearful that the "test would label me as gay." This led to a sensitive discussion of his slight elevation on Scale 5 (Mf, Masculinity–Femininity) to ensure that Leo would not misunderstand it. The counselor avoided using the terms *masculinity* and *femininity* to describe the scale. Instead, he simply referred to the scale as "Scale 5" and interpreted Leo's results as being in the typical range for college-educated men, who typically have higher interests in aesthetics than men in the general population. The counselor also emphasized how this score echoed Leo's artistic interests that had appeared on his Strong profile.

Outcomes

At the completion of counseling, Leo was still struggling with some residual symptoms of depression but had responded well to an informal approach to cognitive therapy that integrated a variety of community resources. The alleviation of his symptoms of depression allowed for the development of positive and realistic beliefs about his overall efficacy as a student and as an HIV-positive gay Latino man. Leo reported that he felt that he was "on the right path" in that he felt more aware of how HIV was impacting his academic and personal lives and he had the social support and tools to continue to address his concerns as they arose.

He stated that his results on the Strong were helpful in affirming his multiple interests in scientific, practical, and creative areas—areas that he would continue to explore through coursework and extracurricular activities. Furthermore, he found reassurance that his results on the Occupational Scales of the Strong showed that he had very similar interests to both engineers and architects. This knowledge strengthened his confidence in his decision to continue with an engineering major but to explore the field beyond mechanical engineering. The counselor discussed with Leo how his profile may become more defined and other interests may emerge as he gained more experience. Leo agreed to return and retake the Strong in a few semesters and to discuss further his future decisions and goals. Leo stated that he planned to continue his involvement in the mentoring program and the community engineers group. He described a greater sense of confidence in his skills with social networking in a professional community. Furthermore, Leo reported greater self-efficacy and motivation as an engineering student.

Overall Leo replaced many of his negative beliefs about his career and life outcomes with newer, more realistic outcome expectations. Leo and the counselor were able to collaboratively set further short-term and medium-term goals. In the short term, Leo changed his major to civil engineering to avoid further delaying his graduation. At termination, Leo was still not sure whether architecture would be a better fit for him and entertained the idea of attending graduate school in architecture or working with an architecture company in some capacity after graduation. He set another short-term goal of obtaining a summer internship through the Hispanic Association of Colleges and Universities at a firm with a staff of architects and civil engineers and an interdisciplinary approach to projects. Leo also established some midrange goals of finishing college on a 5-year plan to allow him to continue his reduced course load and to increase the amount of time he would have to visit his family.

Implications and Recommendations for Therapists

Leo's case illustrates the need for mental health professionals conducting personality and career assessments to be aware of intersecting multiple identities (e.g., sexual identity, cultural identity, health status, economic variables). Providing interpretations and interventions to a diverse population requires more than making simplistic adjustments to assessment tools—rather, a greater collaboration with the client is needed to reach an interpretation that is ethical, valid, and useful. In providing this interpretation to Leo, the counselor took great care to deliver information in a way that kept alive various parts of Leo's identity and his distinct values and cultural norms. In addition, therapists are challenged to provide the results of psychological assessments in a way that empowers clients to use available resources to advocate for themselves in academic and workplace settings and to seek mentorship and opportunities from the communities of which they are members.

References

Association for Assessment in Counseling. (2003). *Responsibilities of users of standardized tests (RUST)*. Alexandria, VA: Author.

Lent, R. W., Brown, S. D., & Hackett, G. (1996). Career development from a social cognitive perspective. In D. Brown, L. Brooks, & Associates (Eds.), *Career choice and development* (3rd ed., pp. 373–421). San Francisco, CA: Jossey-Bass.

Prince, J. P. (1997). Assessment bias affecting lesbians, gay men, and bisexuals. *Measurement and Evaluation in Counseling and Development, 30,* 82–87.

Chapter 31

When the Political and the Personal Collide: Lesbian, Gay, Bisexual, and Transgender People as Political Targets

Glenda M. Russell

In recent decades, American voters have gone to the polls more than 100 times to vote on the rights of lesbian, gay, bisexual, and transgender (LGBT) people. More often than not, the outcomes of those votes have not been favorable for LGBT people or their rights (Gamble, 1997). These elections—and the campaigns that precede them—represent paradigm cases of homophobia and heterosexism. The elections exploit the existing homophobia in U.S. society and stand as witness to the need, articulated in the Competencies for Counseling Gay, Lesbian, Bisexual and Transgendered (LGBT) Clients, to "understand that heterosexism pervades the social and cultural foundations of many institutions and traditions and may foster negative attitudes toward LGBT persons" (Association for Lesbian, Gay, Bisexual and Transgender Issues in Counseling, 1997, "Social and Cultural Foundations," Competency 2).

Therapeutic work with LGBT people confronting anti-LGBT campaigns and elections rests on a number of considerations that have been derived from previous research. Campaigns and elections often have a negative impact on LGBT people. They have the capacity to "undermine the healthy functioning of . . . LGBT persons" (Association for Lesbian, Gay, Bisexual and Transgender Issues in Counseling, 1997, "Social and Cultural Foundations," Competency 1) for a variety of reasons related to the position of LGBT people as psychological, social, and political targets (e.g., Hatzenbuehler, Keyes, & Hasin, 2009; Riggle, Rostosky, & Horne, 2009; Russell, 2000). The failure to understand the potential for this negative impact is likely to leave LGBT people mystified by the psychological reactions they and others experience. At worst, this failure to understand the potential impact can lead to victim blaming (e.g., the suggestion that something is "wrong" with the person who has negative responses to being a political target rather than that something was wrong with a process that targeted a group of people).

Intervention

An intervention designed to help LGBT people overcome the negative impact of homonegative politics entails two major elements. The first involves cognitive reframing, a critical countermeasure to the negative experience of being the target of anti-LGBT rhetoric. The second includes a variety of specific measures, both cognitive and behavioral. Some of these fit within the general rubric of active coping, and some are specific to the content of anti-LGBT politics.

The cognitive reframe provides an alternative to the sense of being personally targeted in a win-or-lose contest. This reframe contextualizes the political event within an expansive perspective from which the particular campaign and election are seen not as the final outcome but as a single moment that is but one part of a much larger movement for equal rights. Other measures in therapy are associated with increasing the strength of an individual's coping capacities. These measures involve a focus on acknowledging the heterosexism implicit in such campaigns, working to counter the internalized homophobia that may be activated by such events (e.g., Levitt et al., 2009), articulating and working through affective responses to the event, and tending to the client's relationship to the LGBT community (e.g., Rostosky, Riggle, Horne, Denton, & Huellemeier, 2010) and to possible heterosexual allies (Russell, 2011).

Client Background

James was a 20-year-old White gay male college student who contacted his university counseling center with concerns about depression. He was assigned to my caseload, and he was aware that I was a lesbian from the beginning of our work together. James was a junior majoring in architectural engineering who reported doing well in his coursework and in his social life at school. He was unable to specify any precipitant for his depression. He suggested that he had begun experiencing intermittent bouts of feeling down—"a vague sense of doom," as he called it—during his most recent summer break with his family in southern California. This intermittent mood had seemed to diminish by the time he returned to Colorado for school in the fall. However, it had returned after a while, and it was severe enough to interfere with James's studying and his everyday enjoyment. James denied any changes in his sleep or appetite. That fact, along with his general presentation and self-description, suggested something other than a biologically based depression.

When I asked James about whether he had experienced depression in the past, he described a period of some months during his years in middle school. He had been on the receiving end of considerable taunts by his classmates. He had been teased because he was smaller than many of the other boys and because he seemed to keep to himself a good deal of the time. Some of the taunts suggested that James was gay. James initially told no one of these experiences. However, as he grew increasingly withdrawn, his parents asked him what was wrong. He told them about the teasing at school, and in the process he told them that he might be gay. His parents were social liberals who also belonged to a liberal Christian denomination. James reported that they "had some adjusting to do" when they learned of their son's sexual orientation. However, they were generally supportive of him and offered James the option of seeing a therapist. They also wanted to talk to the middle school principal about the harassment by classmates, but James insisted that it would only make matters worse.

James took his parents up on the offer of seeing a therapist, and he did so for what he estimated was about a year. James recalled that he had used the therapy to talk about the harassment and about how to deal with his classmates. He had also explored his sexual orientation, and the therapist had given him some helpful resources and concrete information about gay men and the gay community.

When James moved from middle school to high school he quickly became a member of the school's gay/straight alliance. That, in combination with moving to a bigger school, helped James to feel more socially integrated. He developed some strong relationships with other gay and lesbian students as well as with heterosexual students. It was also in high school that James began to pinpoint his interests in both architecture and engineering. By his last 2 years in high school, he felt very comfortable with himself and comfortable with his position at school. He was successful academically and was able to gain admission to his first choice of university. When he left California to begin college, he left a number of solid friendships as well as happy memories of his high school years.

Upon arriving at his new university, James had a relatively uneventful transition. He loved his classes, had a few friends in his residence hall, and joined a student club that attracted engineering majors in particular. James's first 2 years went very well, and he had secured a prized internship for his junior year. He also had a small but comfortable cadre of friends. Although he was enjoying his classes and the internship in this junior year, he kept encountering his vague sense of doom.

Therapy With James

I worked with James in brief therapy, the duration established by the counseling center where he sought help. My work in this time-limited frame was different than it would have been in a more open-ended therapy relationship; in particular, there was virtually no focus on our relationship in this brief format. After reviewing mandatory disclosure information, James and I spent much of the first session exploring both his current situation and his history. He was frankly baffled by his bouts of depressive-like symptoms, and so was I. I asked him questions about his classes, his social life at home and at school, his career plans, his family, and his sexual orientation. None of the questions yielded an answer to our now-shared curiosity about his bouts with "doom," as we began to call it. At the end of our first meeting I asked James to monitor his thinking over the next week, suggesting he pay particular attention to what he was thinking or feeling when he became aware of the doom experience.

When he came to our next session, James brought a brief list of situations in which he felt aware of the doom. As he went through the list, I asked whether any of the issues had been relevant during the previous summer when the depressive feeling had first emerged. Nothing rang a bell—nothing, that is, until James spoke of one item on the list. He had been walking between classes and had heard two male students laughing and talking about "faggots." James was unsure what the context of their conversation was, but he knew he was bothered by the mix of antigay language and laughter.

James denied any current difficulties associated with his sexual orientation. I asked him to elaborate on his experiences in middle school. It clearly had been a stressful time for him. As he talked, James moved ahead in time to mention Proposition 8 in his home state of California; the passage of Proposition 8 had stripped same-sex couples of the recently granted right to marry. As he spoke about the election, James spontaneously mentioned that such elections meant that the majority could overrule the rights of the minority, which made him feel "doomed." I visibly reacted to his use of the word *doomed*, and he immediately knew why.

I asked James to tell me how much he knew about the campaign that had led up to that election, which had occurred several weeks before our first meeting. He spoke with anger about certain campaign materials he had seen before he had left California. He talked about his frustration that people could not understand that "gay people are just people." He said that he had always wanted to get married and maybe raise children with a partner. For a while, it had looked like that would be possible in his home state. Now it was not. Moreover, he had been thinking lately that he did not want to return to California, that he instead might try graduate school in Massachusetts, where marriage is available to same-sex couples.

James spent the remainder of the session describing a host of reactions to the campaign about and passage of Proposition 8. He described pain and alienation and anger. I said little, recognizing that he seemed to have stumbled on (at least) one source of his feelings of doom. It was clear that he needed to talk through some of the affective charge he had been experiencing. As that session wound down, I asked James what he thought about his doom now. He had already decided that Proposition 8 was very relevant to his depressive symptoms. Certainly the timing was more than suggestive. James had been depressed watching the campaign heat up while he was in California during the summer. His depression had improved when he left California for school, which greatly reduced his exposure to the campaign. His symptoms were exacerbated soon after Proposition 8 passed. James went back and forth between wondering why people had to be so "mean" and expressing his anger about the unexpected outcome of the Proposition 8 election. I intentionally took a mirroring stance during James's litany of feelings. He knew what his feelings were, he knew what gave rise to them, and he knew how to articulate them. My job was to help him articulate those feelings and then to reflect them back to him.

At our next session James reported that he had called a friend from his high school gay/straight alliance to talk about the passage of Proposition 8. His friend, Martin, was going to college in California and had been involved in the campaign to defeat Proposition 8. Martin described his campaign experiences to James; he also told him about the very visible activism that had taken place after the election. James was fascinated by his friend's reports. He had never thought of himself as particularly political, but he expressed regret at not having been in California to take part in the public outrage about Proposition 8.

I asked James how much contact he had with the LGBT community on campus. He said he knew a few gay men in his major and a lesbian student couple whom he had met through a friend in his engineering club. But he had sought no contact with the broader LGBT community. I suggested to James something that was apparent from research in a variety of contexts: Contact with the gay community can be helpful to LGBT people in the best of times and especially in the worst of times, when voters deny them equal rights (Russell & Richards, 2003). James immediately saw the connection between this statement and the relief and excitement he felt when he talked with Martin about Proposition 8. We discussed several on-campus LGBT-oriented student groups. James seemed intrigued by the possibility of becoming more involved, but he also expressed concern about spending too much time away from his studies.

At one point in the conversation James referred to the Proposition 8 election as a "catastrophe." I asked how he saw it as a catastrophe. He replied that it had made it unlikely that gay people would ever be able to marry in California or even gain other rights. I viewed James's statement as an invitation to begin reframing his understanding of the election's outcome. I asked him whether he knew that Massachusetts couples' access to marriage equality had been repeatedly threatened, even after it was granted by the court. He said that he knew virtually nothing about how marriage rights had been won there. I gave a 4- to 5-minute minilecture on the story of marriage equality in the Bay State. I emphasized the ups and downs, the victories, the losses and squeakings by, and the amazing work that had been done by both LGBT people and our heterosexual allies.

James was intrigued by the minihistory lesson, and he asked for several specific details. I suggested a couple of resources he might consult to find out more information, but I was more interested in talking with James about the reframe. I suggested to him that the Massachusetts story was a good illustration of how social change tends to happen. It is not anything like a straight line. It is a process that entails victories and defeats, dead ends and lost efforts, the exhilaration of success, and the frequent fear that it will all end in failure.

James wondered, as much to himself as to me, why anyone would want to do it. I asked why he and his friends went out of their way to keep the gay/

straight alliance going in their high school. Without hesitation he said it was because it "meant something; it made a difference." He continued, "We felt better. We helped one another. We weren't alone. We had support. We did the Day of Silence [an annual event in schools nationwide when LGBT and ally students do not speak for a day to call attention to how often LGBT students are silenced on a regular basis], and kids in the school got a lot more awareness about gay issues."

I asked James to contrast how he had felt in high school with how he had felt in middle school. He spoke of loneliness and isolation in middle school and of his fears, first that he was gay and later that others would know that he was gay. High school, in contrast, was "way different, totally different." He was out and not at all lonely or isolated. He no longer lived in fear that others would find out he was gay. He felt "more comfortable in [his] own skin." He ended with, "In some ways, having the gay/straight alliance helped me to feel like being gay was no big deal."

I suggested that being gay both *is* and *is not* a big deal. It is not a big deal when it is just a part of who we are. But it is a big deal when we run into homophobia and heterosexism in the world. James was on a roll, but our time was up.

At our next session James reported that he had gone online twice during the intervening week to read what he could about the election. Having been in Colorado when California voters had passed Proposition 8, he knew about the outcome, of course, and he recalled that he had been shocked by it. But otherwise he had not thought much about it. He was busy at school, and it seemed to have had no immediate effect on him. I asked him what he had discovered through his online searches. Now it was James's turn to offer me a minihistory lesson. He was enthralled by what he had learned, and he was certainly tracking the ups and downs of marriage equality in his home state. James was also angry about what he had read. He was angry not only about the outcome of the election but also about campaign messages, about how not enough gay people took it seriously, about how most heterosexuals didn't "get it," about why there can be elections in which the majority votes away the rights of a minority.

I listened as James led us both through the objects of his anger. They all made sense, even as I privately thought that he overstated the case in a couple of instances. I talked with him about how anger was a reasonable response to the perception of being violated, and I asked him to consider exactly how he personally had been violated by Proposition 8. James was able to say how the election—and the events surrounding it—had made him feel: singled out, targeted, misunderstood and misrepresented, treated unfairly ("when they don't even know who I am!"), "pissed off," isolated, helpless.

I asked James whether he had ever felt that way before. He drew an easy thread to his middle school experiences of being harassed. But as he drew the connection he was less angry now, more in touch with the pain. I reflected on the commonalities in his response to Proposition 8 and his response to what had happened in middle school. They were as clear to James as they were to me. I asked him what the two experiences had in common, and

James went through a number of the feelings he had described earlier. I waited. James added a couple of other parallels in the two experiences.

I waited again. And then I asked James whether he could think of any other commonalities. He did not think so, he said. I suggested that both situations were unfair and painful because of precisely the same ingredient—bias or prejudice. James ran with the idea, only he substituted "homophobia" as the attribution. We spent the remainder of the session discussing homophobia—what it looks like, where it comes from, why some people seem to be more homophobic than others. James was hungry to understand what homophobia was all about.

As we talked James seemed to become more comfortable talking about homophobia as a phenomenon in the world. I asked him whether he knew who Steven Biko was; he did not. I told him that Biko was a freedom fighter against apartheid in South Africa who really understood racism in the world. But Biko, I told James, also understood that oppression is not just an external phenomenon. It also affects people internally; it affects how we think. I told James about an incisive observation Biko had made (a copy of which I keep in a small frame in my office): "The most potent weapon in the hands of the oppressor is the mind of the oppressed." Again I waited.

James began to work with his reaction to the Biko quote. He talked about how he felt on reading the few pieces of pro-Proposition 8 campaign materials that he had seen online and during his time in California the previous summer. He allowed as how he had read the materials quickly and pushed them out of his mind as "trash" and "ridiculous." I asked whether he remembered what they said, and he recalled brief snippets. Without using the term, I began working with James on internalized homophobia. We began with the campaign materials but quickly branched out to discuss other homophobic messages he had heard along the way. We talked about each one: how he reacted to it, its validity, how much he had applied it to the process of constructing his understanding of himself, how easy or difficult it was to let it go.

Not surprisingly, James eventually made his way to the taunts he had heard in middle school. For the first time in our work together he talked about his small stature. It was clear that he had internalized a conflation between his small size and his sexual orientation. He seemed visibly relieved to talk about his size in those terms. When I commented on his reaction, he roamed around a bit before describing a memory: He had worried that others would know he was gay solely because he was so small. His early adolescent mind had assumed that his stature was wholly a function of his sexual orientation and that everyone would automatically know he was gay by seeing that he was small. We talked about how out of his control that must have felt for James. I asked whether he had ever discussed it with his therapist. He had not, although he was unsure whether he assumed that the therapist would already know the "obvious fact" that the two characteristics were connected and/or whether he was too ashamed to acknowledge it to anyone.

As James left my office I wondered whether he looked taller. When he returned the next week he was certainly louder. He and his friend

Martin had had several phone and texting conversations about homophobia and internalized homophobia (James had apparently picked up the term somewhere in these conversations). He also talked about how homophobia "got into [his] head" and how he could resist it. James brought up the idea of the campus groups again. He had decided that he wanted to connect with a bigger group of LGBT friends. I reflected that having contact with other LGBT folks was often a good way to fight internalized homophobia. He would see a bigger cross-section of LGBT people, including people he would like and value, both of which would provide great counters to negative stereotypes. He would find some support to ease his sense of isolation. Perhaps he would find others who were working to resist internalized homophobia—something that often works especially well in groups.

In our sixth session James reported that he had gone to one of the campus LGBT groups but was not sure he liked it. It felt "too political" for him. He had already decided to try an alternative group that had been described as "more of a social group." James quickly changed the topic. He told me that he had had a long conversation with both of his parents about his reaction to Proposition 8. James said it was difficult to bring it up. After all, his parents had been generally very supportive of him—"never any freak-outs about me being gay." Nonetheless, as he was talking with Martin about all of the postelection activity in California, he started wondering why his parents had never participated in any of it. In fact, he realized, they had never even mentioned the election to him, even though they had talked excitedly with him about Barack Obama's winning the presidency on the same day.

As James reported it, his parents were able to listen to his complaints, though he thought his dad sounded "a little defensive at first." He explained to them that he had realized he had been very upset by the passage of Proposition 8 and about what he might have lost for his own future. Both of his parents apologized for not having considered how Proposition 8 might have felt to their gay son. In our session James mentioned that he hoped they would take it seriously now and would "get involved," but he had been afraid to make that request directly of his parents.

James and I discussed his relationships with other heterosexuals. He had the benefit of having had straight allies as friends in his gay/straight alliance in high school. Thus, he was aware that some straight people could be supportive. I suggested to him that some straight people really want to support equality but they don't always know how. I added that sometimes asking is all it takes. James looked me in the eye and inquired, "You think I should ask my parents to get involved, right?" I hedged a moment and then said, "It might help, yes. It might help them, and it might help you."

I used the opportunity to return our focus to the cognitive reframe of the Proposition 8 election. I spoke of how much change had occurred not just in the fight for marriage equality but also with regard to LGBT rights in general. I told James that these changes happened because LGBT people worked and insisted, because we understood what homophobia is and how unfair it is, because we joined with people—straight and LGBT—from other oppressed groups, because we worked with straight allies, because we refused to give up. I added that when we look at all this change—all this progress—it is easier to be optimistic, even in the face of such painful disappointments as Proposition 8. James said little in response. I was a bit worried that in my eagerness to make sure he understood the reframe, I had taken too much of a didactic stance. I wondered whether I had pushed too fast because I was aware that our next session would be our final one.

James came in for that session with the news that he had visited a second LGBT campus group. He liked it more than the first group but still found something missing. On Sunday he went to his local church—something he had done infrequently since moving to Colorado. He returned Sunday evening for a meeting of the weekly discussion group on gay spirituality. He reported that the group included straight people as well as LGBT people and that he would continue to attend. I silently considered that his group might be really good for James; it could help him integrate his spiritual life with his sexual orientation, an issue we had not even touched on in this brief therapy and one that is often interwoven with internalized homophobia and with feelings of isolation.

James said that he would be going back to the on-campus social group as well. Through a broad grin, he told me that he had met another student whom he found attractive, and he wanted to have a chance to "get to know him better." I acknowledged that we had not discussed dating and relationships since our first session (when I was gathering James's history). James said he had dated a couple of guys in high school but had been too preoccupied with school work since coming to the university. He thought it was time he started dating again.

James brought up another topic. He said that he had been thinking about what I had said about how change happens. In fact, he had talked with Martin about it as well. He wondered how he could be part of that when he was "not very political." I reminded him of his own experience with change, his comments about how his high school gay/straight alliance had "made a difference." I suggested that change happens on many levels and that we make change in many ways—through our relationships, through what we talk about, how we vote, what kind of place we work at, what we ask of others (he smiled when I said this), how we spend our money. Any of these can be "political."

James came back with his own measure of change: "What we think about in our heads."

"Touché," I responded.

I asked James what he thought he would do if he lived in a place where another election about LGBT rights were held. He said he was not sure how "political" he would be, but he knew he would give money and maybe do some "behind-the-scenes" work. And he would talk with his family and friends. He added that he would "do something, for sure." He would not ignore it, which was how he characterized his approach to the Proposition 8 election.

"How do you think you'll react if we lose again?"

"I'll hate it." After a pause, James elaborated, "I don't think I'll get depressed—the 'doom' thing again. I would hate it, but I'd know why I felt so bad. And I'd know it's part of something bigger, part of how change happens. Besides, I'd have friends to yell about it with."

"It wouldn't be a catastrophe?"

"No . . . well maybe some, but not a huge catastrophe. I know that much now."

I said, "You know something else too." He waited for me to go on. "You know that even awful events can make for a lot of growth. Look at the organizing that went on in California after the election—the things you read about online and talked with Martin about. Look at how active Martin got, look at what your parents have learned, look at how you have changed."

He felt more "together" as a gay person, he said. (I was thinking of how much he had integrated his sexual orientation and, with it, his experiences in middle school.) He said he was working to juggle his Sunday evening meetings and the student social group with his school work, but he thought he could pull it off—especially because he wasn't carrying the "doom thing" around with him anymore. He left the session with an apparent sense of his own good work.

Conclusion

My work in therapy with James illustrates both the toll that anti-LGBT politics can take on LGBT individuals and how unnoticed this toll can be to them. The case also suggests how experiences with anti-LGBT politics can revive old conflicts and pain related to sexual orientation or gender identity (and often to other areas of a person's life as well). In a more positive vein, almost two decades of research into the impact of anti-LGBT politics has suggested some of the ways in which counselors can help LGBT clients exposed to negative campaigns and elections. Prominent in this therapeutic work are reframing these events in a larger sociopolitical context and working to develop general and LGBT-specific coping skills. As James's case illustrates, this work requires that counselors be open to seeing and intervening in areas where personal identity and political realities collide.

References

Association for Lesbian, Gay, Bisexual and Transgender Issues in Counseling. (1997). *Competencies for counseling gay, lesbian, bisexual and transgendered (LGBT) clients.* Alexandria, VA: Author.

Gamble, B. S. (1997). Putting civil rights to a popular vote. *Journal of Political Science, 41,* 245–269.

Hatzenbuehler, M. L., Keyes, K. M., & Hasin, D. S. (2009). State-level policies and psychiatric morbidity in lesbian, gay, and bisexual populations. *American Journal of Public Health, 99,* 2275–2281.

Levitt, H. M., Ovrebo, E., Anderson-Cleveland, M. B., Leone, C., Jeong, J. Y., Arm, J. R., . . . Horne, S. J. (2009). Balancing dangers: GLBT experiences in a time of anti-GLBT legislation. *Journal of Counseling Psychology, 56,* 67–81.

Riggle, E. D. B., Rostosky, S. S., & Horne, S. G. (2009). Marriage amendments and lesbian, gay, and bisexual individuals in the 2006 election. *Sexuality Research and Social Policy, 6,* 80–89.

Rostosky, S. S., Riggle, E. D. B., Horne, S. G., Denton, F. N., & Huellemeier, J. D. (2010). Sexual minorities' psychological reactions to the 2006 marriage amendments. *American Journal of Orthopsychiatry, 80,* 302–310.

Russell, G. M. (2000). *Voted out: Psychological consequences of anti-gay politics.* New York, NY: New York University Press.

Russell, G. M. (2011). Motives of heterosexual allies in collective action for equality. *Journal of Social Issues, 67,* 376–393.

Russell, G. M., & Richards, J. A. (2003). Stressor and resilience factors for lesbians, gay men, and bisexuals confronting antigay politics. *American Journal of Community Psychology, 33,* 313–328.

Appendix A

Competencies for Counseling Gay, Lesbian, Bisexual and Transgendered (LGBT) Clients

As more and more sexual minorities seek counseling services for assistance with their life challenges, all counselors need to be well versed in understanding the unique needs of this diverse population. The Association for Lesbian, Gay, Bisexual and Transgender Issues in Counseling (ALGBTIC) developed the competencies that follow in order to promote the development of sound and professional counseling practice.

When integrated into graduate counseling curricula, these competencies will assist counselors-in-training in the examination of their personal biases and values regarding LGBT clients, expand their awareness of the world views of sexual minorities, and lead to the development of appropriate intervention strategies that insure effective service delivery.

Human Growth and Development

Competent Counselors will:

- understand that biological, familial, and psychosocial factors influence the course of development of GLB orientations and transgendered identities.
- identify the heterosexist assumptions inherent in current life span development theories and account for this bias in assessment procedures and counseling practices.
- consider that, due to the coming out process, LGBT individuals often may experience a lag between their chronological ages and the developmental stages delineated by current theories.
- recognize that identity formation and stigma management are ongoing developmental tasks that span the lives of LGBT persons.

Note. Reproduced with permission of the Association for Lesbian, Gay, Bisexual and Transgender Issues in Counseling.

- know that the normative developmental tasks of LGBT adolescents frequently may be complicated or compromised by identity confusion; anxiety and depression; suicidal ideation and behavior; academic failure; substance abuse; physical, sexual, and verbal abuse; homelessness; prostitution; and STD/HIV infection.
- understand that the typical developmental tasks of LGBT seniors often are complicated or compromised by social isolation and invisibility.
- affirm that sexual minority persons have the potential to integrate their GLB orientations and transgendered identities into fully functioning and emotionally healthy lives.

Social and Cultural Foundations

Competent counselors will:

- acknowledge that heterosexism is a worldview and value-system that may undermine the healthy functioning of the sexual orientations, gender identities, and behaviors of LGBT persons.
- understand that heterosexism pervades the social and cultural foundations of many institutions and traditions and may foster negative attitudes toward LGBT persons.
- recognize how internalized prejudice, including heterosexism, racism, and sexism, may influence the counselor's own attitudes as well as those of their LGBT clients.
- know that the developmental tasks of LGBT women and people of color include the formation and integration of their gender, racial and sexual identities.
- familiarize themselves with the cultural traditions, rituals, and rites of passage specific to LGBT populations.

Helping Relationships

Competent counselors will:

- acknowledge the societal prejudice and discrimination experienced by LGBT persons and assist them in overcoming internalized negative attitudes toward their sexual orientations and gender identities.
- recognize that their own sexual orientations and gender identities are relevant to the helping relationship and influence the counseling process.
- seek consultation or supervision to ensure that their own biases or knowledge deficits about LGBT persons do not negatively influence the helping relationship.
- understand that attempts to alter or change the sexual orientations or gender identities of LGBT clients may be detrimental or even life-threatening, and, further, are not supported by the research and therefore should not be undertaken.

Group Work

Competent counselors will:

- be sensitive to the dynamics that occur when groups are formed that include only one representative of any minority culture and consider the necessity of including supportive allies for LGBT clients when screening and selecting group members.
- establish group norms and provide interventions that facilitate the safety and inclusion of LGBT group members.
- shape group norms and create a climate that allows for the voluntary self-identification and self-disclosure of LGBT participants.
- intervene actively when either overt or covert disapproval of LGBT members threatens member safety, group cohesion and integrity.

Career and Lifestyle Development

Competent counselors will:

- counter the occupational stereotypes that restrict the career development and decision-making of LGBT clients
- explore with LGBT clients the degree to which government statutes and union contracts do not protect workers against employment discrimination based on sexual orientation and gender identity.
- help LGBT clients make career choices that facilitate both identity formation and job satisfaction.
- acquaint LGBT clients with sexual minority role models that increase their awareness of viable career options.

Appraisal

Competent counselors will:

- understand that homosexuality, bisexuality, and gender nonconformity are neither forms of psychopathology nor necessarily evidence of developmental arrest.
- recognize the multiple ways that societal prejudice and discrimination create problems that LGBT clients may seek to address in counseling.
- consider sexual orientation and gender identity among the core characteristics that influence clients' perceptions of themselves and their worlds.
- assess LGBT clients without presuming that sexual orientation or gender identity is directly related to their presenting problems.
- differentiate between the effects of stigma, reactions to stress, and symptoms of psychopathology when assessing and diagnosing the presenting concerns of LGBT clients.
- recognize the potential for the heterosexist bias in the interpretation of psychological tests and measurements.

Research

Competent counselors will:

- formulate research questions that acknowledge the possible inclusion of LGBT participants yet are not based on stereotypic assumptions regarding these subjects.
- consider the ethical and legal issues involved in research with LGBT participants.
- acknowledge the methodological limitations in regard to research design, confidentiality, sampling, data collection, and measurement involved in research with LGBT participants.
- recognize the potential for heterosexist bias in the interpretation and reporting of research results.

Professional Orientation

Competent counselors will:

- know the history of the helping professions including significant factors and events that have compromised service delivery to LGBT populations.
- familiarize themselves with the needs and counseling issues of LGBT clients and use nonstigmatizing and affirming mental health, educational, and community resources.
- recognize the importance of educating professionals, students, supervisees, and consumers about LGBT issues and challenge misinformation or bias about minority persons.
- use professional development opportunities to enhance their attitudes, knowledge, and skills specific to counseling LGBT persons and their families.

Appendix B

American Counseling Association Competencies for Counseling With Transgender Clients

Approved by ALGBTIC Board on September 18, 2009
and endorsed and adopted by the American Counseling
Association Governing Council on Novembr 7, 2009

Authors

ALGBTIC Transgender Committee: Theodore R. Burnes, (Chair), Anneliese A. Singh, (Presidential Initiative), Amney J. Harper, Brandon Harper, William Maxon-Kann, Denise L. Pickering, Sean Moundas, Thomas R. Scofield, Alex Roan, and Julia Hosea (Committee Members Emeriti)

Reviewers

Lore M. Dickey, Dara Hoffman, Joanne Keatley, Arlene Lev, Vel S. Mckleroy, Jesse Mcnulty, and Stacee Reicherzer

This document contains suggested competencies for use in counseling with transgender clients. These competencies are geared toward professionally trained counselors who work with transgender individuals, families, groups, or communities. These competencies are based on a wellness (e.g., Myers & Sweeney, 2005), resilience (Singh, Hays, & Watson, in press; Singh & McKleroy, in press), and strength-based approach (e.g., Bockting, Knudson, & Goldberg, 2007; Carroll, 2010; Lev, 2004; Vanderburgh, 2009) for working with transgender clients. The authors of these competencies come from diverse theoretical and professional backgrounds in working with transgender clients, advocating for transgender communities, and having relationships with transgender people.

Across this diversity of perspectives and experiences, the authors share a common approach of affirming that all persons have the potential to live fully functioning and emotionally healthy lives throughout the life span along

Note. From American Counseling Association. (2010). Competencies for Counseling With Transgender Clients. *Journal of LGBT Issues in Counseling, 4,* 135–159. doi:10.1 080/15538605.2010.524839. Copyright 2010 by Routledge, Taylor & Francis Group. Reprinted with permission.

the full spectrum of gender identity and gender expression. The authors advocate using a strength-based approach to highlight the strengths and resilience transgender individuals may have despite the significant experiences of multiple oppressions transgender people may have experienced. Further, the authors believe that counselors are in the unique position to endeavor to make institutional changes in the environments in which they work to develop safer counseling settings for transgender people.

Theoretical Framework

The authors developed a theoretical framework from which they constructed these competencies. This framework in part stemmed from the authors' acknowledgment of their biases—their own and those of the society in which they live. The authors chose to be transparent about their theoretical framework to not only share their assumptions about transgender people, but also to acknowledge that all individuals hold biases of which they are not yet aware. Therefore, the authors met as a committee weekly or biweekly for over a year to identify these biases and develop strength-based competencies. The authors also sought the expertise of seven independent reviewers who ranged in their experiences of practice, supervision, training, research, and advocacy with transgender concerns in counseling.

The authors conceptualized this approach from a theoretical orientation of counseling that integrates multicultural (Sue & Sue, 2008), social justice (Goodman et al., 2004), and feminist (Worell & Remer, 2003) approaches, which each acknowledge the influence of privilege, power, and oppression on clients' lives. These theoretical approaches provide a lens for identifying, documenting the experiences of, and working to meet the needs of transgender clients. These approaches also provide a framework for the macrolevel implications for working with transgender individuals and communities and allowed the authors to recognize how gender identity intersects with a client's multiple sociocultural identities (e.g., race, ethnicity, sexual orientation, etc.).

In addition to their theoretical orientation to counseling, the authors strived to incorporate counselors' multiple professional roles into the theoretical framework of these competencies. For example, the importance of social justice and advocacy as part of counselors' work with transgender clients is acknowledged (e.g., Carroll, 2010). In developing these competencies, the authors referenced the original lesbian, gay, bisexual, and transgender (LGBT) competencies (Association for Lesbian, Gay, Bisexual and Transgender Issues in Counseling [AGLBIC], 2003), the ACA *Advocacy Competencies* (Lewis, Arnold, House, & Toporek, 2003), and the ACA multicultural competencies (Sue, Arredondo, & McDavis, 1992) to ensure that the current transgender competencies are grounded in the counselor role of advocacy that also integrates a multicultural approach to wellness.

An additional and important aspect of the authors' theoretical framework stemmed from the authors' beliefs about how these competencies should be used. These competencies should not be used in lieu of professional training in working with transgender clients, and supervision of trainees by licensed professionals. Consultation among and with professionals is essential and provides ongoing continuing education for individuals working with transgender clients. There are established World Professional Association of Transgender Health (WPATH) Standards of Care (Meyer et al., 2001—previously known as the Harry Benjamin Standards of Care) for working with transgender clients, and the authors do not intend that these competencies replace the WPATH Standards of Care, but rather that they complement them and are used in the training of counselors and establishing best practices in the counseling field with transgender clients.

Best practices for professional counselors working with clients from historically marginalized communities (e.g., AGLBIC, 2003) articulate the need for counselors to be familiar with all eight domains of these competencies to demonstrate cultural competence with transgender clients. Further, although there may be overlap among the different areas of these competencies, it will be important to review all areas to incorporate common themes of the areas as well as counseling strategies that are unique to particular sections.

Transgender-Affirmative Language

In addition to their theoretical framework, the authors consulted many different theoretical and empirical sources (e.g., Bockting & Coleman, 2007; Feinberg, 1996; Green & Dickey, 2009; Lombardi, 2001; Sue, Arredondo, & McDavis, 1992) and the seven reviewers of this document (see Appendix B to identify appropriate, transgender-affirmative language to use in these competencies). The authors of this document recommend the following as a growing list of some of the least restrictive terms available for use with transgender people, which are excerpted with permission from the Lambda Legal (2008) publication *Bending the Mold: An Action Kit for Transgender Youth* (see Appendix A). Although specific terms are used throughout the document, it is important to recognize the continuous evolution of language is to be expected with regard to working with transgender clients as there are many terms that are used within transgender communities.

Despite identifying and using a common language that was pervasive throughout the competencies, the authors thought it important to note that language in transgender (and any cultural) communities varies and that these competencies would not dictate "accurate" or "correct" language. In addition to language surrounding constructs of gender identity and expression, the authors also recognize that the correct use of self-identified, gender-affirming pronouns for transgender clients are also important. For example, the use of gender-neutral pronouns such as "ze" and "hir" are a critical addition to counselors' vocabulary when working with some transgender clients. It is important to honor the set of pronouns that clients may identify with and/or select—and to use these pronouns throughout the counseling process. At the same time, counselors should also be aware that some transgender individuals do not identify with gender-neutral pronouns and identify with traditional gender pronouns. Specifically, any language used by the counselor should be directed by the client and should affirm the client's self-identified gender throughout the transition process, especially in instances where the counselor's perception of the client's gender identity and expression and the client's actual gender identity and expression differ.

The authors asserted that it was important to note that transgender people have been historically marginalized and pathologized by diagnostic and assessment systems. Then, the authors recognized that they would need to position themselves within the range of counseling approaches (e.g., pathology-based vs. strength-based) with transgender clients. Drawing from the minority stress model (Meyer, 2003), the authors believe that gender identity is in no way a mental disorder and articulate this view by placing *disorder* in quotes throughout the competencies (e.g., gender identity "disorder"), to draw attention to their critique of pathologizing gender identity.

Due to heterosexism and transphobia being referenced throughout the document and being central concepts to the minority stress model, it is important to clarify the difference between the two terms. *Transphobia* describes the irrational fear and hatred of all those individuals who transgress, violate, or blur the dominant gender categories in a given society, which may be experienced by transgender individuals in different ways from microaggressions to violence. The authors encourage counselors to also consider that *transprejudice* is often a more helpful term to use when describing the actual discrimination that transgender people experience. *Heterosexism*, on the other hand, describes the assumption that everyone is heterosexual or should be. Although many transgender individuals identify as heterosexual, they may still experience heterosexism because embedded within heterosexism is a narrow binary gender system that transgender individuals may be seen as outside of or they are questioned about their status of being a "real" man or woman. Therefore, ze/she/he may be heterosexual yet experience heterosexism through microaggressions, discrimination, harassment, violence, and so on because of being incorrectly viewed as gay, lesbian, and/or bisexual.

An important consideration in working with transgender individuals is how family is defined. Due to the heterosexism, transprejudice, transphobia, and transnegativity many transgender individuals experience, it is common for transgender people to be rejected from their family of origin; there may be conflict and/or separation from nuclear and extended families. Transgender individuals may therefore find and define family by those who perform the roles of family, despite biological or legal adoption within a family unit. This broader definition of *family* should be honored and integrated into the counseling process as the individual chooses. Within the transgender community, this is usually referred to as "family of choice," and also the authors urge counselors to honor how individuals define and label family for themselves.

Limitations of Competencies

Although this document attempts to provide a comprehensive list of competencies in counseling transgender clients, the authors also want to acknowledge that this project has limitations in its scope. These competencies are intended to be a foundation, and the authors encourage counselors to continually develop resources and knowledge that build upon limitations. Some particular limitations the authors would like to note regarding this project are specific populations and differences related to what some may label as a gender transition.

With regards to specific populations, the competencies did not permit for an in-depth application to counseling transgender youth, the elderly, or working with the family and loved ones of transgender individuals. Although many items in these competencies will be relevant for working with transgender youth and family and loved ones of transgender individuals, because it was not the focus, there are considerations that require further attention and commentary. The authors have attempted to address this issue through providing resources at the end of the document.

An additional limitation that the authors felt important to note is that the document does not break down the competencies by the specific experiences of identifying as male-to-female (MTF) or female-to-male (FTM) and those who identify with other gender descriptions (e.g., genderqueer). For instance, an important difference to note is the experiences relating to the loss of male privilege for MTF transgender individuals and the gain of male privilege for FTM transgender individuals. These experiences also vary within the range of gender identity and expression and are based on the individual's experience (e.g., how gaining male privilege is experienced by a FTM will vary widely, such as how other identities such as race/ethnicity intersect with their gender identity). Not every transgender individual will decide to make a medical and/or social transition from MTF or FTM, not all transgender people identify with the word *transition*, and not all transgender individuals identify within the current gender binary (male or female). Ze/she/he instead may identify as genderqueer, androgynous, gender-fluid, and so on. Regardless, it is important for counselors to be aware of the pressure all individuals experience related to fitting into the narrow gender binary and the additional challenges transgender people might face when stepping out of these gender confines.

Organization of Competencies

Using the theoretical framework articulated above, the authors developed domains of competencies for counseling with transgender clients. The competencies are organized according to the Council for Accreditation of Counseling and Related Educational Programs standards (CACREP; 2009). They are divided into eight domains that align with the eight training domains of CACREP standards, as the expectation that the CACREP standards are the minimum standards for the delivery of ethical and competent counseling supervision and training of the counseling profession. In this document, the authors have encouraged counselors to move beyond competence into the role of conscientious consumers of these standards by becoming social change agents and allies for transgender clients. It was the authors' intention that counselors will recognize and celebrate the rich histories, lives, and pride of transgender clients and communities. The competencies incorporated a multicultural counseling competency framework that includes knowledge, skills, and awareness (KSA) areas (Sue et al., 1992). This framework was used for the LGBT competencies (AGLBIC, 2003), and the authors find it appropriate to similarly structure these competencies for working with transgender clients as a beginning step. Although the KSA structure was the existing framework for organizing these competencies, the authors also recognized that this document will evolve and require revision over time. Thus, these competencies will require periodic evaluation and revision to reflect current theory, research, practice, and counseling frameworks regarding transgender clients. Therefore, the authors also set an intention to welcome feedback from those reading and using these competencies. This feedback may be e-mailed to the current ALGBTIC president (e-mail found at www.algbtic.org) at any time, which will then be directed to the ALGBTIC Transgender Committee chair. The authors also recognized that there are also many interactions among the three areas of the KSA competence model, and therefore all eight domains of these competencies respectively integrate all three areas (vs. identifying specific and respective competencies of knowledge, skills, and awareness for each of the eight CACREP domains).

Using an organizational structure that integrates the eight CAREP domains and draws from the content and spirit of the ACA multicultural (Sue et al., 1992) and the ACA *Advocacy Competencies* (Lewis et al., 2003), the authors recognized that it is inevitable that references for various CACREP domains and KSA areas overlap and could become cumbersome in utilizing the competencies. Therefore the authors have listed all references at the end of the entire document for readers' reference and further professional development. Also, the authors made no links in the body of the text to specific references. Rather, counselors should use the reference section as critical tools to obtain resources for their continued professional development in theory, research, practice, training, advocacy, and resilience of transgender clients.

Foundational Literature

As part of the initial development of these competencies, the authors recognized the importance of using empirical research as a basis from which the competencies could be identified. Such a process stemmed in part from calls from the professional literature that stressed the importance of using current empirical and theoretical literature in the development of guidelines for multicultural practice and training (Association for Assessment in Counseling and Education, 2002). The authors also included sources in their review of the literature with which they believed readers should engage for their own professional development as counselors use these competencies.

- American Counseling Association *Advocacy Competencies* (Lewis et al., 2003)
- American Counseling Association multicultural competence (Sue et al., 1992)
- American Counseling Association Ethics Code (2005)
- Council for Accreditation of Counseling and Educational Related Programs (2009)
- World Professional Association of Transgender Health standards of care (Meyer et al., 2001)
- American Psychological Association *Report of the Task Force on Gender Identity and Gender Variance* (2009)

A. Human Growth and Development

Competent counselors will:

- A. 1. Affirm that all persons have the potential to live full functioning and emotionally healthy lives throughout their life span while embracing the full spectrum of gender identity and expression, gender presentation, and gender diversity beyond the male-female binary.
- A. 2. Identify how respective developmental periods throughout the life span (e.g., youth, adolescence, elderly) may impact the concerns and process that transgender clients present in counseling.
- A. 3. Affirm transgender mental and medical health care (e.g., hormone therapies, sex reassignment surgery, safe and transgender-positive general medical services) through the entire life span, not just during the initial assessment process or during transition.
- A. 4. Understand the biological, familial, social, cultural, socioeconomic, and psychological factors that influence the course of development of transgender identities.
- A. 5. Identify the gender-normative assumptions present in current lifespan development theories and address these biases in assessment and counseling practices.
- A. 6. Understand how stigma and pressures to be gender conforming may affect personality development even in the face of the resiliency and strengths of transgender individuals. Further, understand how these factors influence decision making in regards to employment, housing, health care, and manifestation of psychological disorders of transgender individuals.
- A. 7. Recognize the influence of other contextual factors and social determinants of health (e.g., race/ethnicity, education, religion and spirituality, socioeconomic status, sexual orientation, role in the family, peer group, geographical region, etc.) on the course of development of transgender identities.
- A. 8. Be informed of the various ways of living consistently with one's gender identity, which may or may not include physical or social gender transition, and how these options may affect transgender individuals throughout their development. Be aware of the sociopolitical

influences that affect the lives of transgender individuals, and that stereotyping, discrimination, and marginalization may shape one's developmental processes, self-esteem, and self-concept.

- A. 9. Recognize that the normative developmental tasks of many transgender individuals may be complicated or compromised by one's self identity and/or sexuality confusion, anxiety and depression, suicidal ideation and behavior, nonsuicidal self-injury, substance abuse, academic failure, homelessness, internalized transphobia and transprejudice, SID/HIV infection, addiction, and other mental health issues.
- A. 10. Understand how transgender individuals navigate the complexities of self and others with regard to intimate relationships throughout the life span.
- A. 11. Understand that the typical developmental tasks of transgender seniors often are complicated or compromised by social isolation and invisibility, medical problems, transgender-related health concerns, family-of-origin conflicts, and often limited career options—especially for those with developmental disabilities.
- A. 12. Recognize that gender identity formation, self-acceptance of transgender identity, and disclosure of transgender status are complex processes and events that are not necessarily permanently resolved and may be experienced repeatedly across one's life span.

B. Social and Cultural Foundations

Competent counselors will:

- B. 1. Understand the importance of using appropriate language (e.g., correct name and pronouns) with transgender clients; be aware that language in the transgender community is constantly evolving and varies from person to person; seek to be aware of new terms and definitions within the transgender community; honor clients' definitions of their own gender; seek to use language that is the least restrictive in terms of gender (e.g., using client's name as opposed to assuming what pronouns the client asserts are gender affirming); recognize that language has historically been used to oppress and discriminate against transgender people; understand that the counselor is in a position of power and should model respect for the client's declared vocabulary.
- B. 2. Acknowledge that the oppression of transgender people is a component of sexism, heterosexism, transphobia, and transprejudice and reflects a worldview and value system that undermines the healthy functioning and autonomy of transgender people.
- B. 3. Understand that transprejudice and transphobia pervades the social and cultural foundations of many institutions and traditions and fosters negative attitudes, high incidence of violence/hate crimes, and overt hostility toward transgender people.
- B. 4. Recognize how internalized prejudice and discrimination (e.g., transphobia, racism, sexism, classism, religious discrimination, ableism, adultism, ageism) may influence the counselor's own attitudes as

well as those of her/his/hir transgender clients resulting in negative attitudes toward transgender people.

- B. 5. Recognize, acknowledge, and understand the intersecting identities of transgender people (e.g., race/ethnicity, ability, class, religion/spiritual affiliation, age, experiences of trauma) and their accompanying developmental tasks. This should include attention to the formation and integration of the multiple identity statuses of transgender people.
- B. 6. Understand how the specific intersection of sexism, heterosexism, and transphobia may affect clients' lives. For example, sexism (how patriarchy promotes gender stereotypes and roles and how power and privilege are distributed to reinforce the binary gender system), transphobia (internalized fears or negative self-concept), transprejudice (discrimination against transgender people), and heterosexism (conflating sexual orientation and gender identity) are different. Counselors should understand also how heterosexism impacts both those who identify as homosexual and heterosexual, because ze/she/he may be viewed as being outside of the gender binary or as "really a man/woman" and therefore are seen as gay, lesbian, and/or bisexual).
- B. 7. Understand how the specific intersection of racism, sexism, heterosexism and transphobia and transprejudice influences the lives of transgender people of color (e.g., increased risk for HIV/AIDS and overrepresentation of transgender people of color in HIV infections) and recognize the negative stereotypes used against transgender people of color.
- B. 8. Acknowledge how classism affects the lives of transgender people through increased rates of homelessness, restricted job opportunities and increased marginalization within the work place, and lack of federal employment protections.
- B. 9. Identify transgender-positive resources (e.g., support groups, websites, brochures) that address multiple identities of transgender people (e.g., youth, differential ability, people of color).
- B. 10. Use empowerment and advocacy interventions (see ACA *Advocacy Competencies*) when necessary and/or requested with transgender clients (e.g., employment and education discrimination, transgender people of color, housing discrimination).
- B. 11. Educate themselves and others about the damaging impact of colonization and patriarchy on the traditions, rituals, and rites of passage specific to transgender people across cultures over time (e.g., Hijras of India, Mahu of Hawaii, Kathoey of Thailand, Two-Spirit of Native American/First Nations people).
- B. 12. Recognize that spiritual development and religious practices may be important for transgender individuals, yet it may also present a particular challenge given the limited transpositive religious institutions that may be present in a given community, and that many transgender individuals may face personal struggles related to their faith and their identity.

C. Helping Relationships

Competent counselors will:

- C. 1. Understand that attempts by the counselor to alter or change gender identities and/or the sexual orientation of transgender clients across the life span may be detrimental, life threatening, and are not empirically supported; whereas counseling approaches that are affirmative of these identities are supported by research, best practices, and professional organizations—such as the American Counseling Association, American Psychological Association.
- C. 2. Recognize that the counselors' gender identity, expression, and concepts about gender are relevant to the helping relationship, and these identities and concepts influence the counseling process and may affect the counselor/client relationship.
- C. 3. Be aware that, although the client is transgender and may have gender-related concerns, the client's primary concern and reason for seeking counseling services may *not* be related to gender identity and/or gender dysphoria.
- C. 4. If gender identity concerns are the reason for seeking treatment, counselors acknowledge experience, training, and expertise in working with individuals with gender concerns at the initial visit while discussing informed consent and seek supervision and consultation as necessary.
- C. 5. Acknowledge with the paucity of research on efficacious theoretical approaches for working with transgender populations, counselors are urged to conduct routine process monitoring and evaluation of their service delivery and reevaluate their theoretical approach for working with transgender individuals.
- C. 6. Acknowledge that, although gender identities and expressions are unique to individuals, they can vary greatly among and across different populations of transgender people. Further, a transgender client's gender identity and/or expression may evolve across their life span.
- C. 7. Acknowledge that physical (e.g., access to health care, HIV/AIDS, and other health issues), social (e.g., family/partner relationships), emotional (e.g., anxiety, depression, substance abuse), cultural (e.g., lack of support from others in their racial/ethnic group), spiritual (e.g., possible conflict between their spiritual values and those of their family's), and/or other stressors (e.g., financial problems as a result of employment discrimination) often interfere with transgender people's ability to achieve their goals. Therefore, it is important assist them with overcoming these obstacles and regulating their affects, thoughts, and behavior throughout this coping process.
- C. 8. Recognize and acknowledge that, historically, counseling and other helping professions have compounded the discrimination of transgender individuals by being insensitive, inattentive, uninformed,

and inadequately trained and supervised to provide culturally proficient services to transgender individuals and their loved ones.

- C. 9. Create a welcoming, affirming environment for transgender individuals and their loved ones by creating a counseling space that affirms
transgender people's identity (e.g., placing transgender-positive maga-
zines and literature in the waiting room, etc.). Respect and attend to the
entire individual—not just his or her gender identity-related concerns.
- C. 10. Facilitate an open discussion to identify the effects of transprejudice and discrimination experienced by transgender clients and assist
them in overcoming potential internalized negative attitudes about
themselves and their gender identities.
- C. 11. Proactively seek consultation and/or supervision from professionals competent in working with transgender individuals (please
refer to WPATH's *Standards of Care* regarding guidelines for professional
competency) to ensure that the counselors' own biases or knowledge
deficits do not negatively affect the helping relationship.

D. Group Work

Competent group counselors will:

- D. 1. Maintain a nonjudgmental, supportive stance on all expressions
of gender identity, gender expression, and sexuality and establish this
as a standard for group members as well.
- D. 2. Facilitate group members' understanding that mental health
professionals' attempts to change a member's gender identity (e.g.,
conversion or reparative therapies) are not supported by research and,
moreover, may have detrimental and/or life-threatening consequences.
- D. 3. Involve members in establishing the group treatment plans,
expectations, and goals, which should be reviewed periodically
throughout the group. These should foster the safety and inclusion
of transgender members.
- D. 4. Provide education and opportunities for social learning about
a wide array of choices regarding coming out and transitioning if
indicated or warranted.
- D. 5. Recognize the impact of power, privilege, and oppression within
the group especially among the counselor and members and between
members of advantaged and marginalized groups.
- D. 6. Consider diversity (e.g., gender identity and expression, sex assigned at birth, sexual orientation, mental and physical ability status,
mental health concerns, race, ethnicity, religion, and socioeconomic class)
when selecting and screening group members and be sensitive to how
these aforementioned diverse identities may affect group dynamics.
- D. 7. Be aware of the unique status of an individual who may be the
only transgender group member and create a safe group environment in which that person can share her or his experiences if feeling
comfortable. In this case, it is especially important to foster a sense
of security within the group through the use of respectful language

toward the transgender member (e.g., correct pronouns and name; gender-affirmative terminology of transition interventions).

- D. 8. In gender-specific groups (e.g., inpatient treatment settings, substance abuse treatment, etc.), counselors should support transgender individuals attending the gender group with which they identify with rather than, for instance, insisting that a transgender person attends a group setting according to the sex that person was assigned at birth.
- D. 9. Acknowledge the impact of institutionalized and personalized transphobia and transprejudice on transgender members' comfort with disclosing and reflecting on their experiences that occur inside and outside of group.
- D. 10. Actively intervene when either overt or covert hostility toward transgender-identified members threatens group security and cohesion. This applies to transgender-specific groups and any group that has transgender members.
- D. 11. Recognize that although group support can be very helpful for transgender clients, peer pressure from group members to conform to specific conceptions of gender identity and expression may emerge within the group and should be addressed by the counselor.
- D. 12. Coordinate treatment with other professionals working with transgender members, while maintaining confidentiality within the group.
- D. 13. Refer clients to other mental and physical health services when either initiated by the group member or due to clinical judgment that the member is in need of these interventions.
- D. 14. Be aware of how their own gender identities, beliefs about gender, and lack of knowledge about transgender issues may affect group processes.
- D. 15. Seek consultation or supervision to ensure that the counselor's potential biases and knowledge deficits do not negatively affect group dynamics.
- D. 16. Will ideally have previous experience working with transgender individuals in non-transgender-specific and transgender-specific groups. If no previous counseling experience with transgender individuals exists, consultation and supervision with mental health professionals who are competent and have more experience working with transgender issues are even more critical.

E. Professional Orientation

Competent counselors will:

- E. 1. Understand and be aware that there has been a history of heterosexism and gender bias in the *Diagnostic and Statistical Manual* (*DSM*). For instance, counselors should have knowledge that homosexuality was previously categorized as a mental disorder and that currently "gender identity disorder" remains in the *DSM*.

  Know the history of how the helping professions have negatively influenced service delivery to transgender individuals, their families, and significant others through heterosexism and gender bias and specifically know the history of when "gender identity disorder" was inserted into the *Diagnostic and Statistical Manual* (*DSM*) and when homosexuality was removed as a mental health disorder.

- E. 2. Acknowledge and address the gatekeeper role and subsequent power that mental health professionals have historically had in transgender clients accessing medical interventions and resulted in mistrust of mental health professionals. This power difference needs to be minimized in the counseling relationship with transgender clients.
- E. 3. Ascertain the needs and presenting concerns of transgender clients, including transgender identity development, gender confusion, gender transition, gender expression, sexuality, anxiety, and depression related to transgender life experiences, family/partner relationships, substance abuse, transgender health issues, and presenting concerns unrelated to gender.
- E. 4. Understand the related ACA ethical guidelines (e.g., nonmaleficence, fidelity, competence, etc.) relevant for counseling individuals who are exploring issues related to gender identity, gender expression, and sexual orientation.
- E. 5. Seek consultation or supervision to ensure that personal biases do not negatively affect the client–therapist relationship or the treatment outcomes of the transgender individual.
- E. 6. Be familiar with and know how to assist transgender clients access community resources where appropriate.
- E. 7. Facilitate access to appropriate services in various settings for transgender individuals by confronting institutional barriers and discriminatory practices.
- E. 8. Seek professional development opportunities to enhance attitudes, knowledge, and counseling skills related to transgender individuals.
- E. 9. Recognize the importance of educating professionals, students, and supervisees about transgender issues and challenge misinformation and bias about transgender individuals.
- E. 10. Support a positive, public dialogue that affirms individual gender expression and gender identity.
- E. 11. Serve as advocates for transgender individuals within professional counseling organizations, and specifically advocate for anti-discrimination policies concerning transgender individuals.
- E. 12. Collaborate with health professionals and other individuals, groups, agencies, as indicated by the individual to provide comprehensive care.

F. Career and Lifestyle Development Competencies

Competent counselors will:

- F. 1. Assist transgender clients with exploring career choices that best facilitate identity formation and job satisfaction.
- F. 2. Recognize that existing career development theories, career assessment tools, employment applications, and career counseling interventions contain language, theory, and constructs that may be oppressive to transgender and gender-conforming individuals.

- F. 3. Acknowledge the potential problems associated with career assessment instruments that have not been normed for the transgender community.
- F. 4. Challenge the occupational stereotypes (e.g., sex work, entertainment careers, etc.) that restrict the career development and professional decision making of transgender clients, or respect decisions to remain in entertainment careers, while also be prepared to affirm that these are valid jobs for those who are satisfied working in these fields.
- F. 5. Acknowledge and understand how the interplay of discrimination and oppression against transgender individuals adversely affect career performance and/or result in negative evaluation of their job performance and thus may limit career options resulting in underemployment, less access to financial resources, and overrepresentation in certain careers.
- F. 6. Demonstrate awareness of the high degree of discrimination that transgender individuals have historically experienced in the workplace and how this discrimination may affect other life areas (e.g., housing, self-esteem, family support).
- F. 7. Demonstrate awareness of and skill in addressing employment issues and challenges for transgender individuals who have experienced a medical and/or social transition, those who may choose to transition, and those who may not opt to transition while in the workplace and recognize the diversity of experiences for transgender individuals who choose to transition while in the workplace.
- F. 8. Explore with clients the degree to which government (i.e., federal, state, and/or local) statutes, union contracts, and workplace policies protect workers against employment discrimination based on gender identity and expression. In cases where there is no protection of transgender employment rights, provide information on advocacy and support efforts.
- F. 9. Link clients with transgender mentors and resources that increase their awareness of viable career options.
- F. 10. Provide employers with consultation and education on gender identity issues and ways to facilitate workplace changes, such as restrooms, locker rooms, staff education, and creating a respectful, inclusive environment.
- F. 11. Assist with empowering transgender individuals to advocate on their own behalf as appropriate in their workplace context (i.e., microlevel or macrolevel) and/or offer to engage in this advocacy with the client's consent if the client would benefit from a direct workplace psychoeducation/training on transgender issues and safety in the workplace.
- F. 12. Advocate for gender identity and gender expression antidiscrimination policies in the workplace as they are applicable on microlevel (e.g., in the workplace) and macrolevels (e.g., in the local and larger communities where we live, with policy makers and legislators, etc.).

G. Appraisal

Competent counselors will:

- G. 1. Determine the reason for counseling services at the initial visit (e.g., exploring gender issues, career issues, relationship issues, evaluation and referral for medical services, or other mental health services).
- G. 2. Identify challenges that may inhibit desired treatment (e.g., cognitive impairment, serious mental health concerns such as psychosis or personality disorders, medical issues, developmental disabilities, etc.).
- G. 3. Understand that gender identity and expression vary from one individual to the next, and that this natural variation should not be interpreted as psychopathology or developmental delay.
- G. 4. Examine the legitimate power that counselors hold as helping professionals, particularly in regards to assessment for body modifications, and seek to share information on the counselor's gatekeeping role (e.g., writing letters supporting body modifications) so it is not a restrictive influence but rather seeks to better serve transgender people's needs.
- G. 5. Understand the power that counselors have in meeting the needs of transgender individuals in regards to making decisions about hormonal or surgical interventions. Therefore, it is important to collaboratively discuss the potential length of counseling services and costs as a part of the informed consent process.
- G. 6. Recognize that the goal of treatment is to provide a comprehensive psychosocial mental health assessment, which should encompass all life areas, for all transgender individuals whether they are seeking medical interventions and/or body modifications.
- G. 7. Examine how their own biases and privilege may influence their assessment with each transgender individual. Such bias might include sexism, heterosexism, transnegativity, promoting medical interventions, or a particular course of treatment.
- G. 8. Utilize supervision and consultation as tools to help counselors minimize biases and avoid misuse/abuse of privilege and power (e.g., in regards to providing approval for transgender individuals to obtain medical treatment and/or body modifications).
- G. 9. Understand how heterosexism and sexism are promoted and maintained within society, and how these dynamics influence the assessment of transgender individuals.
- G. 10. Consider in the differential diagnosis process how the effects of stigma, oppression, and discrimination contribute to psychological symptoms but do not necessarily indicate pathology for transgender individuals. Consider these effects when collaboratively deciding client's readiness for body modifications.
- G. 11. Apply ethical standards when utilizing assessment tools such as tests, measurements, and the current edition of the *DSM-IV-TR*, and recognize that these assessments have often not been normed

with transgender people. As many assessments are also products of a sexist and heterosexist culture and may reinforce a pathological or transgender-negative perspective on transgender people, determine which assessments are in the best interest of transgender people (i.e., ones that do not equate mental health with being gender conforming) and employ a collaborative assessment approach when possible.

- G. 12. Be sensitive to and aware of the ongoing debate regarding gender identity "disorder" being listed as a medical condition in the current edition of the *DSM* and be willing to communicate to transgender individuals the position the helping professional takes, and to have open and honest discussions about how this may affect the work you do together.
- G. 13. Be familiar with WPATH's *Standards of Care* principles to guide but not dictate treatment for individuals with gender identity and expression concerns, including gender dysphoria.
- G. 14. Be prepared to face ethical dilemmas with the appraisal of transgender people, especially because theories and practices with transgender people continue changing and evolving, and creating many ethical dilemmas.
- G. 15. Seek out the perspectives and personal narratives of the transgender community as essential components to fully understanding appropriate assessment of transgender people.
- G. 16. Recognize that the presence of a co-occurring mental or physical health disorder does not necessarily preclude counseling for gender concerns or medical treatments but may or may not require stabilization or additional treatment.
- G. 17. Recognize that transgender people with mental health concerns (e.g., severe mental health issues such as personality disorders) and/or cognitive challenges experience significant bias and discrimination and may benefit from discussions about the impact of mental health stigma on their daily lived experiences and their selection of body modifications.

H. Research

Competent counselors will:

- H. 1. Be aware of existing transgender research and literature regarding social and emotional well-being and difficulties, identity formation, resilience and coping with oppression, as well as medical and nonmedical treatment options.
- H. 2. Consider limitations of existing literature and existing research methods regarding transgender individuals such as sampling, confidentiality data collection, measurement, and generalizability (e.g., LGB literature applying results and content to transgender individuals).
- H. 3. Be aware of the gaps in literature and research regarding understanding the experiences of and assisting of transgender individuals and family members.

- H. 4. Have knowledge of qualitative, quantitative, and mixed methods research processes and potential future research areas related to transgender concerns in counseling (e.g., individual experiences of transgender people, counselor awareness and training on transgender concerns, reduction of discrimination toward transgender individuals, advocacy opportunities for positive social change in the lives of transgender individuals).
- H. 5. Consider how critical consumption of research may assist with understanding needs, improving quality of life, and enhancing counseling effectiveness for transgender individuals.
- H. 6. Formulate research questions collaboratively with transgender individuals and communities, taking into account transgender participants and transgender issues/concerns.
- H. 7. Construct surveys or any data-gathering forms that include gender demographic information options that provide participants with the opportunity to disclose their declared or affirmed gender identity while concurrently not conflating gender identity and sexual orientation.
- H. 8. Be familiar with current transgender-affirmative terminology and be aware of the importance of using the least restrictive gender language that adheres to participants' declared or affirmed pronouns/names.
- H. 9. Involve transgender-identified individuals in research regarding transgender issues/concerns when appropriate and possible—while attending to and being reflective of transgender research participants' lived experiences.
- H. 10. Recognize research is never free of positive or negative bias by identifying the potential influence personal values, gender bias, and heterosexism may have on the research process (e.g., participant selection, data gathering, interpretation of data, reporting of results, *DSM-IV-TR* diagnosis of gender identity "disorder"), and seek to address these biases in the best manner possible.
- H. 11. Make transgender-focused research available to the transgender community served by making a study's results and implications accessible for the community, practitioners, and academics alike.

References

American Counseling Association. (2005). *ACA code of ethics*. Retrieved from http://www.counseling.org/Resources/CodeOfEthics/TP/Home/CT2.aspx

American Counseling Association. (2009). *Competencies for counseling with transgender clients*. Alexandria, VA: Author.

American Psychiatric Association. (2000). *Diagnostic and statistical manual of mental disorders* (4th ed., text revision). Washington, DC: Author.

American Psychological Association, Task Force on Gender Identity and Gender Variance. (2009). *Report of the Task Force on Gender Identity and Gender Variance*. Washington, DC: Author.

Association for Assessment in Counseling and Education (2002). *Standards for educational and psychological testing: What counselors need to know.* Alexandria, VA: Author.

Association for Lesbian, Gay, Bisexual and Transgender Issues in Counseling. (2003). *Competencies for counseling gay, lesbian, bisexual, and transgender (LGBT) clients.* Retrieved from http://www.algbtic.org/resources/competencies.html

Beh, H., & Diamond, M. (2005). Ethical concerns related to treating gender nonconformity in childhood and adolescence: Lessons from the Family Court of Australia. *Health Matrix: Journal of Law-Medicine, 15,* 239–283.

Bockting, W. O. (1997). The assessment and treatment of gender dysphoria. *Directions in Clinical & Counseling Psychology, 7,* 1–23.

Bockting, W. O., & Coleman, E. (2007). Developmental stages of the transgender coming out process: Toward an integrated identity. In R. Ettner, S. Monstrey, & E. Eyler (Eds.), *Principles of transgender medicine and surgery* (pp. 185–208). Binghamton, NY: Haworth Press.

Bockting, W. O., & Fung, L. C .T. (2005). Genital reconstruction and gender identity disorders. In D. Sarwer, T. Pruzinsky, T. Cash, J. Persing, R. Goldwyn, & L. Whitaker (Eds.), *Psychological aspects of reconstructive and cosmetic plastic surgery: Clinical, empirical, and ethical perspectives* (pp. 207–229). Philadelphia, PA: Lippincott, Williams & Wilkins.

Bockting, W. O., & Goldberg, J. (2006). *Multidisciplinary guidelines for transgender care.* Binghamton, NY: Haworth Medical Press.

Bockting, W. O., Knudson, G., & Goldberg, J. M. (2007). Counseling and mental health care for transgender adults and loved ones. *International Journal of Transgenderism, 9*(3/4), 36–82.

Brown, G. R. (1994). Women in relationships with cross-dressing men: A descriptive study from a nonclinical setting. *Archives of Sexual Behavior, 23,* 515–530.

Bruce, D., Ramirez-Valles, J., & Campbell, R. T. (2008). Stigmatization, substance use, and sexual risk behavior among Latino gay and bisexual men and transgender persons. *Journal of Drug Issues, 38,* 235–260.

Carroll, L. (2010). *Counseling sexual and gender minorities.* Upper Saddle River, NJ: Merrill/Pearson.

Chen-Hayes, S. F. (2003). Counseling and advocacy with transgender and gendervariant persons in schools and families. *Journal of Humanistic Counseling, Education, & Development, 40,* 34–49.

Clements-Nolle, K., Marx, R., & Katz, M. (2006). Attempted suicide among transgender persons: The influence of gender-based discrimination and victimization. *Journal of Homosexuality, 51,* 53–69.

Coolidge, F. L., Thede, L. L., & Young, S. E. (2002). The heritability of gender identity disorder in a child and adolescent twin sample. *Behavior Genetics, 32,* 251–257.

Costa, L., & Matzner, A. (2007). *Male bodies, women's souls: Personal narratives of Thailand's transgendered youth.* Binghamton, NY: Haworth Press.

Council of Accredited Counseling and Education Related Programs. (2009). *2009 standards.* Retrieved from http://www.cacrep.org/doc/2009%20Standards%20with%20cover.pdf

Crethar, H. C., Torres Rivera, E., & Nash, S. (2008). In search of common threads: Linking multicultural, feminist, and social justice counseling paradigms. *Journal of Counseling & Development, 86,* 269–278.

Currah, P. (2006). Gender pluralism under the transgender umbrella. In P. Currah, R. M. Jung, & S. Minter (Eds.), *Transgender rights* (pp. 3–31). Minneapolis, MN: University of Minnesota Press.

Currah, P., Juang, R. M., & Minter, S. (2006). Introduction. In P. Currah, R. M. Juang, & S. Minter (Eds.), *Transgender rights* (pp. xiii–xxiv). Minneapolis, MN: University of Minnesota Press.

Currah, P., Minter, S., & Green, J. (2000). *Transgender equality: A handbook for activists and policy makers.* Washington, DC: Policy Institute of the National Gay and Lesbian Task Force/San Francisco, CA: National Center for Lesbian Rights.

Dahl, M., Feldman, J., Goldberg, J. M., & Jaberi, A. (2006). Physical aspects of transgender endocrine therapy. *International Journal of Transgenderism, 9*(3/4), 111–134.

D'Augelli, A. R., Grossman, A. H., & Starks, M. T. (2006). Childhood gender atypicality, victimization, and PTSD among lesbian, gay, and bisexual youth. *Journal of Interpersonal Violence, 21,* 1462–1482.

DiClemente, R. J., & Wingood, G. M. (1995). A randomized controlled trial of an HIV sexual risk reduction intervention for young African-American women. *Journal of the American Medical Association, 274*(16), 1271–1276.

Edney, R. (2004). To keep me safe from harm? Transgender prisoners and the experience of imprisonment. *Deakin Law Review, 9,* 327–338.

Ehrbar, R., Witty, M., Ehrbar, H. B., & Bockting, W. O. (2008). Clinician judgment in the diagnosis of gender identity disorder in children. *Journal of Sex & Marital Therapy, 34,* 385–412.

Elze, D. E. (2007). Research with sexual minority youths: Where do we go from here? *Journal of Gay & Lesbian Social Services, 18*(2), 73–99.

Fassinger, R. E., & Arsenau, J. R. (2007). "I'd rather get wet than be under that umbrella": Differentiating the experiences and identities of lesbian, gay, bisexual, and transgender people. In K. J. Bieschke, R. M. Perez, & K. A. Debord (Eds.), *Handbook of counseling and psychotherapy with lesbian, gay, bisexual and transgender clients* (2nd ed., pp. 19–50). Washington, DC: American Psychological Association.

Feinberg, L. (1996). *Transgenderwarriors: Making history from Joan of Arc to RuPaul.* Boston, MA: Beacon Press.

Garofalo, R., Deleon, J., Osmer, E., Doll, M., & Harper, G. W. (2006). Overlooked, misunderstood and at-risk: Exploring the lives and HIV risk of ethnic minority male-to-female transgender youth. *Journal of Adolescent Health, 38,* 230–236.

Goodman, L. A., Liang, B., Helms, J. E., Latta, R. E., Sparks, E., & Weintraub, S. R. (2004). Training counseling psychologists as social change agents: Feminist and multicultural principles in action. *Counseling Psychologist, 32,* 793–837.

Green, E., & dickey, l. m. (2009). *Considerations for research with trans subjects and communities.* Retrieved from http://www.trans-academics.org/considerationsresearch

Grossman, A. H., & D'Augelli, A. R. (2006). Transgender youth: Invisible and vulnerable. *Journal of Homosexuality, 51*, 111–128.

Grossman, A. H., & D'Augelli, A. R. (2007). Transgender youth and life-threatening behaviors. *Suicide and Life-Threatening Behavior, 37*, 527–537.

Grossman, A. H., D'Augelli, A. R., Howell, T. J., & Hubbard, S. (2005). Parents' reactions to transgender youths' gender nonconforming expression and identity. *Journal of Gay and Lesbian Social Services, 18*, 3–16.

Grossman, A. H., D'Augelli, A. R., & Salter, N. P. (2006). Male- to-female transgender youth: Gender expression milestones, gender atypicality, victimization, and parents' responses. *Journal of GLBT Family Studies, 2*, 71–92.

Herbst, J. H., Jacobs, E. D., Finlayson, T. J., McKleroy, V. S., Neumann, M. S., & Crepaz, N. (2008). Estimating HIV prevalence and risk behaviors of transgender persons in the United States: A systematic review. *AIDS & Behavior, 12*, 1–17.

Human Rights Campaign. (2008). *Statewide employment laws and policies.* Washington, DC: Author. Retrieved from http://www.hrc.org/documents/EmploymentLawsand Policies.pdf.

Human Rights Campaign Foundation. (2008). *Transgender inclusion in the workplace* (2nd ed.). Washington, DC: Author. Retrieved from http://www.hrc.org/documents/HRC FoundationTransgender Inclusion in the Workplace 2ndEdition - 2008.pdf

Kenagy, G. P., & Bostwick, W. P. (2005). Health and social service needs of transgender people in Chicago. In W. O. Bockting & E. Avery (Eds.), *Transgender health and HIV prevention: Needs assessment studies from transgender communities across the United States* (pp. 57–66). Binghamton, NY: Haworth Medical Press.

Kenagy, G. P., & Hsieh, C. M. (2005). The risk less known: Female-to-male transgender persons' vulnerability to HIV infection. *AIDS Care, 17*, 195–207.

Korell, S. C., & Lorah, P. (2007). An overview of affirmative psychotherapy and counseling with transgender clients. In K. J. Bieschke, R. M. Perez, & K. A. DeBord (Eds.), *Handbook of counseling and psychotherapy with lesbian, gay, bisexual, and transgender clients* (pp. 271–288). Washington, DC: American Psychological Association.

Lambda Legal. (2008). *Bending the mold: An action kit for transgender youth.* Retrieved from http://www.lambdalegal.org/.../bending...mold/order-bendingthe-mold.html

Lev, A. I. (2004). *Transgender emergence: Therapeutic guidelines for working with gender-variant people and their families.* Binghamton, NY: Haworth Clinical Practice Press.

Lewis, J., Arnold, M., House, R., & Toporek, R. (2003). *Advocacy competencies* [Electronic version]. Retrieved from http://www.counseling.org/Resources/Competencies/Advocacy Competencies.pdf

Lombardi, E. (2001). Enhancing transgender health care. *American Journal of Public Health, 91*, 869–872.

Lombardi, E. L., Wilchins, R. A., Priesing, D., & Malouf, D. (2001). Gender violence: Transgender experiences with violence and discrimination. *Journal of Homosexuality, 42*, 89–101.

Martin, J., & Meezan, W. (2003). Applying ethical standards to research and evaluations involving lesbian, gay, bisexual, and transgender populations. *Journal of Gay & Lesbian Social Services, 15*, 181–201.

Meezan, W., & Martin, J. (2003). *Research methods with gay, lesbian, bisexual, and transgender populations.* New York, NY: Haworth Press.

Meyer, I. H. (2003). Prejudice, social stress, and mental health in lesbian, gay, and bisexual populations: Conceptual issues and research evidence, *Psychology Bulletin, 129*, 674–697.

Meyer, W., Bockting, W., Cohen-Kettenis, P., Coleman, E., Diceglie, D., Devor, H., et al. (2001, January-March). Harry Benjamin International Gender Dysphoria Association's the standards of care for gender identity disorders (6th Version). *International Journal of Transgenderism, 5*(1). Retrieved from http://www.wpath.org/publications standards.cfm

Meyers, J. E., & Sweeney, T. J. (2005). *Counseling for wellness: Theory, research, and practice.* Alexandria, VA: American Counseling Association.

National Center on Transgender Equality. (2008). ENDA by the numbers. Retrieved from http://www.nctequality.org/Issues/employment.html

Nemoto, T., Operario, D., Keatley, J., Han, L., & Soma, T. (2004). HIV risk behaviors among male-to-female transgender persons of color in San Francisco. *American Journal of Public Health, 94*, 1193–1199.

Newman, L. K. (2002). Sex, gender and culture: Issues in the definition, assessment and treatment of gender identity disorder. *Clinical Child Psychology & Psychiatry, 7*, 352–359.

O'Neil, M. E., McWhirter, E. H., & Cerezo, A. (2008). Transgender identities and gender variance in vocational psychology: Recommendations for practice, social advocacy, and research. *Journal of Career Development, 34*(3), 286–308.

Pickering, D. L. (2005). Counselor self-efficacy with transgendered clients: Implications for training. *Dissertation Abstracts International*, DAI-A 66/10, 3577.

Sanchez, F. J., & Vilain, E. (2009). Collective self-esteem as a coping resource for male-to-female transsexuals. *Journal of Counseling Psychology, 56*(1), 202–209.

Sausa, L. A. (2005). Translating research into practice: Trans youth recommendations for improving school systems. *Journal of Gay and Lesbian Issues in Education, 3*(1), 15–28.

Schram, T. H. (2006). *Conceptualizing and proposing qualitative research.* Columbus, OH: Person.

Sell, R. L., & Dunn, P. M. (2008). Inclusion of lesbian, gay, bisexual and transgender people in tobacco use-related surveillance and epidemiological research. *Journal of LGBT Health Research, 4*(1), 27–42.

Singh, A. A., Hays, D. G., & Watson, L. (in press). Strategies in the face of adversity: Resilience strategies of transgender individuals. *Journal of Counseling and Development.*

Singh, A. A., & McKleroy, V. S. (in press). "Just getting out of bed is a revolutionary act": The resilience of transgender people of color who have survived traumatic life events. *International Journal of Traumatology.*

Sue, D. W., Arredondo, P., & McDavis, R. J. (1992). Multicultural counseling competencies and standards: A call to the profession. *Journal of Counseling &Development, 70*, 477–486.

Sue, D. W., & Sue, D. (2008). *Counseling the culturally different: Theory and practice* (5th ed.). New York, NY: Wiley.

Suppe, F. (1984). Classifying sexual disorders: The Diagnostic and Statistical Manual of the American Psychiatric Association. *Journal of Homosexuality, 9*, 9–28.

Vanderburgh, R. (2009). Appropriate therapeutic care for families with pre-pubescent transgender/gender-dissonant children. *Child & Adolescent Social Work Journal, 26*, 135–154.

White, C. H., & Goldberg, J. M. (2006). Social and medical transgender case advocacy. *International Journal of Transgenderism, 9*(3/4), 197–217.

Wiersma, W., & Jurs, S. G. (2009). *Research methods in education.* Boston, MA: Pearson.

Worell, J., & Remer, P. (2003). *Feminist perspectives in therapy: Empowering diverse women.* New York, NY: Wiley.

Yalom, I. D., & Leszcz, M. (2005). *The theory and practice of group psychotherapy* (5th ed.). New York, NY: Basic Books.

Yuksel, S., Kulaksizoglu, B., T'urksoy, N., & Sahin, D. M. (2000). Group psychotherapy with female-to-male transsexuals in Turkey. *Archives of Sexual Behavior, 29*, 279–290.

Appendix A

The authors of this document recommend the following as a growing list of some of the least restrictive terms available for use with transgender people, which are derived from the Lambda Legal (2008) publication, *Bending the Mold: An Action Kit for Transgender Youth* and reproduced below with permission of Lambda Legal.

Biological Sex, Sex: a term used historically and within the medical field to refer to the chromosomal, hormonal, and anatomical characteristics that are used to classify an individual as female or male.

Classism: a system of institutionalized practices and individual actions that benefits people who have wealth and power.

Crossdresser: a person who, on occasion, wears clothing associated with another sex, but who does not necessarily desire to change his or her sex. Many crossdressers identify as heterosexual but can have any sexual orientation.

Drag King / Drag Queen: a performer who wears the clothing associated with another sex, often involving the presentation of exaggerated, stereotypical gender characteristics. The performance of gender by drag queens (males in drag) or drag kings (females in drag) may be art, entertainment, and/or parody.

FTM (Female to Male), Transgender Man: terms used to identify a person who was assigned the female sex at birth but who identifies as male.

Gender: a set of social, psychological, and emotional traits, often influenced by societal expectations, that classify an individual as feminine, masculine, androgynous, or other.

Gender Binary: the concept that everyone must be one of two genders: man or woman.

Gender expression: The outward manifestation of internal gender identity, through clothing, hairstyle, mannerisms, and other characteristics.

Gender Identity: the inner sense of being a man, a woman, both, or neither. Gender identity usually aligns with a person's sex but sometimes does not.

Gender Dysphoria: an intense, persistent discomfort resulting from the awareness that the sex assigned at birth and the resulting gender role expectations are inappropriate. Some consider gender dysphoria to be a symptom of gender identity disorder, a health condition recognized by the American Psychiatric Association. Many transgender people do not experience gender dysphoria.

Genderqueer: a term used by some people who may or may not identify as transgender, but who identify their gender as somewhere on the continuum beyond the binary male/female gender system.

Gender-Nonconforming: behaving in a way that does not match social stereotypes about female or male gender, usually through dress or physical appearance.

Gender Role: the social expectation of how an individual should act, think, and feel, based upon the sex assigned at birth.

Gender Transition: the social, psychological, and medical process of transitioning from one gender to another. Gender transition is an individualized process and does not involve the same steps for everyone. After gender transition, some people identify simply as men or women.

Hormone Therapy: administration of hormones and hormonal agents to develop characteristics of a different gender or to block the development of unwanted gender characteristics. Hormone therapy is part of many people's gender transitions and is safest when prescribed and monitored by a health care professional.

MTF (Male to Female), Transgender Woman: terms used to identify a person who was assigned the male sex at birth but who identifies as female.

Oppression: the acts and effects of domination of certain groups in society over others, caused by the combination of prejudice and power. Systems of oppression include racism, sexism, homophobia, and transphobia.

Post-Op, Pre-Op, Non-Op: terms used to identify a transgender person's surgical status. Use of these terms is often considered insulting and offensive. Surgical status is almost never relevant information for anyone except a transgender person's medical providers.

Privilege: social and institutional advantages that dominant groups receive and others do not. Privilege is often invisible to those who have it.

Racism: a system of institutionalized practices and individual actions that benefits white people over people of color.

Sex Reassignment Surgery (SRS): any one of a variety of surgeries involved in the process of transition from one gender to another. Many transgender people will not undergo SRS for health or financial reasons, or because it is not medically necessary for them.

Sexism: a system of institutionalized practices and individual actions that benefits men over women.

Transgender or Trans: an umbrella term used to describe those who challenge social gender norms, including genderqueer people, gendernonconforming people, transsexuals, crossdressers, and so on. People must self-identify as transgender for the term to be appropriately used to describe them.

Transphobia: the irrational fear of those who challenge gender stereotypes, often expressed as discrimination, harassment, and violence.

Transsexual: a person who experiences intense, persistent, long-term discomfort with their body and self-image due to the awareness that their assigned sex is inappropriate. Transsexuals may take steps to change their body, gender role, and gender expression to align them with their gender identity.

Appendix B

List of reviewers and their affiliations:

lore dickey, MA, counseling psychology doctoral student at the University of North Dakota

Dara Hoffman, MA, LPC, professional counselor in private practice

Joanne Keatley, PhD, director of the Center for Excellence of Transgender HIV Prevention at The University of California, San Francisco

Arlene Lev, LCSW, social worker and author of *Transgender Emergence*

Vel S. McKleroy, MPH, behavioral scientist at The Centers for Disease Control and Prevention and Transgender Working Group Leader

Mr. Jesse McNulty, MS, special education school teacher, feminist activist, and Georgia Safe Schools Coalition member

Stacee Reicherzer, PhD, LPC, professional counselor and Walden university counselor educator